THE

INTUITIONS OF THE MIND

INDUCTIVELY INVESTIGATED.

BY THE

REV. JAMES M'COSH, LL.D.,

PROFESSOR OF LOGIC AND METAPHYSICS IN QUEEN'S COLLEGE, BELFAST,

AUTHOR OF 'THE METHOD OF THE DIVINE GOVERNMENT PHYSICAL AND MORAL,' AND JOINT AUTHOR OF 'TYPICAL FORMS AND SPECIAL ENDS IN CREATION.'

NEW YORK:
ROBERT CARTER AND BROTHERS,
530, BROADWAY.
1860.

JOHN EDWARD TAYLOR, PRINTER,
LITTLE QUEEN STREET, LINCOLN'S INN FIELDS, LONDON.

CONTENTS.

INTRODUCTION.

Page
AIM OF THE WORK AND METHOD OF INQUIRY 1

Part First.

GENERAL VIEW OF THE NATURE OF THE INTUITIVE CONVICTIONS OF THE MIND.

BOOK I.

GENERAL PROPOSITIONS REGARDING INTUITIONS.

CHAPTER I.

NEGATIVE PROPOSITIONS.

Sect. I. No Innate Mental Images or Representations 13
Sect. II. No Innate, Abstract, or General Notions 16
Sect. III. No *A Priori* Forms imposed by the Mind on Objects 19
Sect. IV. The Intuitions are not immediately before Consciousness as Laws or Principles 21

CHAPTER II.

POSITIVE PROPOSITIONS.

Sect. I. There are Intuitive Principles operating in the Mind . 23
Sect. II. The Native Convictions of the Mind are of the Nature of Perceptions or Intuitions 29
Sect. III. Intuitive Convictions rise on the Contemplation of Objects presented or represented to the Mind 30

Page

Sect. IV. The Intuitions of the Mind are primarily directed to Individual Objects 31
Sect. V. The Individual Intuitive Convictions can be generalized into Maxims, and these are entitled to be represented as Philosophic Principles 33

BOOK II.

CHARACTER OF INTUITIONS AND METHOD OF EMPLOYING THEM.

CHAPTER I.

MARKS AND PECULIARITIES OF INTUITIONS.

Sect. I. Tests 37
Sect. II. Different Aspects of Intuitions, and their Theoretical Characters 41
Sect. III. Certain Misapprehensions in regard to the Character of Intuitive Convictions 55
Sect. IV. Certain Practical Characteristics 59

CHAPTER II.

METHOD OF EMPLOYING INTUITIVE PRINCIPLES.

Sect. I. The Spontaneous and Reflex Use of Intuitive Principles 62
Sect. II. Sources of Error in Metaphysical Speculation . . , 69
Sect. III. Conditions of the Legitimacy of the Appeal to Intuitive Principles 76
Sect. IV. Method of Investigating and Interpreting our Intuitions 85
Sect. V. What Explanation can be given of the Intuitions of the Mind 92

CHAPTER III.

(SUPPLEMENTARY.) BRIEF CRITICAL REVIEW OF OPINIONS IN REGARD TO INTUITIVE TRUTHS 98

Part Second.

PARTICULAR EXAMINATION OF THE INTUITIONS.

BOOK I.

PRIMITIVE COGNITIONS.

CHAPTER I.

BODY AND SPIRIT.

Page
Sect. I. The Mind begins its Intelligent Acts with Knowledge. The Simple Cognitive Powers 119
Sect. II. Our Intuitive Cognitions of Body 122
Sect. III. Some Distinctions to be attended to in regard to our Cognition of Body 133
Sect. IV. The Qualities of Matter known by Intuition 145
Sect. V. Our Intuitive Cognition of Self or of Spirit 148

CHAPTER II.

ANALYSIS OF OUR PRIMITIVE COGNITIONS.

Sect. I. (*Preliminary.*) *On the Nature of Abstraction and Generalization* 157
Sect. II. On Being 161
Sect. III. On Substance 164
Sect. IV. On Mode, Quality, Property, Essence 173
Sect. V. On Personality 180
Sect. VI. On Extension 183
Sect. VII. On Number 184
Sect. VIII. On Motion 185
Sect. IX. On Power 187
Sect. X. (*Supplementary.*) *The Various Kinds of Power known by Experience* 187

BOOK II.

PRIMITIVE BELIEFS.

CHAPTER I.

Their General Nature 196

Page

CHAPTER II.

TIME AND SPACE 202

CHAPTER III.

THE INFINITE 214

CHAPTER IV.

THE EXTENT, TESTS, AND POWER OF OUR NATIVE BELIEFS . 231

BOOK III.

PRIMITIVE JUDGMENTS.

CHAPTER I.

THEIR GENERAL NATURE, AND A CLASSIFICATION OF THEM . 236

CHAPTER II.

RELATIONS INTUITIVELY OBSERVED BY THE MIND.

Sect. I. Relation of Identity 242
Sect. II. Relation of Whole and Parts 247
Sect. III. Relations of Space 250
Sect. IV. The Relations of Time 252
Sect. V. The Relations of Quantity 252
Sect. VI. The Relations of Resemblance 255
Sect. VII. Relations of Active Property 257
Sect. VIII. Relation of Cause and Effect 258

BOOK IV.

MORAL CONVICTIONS.

CHAPTER I.

GENERAL VIEW OF THE MOTIVE AND MORAL POWERS.

Sect. I. The Appetencies, the Will, and the Conscience . . . 279
Sect. II. (*Supplementary.*) *On the Beautiful* 288

CHAPTER II.

CONVICTIONS INVOLVED IN THE EXERCISES OF CONSCIENCE.

Sect. I. Convictions as to the Nature of Moral Good 290
Sect. II. On Sin and Error 297
Sect. III. Relation of Moral Good and Happiness 302

Page

CHAPTER III.

The Freedom of the Will 308

Part Third.

INTUITIVE PRINCIPLES AND THE VARIOUS SCIENCES.

BOOK I.

METAPHYSICS.

CHAPTER I.

Metaphysics, Gnosiology, and Ontology 315

CHAPTER II.

GNOSIOLOGY.

Sect. I. On Knowledge 322
Sect. II. On the Origin of our Knowledge and Ideas 326
Sect. III. Limits to our Knowledge, Ideas, and Beliefs 334
Sect. IV. Relation of Intuition and Experience 340
Sect. V. On the Necessity attached to our Primary Convictions . 345
Sect. VI. (*Supplementary.*) *On the Distinctions between the Understanding and the Reason; between* a priori *and* a posteriori *Principles; between Form and Matter; between Subjective and Objective; between the Logical and Chronological Order of Ideas; between the Cause and Occasion of Innate Ideas* . . 351

CHAPTER III.

ONTOLOGY.

Sect. I. On Knowing and Being 358
Sect. II. On Idealism 362
Sect. III. On Scepticism 374
Sect. IV. On the Conditioned and the Unconditioned 385
Sect. V. (*Supplementary.*) *The Antinomies of Kant* 388
Sect. VI. (*Supplementary.*) *Examination of Mr. J. S. Mill's Metaphysical System* 390

BOOK II.

METAPHYSICAL PRINCIPLES INVOLVED IN THE SCIENCES.

CHAPTER I.

Page

Distinction between the Demonstrative or Formal and the Material or Inductive Sciences 395

CHAPTER II.

THE MENTAL SCIENCES.

Sect. I. Classification of the Mental Sciences 400
Sect. II. Logic 402
Sect. III. Ethics 406

CHAPTER III.

Mathematics 409

CHAPTER IV.

Intuitive Principles involved in the Physical Sciences 415

CHAPTER V.

APPLICATION TO THEOLOGY.

Sect. I. Faith and Reason 419
Sect. II. Natural Theology. The Theistic Argument 427
Sect. III. On the Immortality of the Soul 441
Sect. IV. Pantheism 446
Sect. V. Christian Divinity 461
Sect. VI. Man as a Religious Being 476
Sect. VII. Rational Theology 480
Sect. VIII. Intuitional Theology 482

ERRATA.

Page 166, line 5 from foot, *for* "Abrici" *read* "Ulrici."
Page 246, line 7 from head, *for* "A is not A" *read* "A is not Not-A."

INTUITIONS OF THE MIND.

INTRODUCTION.

AIM OF THE WORK AND METHOD OF INQUIRY.

According to one class of speculators, the mind derives all its knowledge, judgments, maxims, from observation and experience. According to another class of thinkers, there are ideas, truths, principles, which originate in the native power, and are seen in the inward light of the mind. These last have been called by a great number of names, such as innate ideas, intuitions, necessary judgments, fundamental laws of belief, principles of common sense, first or primitive truths; and diverse have been the accounts given of them, and the uses to which they have been turned. This is a controversy which has been from the beginning, and which is ever being renewed in one form or other. It appears to me that this contest is now, and has ever been, characterized by an immense complication of confusion; and confusion, as Bacon has remarked, is more difficult to rectify than open error. I am not, in this treatise, to plunge at once into a thicket, in which so many have lost themselves as they sought to find or cut a way through it. But my aim throughout is to ascertain what are the actual laws or principles in the mind denoted by these various phrases, what is their mode of operation, what the rule which they follow, and the purpose which they are competent to serve.

As the result, it will appear that there are in the mind such existences and powers as primary perceptions and fundamental laws of belief, but that they are very different in their nature from the account which is often given of them, and that they are by no means fitted to accomplish the ends to which they have been turned in metaphysical and theölogical speculation. I would as soon believe that there are no such agents as heat, chemical affinity, and electricity in physical nature, as that there are no immediate perceptions and native-born convictions in this mind of ours. I look indeed on the one kind of agents, like the other, to be among the deepest and most potent at work in this world, mental and material; and yet the one class, like the other, while operating every instant on soul or body, are apt to hide themselves from the view. Indeed they discover themselves only by their effects, and their law can be detected only by a careful observation of its actings; and it should be added, that both are capable of evil as well as good, and are to be carefully watched and guarded in the use which is made of them.

The prejudice against native and necessary principles has arisen to a great extent from the extravagant account which has been rendered of them, and from the vain, the ambitious, and often pernicious purposes which they have been made to serve. It is to be hoped, that by a clear determination of their exact nature, and of the rules of their operation, and by a judicious exposition of the method by which alone they can be discovered, and of the restrictions which should be laid on their employment, the feeling against them on the part of so many, philosophers and non-philosophers, may be dispelled; while at the same time rash speculators are prevented from employing them for the furthering of pretentious ends to which they have no legitimate reference.

In inquiring into the evidence of their existence, into the place which they hold in the constitution of the mind, the laws by which they are guided, and the way in which they manifest themselves, I am to proceed throughout in the Method of Induction. I profess to prosecute the investigation in the way of the observation of facts—with an accompanying analysis and co-ordination, but still of facts, which have been carefully observed. It has often been shown that the method of induction admits, *mutatis mutandis,* of an application to the study of the human mind, as well as to that of the material universe. The difference in the application lies mainly in this, that in the one case we use self-consciousness, or the internal sense, whereas in the other we employ the external sense as the organ or instrument. I certainly do not propose to find out the intuitions of the mind by the bodily eye, aided or unaided by the microscope, nor discover their mode of operation by the blowpipe. They are in their nature spiritual, and so sense cannot touch them, nor see them, nor hear them, nor can the telescope in its widest range detect them. Still they are *there* in our mental nature; there is an eye of wider sweep than the telescope, and more searching than the microscope, ready to be directed towards them. By introspection we may look on them in operation; by abstraction or analysis we may separate the essential peculiarity from the rough concrete presentations; and by generalization, rise to the law which they follow.

But let me not be misunderstood. The method pursued, as it is not on the one hand to be confounded with an ambitious transcendentalism which declines to ask help from observation, so it is as little on the other hand to be identified with a miserable sensational empiricism. I do not expect to discover what are the native principles of the mind by *à priori* speculation, but neither do I profess by observation to lay or construct a foundation on which to rear fundamental truth. I am not, therefore, to be lightly charged with a contradiction, as if I resorted to experience for a basis or ground of principles which I represent as original and independent. I employ induction simply as a *mean* or *method* of finding laws which are prior to induction, otherwise induction could not find them. Experience is not supposed by me to furnish the ground of necessary truth; all that it can do is to supply the facts which enable us to discover the truth, and that the truth is necessary. I allude to this objection, not with the view of formally meeting it here, but in order to show that it has not been overlooked, and then adjourn the discussion of it to its appropriate place. It will come out, in the course of our survey, that while there are regulative principles in the mind, operating altogether independently of any reflex notice we may take of them, and not depending for their authority on our induction of them, it is at the same time true that they can become known to us as general principles only by inward observation, and can be legitimately employed in philosophic speculation only on the condition of being rigidly inducted. By observation we may rise to the discovery of mental principles which do not in themselves depend on observation, but which have a place in our constitution anterior to our observation of them, and are there, as observation discovers, native, necessary, and universal.

In some respects, it is an unfortunate time for giving forth such a work to the world. Every age, like the seed, is at one and the same time the product of combined influences in the past, and the germ of life for the future.

In this present age, two manner of principles, each of the character of a different parent, are struggling for the mastery; the one earth-born, sensational, empirical, utilitarian, deriving all ideas from the senses, and all knowable truth from man's limited experience, and holding that man can be swayed by no motives of a higher order than the wish to secure pleasure or avoid pain; the other, if not heaven-born, at least cloud-born, being ideal, transcendental, pantheistic, attributing man's loftiest ideas to an inward light, appealing to principles which are discovered without the trouble of observation, and issuing in a belief in the good, instead of a belief in God. Each of these views has its keen partisans, either violently attacking one another, or regarding each other with silent contempt, while the great body of reading men are professedly indifferent,—those who claim to be neutral, however, being all the while unconsciously in the service either of the one or other, commonly of the lower or earthly, just as those who profess to belong neither to God nor Mammon, do in fact belong to Mammon.

What then can be expected of the reception of such a work in such an age? A large body, even of the thinking portion of the community, are prejudiced against all such discussions, as fruitless of good in every circumstance, and in some forms productive of mischief. I suspect the great mass of those who call themselves practical men, and the majority of those addicted to the study of the physical sciences, will be further prepossessed against this treatise as defending a doctrine which they thought had been long ago and for ever exploded by Locke. On the other hand, those most inclined to favour such pursuits are, for the most part, committed and pledged to extreme views, and can scarcely be expected to look with a favourable eye on a work which, professedly built on pure observation, declines to follow any school,—indeed, proclaims that as schools and sects, with their separate standpoints and watchwords, have long ago ceased in physical science, so it is time they should disappear in the field of mental science likewise; that those who prosecute the study, calling no man master, may look, without prepossession, into the volume spread out before them in their own soul, and read it with the eye of consciousness. Nearly all confessed metaphysicians will assert that I am degrading high philosophy in making it submit to the method of induction, and that the restrictions which I would lay upon speculation must deprive it of its most fascinating charms; while hundreds of eager youths, walking hopefully on the high *à priori* road, and expecting that the next turn—which they already see not far in front—must open on the great ocean of absolute truth, will feel as if they were unmercifully stopped and turned back at the very time when the long looked-for scene was about to burst gloriously on their view.

But regarded under some other aspects, this is an age in which such a work (I would on this account as well as many others it were only worthy of its subject) is especially needed. Every nation awakened to intelligence must have a philosophy of some description. Whatever men may profess or affect, they cannot in fact do without it; and if any age or nation, arrived at civilization, will not form or adopt a high and elevating philosophy, it will assuredly fall under the power of a low and a debasing one. It oftens happens that a profession of contempt for all metaphysics as being futile and unintelligible, is often an introduction to a discussion which is metaphysical without the parties knowing it (as the person in the French play had spoken prose all his life without being aware of it); and of such metaphysics it will commonly be found that they are futile and unintelligible enough. Often is Aristotle denounced in language borrowed from himself, and the Schoolmen are disparaged by those who are all the while using distinctions which they have cut with sharp chisel in the rock, never to be effaced. There are persons speaking with contempt of Plato, Descartes, Locke, and all the metaphysicians who are taking advantage of the great truths which they have discovered. I could easily show that in our very sermons from the pulpit, and orations in the senate, and pleadings at the bar, principles are ever and anon appealed to which have come from the heads of our deepest thinkers, in ages long gone by, and who may now be forgotten by all but a few antiquarians in philosophy. Natural science itself is, in the hands of its most advanced votaries, ever touching on the borders of metaphysics, and compelling our physicists to rest on certain fundamental convictions as to extension and force. The truth is, in very proportion as material science advances, do thinking minds feel the need of something to go down deeper and mount up higher than the senses can do—of some means of settling those anxious questions which the mind is ever putting in regard to the soul, and the relation of the universe to God, and of a foundation on which the understanding can ultimately and confidently repose. Whatever the superficial may think, philosophy is an underlying power, of vast importance because of mighty influence. It is because it is fundamental and radical, that it is unseen by the vulgar, who notice only what is above the surface. Let us see that the foundation be well laid, that the root be properly planted. That foundation must be secure which is founded in our mental constitution; that is the proper root which is planted by our Maker.

In determining the precise nature of the mental intuitions, we may hope to be able to settle what they can do, and, as no less important, what they cannot do. Thus do

I hope to contribute my little aid in elevating the low, and in bringing down the presumptuous tendencies of the age; thus would I raise the downward, and at the same time lower the proud look; thus would I keep men from poring ever on the dust of the earth on the one hand, and on the other hand from attempting, Icarus-like, to mount in a flight which must issue in a lamentable fall. Thus would I seek to raise the view-position of some reckoned by themselves and others the wiser and more sober, who are digging for ever in the mere clay of material existence, and who, believing in nothing but what can be seen and touched, never rise to the contemplation of moral and spiritual, of immutable and eternal truth; and thus too would I save the more promising of our intellectual youths from falling under the power of a boasting *à priori* intuitionalism, which is alluring them on by gilded clouds, which will turn out to be damp and chill after they have taken infinite pains to climb to them and to enter them.

In Germany, in Britain, in the United States of America,—alas! France, with its finest minds ground down by a military despotism necessitated by an unprincipled democracy, has ceased to be a country of independent thought, and so cannot be named in such a connection, —thought is in a transition, and therefore a very restless state. In Germany, the high transcendental, intuitional, or dialectic method, has wrought itself out—has cropped out to the surface in thinness and brittleness; and in the reaction, eminent professors are lecturing to half-empty benches; and books which if published twenty years ago would have moved thought to its greatest depths, can now find little sale, few readers, and scarcely any believers; while in the absence of a judicious philosophy, accepted and influential, a plausible materialism, acknowledging no existence but matter and force, is making considerable progress on the pretence of furnishing what the old metaphysics never yielded, something tangible and therefore solid. In the English-speaking nations there coexists with the old experiential spirit engendered by Locke, and the sensational spirit imported from France, a determined recoil, especially among certain musing and impulsive youths, against Lockism, and sensationalism, and the bony and haggard forms of physicism, which have become denuded of all truth, intellectual, moral, and religious, transcending sense and experience; and there is strong tendency towards an idealism, which, all decked and radiant, is seeking to win them to its embrace. It is surely possible that there may be some disturbed by the din of these controversies, and shunning both extremes, who may be prepared to welcome an attempt to discover—not, certainly, all truth (which is precluded to the human mind), but, by a sure method—that of observation and facts—a sure foundation, laid by God himself, and on which other truths may be laid, and on which they may firmly rest.

I would not have taken such pains (as I can say conscientiously I have done) with this treatise, had I not been persuaded that it embodies important truth. At the same time I feel that in discussing so many and such abstruse topics, confusion and error may have crept in. My conviction indeed is very strong as to the accuracy of the general views unfolded in the First and Third of the three Parts into which the work is divided. There is more room for doubt and hesitation as to the discussions on the more particular topics in the Second Part. In regard to these, I would not only give—what indeed I know I cannot withhold—full freedom to others to differ from me, but I reserve to myself the right to improve, to modify, to correct, if need be, the views here set forth, should I receive new light on further reading and reflection. I make this admission and claim this prerogative the more readily, as in doing so I may be in the better position to maintain that oversights and errors in these details will not be found after all to affect the general principles expounded in this volume, and their application to every form of speculation, philosophic and religious.

Note.—In thinking out this Work, I have made free but not unacknowledged use of the works of the great thinkers, both of ancient and modern times, both of the Continent and of Britain, who have pondered on these topics. Among later metaphysicians I have specially to acknowledge my obligations to the erudition, the unsurpassed logical power, and the profound observation, of the late Sir William Hamilton. I have also derived advantage, in the discussion of certain points, from the writings of living authors, British and Continental, who will be quoted or referred to at the proper places. In making this acknowledgment, I do not profess to belong to the school of any eminent man of the past or present, nor to any school, except the one which will attend to nothing but facts. I claim to have so far caught the spirit of those who have gone before, as to be resolute to maintain my independence, and I have not scrupled to state wherein I differ from those whose writings have yielded me the most valuable thoughts and suggestions. I have so constructed the work as to put incidental discussions and criticisms in Chapters and Sections, *Preliminary* and *Supplemental,* printed in smaller type.

PART FIRST.

GENERAL VIEW OF THE NATURE OF THE INTUITIVE CONVICTIONS OF THE MIND.

BOOK I.

GENERAL PROPOSITIONS REGARDING INTUITIONS.

CHAPTER I.

NEGATIVE PROPOSITIONS.

SECT. I. NO INNATE MENTAL IMAGES OR REPRESNTATIONS.

THE mind of man has the power of imaging or representing, in old forms by the memory, or in new forms by the imagination, whatever it has at any time known or experienced. To this mental property the Aristotelian phrase 'phantasy,' in use till last century, and revived of late by Sir William Hamilton,* might be appropriately applied, and then we should have the old term 'phantasm' (not 'phantom,' which might continue to denote the spectre) ready to designate the mental result, or the idea in consciousness. Having seen a given mountain, I can recall it at any time. Not only so, but I can put what I have experienced in an indefinite number of new shapes and colours. Having seen Mont Blanc, I can, when it pleases me, bring it up before me in all its bulk, supported by its snow-capped buttresses and flanked by its glancing glaciers; but I can do more, I can picture a mountain covered, not with ice, but with silver, or a mountain

* See his edition of Reid's Works, p. 291.

reaching up to the moon. I can reproduce in like mode whatever has been brought under my notice by any of the other senses. I can recall and reconstruct the bodily sensations,—the sounds, the colours, the tastes,—which I have at any time experienced. Milton, when he wrote 'Paradise Lost,' had lost the power of beholding colours, but he had still the capacity of imaging them to himself, or delineating them to others, as he did in his picture of the garden of Eden. A late distinguished poet never had the sense of smell, except for one brief but enjoyable space, when it awoke as he stood in a garden with flowers; but he must have been able ever after to realize what odours meant. It is to be carefully noted that this reproductive power reaches not only over all that has been acquired by the bodily senses, but over all that has been obtained by consciousness or the inward sense. I can recall the joys, the hopes, the sorrows, the fears, which at some former time may have moved my bosom. I can do more: I can picture myself, or picture others, in new and unheard-of scenes of gladness or of grief. Not only can I represent to myself the countenance of my friend, I can have an idea of his character and dispositions. I can form a mental picture of the outward scenes in which Shakspeare or Walter Scott place their heroes or heroines; but I can also enter into their thoughts and feelings.

But all these ideas, in the sense of phantasms, are reproductions of past experience in old forms or new dispositions. He who has had the use of his eyes at any time, can ever after understand what is meant by the colour of scarlet, but the person born blind has not the most distant idea of it in the sense of image, and if pressed for an answer to the question what he supposes it to be, he can come no nearer the reality than the man mentioned by Locke, who likened it to the sound of a trumpet; or than the blind boy of whom I have heard, who when asked whether he would prefer a lilac-coloured or a brown-coloured book, offered as a prize, decided for the lilac, as he supposed it must resemble the lilac-bush, whose odour had been so agreeable to him. Having experience of cogitations and sentiments of our own, we apprehend and appreciate those of others. Having a spiritual nature ourselves, we can form some idea of that Great Spirit in whose image we can claim to have been fashioned. But there may be attributes possessed by God of which we can form as little idea as the deaf man can of sounds, or the man without smell can of odours; they may be attributes to which we possess nothing like, and which we may be incapable of representing even in imagination. Niebuhr, the traveller, had often brought before him in his old-age the scenes of Eastern lands, but it was because he had witnessed them in his youth; and even we who have never been in those countries can so far understand the descriptions in his travels, because we have had the elements of them in our own experience; but there may be scenes in heaven which it hath not entered into the heart of man to conceive, inasmuch as nothing similar has passed under his notice in this lower world.

Now the proposition advanced in this Section is that the soul is not born unto this world with a stock of such phantasms, ready to come out on occasions presented. I rather think that this is the sense in which the phrase is understood by those who give Locke the credit of exploding the doctrine of "innate ideas" for ever. Taking 'idea' in the sense of 'image,' they say, what can be so unreasonable as to suppose that the mind comes into the world with such impressions ready to start forth, like writing with invisible ink, or like sun-pictures when exposed to certain chemical agencies. Locke, who

I suspect took 'idea' very much in the sense of mental image, or representation, may very possibly claim to have for ever set aside this view. But his credit in this respect is not very great after all. For I rather think no philosopher of influence ever propounded such a doctrine, formally or explicitly. It is quite conceivable, indeed, that Plato might have consistently held some such doctrine. He might have maintained that the soul did come into the world with such ideas; but then he would have ascribed them to experience acquired in a previous state of existence. But Plato's doctrine of ideas, while I believe it, in many aspects of it, to be as true as it is sublime, is apt to run into myths and fancies in the expression, so that it is difficult to give a thoroughly consistent exposition of it. By 'idea' he meant a pattern in or before the Divine Mind from all eternity; and he supposes a course of philosophic abstraction to be quite as necessary as reminiscence to call up such ideas into consciousness. But whether the view which I am opposing has or has not been entertained by men of eminence, it is expedient to notice it, in order at the very commencement to remove it out of the way as an encumbrance.

Sect. II. No Innate Abstract or General Notions.

This proposition is not the same as that illustrated in last Section. A mental picture of a mountain is one thing, and a general notion of the class mountain is a very different thing. All our cognitions by the senses or the consciousness, and all our subsequent images of them in memory or imagination, are singular and concrete; that is, they are of individual things, and of things with an aggregate of qualities. I can see or picture to myself an individual man of a certain form or character, but I cannot perceive nor adequately represent in the phantasy the class man. I can see or imagine a piece of magnetized iron, but I cannot see or imagine the polarity of the iron apart from the iron.

Still the mind has the high capacity of forming abstract and general notions. Out of the concrete it can form the abstract notion. I can see or image a lily only as with both a shape and colour, but I can in thought contemplate its whiteness apart from its form. Having seen a number of beasts with four limbs, I can think about a class of animals agreeing in this, that they are all quadrupeds. It appears then that the mental image and the abstract or general notion are not the same. The former is an exercise of the reproductive powers, recalling the old or putting the old in new collocations. The other is the result of an exercise of thought, separating the part from the whole, or contemplating an indefinite number of objects as possessing common qualities. If the one may be called the phantasm; the other, in contradistinction, may be denominated the notion or concept; or, to designate it more unequivocally, the logical notion or concept.

But it is quite as true of the abstract and general notions, as of the mental representations of the individual, that they are not in the soul when it comes into the world. It has been the avowed doctrine of the great body of philosophers, that the mind starts with the singular and the concrete. All our abstract notions are the result of a process in which we separate in thought the part from the whole; say the quality, from the substance presenting itself with its qualities,—say transparency, contemplated apart from the transparent ice or glass. All our general notions are the product of a process in which we contemplate objects as possessing common attributes, —say philosophers, as men agreeing in this, that they are seekers of wisdom.

It is, as I reckon it, the true merit of Locke that, in

the second book of his Essay on the Human Understanding, he shows how in the ideas we form of such objects as space, time, substance, cause, and infinity, and in the general maxims employed in speculation, such as that "it is impossible for the same thing to be and not to be at the same time," there is involved a process of the understanding founded on a previous experience.* It will be acknowledged that the soul is not born into the world with such abstract ideas as those of hardness, or organic action, or life, nor such general notions as those of mineral, plant, animal. This is admitted by all. But it is equally true that the soul of the infant has not yet in an abstract or general form those ideas which certain meta-

* Wherein lie the defects of Locke will come out as we advance (see more especially Part I. Book II. Chap. III., and Part III. Book I. Chap. II., sect. ii.); but I think he is invincible when he shows that children do not start with general maxims consciously before them, and that savages are not in possession of them. Thus, speaking of the maxim, "It is impossible for the same thing to be and not to be," he says, "A great part of illiterate people and savages pass many years of their rational age without ever thinking on this and the like general propositions" (Essay, bk. i. ch. xi. s. 12). "There is no knowledge of these general and self-evident maxims in the mind till it comes to the exercise of reason" (*ib.*, s. 14). Speaking of more particular self-evident propositions, which are assented to at first hearing, as that one and two are equal to three, he says, "They are known and assented to by those who are utterly ignorant of these more general maxims, and so being earlier in the mind than those (as they are called) first principles, cannot owe to them the assent wherewith they are received at first hearing" (s. 20). "For though a child quickly assents to this proposition, that an apple is not fire, when he has got the ideas of these two different things distinctly imprinted on his mind, and has learned that the names apple and fire stand for them, yet it will be some years after, before the same child will assent to this proposition, that it is impossible for the same thing to be and not to be" (s. 23). "He that will say children join these general abstract speculations with their sucking-bottles and their rattles, may perhaps with justice be thought to have more passion and zeal for his opinion, but less sincerity and truth, than one of that age" (s. 25). "Such kind of general propositions are seldom mentioned in the huts of Indians; much less are they found in the thoughts of children, or any impressions of them on the minds of naturals" (s. 27).

physicians describe as innate, as those of the *ego* and the *non-ego*, extension and potency, mind and matter, cause and effect, infinity and moral good. We reach the abstract idea of hardness by specially fixing the attention on one of the qualities of body. In like manner it is necessary, in order to attain the idea of space, to separate in thought the space from body known as occupying space. We get the idea of bodily substance by considering the permanent being apart from that which changes in the bodies falling under our notice. It is one of the aims of this treatise to specify the way in which the mind gets these ideas in the concrete and singular. But for the present I am seeking to have rubbish removed, that there may be free space whereon to lay a foundation. And I think it of vast moment to have it admitted that every abstract notion implies a process of separation, that every general notion implies a process of comparison, and that both one and other proceed on a previous knowledge which has come within the range of our consciousness.

Sect. III. No *a priori* Forms imposed by the Mind on Objects.

This proposition is laid down in opposition to a view which has been extensively and resolutely entertained of late years. Traces of it in a looser form may be detected at a much earlier date, but it may be regarded as formally introduced into philosophy by Kant, in his great work on the Kritick of Pure Reason. Suppose that the eyes, in every exercise of vision, were to start with a lens of a particular shape and colour, every object seen would take a predetermined form, and appear in a special hue. It is thus, according to Kant, that the mind sets out with certain forms which it imposes on phenomena,—that is, on appearances presenting themselves. In every primary cognition the mind imposes two Forms, one of Space and another of Time, on the phenomena presented empirically or *a posteriori*. Again, in comparing its cognitions, it sets them in a number of frameworks, called Categories, such as that of Quantity, Quality, Relation (including Substance and Accident, Causality and Dependence), and Modality, which have a reality not objectively in things but subjectively in the mind. A yet higher formative power brings these categories into unity in three Ideas of Pure Reason, those of Substance, Interdependence of Phenomena, and God, in which all objective reality has disappeared. These forms of the senses, categories of the understanding, and ideas of pure reason, constitute the *a priori* as distinguished from the *a posteriori* elements in the mental exercises.

It would carry us prematurely into very deep topics, with very ramified connections, were I at this early stage to criticize this doctrine in all its extent and bearings. It must suffice for the present to affirm that so far as it declares that the mind in cognition gives to the object what is not in the object, it is an unnatural doctrine, and is fraught with far-reaching consequences of a perilous character. The doctrine which I hope to establish is that the intuitive or cognitive powers do not impose forms on the objects, but are simply the agents or instruments by which we are enabled to discover what is in the objects. The mind, in looking at a material object, does not superinduce extension on it, but it observes that it is in space and must be in space. It does not carry within it a chain wherewith to connect events by a law of causation, but it has a capacity to discover that events are so connected and must be so connected. The capacity of cognition in the mind is not that of the bent mirror, to reflect the object under modified forms, but of the plane mirror, to reflect it as it is in its proper shape and colour. The truth is perceived by the mind, not formed; it is cognized, and not created. There must of course be a correspondence between the subject, mind, and the object, material or mental, contemplated; but it is a correspondence whereby the one knows and the other is known. This seems to me to be our natural, intuitive, and necessary conviction, and he who departs from it is landed in thickening difficulties on every side, and in particular cannot possibly defend himself from the assaults of scepticism; for if the mind can in respect of what it apprehends in the object create so much, why not suppose that it creates all? If it can create the space in which the object is perceived, why not suppose that it can create the object itself? This was the conclusion drawn by Fichte, who, carrying out the principles of Kant a step further, made the whole supposed external object a mere projection of the mind. There is no satisfactory or consistent way of avoiding this consequence but by adhering to the natural doctrine, and holding that the mind is so constituted as to know the object as it is, under the aspects in which it is presented to it.

Sect. IV. The Intuitions are not immediately before Consciousness as Laws or Principles.

I am to labour to show, in coming Sections, that there are intuitive principles in the mind regulating cognitions, beliefs, and judgments, whether intellectual or moral. My present position is, that operating in the mind as native laws or rules, they are not, as such, before the consciousness.

Every one speaks of there being in the mind capacities, powers, or faculties, such as the memory, or the imagination, or the reason, yet no one is immediately conscious of these mental powers. We are conscious of remembering a given event, of imagining a given scene, of discovering a given relation, but not of the mental power from which the acts proceed. Such considerations show that there may be operating in the mind faculties which do not fall directly under the internal eye. What is true of the faculties is true of the intuitive potencies of the mind. Indeed the intuitive principles of the mind are very closely related to the faculties. I have seldom however seen the precise relation between them distinctly pointed out. One class of investigators, such as Locke, treat of the faculties; another class, such as the German metaphysicians who have ramified from Kant, of *a priori* principles in the mind; while a third class, such as the Scottish school which has sprung from Reid, admit both into their system, but without explaining their connection. To me it appears that the intuitive or necessary principles of the mind are just the fundamental principles or regulative laws of the faculties. But without dwelling on this at present, it is enough to announce that the necessary principles, like the faculties of the mind, do not come immediately under the cognizance of consciousness. The individual actings do indeed fall directly under reflection or the internal sense. Thus we are conscious that the mind, on discovering a given effect, judges and decides that it must have a cause, and looks for a cause; but it has not meanwhile before it the general principle that every effect has a cause, or the principle of causation expressly formalized. Being convinced that we exist, we cannot be made to believe that we do not exist; but this is not because we have consciously before us the principle of contradiction, 'that it is impossible for the same thing to be and not to be at the same time.' It will be shown forthwith that we arrive reflexly at a knowledge of the intuitive principle, which operates spontaneously, by the observation and generalization of its individual acts or energies. My present purpose is gained if it is shown that such metaphysical principles as causation and contradiction are not directly before consciousness as rules, laws, or principles.

CHAPTER II.

POSITIVE PROPOSITIONS.

SECT. I. THERE ARE INTUITIVE PRINCIPLES OPERATING IN THE MIND.

I DO not propose to bring a full or satisfactory proof of this assertion in this short Section; the evidence will be found in the Second Part, in which our intuitive convictions are unfolded and discussed in detail. All that I profess to do at this stage is, to announce and explain certain positions which I hope to establish as we proceed, and answer some preliminary objections which are likely to occur to the English reader. To illustrate my meaning I must refer to certain convictions which I suppose to be intuitive, such as those regarding Space and Time, Substance, Quality, Cause and Effect, and Moral Good; all of these will be treated in detail in subsequent parts of the volume.

(1.) The first position I would lay down is that the mind must have something native or innate. The word innate is apt to be obnoxious to English ears; it is associated with views which Locke is supposed to have set aside for ever; and the revival of it will appear to some like the raising of a carcase from the grave to which it had been happily consigned. I have no partiality for a phrase which has been employed to set forth doctrines which it will be one object of this Work to undermine. To the phrase 'innate ideas' I take strong objections, which will come out as we advance. To the term 'innate,' if it were employed to qualify the proper noun, I see no objections; but if any are offended with it, the word 'native' will serve our purpose as well. All that either phrase denotes is, that there is something—at present I do not say what—in man's soul at the time it is born.

In this respect it is like the bodily substances which fall under our notice. These bodies are something and have something. This piece of iron which I hold in my hand is not a nonentity; it is an existence; it occupies space; it resists pressure; it has a colour. The soul of man is also an existence; it knows; it understands; it grieves; it rejoices. The capacity which it has of doing so may be described as native and original.

In this respect it is like the bodily frame when it comes forth from the womb. That body is not all which it is afterwards to become. Yet it is not, even at this early stage, a nonentity; it is not a nothing about to grow into something. Already that frame has a structure, a form, and most wondrous properties. And just as little is the soul, when it awakes to consciousness, a nonentity; even at this point, it is an existence, a something, and is possessed of something which may be called innate or connate.

Even on the supposition that it is like a surface of wax or a sheet of white paper, ready to receive whatever is impressed or written on it, it must have something inborn. If the mind have but a power of impressibility, it has in this something innate. The very wax and paper, in the inadequate illustration referred to, have capabilities, the capacity of taking something on them, and retaining it. But such comparisons have all a misleading tendency.

Surely the mind has something more than a mere receptivity! It is not a mere surface, on which matter may reflect itself as on a mirror: our consciousness testifies that, in comparison with matter, it is active; that it has an original, and an originating potency.

(2.) A second position may be maintained; that this something has rules, laws, or properties. Matter, with all its endowments, inorganic and organic, is regulated by laws which it is the office of physical and physiological science to discover. All the powers or properties of material substance have rules of action; for example, gravitation and chemical affinity have regulations which can be expressed in quantitative proportions. That mind also has properties, is shown by its action; and surely these properties do not act capriciously or lawlessly. There are rules involved in the very constitution of the active properties, and these rules are not beyond the possibility of being discovered and expressed. The senses indeed cannot detect them, but they may be found out by internal observation. Nor does it appear that this law can be discovered immediately by consciousness, any more than the law of gravitation can be perceived by the eye. But the operations of the mental properties are under the eye of consciousness just as those of gravitation are under the senses; and by careful observation, analysis, and generalization, we may from the acts reach the laws of the acts. He who has reached the exact expression of our mental properties, is in possession of a law which is native or innate.

(3.) As a third position, it is capable of being established that the mind has original perceptions, which original perceptions may be described as intuitive. Every one will acknowledge that the mind has perceptions through the senses, and I shall endeavour to show, as we advance, that it has perceptions of the understanding and of the moral faculty: some of these perceptions are, no doubt, secondary and derivative, but the secondary imply primary perceptions, and the derivative original ones. Thus perception of distance by the eye may be derivative: but it implies an original perception, by the eye, of a surface. It is by a process of reasoning that I know that the square of the hypothenuse of a right-angled triangle is equal to the square of the other two sides: but this reasoning proceeds on certain axiomatic truths whose certainty is seen at once, as that "if equals be added to equals, the wholes are equal." Let it be observed that we are now in a region in which are loftier properties than those possessed by inert matter; still these higher have rules as well as the lower or material properties. The original perceptions by sense, or reason, or moral power, have all their laws, which it should be the business of psychology or of metaphysics to discover and determine. These original perceptions may be represented as intuitions inasmuch as they look immediately on the object or truth. The rules or laws which they obey may be described as intuitive principles; it is the office of mental science to discover them by a process of introspection, abstraction, and comparison.

(4.) It is possible to defend a fourth position, that the mind can discover necessary and universal truth. Not that I propose to substantiate this statement at this stage of our inquiries, still I may announce it, and show how it is not impossible to establish it. The mind declares that these two straight lines before it do not enclose a space. It does more: it declares of every other two straight lines conceived, that they cannot enclose a space. It says of these two straight lines, that if they proceed an inch without being nearer each other, that they will proceed an ell, a mile, or a myriad of miles, without being nearer; nay, it declares of all such parallel lines, that they may be prolonged for ever without meeting. These are specimens of a large class of truths, which the mind perceives to be true, and necessarily true. There are logical truths—such as that whatever is predicated of a class may be predicated of all the members of the class, and moral truths—such as that sin is deserving of reprobation, which are also necessary and universal. But if the mind may—as I maintain that it can and does—rise to the discovery of such truths, it must be by native laws, the expression of which will give us metaphysical science, just as the expression of the laws which material phenomena obey gives us physical science.

But it will be said that we discover all this by experience. We are not at this stage of inquiry in circumstances to have the relation between intuition and experience definitively pointed out. But

(5.) It may be stated, as a fifth position, that the very acquisition of experience implies native laws or principles. So far from experience being able to account for innate principles, innate principles are required to account for the treasures of experience. For how is it that man is enabled to gather experience? How is he different in this respect from the stock or the stone, from the vegetable or the brute, which can acquire no experience, at least no such experience? Plainly because he is endowed with capacities for this end; and these faculties must have some law or principle on which they proceed. Experience, in the narrow sense, must mean, what we have personally noticed. Even in noticing this, there must be faculties, with principles involved in them, at work. But a personal experience would of itself be valueless to man; it would not and could not enable him to rise from the known to the unknown, to argue from the past to the future. But man can from the known discover the unknown, from the past he can anticipate the future; and when he does so, he must proceed on some principle which is capable of exposition, and ought to be expressed. And if man be capable, as I maintain he is, of reaching necessary and universal truth, he must proceed on principles which can never be derived from experience. Twenty times have we tried, and found that two straight lines do not enclose a space: this does not authorize us to affirm that they never can enclose a space, otherwise we might argue that, because we had seen a judge and his wig twenty times together, they must therefore be together through all eternity. A hundred times have I seen a spark kindle gunpowder: this does not entitle me to declare that it will do so the thousandth or the millionth time, or wherever the spark and the gunpowder are found. The gathered knowledge and wisdom of man, and his power of prediction, thus imply more than experience: they presuppose faculties to enable him to gather experience, and in some cases involve necessary principles which enable him, and justify him, as he acts on his ability, to rise from a limited experience to an unlimited and necessary law.

But it may be urged that we reach these results by reasoning. I reply that

(6.) A sixth position may be established, that reasoning proceeds on principles which cannot be proved by reasoning, but must be assumed, and assumed as seen intuitively to be true. In all ratiocination there must be something from which we argue. That from which we argue is the premiss,—in the Aristotelian analysis of argument, it is the two premisses. But as we go back and back, we must at length come to something which cannot be proven. That which cannot be proven must be assumed, but surely not assumed capriciously; if assumed capriciously, it can yield no proper foundation, and if not assumed arbitrarily, it must be according to some rule or principle which should be expounded and stated by the metaphysician. How can we reason but from what we know? and in going back we come to truths which we know directly, that is, by intuition, and the law of this intuition should be evolved. It might further be shown that there must be a mental principle involved—it is the Dictum in the Aristotelian account of reasoning—in the process by which we connect the conclusion with the premisses; for were there no such principle, the ratiocination would be arbitrary, and it would be vain for any man to endeavour to convince his neighbour, or even to try to keep himself consistent. Such considerations as these show that at the foundation of argument, and at every stage of the superstructure, there are mental principles involved which are either intuitive or depend on principles which are intuitive.

Sect. II. The Native Convictions of the Mind are of the Nature of Perceptions or Intuitions.

In some cases there are external objects presented; the mind looks upon them, and the conviction at once springs up. Thus it is that it knows immediately this particular body, this paper or table, as occupying space. In other cases it is something within the mind that is contemplated; it is self in some particular exercise,—say thinking or feeling. In many instances the object presented in the mind is the result of a prior mental process. Thus, having at a former time seen two straight lines, we now, in our thinking moods, image or represent them; and the mind, on the contemplation, proclaims at once that they cannot enclose a space. Or we have occasion to consider some particular voluntary sentiment of a fellow-man,—say his cherishing malice against another man, and we proclaim it to be evil, condemnable. In this last instance the act contemplated is not, properly speaking, under our immediate view, for it is in the breast of a neighbour, but it is represented to us in our minds, and looking on this representation the mind pronounces a decision. In every case these convictions seem to be of the nature of perceptions, that is, something is presented to us, and the cognition, belief, or judgment is formed. It is on this account that I have, in the title of this Treatise, chosen to call them Intuitions. As we advance, we shall find other distinctive characters, the expression of which yields other epithets; but the term Intuitions, that is, perceptions formed by looking in upon objects, seems to bring out the original quality of the native convictions of the mind.

Sect. III. Intuitive Convictions rise on the Contemplation of Objects Presented or Represented to the mind.

Metaphysicians have often given such an account of them as to leave the impression that the mind creates them independent of objects, or that, at the utmost, experience furnishes merely the occasion, on the occurrence of which the mind fashions them by its own inherent power. I shall have occasion to show that the relation between the intuitive powers and objects is of a much closer and more dependent character than this account would lead us to suppose. In intuition we look into the object, we discover something in it, or belonging to it, or we discover a relation between it and some other object. Were the object taken away, the perception would be meaningless, indeed it would altogether cease. Intuition is a perception of an object, and of something in it or pertaining to it. Perception, without something looked into, would be as contradictory as vision without an object seen, or touch without an object felt. In our cognitions we know objects, or qualities of objects, we know self as thinking, or body as extended. In belief we entertain a trust regarding certain objects that they are so and so,—of time, for example, that it can come to no end. In judgment we discover certain relations between two or more objects, as that a mode implies a substance. Our intuitive convictions are thus not ideas, notions, judgments, formed apart from objects, but are in fact discoveries of something in objects, or relating to them.*

SECT. IV. THE INTUITIONS OF THE MIND ARE PRIMARILY DIRECTED TO INDIVIDUAL OBJECTS.

I shall have occasion to show, when I come to distinguish and classify the intuitions, that some are of the nature of cognitions and beliefs, while others are of the nature of judgments. But whatever be their distinctive nature, they always, as intuitions, primarily contemplate objects as individuals. If I know, or believe in anything, it is an existing thing, that is, as singular. If I form an intuitive judgment, that is, make a comparison, it is still in regard to two or more objects considered as singulars; and so far as we pass beyond this, there is always, as I shall endeavour to show, a discursive process involved.

A very different account is often given, if not formally, at least implicitly, of intuition or of intuitive reason. Man is represented as gazing immediately on the true, the beautiful, the good, meaning in the abstract, or in the general. It is admitted that there must be some sort of experience, some individual object presented as the occasion, but the mind, being thus roused into activity, is represented as contemplating, by direct vision, such things as space and time, substance and quality, cause and effect, the infinite, and moral good. I hope to be able to

* Locke laid strong hold of the features specified in this Section and the last; see *infra*, Part I. Book II. Chap. III.

show that this theory is altogether mistaken. Our appeal on this subject must be to the consciousness and the memory, and these give a very different account of the process which passes through the mind when it is employed about such objects. Intuitively the mind contemplates a particular body as occupying space and being in space, and it is by a subsequent intellectual process, in which abstraction acts an important part, that the idea of space is formed. Intuitively the mind contemplates an event as happening in time, and then by a further process arrives at the notion of time. The mind has not intuitively an idea of cause or causation in the abstract, but discovering a given effect, it looks for a specific cause. It does not form some sort of vague notion of a general infinite, but fixing its attention on some individual thing,—such as space, or time, or God,—it is constrained to believe it to be infinite. The child has not formed to itself a refined idea of moral good, but contemplating a given action it proclaims it to be good or evil. The same remark holds good of the intuitive judgments of the mind, that is, when it compares two or more things, and proclaims them at once to agree or disagree. I do not, without a process of discursive thought, pronounce, or even understand, the general maxim that things which are equal to the same things are equal to one another, but on discovering that first one bush and then another bush are of the same height as my staff, I decide that the two bushes are equal to one another.

It will be shown in next Section that the mind has the power of generalizing the individual cognitions or judgments of the intuitions, and in doing so it may arrive at most important truth. It will come out, too, that intuition may fasten on the general proposition and pronounce decisions in which it is involved. But in the formation of the general maxim, there is a process of logical thought involved for which the intuition is not responsible. It is only in the form of convictions regarding individuals presenting themselves that our intuitions manifest themselves in all men—in children and savages for instance. The boy decides that the ball which he holds in his hand cannot be at the same time in the hand of some other boy who may pretend to have it; but he has not meanwhile consciously before him the formula that it is impossible for the same body to be in two places at the same time. The individual conviction is in all men when the objects are pressed on their attention, the general maxim is the result of thought and especially of abstraction and generalization. By drawing this distinction we are able to maintain that these intuitions are native and in all minds, and yet save ourselves from the absurdity in which so many metaphysicians land themselves when they speak of children or infants as employed in contemplating the *ego* and the *non-ego*, personality, externality, subject, and object. The particular conviction is formed by all in a concrete form when the appropriate objects present themselves; but the abstract formula is fashioned by those addicted to reflection, and is not even understood except by those whose minds are matured and cultivated.

SECT. V. THE INDIVIDUAL INTUITIVE CONVICTIONS CAN BE GENERALIZED INTO MAXIMS, AND THESE ARE ENTITLED TO BE REPRESENTED AS PHILOSOPHIC PRINCIPLES.

The native principles in the soul are analogous to the physical laws operating in external nature. Both one and other act at all times, on the necessary conditions being supplied. Like the physiological processes of respiration and the circulation of the blood, the intuitions do not depend for their operation on any voluntary determination of the human mind, and they act whether we observe them or no; indeed they often act best when we are taking no notice of them. We cannot command their exercise on the one hand, nor prohibit it on the other. A greater or less number of them are working in the soul at every waking moment of our existence. It is always to be remembered indeed that they are mental and not material laws; but, making allowance for this, they may be regarded as operating very much like the great physical or physiological laws of chemical affinity, or of nervous irritability, or of the reflex nervous system. As they act in an analogous manner, so they may be discovered in much the same way as the laws of the material universe, that is, by the method of induction.

The laws of matter are discovered by the observation and generalization of their individual operations. With the exception of a few metaphysicians of the schools of Schelling or Hegel, no one now maintains that these laws can be discovered by *a priori* speculation. Nor can they be detected by mere sense,—by eye, or touch, or ear; no man ever yet saw, or touched, or heard, a law of nature. All that falls under the perception of the senses are individual facts, and those generally concrete or complex; that is, the object is presented as exhibiting more than one quality at the same time, or the effect is the result of a variety of causes. In order to reach the law by an observation of the facts, there is need first of all of a judicious analysis, or, as Bacon calls it, the necessary "rejections and exclusions," or the separation and setting aside of the extraneous matter of the mixed phenomenon; that is, the matter which does not belong to the law or agent we are seeking to discover. Having made these appropriate rejections, we now generalize the facts—that is, find out where they agree—and thus arrive at the discovery of the physical law.

It is in much the same way, *mutatis mutandis*, that we discover the laws of our original and native convictions. I boldly affirm that it is as impossible to determine them as it is to settle the laws of the external universe by *a priori* cogitation or logical division and dissection. As they cannot be elaborated by speculation on the one hand, so neither do they fall under the immediate cognizance of consciousness on the other. All that comes under the consciousness is individual: it is an object now present; it is the mind in some state or mode. But our modifications of mind at any given moment are always more or less complex; that is, there is more than one property in exercise, though of course combined in the unity of the mind. But, by a sharp analysis, it is always possible to separate the different elements, and fix the attention exclusively on that which alone pertains to the law or property we are seeking to evolve. Examining carefully the nature of the acts which seem to flow from the same principle, we generalize them; and, if we do so accurately, we obtain the exact nature of the principle, and can embody it in a verbal expression.

The principle thus discovered and enunciated is properly a metaphysical one; it is a truth above sense, a truth of mind, a truth of reason. It is different in its origin and authority from the general rules reached by experience, such as the law of gravitation, or the law of chemical affinity, or the law of the distribution of animals over the earth's surface. These latter are the mere generalizations of an experience necessarily limited; they hold good merely in the measure of our experience, and as experience can never reach all possible cases, so the rule can never be absolute; we can never say that there may not be exceptions. Laws of the former kind are of a higher or deeper nature, they are the generalization of convictions carrying necessity with them, and a consequent universality in their very nature. They are entitled to be regarded as in an especial sense philosophic principles, being the ground to which we come when we follow any system of truth sufficiently far down, and competent to act as a basis on which to erect a superstructure of science. They are truths of our original constitution, having the sanction of Him who hath given us our constitution, and graven them there with His own finger.

It is ever to be borne in mind, however, that the detection and exact expression of these intuitive principles is always a delicate and is often a most difficult operation. Did they fall immediately under the eye of consciousness, the work would be a comparatively easy one; we should only have to look within in order to see them. But all that consciousness can notice are their individual exercises mixed up one with another and with all other actings of the mind. It requires a microscopic eye, and much analytic skill, to detect the various fibres in the complex structure, and to follow each through its various windings and entanglements to its source.

BOOK II.

CHARACTER OF INTUITIONS, AND METHOD OF EMPLOYING THEM.

CHAPTER I.

MARKS AND PECULIARITIES OF INTUITION.

SECT. I. TESTS.

BUT how are we to distinguish a primitive conviction which does not need probation, and which we may not even doubt, from propositions which we are not required to believe till evidence is produced? Are we entitled to appeal, when we please and as we please, to supposed first truths? Have we the privilege, when we wish to adhere to a favourite opinion, to declare that we see it to be true intuitively, and thus at once get rid of all objections, and of the necessity for even instituting an examination? May we, when hard pressed, or defeated in argument, resort, as it suits us, to an original principle which we assume without evidence, and declare to be beyond the reach of refutation? It is one of the aims of this treatise to limit the confidence we put in our supposed intuitions, and lay a stringent restraint on the appeal to truths which are represented as above probation. There can be tests propounded sufficient to determine with precision what convictions are, and what convictions are not, entitled to be regarded as intuitive, and these tests are such that they admit of an easy application, requiring only a moderate degree of careful consideration of the maxim proffered as claiming our assent.

1. *The primary mark of intuitive truth is self-evidence.* It must be evident, and it must have its evidence in the object. The mind, on the bare contemplation of the object, must see it to be so and so, must see it to be so at once, without requiring any foreign evidence or mediate proof. That the planet Mars is inhabited, or that it is not inhabited, is not a first truth, for it is not evident on the bare contemplation of the object. That the isle of Madagascar is inhabited, even this is not a primary conviction; we believe it because of secondary testimony. Nay, that the three angles of a triangle are together equal to two right-angles, is not a primitive judgment, for it needs other truths coming between to carry our conviction. But that there is an extended object before me when I look at a table or a wall, that I who look at these objects exist, and that two marbles added to two marbles here will be equal to two marbles added to two marbles there,—these are truths that are evident on the bare contemplation of the objects, and need no foreign facts, or considerations derived from any other quarter, to establish them.

But it may be asked, can we certainly know what truths are self-evident? Are we not liable to be deceived, especially by education and prepossessions? Have not some declared propositions to be self-evident, which have afterwards been positively disproved? The reply is, that if we devote our minds earnestly to the object, we cannot readily go astray. No doubt, it is possible to fall into error in the application of this test, as in the application of any other; but this can take place only by negligence, by refusing to go round the object to which the conviction refers, and to look upon it as it is in itself, and in all its aspects. In specifying this test as the fundamental one, I do not mean that it can be applied without much and careful inspection. It is fortunate that we have a secondary test to determine the presence of the primary characteristic.

2. *Necessity is a secondary mark of intuitive truth.* I am not inclined to fix on this as the original or essential characteristic. I shrink from maintaining that a proposition is true because we must believe it. A proposition is true as being true, and certain propositions are seen by us to be self-evidently true. I would not ground the evidence on the necessity of belief, but I would ascribe the irresistible nature of the conviction to the self-evidence. As the necessity flows from the self-evidence, so it may become a test of it, and a test not difficult of application.

When an object or truth is self-evident, necessity always attaches to our convictions regarding it. And according to the nature of the conviction, so is the necessity attached. We shall see that some of the convictions are of the nature of knowledge, others of the nature of belief, a third class of the nature of judgments, in which we compare objects known or believed in. In the first our cognition is necessary, in the second our belief is necessary, in the third our judgment is necessary. I know self as an existing thing: this is a necessary cognition; I must entertain it, and never can be driven from it. That space exceeds my widest imagination of space: this is a necessary belief, I must believe it. That every effect has a cause: this is a necessary judgment; I must decide in this way. Wherever there is such a conviction, it is a sign of an intuitive perception. Necessity too may be employed in a negative form, and this is often the most decisive form. If I know immediately that there is an extended object before me in the book which I read, I cannot be made to know that there is not an extended object before me. If I must believe that time had no beginning, I cannot be made to believe that it has had a beginning. Necessitated as I am to decide that two parallel lines cannot meet, I cannot be made to decide that they can meet. Necessity as a test may thus assume two forms, and we may take the one best suited to our purpose at the time. In the use of a very little care and discernment, this test will settle for us as to any given truth, whether it is or is not self-evident.

3. *Catholicity may be employed as a tertiary test.* By catholicity is meant that the conviction is entertained by all men, or at least by all men possessed of intelligence, when the objects are presented. I am not inclined to use this as a primary test. For in the first place it is not easy to ascertain, or at least to settle absolutely, what truths may claim this common consent of humanity; and even though this were determined, still it might be urged in the second place that this does not prove that it is necessary or original, but simply that it is a native property,—like the appetite for food among all men,—and would still leave it possible for opponents to maintain that there may be intelligent beings in other worlds who accord no such assent, just as we can conceive beings in the other parts of the universe who have no craving for meat or drink. But while not inclined to use catholicity as a primary test, I think it may come in at times as an auxiliary one. For what is in all men, may most probably come from what is not only native, but necessary; and must also in all probability be self-evident, or at least follow very directly from what is self-evident. Catholicity, when conjoined with necessity, may

determine very readily and precisely whether a conviction is intuitive.

Important purposes are served by the combination of these two tests: that is, necessity and catholicity. By the first we have a personal assurance which can never be shaken, and of which no one can deprive us. Though the whole world were to declare that we do not exist, or that a cruel action is good, we would not give up our own personal conviction in favour of their declaration. By the other principle we have confidence in addressing our fellow-men, for we know that there are grounds of thought common to them and to us, and to these we can appeal in reasoning with them. By the one I am enabled, yea, compelled, to hold by my personality, and maintain my independence; by the other I am made to feel that I am one of a large family, every member of which has the same principles of belief as I myself have. The one gives me the argument from private judgment, the other the argument from common or catholic consent. The concurrence of the two should suffice to protect me from scepticism of every kind, whether it relate to the world within or the world without, whether to physical or moral truths.

These marks are as clear and as easily applied, and are quite as decisive for testing reason in its primary or intuitive exercise, as the syllogism is in testing reason in its secondary or derivative operation; that is, as inference or reasoning.

SECT. II. DIFFERENT ASPECTS OF INTUITIONS, AND THEIR THEORETICAL CHARACTERS.

Hitherto we have been approaching our subject by a somewhat winding path, catching glimpses of the position of the building, and of some of its principal turrets. We may now walk up directly to it, and take a survey of its general form, and ascertain the mode of entering it, with the view of afterwards exploring its apartments one by one. It will be found to present three sides, sides of one fabric, but each with its peculiarities.

The intuitions may be considered *first* as laws, rules, principles regulating the original action and the primitive perceptions of the mind. Or *secondly*, they may be regarded as individual perceptions, or convictions manifesting themselves in consciousness. Or *thirdly*, they may be contemplated as abstract notions, or general rules elaborated out of the individual exercises. We cannot have a distinct or adequate view of our intuitions unless we carefully distinguish these the one from the other. The whole of the confusion, and the greater part of the errors, which have appeared in the discussions about innate ideas and *a priori* principles, have sprung from neglecting these distinctions, or from not carrying them out consistently. In each of these sides the intuitions present distinct characters, and many affirmations may be properly made of the original principles of the mind under one of these aspects, which would by no means hold good of the others.

I. They may be contemplated as LAWS, RULES, OR PRINCIPLES GUIDING THE MIND. Hence they have been called *κοιναὶ προλήψεις, κοιναὶ ἔννοιαι, πρῶται ἔννοιαι*, forms and regulative principles. Under this aspect

(1.) *They are native.* Hence they have been called natural, innate, connate, implanted, constitutional. All these phrases point to the circumstance that they are not acquired by practice, nor the result of experience, but are in the mind naturally, as constituents of its very being, and involved in its higher exercises. In this respect they are analogous to universal gravitation and chemical affinity, which are not produced in bodies as they operate, but are in the very nature of bodies, and the springs of their action. It is thus—that is, by an original property of his being—that man is led to look on body as occupying space, on any given effect as having a cause, and on certain actions as being morally good or evil.

(2.) *They are regultaive.** They rule the mind in its original and primitive energies, both of thought and belief. They lead the mind, for example, on discovering a quality, to connect it with substance; on contemplating time, to declare that it cannot have had a beginning; and on having a vicious action brought before it, to decide that it is deserving of punishment. This characteristic is brought before us by the phrases so often applied to them,—forms, laws, rules, canons, and principles. They lead and guide the deeper mental action, just as the chemical and vital properties conduct and control the composition of bodies and the organization of plants. It is to be carefully noticed that, as regulative principles, they are not dependent, in themselves or in their action, on our observation of them; indeed they must be guiding the mind before we can observe them; still less are they dependent on the will of the possessor, which has merely an indirect control over them, and this only by bringing before the cognitive or representative powers of the mind the objects which evoke them.

(3.) They are *catholic, or common.* That is, they are

* The phrase Regulative has been used by Kant in Kr. d. r. Ver. transcen. Doc. der Urtheilskraft, ch. iii., where he speaks of certain principles as being constitutive and others regulative. The distinction proceeds on certain Kantian views, and cannot be admitted by any natural realist. Sir W. Hamilton has adopted the phrase Regulative ('Metaphysics,' Lect. 38), and agrees so far with Kant that he reckons many of the regulative principles of the mind, such as those about space and time and cause, as guaranteeing no objective reality. The phrase is a good one, but in adopting it, care must be taken to dissociate it from all the peculiarities of the Kantian and Hamiltonian philosophy. The regulative principles guide the mind so as that it discovers what is in things, whereas, according to Kant, they guarantee nothing as to things.

in every human mind. Not that they are in all men as formalized principles; under this aspect, as we shall see forthwith, they come before the minds of comparatively few. Some of them are perhaps not even manifested in all minds; certainly some of them are not manifested, in their higher forms, in the souls of all. In infants some of them have not yet made their appearance, and among persons low in the scale of intelligence, they do not come out in their loftier exercises; just as the plant does not come all at once into full flower,—just as the plant, in unfavourable circumstances, may never come into seed at all. Still the capacity is there, needing only favourable circumstances—that is, the appropriate objects pressed on the attention—to foster it into developed forms. Under this aspect, the epithets common, catholic, have been applied to them; they have been represented as the universal attributes of humanity, and as belonging to man as man.

But it is to be specially noticed that in this whole general view of them, they are not before consciousness as principles. They do indeed come out into consciousness, not however as laws, but as individual convictions. This negative characteristic has been often referred to when they have been spoken of as latent, occult, hiding themselves, as roots covered up in the substance of the soul, as foundations beneath the ground, as faculties requiring to be developed, and as evoked into exercise only on the occasion of experience.

II. They may be contemplated as CONVICTIONS MANIFESTED IN CONSCIOUSNESS. Hence they are called especially intuitions, spontaneous or natural convictions, innate ideas, and primitive beliefs and judgments. It is only under this aspect that we can directly apply to them the tests of intuition specified in last Section. Under what restriction they apply to our intuitions as regulative or as generalized principles may be afterwards pointed out. We have already in our survey gathered what are some of the characteristics of these our conscious convictions; still, what we before enounced will require to be formally stated in its proper place alongside of some other theoretical characteristics, to be now unfolded.

(1.) *They are perceptions.* This feature was caught and has been expressed by those who speak of them as perceptions, apperceptions, senses, apprehensions, and who represent them as seeing, looking, regarding, contemplating.

(2.) *They look at objects.* Hence they have been represented as comprising knowledge, cognition, and discernment. It is of the greater moment to bring out this characteristic, from the circumstance that they have often been too much dissociated from objects. In reading some of the exaggerated accounts of them, the impression is apt to be left that they are formed by the native power of the mind, independent of objects altogether; and even in more guarded statements, the presentation of objects is spoken of as merely the occasion on which they spring up.* In opposition to all this, I maintain that they are perceptions of objects, of objects themselves or something in objects. Sometimes the objects are external to the mind, as when I intuitively look on body as extended or on space as having no limits. In other cases the objects are within the mind, as when I look on self, and discover that it has being and personality, or on a certain representation in the mind, say of a benevolent action, which I discern to be good. Or the intuition may manifest itself in the form of judgments or comparisons; but even in such, it is a perception of objects as having points of relation. It is the very nature of the regulative principles of the mind that they

* This view is examined *infra*, Part III. Book I. Chap. II. sect. v., *Supplementary*.

lead us to look at objects, and to discover what is in them.

(3.) *They look at objects as singulars.* In this respect they are analogous to the senses and consciousness, and have often been characterized as senses and as consciousnesses. This peculiarity has already been explained in a general way.

(4.) *They are immediate.* That is, our minds, in intuition, gaze directly on the object. Hence they have been called feelings,—language which may be allowed if meant merely to express that they are analogous to feeling or touch as it feels or handles an object, but which is of a most misleading character if intended to signify that they are of the nature of emotions. Under this aspect they have been called visions, inspirations, revelations. Hence too the special name Intuitions applied to them, to denote that they see the object as it were face to face, and with nothing coming between to aid the view on the one hand, or obstruct it on the other. This character it is which affords what I have described as the primary test, that is, self-evidence.

In the case of many objects, we cannot look on them directly. Thus we who live in the nineteenth century cannot be spectators of the events which happened in the first century. When dwelling in these islands, we cannot gaze on the Himalayas or Andes; we can contemplate such objects only indirectly, and through something else as a medium. But in every intuition we look at once on the corresponding object: it is thus we are conscious immediately of self in action; thus that we gaze on body as occupying space; thus that we regard space as unbounded; thus that we regard a certain disposition as good or as evil.

But to prevent misapprehension it is necessary here to offer an explanation. When I say that the object is present, I do not mean by this that the object must be a bodily one, or one external to the mind. The object may quite as frequently be a mental as a material one. The object may even be represented, in a loose and inaccurate sense, as an absent one. Thus I may pronounce of an event which happened far away, in India, that it must have had a cause, and of a deed of self-sacrifice, done a thousand years ago, that it must have been good. But then it is not, properly speaking, to the distant event that the intuition looks, but to the representation of it in the mind. It is only mediately, through the representation, that the intuition can refer to the actual occurrence, and this on the supposition that the representation is correct; and if the representation be erroneous, or even mutilated, or imperfect, it cannot be legitimately applied to the event. Correctly speaking, the object is always present when the intuition gazes on it; it is either a bodily object immediately before the mind, or it is a presentation or representation within the mind itself.

(5.) *There is a conviction of necessity attached to every one of them.* Hence they have been described as irresistible, unavoidable, compelling belief, and not admitting of doubt or dispute. We have already had this character under our notice, and it may yet come before us in its applications, and in regard to the supposed diversity in the necessity as attached to different convictions, and it is not needful to enter more minutely into its nature in this general survey. It should be carefully noticed that the necessity attaches itself directly only to our individual perceptions. The general formula carries with it no such conviction till it is shown that it has been correctly formed. There may be legitimate doubts and disputes as to many proposed philosophic maxims, as to whether they are or are not correct. Still, as will be shown, the necessity being in the singulars, goes up into the universals on the condition of the universal being properly formed.

(6.) *They are original and independent.* Hence they have been called first, primary, or primitive truths, and been described as origins, ἀρχαί, or original principles, seeds, roots, and starting-points, and characterized as underived, independent, self-sufficient. The mind spontaneously starts with such, it sets out from them, and in doing so, feels that it has need of no probation or foreign support of any kind.

A large body of our convictions, even of the surest, are derived; they are dependent on something else. Thus we are dependent for our historical information on the testimony of our fellow-men; for our belief in the great mysteries opened in the Bible, on the testimony of God; for our conviction of the propositions in the Sixth Book of Euclid, on the prefixed axioms, and on the propositions in the other five books, and generally for the last conclusion of a chain of reasoning, on all the links which have preceded. But in intuition, or, as it may be called, intuitive reason, our conviction hangs on nothing else. That the whole, orange or earth, is equal to the sum of its several parts, is a truth which depends on no other.

There may be many asseverations to which we do not give our assent till evidence of some kind is furnished. There may be true propositions from which we withhold our concurrence till they are proven. Very possibly there may be inhabitants on that other side of the moon which no human eye has seen, but I wait for evidence before I give a decision one way or another. It seems very certain that there have been volcanoes in the moon, but men did not give their credence till traces of eruptive formations were discovered by the telescope. But there are propositions which do not require proof, even as they do not admit of proof, and yet our conviction of them, to say the least of it, is as strong as of the truths most firmly established by probation. There are some apprehensions, some propositions, in regard to which the mind sees that it needs mediate proof in order to convince it that they imply a reality or a truth; but there are others, in regard to which it sees that they have in themselves all that is needful to gain our assent. There are some truths for which reason demands support before it will give its adhesion to them; there are others, in regard to which reason says, that they do not require to be borne up by any external evidence. It is not because of any defect in the veracity of intuitive truths, that they do not admit of probation; it is rather because of the fullness and strength of their veracity. It is, in a sense, owing to a deficiency in certain truths, or rather, a deficiency in our minds with respect to them, that they require something to lean on. Thus it is because of some defect or perplexity in the truth (to us), that mathematicians cannot solve, except approximately, the problem of three bodies attracting each other. It is because of the self-sufficiency of certain truths, such as that the thinking *me* exists, and that extended bodies exist, and that gratitude is a virtue, it is because our minds are so constituted as to see them at once, that they require no proof; we need no other light in which to see them, they shine in their own light.

But let us properly understand and limit this account given of them; when they are said to be independent, it does not mean that they are independent of objects: we have before seen that our intuitions are perceptions of or regarding objects.

(6.) *Some of them are catholic,—that is, in all men.* Hence they have been described as common ideas and notions. We have seen that as regulative powers they are in all men, without exception. But all of them do not, therefore, come forth in actual energies; many of them in their developed and manifested form are the result of growth, and some of them seem to lie dormant in many minds from the want of proper fostering circumstances. Still, there are some of them, such as the intuition of self and the intuition of body in space, which are formed by all men in their individual and concrete form.

III. They may be contemplated as NOTIONS OR PRINCIPLES FORMED BY ABSTRACTION AND GENERALIZATION. Under this aspect they are *πρῶτα νοήματα*, *naturæ judicia*, *a priori* notions, definitions, maxims, and axioms.

Thus considered they cannot be represented as common or universal in the sense of being in all men. If we look to the hundreds of millions of human beings on the face of the earth, including infants, children, savages and the unreflecting masses, there is but a very small minority of the family of man who have ever had such notions or maxims before them. Every human being, if he sees an object before him, will refuse to give his assent to the assertion that this object does not exist; but how few beyond the limited circle of professed metaphysicians have ever had consciously before them the principle that it is impossible for the same thing to be and not to be at the same time. Millions of men, women, and children are every hour acting on the intuition of causation—are taking food, for example, in the belief that it will nourish them, though they never have had the principle consciously before them, and know not so much as that there is a principle of causation. But under this view,

(1.) *The General Maxim is Necessary, on the condition of the generalization out of the individual convictions being properly formed.* It is to be constantly kept in mind, that the necessity attaches in the first instance to the singular conviction looking to its objects. But the necessity being in the individuals, may be made to go up into the general, provided the general has been legitimately drawn from the individuals. With this proviso, a very important one however, the maxim is not only true, it is necessarily true, it cannot be otherwise. If any one were to lay down the principle that "everything must have a cause," he would not be announcing a necessary truth; for while there is a necessary conviction in every exercise of mind regarding causation, he has not seized it properly, nor expressed it correctly. But if the maxim that "everything which begins to be must have a cause" be, as I maintain it is, the proper generalization of the peculiarity of the individual conviction, it may be regarded as a necessary one. In this respect it differs from the general laws of nature reached by observation; as for example, that hydrogen chemically combines with oxygen in the proportion of one to eight. We cannot, from the bare contemplation of hydrogen and oxygen, say that they must unite in any particular proportion, or that they shall unite at all. The law is reached by the pure observation of particular cases, and these, however many, are still limited in number; for all the particular cases, that is, of the mutual action of hydrogen and oxygen in the universe, never can fall under our notice. The law may, after all, be a mere modification of a higher and wider law; there may be exceptions to it in other worlds; it is in no sense absolutely or universally certain. But on the bare contemplation of two given straight lines, I perceive, without any succession of trials, that they cannot enclose a space. I perceive that this would be true of any other two straight lines that could fall under my notice, and thus I reach the general maxim that no two straight lines can enclose a space, a maxim admitting of exceptions at no time and at no place. In regard to the one class of general truths, I have formed a law from a necessarily limited, out of an indefinite number of cases. In regard to the other, our generalizations are of convictions in our own mind, each of which carries necessity in it. In order to the formation of the latter, we have not to go out in search of external instances in the mental or material world, nor to number and to weigh such; we have all the elements in each of our convictions; and if we generalize properly, by what in some cases is an easy, but in others a somewhat difficult process, we reach general truths, which have the same necessity as the individual convictions.

(2.) *They are Universal, Immutable, Eternal:* only however on the same condition as they are necessary, that is, on the understanding that the general maxim is duly fashioned out of the individual convictions. But here it will be necessary to distinguish between two applications of the word 'universal' which have often been confounded. Sometimes a principle is called universal because it is in all men or avowed by all men. I have in this treatise adopted the word 'catholic,' or 'common,' to express this property of intuition. But when we say a truth is universal, we may mean that it is universally true, that is, admits of no exceptions, and it is in this latter application I use the word 'universal.' Universality in this sense follows from necessity; the maxim which is necessarily, must be universally, true.* It is only in this

* That a truth is accepted by common or catholic consent, and that it is without exception, are not the same, though they have often been confounded under the one epithet 'universal.' Sir W. Hamilton says (Note A. p. 754, Reid's Works), "Necessity and universality may be regarded as coincident; for when a belief is necessary, it is, *eo ipso*, universal; and that a belief is universal is a certain index that it must be necessary (see Leibnitz, 'Nouveaux Essais,' lib. i. s. 4)." Hamilton means by universality, universality of belief; which also Leibnitz means in the passage referred to—the language he uses is, "consentement universel."

meaning that the term can be applied to the maxims which express in a general form the law of our intuitive convictions. Such maxims admit of exceptions at no time and in no place. They are true in our own land, but they are true also in other lands; true in our world, they are true in all other worlds; true in all ages of time, they are equally true through all eternity. Hence they have been called expressively unchangeable, imperishable, and eternal truths.

(3.) *They are fundamental.* Hence they have been described as radical, as grounds or foundations, and called fundamental laws of thought and belief. They are the truths we come to, when we analyze a discussion into its elements. We may even set out with them in argument or in speculation, provided we have adequately generalized them. All demonstrated and derived truths will be found, if we pursue them sufficiently far down, to be resting on such fundamental truths. In controversies on profound topics, especially in theology and metaphysics, those who engage in them feel themselves ever coming down to a ground beneath which they cannot get. In searching into the structure of argument, we find,

But it is surely conceivable (I do not say, actual), that a conviction might be necessary to one man and not to all men; and there are in fact beliefs in man, which are universal, such as that the sun will rise tomorrow, which are not necessary. Kant used 'universal' in the sense of 'true without exception,' and very properly remarks, that the necessity and universality belong inseparably to each other, but that sometimes the one and sometimes the other test admits of the easier or more effective application. "Nothwendigkeit und strenge Allgemeinheit sind also sichere Kennzeichen einer Erkenntniss *a priori*, und gehören auch unzertrennlich zu einander. Weil es aber im Gebrauche derselben bisweilen leichter ist, die empirische Beschränktheit derselben, als die Zufälligkeit in den Urtheilen, oder es auch mannigmal einleuchtender ist, die unbeschränkte Allgemeinheit, die wir einem Urtheile beilegen, als die Nothwendigkeit desselben zu zeigen, so ist rathsam, sich gedachter beider Kriterien, deren jedes für sich unfehlbar ist, abgesondert zu bedienen" (K. d. r. V., Einleit. Auf. 2. Werke, bd. ii. p. 697: Rosenkranz).

as we follow it from conclusion to premiss, hanging on a premiss which is self-supporting. The sceptic is ever compelling the philosopher to go down to these depths. The dogmatist, in building his structure, is entitled to start with them as assumptions,—he must be the more careful that what he builds on be really the rock. On them other truths may rest, but they themselves rest on none. There may ever be an appeal to them, but there can never be an appeal from them.

Now in order to avoid confusion, and the error which springs from confusion, it is essential that we go round these three sides of this shield of truth, that we read what is on each, and carefully distinguish the inscriptions. If any one having occasion to employ intuition neglect to do this, he will ever be liable to affirm of the intuition under one aspect, what is true of it only in another, or to turn the wrong side towards the weapons of the assailant while he keeps the wrong side towards himself. When we are required to speak of them distinctively, our intuitions under the first aspect may be called native laws or regulative principles; under the second aspect, native, spontaneous, or necessary convictions; under the third aspect, universal truths or formalized maxims.

As Innate or Regulative Principles they are in all men at all ages; but it is wrong to represent them as being before the consciousness, as being immediately under our notice, as capable of being discovered without abstraction or generalization, or observation, or trouble of any kind. It is wrong to represent them as ideas in the Lockian sense of the term, that is, as apprehensions before consciousness.

As Spontaneous Convictions they are immediately under the eye of consciousness, but there they are not in the form of philosophic principles, nor can we say of every one of them they appear in all men, and from their earliest infancy.

As Universal Truths or General Maxims they are in an especial sense philosophic principles, but then as such they are known only to comparatively few; they can be appealed to in argument only on the condition that their law has been gathered by induction, and carefully expressed, and while there can be no dispute as to the spontaneous convictions, there may be disputes as to whether they have been properly generalized.*

At the same time these are after all only the diverse aspects of one great general fact, and they have relations all to each, and each to all. There is first a mind with its native capacities, each with its rule of action. In due time these come out into action, some of them at an earlier, and some of them at a later date, on the appropriate objects being presented, and the actions are before consciousness. As being before consciousness we can observe them by reflection, and discover the nature of the law which has all along been in the mind, and in its very constitution.

SECT. III. CERTAIN MISAPPREHENSIONS IN REGARD TO THE CHARACTER OF INTUITIVE CONVICTIONS.

Looking on the above as the properties and marks of the intuitive convictions of the mind, we see that a wrong account is often given of them.

1. It is wrong to represent them as unaccountable feelings, as blind instincts, as unreasonable impulses. They have nothing whatever of the nature of those feelings or emotions which raise up excitement within us, and attach us to certain objects, and draw us away from

* In writing this Section, I have kept before me throughout Hamilton's famous Note A, and have freely borrowed from it. But Hamilton has not distinguished between these Three Aspects of Common Sense.

others. Nor should they be put under the same head as the instincts which prompt us to crave for food when we are hungry, or which lead the dog to follow his master. In such cases the parties obey an impulse, which is not accompanied with knowledge or judgment of any kind, whereas in the perceptions of intuition there is always knowledge involved, and this the most certain of all, immediate knowledge, and in many of them there is judgment looking directly on the objects compared. So far from being unreasonable, they involve a primary exercise of reason superior to all secondary or derivative processes, which ever depend on the primary, and are often inferior in certainty, and can, in no circumstances, rise higher than the fountain from which they have flowed.

2. It is wrong to represent man, so far as he yields to these convictions, as being under some sort of stern and relentless fatality which compels him to go, without yielding him light of any kind. No doubt they constrain him to acknowledge the existence of certain objects, and the certainty of special truths; but this, not by denying him light, but by affording him the fullest conceivable light, such light that he cannot possibly mistake the object or wander from the path. No doubt he cannot have mediate proof, but it is because he has what the faculties which judge of proof declare to be vastly higher, immediate evidence, or self-evidence. We need no secondary proof, for we have primary, to convince us that two parallel lines can never meet. Our intuitions do not compel us against the reason, but they convince us in the highest exercise of reason, and they lead us not against, but by the assent of our clearest and profoundest intelligence. No man is ever, even in his most wayward moods, spontaneously tempted to complain because bound to yield to these convictions.

When he reflects on their nature, he should rejoice because such is his constitution that he is led to follow and obey them.

3. It is wrong to represent these self-evident truths as being truths merely to the individual, or truths merely to man, or beings constituted like man. There are some who speak and write as if what is truth to one man might not be truth to another man; as if what is truth to mankind might not be truth to other intelligent beings.* This account might be correct if the convictions were borne in upon the mind by a blind natural impulse. But what we perceive by an original intuition

* It is not easy to determine the precise philosophy of the Sophists, if indeed they had a philosophy. The doctrine of Heraclitus was that all is and is not; that while it does come into being, it forthwith ceases to be. Protagoras, proceeding on this doctrine, declared, Φησὶ γάρ που πάντων χρημάτων μέτρον ἄνθρωπον εἶναι, τῶν μὲν ὄντων, ὡς ἔστι, τῶν δὲ μὴ ὄντων, ὡς οὐκ ἔστιν. This Socrates expounds as meaning ὡς οἷα μὲν ἕκαστα ἐμοὶ φαίνεται, τοιαῦτα μέν ἐστιν ἐμοί, οἷα δὲ σοί (Plato, Theætetus, 24: Bekker). Aristotle represents Protagoras as maintaining that τὰ δοκοῦντα πάντα ἐστὶν ἀληθῆ καὶ τὰ φαινόμενα (Metaph. lib. iii. c. 5: Bonitz). Again, lib. x. c. 6, this καὶ γὰρ ἐκεῖνος ἔφη πάντων χρημάτων εἶναι μέτρον ἄνθρωπον, οὐθὲν ἕτερον λέγων ἢ τὸ δοκοῦν ἑκάστῳ τοῦτο καὶ εἶναι παγίως. It will be observed that in these accounts there is an interpretation put on the language of Protagoras. But there can be no doubt that Plato, and Aristotle too, laboured each in his own way to show, in opposition to these views, that there was a reality and a truth independent of the individual and of appearance. (See *infra*, Chap. III.) It is an instructive circumstance that the Sensationalist School has reached in our day the very position of the Sophists, and regard it as impossible to reach independent and necessary truth, if indeed any such truth exists. We might expect that such men would seek to justify the Sophists, and disparage the high arguments of Plato. Cudworth, speaking of the theoretical universal propositions in geometry and metaphysics, has finely remarked that it is true of every one of them whenever "it is rightly understood by any particular mind, whatsoever and wheresoever it be: the truth of it is no private thing, nor relative to that particular mind only, but is ἀληθὲς καθολικὸν, 'a catholic and universal truth,' as the Stoics speak, throughout the whole world; nay, it would not fail to be a truth throughout infinite worlds, if there were so many, to all such minds as would rightly understand it" (Immutable Morality, bk. iv. c. v.).

is a reality or is a truth; we know it to be so, we judge it to be so. And it is a reality, a truth, whether others know and acknowledge it or no. It is a truth, not merely to me or you, but to all men; not only to all men, but to all intelligences capable of discovering truths of that particular nature. That two lines cannot enclose a space, is a truth everywhere, in the planet Mars as well as in the planet Earth. That ingratitude is morally evil, must hold good in all other worlds, as well as in this world of ours, where sin so much abounds. Another misapprehension, of a different character, must also be rectified.

4. It is wrong to represent all our intuitive convictions as being formed within us from our birth. The account given of them by some would leave the impression on the mind that they must all appear in infancy. This is commonly the view taken by those who throw ridicule upon them. What can be so preposterous, they say, as to suppose that babies are meditating on the infinite from the time they escape from the womb, and distinguishing between good and evil before they know the right hand from the left? The account which has been given, in these chapters, of our original convictions, shows how they may not all appear from our earliest years. They are formed, we have seen, on the contemplation of objects presenting themselves from without or from within. Some of these objects press themselves, I believe, on the notice from the very first action of the soul, and the intuitions directed to these are exercised with the very first exercises of intelligence. From the very dawn of existence the infant must envisage self, and body acting on self. But there are other convictions which cannot be formed till a later date, because the objects to which they relate cannot be presented till the intelligence is advanced. Thus I believe that the

conviction of moral good and evil arises on the presentation of voluntary actions done by intelligent beings, and the mind must have made progress before it can form such a notion, and look into it to see what is involved in it. The intuition in regard to the infinite is called forth only when we contemplate such objects as space and time, or God, and the comprehension of these implies a considerable maturity of intelligence. We thus see that though all our intuitive convictions are native, yet some of them are the result of growth. Some of them do not appear in infancy; some of them appear in children, and among persons low in the scale of understanding, such as savages, only in a very low and rudimentary form. All of them are capable of growing with the growth of our intelligence, and even with the growth of our voluntary and emotional nature. Some of them are at one and the same time natural, and the issue of a long development—like the flower and the fruit, which are in the plant from its embryo, but may not be actually formed till there has been a stalk and branches, and leaves and buds.

Sect. IV. Certain Practical Characteristics.

From the theoretical characters there flow some others of a more practical nature.

1. All men who have had their attention addressed to the objects, are in fact led by spontaneous conviction, and this, whatever be their professed speculative opinions. This follows from the circumstance that they are self-evident, and that men, all men, must give their assent to them. The regulative principles being essential parts of man's nature, we find all men under the influence of them. Being irresistible, no man can deliver himself from them. They are ever operating spontaneously, and that whether men do or do not acknowledge them

reflexly. In this respect the philosopher and the peasant, the dogmatist and the sceptic are at one. The metaphysician who has detected and formalized the principle, is not in a better position than the mechanic who acts on the principle without knowing that there is a principle. The sceptic who denies the principle is notwithstanding convinced of the individual truth when it is pressed upon his notice, quite as implicitly as the philosopher who is strenuously defending it.

2. These self-evident truths cannot be set aside by any other truth, real or pretended. They could be overthrown only by some truth higher in itself, or carrying with it greater weight. But there is no such truth, there can be no such truth. There are indeed co-ordinate principles,—all self-evident truths are in respect of veracity of equal rank,—but not even on the supposition that the one contradicted the other, could we set aside either. The result in which such a contradiction should land us, is not a selection of one or other, but absolute scepticism, always along with implicit spontaneous faith in both principles. I shall have occasion to show that we are not landed in any such lamentable issue, and that all attempts to prove that intuitive truths contradict each other have lamentably failed.

It follows that when an apparent contradiction arises between what seems a self-evident truth and any other supposed truth, we are to examine the evidence which we have for both. It is thus that the mathematician acts when his demonstrations seem to be contradictory. He does not allow himself to imagine that truth can be inconsistent; he goes over his demonstrations to find out what error he has himself committed. If one fundamental principle seems to be inconsistent with another fundamental principle, we are to examine whether both are certainly fundamental, and can be shown to be so by the proper tests, and in particular whether they have been properly generalized and expressed. In all such cases it will be found either that one at least of the principles is not intuitively certain—indeed neither of them may be so; or, as is more common, we may not have properly stated the primitive principle, and the seeming inconsistency lies not in the principles themselves, but in our expression of them.

Or, again, the apparent contradiction may lie between a primitive principle and a derivative one. In such a case it is certain that if what seems a primitive principle be truly so, and if we have put it in the proper form, it can never be displaced or overthrown by any secondary one. For if we follow that derivative principle to its foundation, we shall find that it cannot be resting on any truth more authoritative than the fundamental one which it is now being employed to undermine, while in the derivation of it, a number of doubtful elements may have entered which must render it by more or fewer degrees less certain than the intuitive truth against which it is set. In all such cases we must examine the supposed first principle, to see that it is a first principle, and that it is properly inducted, and review the derivative principle in order to determine the nature of the evidence by which it is supported. By such a sifting process the seeming contradiction will in all probability disappear; but if it still continue, we are of course shut up to the alternative of adhering to the fundamental truth, and laying aside the derivative one, as being inferior in authority and certainty.

CHAPTER II.

METHOD OF EMPLOYING INTUITIVE PRINCIPLES.

SECT. I. THE SPONTANEOUS AND REFLEX USE OF INTUITIVE PRINCIPLES.

FROM the account which has been given of the Intuitions, it appears that they may operate—indeed they are ever operating—of their own accord, and without our prompting them into exercise by any voluntary act; and it appears, too, that we may generalize the individual actings, discover the rule of their operation, and then proceed to use them in deduction and in speculation. The former of these may be called the Spontaneous Action, and the latter the Reflex Application of the Intuitions. In their spontaneous exercise they are regulating principles, regulating thought and belief, and operating whether we observe them or no. But in this operation our convictions all relate to singulars, and so cannot be directly used in philosophic speculation. In order to their scientific application, there is need of careful reflex observation and generalization. In order to their spontaneous perception it is not requisite that their nature should be determined, they act best when we look simply at the object and take no introspection of them. But to a legitimate application of them in philosophy, it is essential that their exact nature, and precise law and rule, be carefully determined. It is all-important, in treating of our intuitions, to draw such a distinction, for much which may be affirmed of them under one of these aspects cannot be affirmed of them in the other.*

* "La raison se développe de deux manières, spontanéité et ré-

1. The spontaneous must always precede the reflex form. We have already noticed the circumstance that in the case of some of them the spontaneous perception begins with the earliest exercise of the intelligence, while in the case of others, though a preparation is made for them from the beginning—just as all the organs of the animal may be said to be in the embryo—it is long before they come out in open manifestation, and in unfavourable circumstances they may never appear in a fully developed form, or in vigorous life. But at whatever time they appear spontaneously, the generalized expression of them must always be later. We cannot generalize them till we have observed them, and we cannot observe them till they are in exercise. The reflex use of them is a scientific process, and cannot begin in the individual or in a nation, till the scientific spirit has been engendered. Even in their native form, some of them appear only in the mature man and in the fully developed mind; in their reflex shape they are found only in individuals and in ages and countries addicted to reflection or inward observation. Indeed, as the discovery, or even the comprehension, of the reflex law implies a special bending back of the eye, from which most men shrink, the process is one which the great mass of mankind never engage in, and which the majority of those who engage in it never follow, except for the sustaining of some favourite dogma, or the repelling of some proffered objection. It must be late in the history of inquiry and

flexion."—"La raison débute par une synthèse riche et féconde, mais obscure : vient après l'analyse qui éclaircit tout en divisant tout, et qui aspire elle-même à une synthèse supérieure, aussi compréhensive que la première et plus lumineuse. La spontanéité donne la vérité; la réflexion produit la science ; l'une fournit une base large et solide aux développements de l'humanité; l'autre imprime à ces développements leur forme la plus parfaite."—"L'erreur vient de la réflexion." (Cousin, Cours de l'Hist. Phil. 11e série, t. i. leç. vi. vii.)

speculation before we can expect to have an expression of the laws of the intuitions expounded simply for its scientific value, or as a body of scientific truth.

2. The intuition, in its reflex, abstract, or general form, is derived from, and is best tested by, the concrete spontaneous conviction. In order to the formation of the definition, maxim, or axiom, we must have objects or cases before us, and we must be careful to observe them, and note what is involved in them.

It is a matter of fact that geometry arose out of mensuration. Men began by measuring fields and heights, and thence proceeded to construct a scientific mode of accomplishing what had been done by practical rules, and I suspect that the enunciation of axioms and some of the more elementary demonstrations, came at a later date than practical rules, or even than certain of the more advanced propositions. We find, in like manner, that a systematized and connected Ethics, proceeding from original principles, and going on to applications, came later in the history of moral philosophy than the practical injunctions of parents, or the moral codes of legislators and the laws of religion. There was reasoning, and even rules of reasoning, before a regular Logic appeared. Metaphysics has arisen out of the contests of opposing sects, or has been interposed as a breakwater against a tide of scepticism.

In all times and circumstances, the most effectual means of testing logical, ethical, and metaphysical principle, is by the application of it to actual cases, which should be as numerous and varied as possible. It is when actual examples are before it that the mind is able to appreciate the meaning of the general formulæ. It is only when it has considered them in their application to a number of diversified instances that the mind is in circumstances to pronounce them to be probably, or approximately, or altogether correct.* Without such observational testing, definition, division, arrangement, and deduction may have rather a tempting and misleading influence. A power of dissection and inference can do as little in metaphysical as in physical investigation, that is, it is of no value at all, or may be positively injurious unless it proceed on a previous collation of facts. Minds of great logical and critical discernment are apt to go further wrong than others who are no philosophers at all, by seizing on some mutilated or imperfectly expressed principle, and carrying it out fearlessly, according to the rules of a rigid deduction. Of all men, those who live in the region of high abstractions, which they never bring down to realities, are most apt to go astray as in snow-drift; and when they do wander, they go faster and further wrong than other men.

At the same time, it is to be observed that the abstraction, or generalization, is not got from an outward object or event which may fall under ocular inspection or instrumental experiment, but from the operations of a mental law, which may be altogether missed by those who are exclusively engrossed with the object at which the mind is looking when the regulative principle is working. Of all men, the ardent sense-observer, or the

* Kant has laid down a very different maxim, declaring that examples only injure the understanding in respect of the correctness and precision of the apprehension. Speaking of examples: "Denn was die Richtigkeit und Präcision der Verstandeseinsicht betrifft, so thun sie derselben vielmehr gemeiniglich einigen Abbruch, weil sie nur selten die Bedingung der Regel adäquat erfüllen (als *casus in terminis*), und überdies diejenige Anstrengung des Verstandes oftmals schwächen, Regeln im Allgemeinen, und unabhängig von den besonderen Umständen der Erfahrung, nach ihrer Zulänglichkeit, einzusehen, und sie daher zuletzt mehr wie Formeln, als Grundsätze, zu gebrauchen angewöhnen" (K. d. r. Vern. Trans. Log., p. 119: Rosen.). This shows that Kant had no correct idea of the way in which the general rule is reached. The same view is evidently taken by many of the formal logicians of our day.

lively picturer of external images, is the most inclined to shrink from reflex inspection, and is the worst fitted to propound or to judge of abstract mental principles.

3. The expression of the abstract or general truth is more or less easy, and is likely to be more or less correct, according to the simplicity of the objects to which the spontaneous conviction is directed. It is evident that some of the intuitive principles of the mind are more difficult to detect and formalize than others. Those which are directed to sensible objects, and simple objects, will be found out more easily, and at an earlier date, than those which look to more complex or spiritual objects. Thus the intuitions regarding space—seen by the eye, and readily pictured in the imagination—were abstracted, and generalized into geometrical definitions and axioms, at an early stage of intellectual culture. It is a vastly more difficult task to express accurately, and in their ultimate form, the intuitive convictions regarding such objects as substance, and quality, and the laws involved in thought and moral perception. Still the war of contending sects, and the assaults of the sceptic, and the insidious underminings of the sophist, would compel men, at an early date, to evolve some sort of logic, and we have the nature of genera and species and definition, chalked out by Socrates, the principle of contradiction employed by Plato, and the formula of reasoning determined, at least approximately, by Aristotle, and, in a looser form, even in India, more than two thousand years ago.* The practical interest collecting round moral questions would also lead to an early enunciation of ethical principle, which, however, owing to the innumerable relations involved in the discharge of duty, would not, at an early stage, take a thoroughly fundamental or rigidly

* See Paper on Indian Logic, by Professor Max Müller, in Appendix to Thompson's 'Outline of the Laws of Thought.'

exact form. The crude nature of the classification embodied in the cardinal virtues, is a proof of the difficulty of expressing the ultimate laws of morality, or the supreme rule of right and wrong. A similar complexity presents itself in all inquiries in which substance and force enter as elements, and hence, while attempts will be made from the commencement of speculation to express first principles in regard to such objects, the rule announced will in general combine a mixture of intuitive and experiential elements, will be able to serve only a provisional purpose, will seldom be more than approximately correct, and will require to be rectified by much subsequent examination and comparison with concrete cases.

4. In their spontaneous action the intuitions never err, properly speaking; but there may be manifold errors lurking in their reflex form and application. I have used the qualified language that *properly speaking* they do not err in their original impulses; for even here they may carry error with them. They look to a representation given them, and this representation may be erroneous, and this error will appear in the result. The mind intuitively declares that on a real quality presenting itself, it must imply a substance; but what is not truly a quality may be represented as a quality, and then it is declared that this quality implies a substance. Thus Sir Isaac Newton and Dr. S. Clarke represented time and space as qualities, (which I regard as a mistake,) and then represented reason as guaranteeing that these qualities implied a substance in which they inhere, which is God. But the error in such cases cannot legitimately be charged on the intuition, which is exercised simply in regard to the presentation or representation made to it.

But there is room for innumerable errors creeping into the abstract or general enunciation and the scientific application of it. For we may have made a most defective, or exaggerated, or totally inaccurate abstraction or generalization of the formula out of the individual exercises, or we may apply it to cases to which it has no legitimate reference. From such causes as these have sprung those oversights, exaggerations, and not unfrequently flagrant and pernicious errors, which have appeared in every form of metaphysical speculation. This is a topic which will fall to be resumed in next Section.

5. The tests of intuitive convictions admit of an application to the abstract and general principle, only so far as the abstraction and generalization have been properly performed. It is only as applied to singulars, that our perceptions can be regarded as intuitive. The tests of intuitions, viz. self-evidence, necessity, and catholicity, apply directly only to individual convictions. To the formalized expression of them, the tests apply only mediately, and on the supposition and condition that the formulæ are the proper expression of the spontaneous convictions.

It is always possible that the abstraction and the generalization have not been correctly executed. In some cases, this is no more than barely possible. Whenever the object is a very simple one, presenting itself very much apart from all other circumstances, there is scarcely the possibility of error creeping in. Hence the assurance which the mind feels in regard to mathematical axioms, and the propositions founded on them by steps every one of which is intuitive. Even in regard to mathematics there may be doubts and contests, but it is only in more recondite topics, such for instance as those into which the idea of infinity enters. But in regard to intuitions which refer to objects which are more complicated, that is, which are mixed up with divers other matters in our comprehension, there may be difficulties in exactly seizing and expressing the principle, and there may therefore be doubts and disputes as to whether any given account of them is correct and adequate. It is self-evident as to this particular quality, that it implies a substance, but there is much obscurity about the general relation of substance and quality. The mind at once declares of this given effect that it must have a cause, but there may be doubts and difficulties as to the proper form in which to put the law of causation. Every man is convinced that he is the same person today as he was yesterday, but how few have had consciously before them the general principle of self and of personality!

SECT. II. SOURCES OF ERROR IN METAPHYSICAL SPECULATION.

All proposed metaphysical principles are attempted expressions of the intuitions in the form of a general law. Now error may at times spring from the assumption of a principle which has no existence whatever in the human mind. I am persuaded however that the errors thus originated are comparatively few, and are seldom followed by serious consequences. In regard to the assumption of totally imaginary principles, I am convinced that there have been fewer mistakes in metaphysical than in physical science. As the intuitions of the mind are working in every man's bosom, it will seldom happen that the speculator can set out with a principle which has no existence whatever; and should he so venture, he would certainly meet with little response. It is possible also for error to arise from a chain of erroneous deduction from principles which are genuine in themselves and soundly interpreted. The mistakes springing from this quarter are likewise, I believe, few and trifling, the more so that those who draw such inferences are generally men of powerful logical mind, and not likely to commit errors in reasoning; and if they did, those who have ability to follow them would be sure to detect them. By far the most copious source of error in philosophic speculation is to be found in the imperfect, or exaggerated, or mutilated expression of principles which really have a place in our constitution. In such cases the presence of the real metal gives currency to the dross which is mixed with it.

In regard to many of our intuitions, the gathering of the common quality out of the concrete and individual manifestations is about as subtle a work as the human understanding can engage in. This arises from the recondite, the complicated, and fugitive nature of the mental states, from which they must be drawn. But from the very commencement of speculation and the breaking out of discussion, attempts have been made to give a body and a form to the native convictions. It is seldom that the account is altogether illusory; most commonly there is a basis of fact to set off the fiction. But the principle is seen and represented only under one aspect, while others are left out of sight. It oftens happens that he whose intuitions are the strongest and the liveliest is of all men the least qualified to examine and generalize them, and should he be tempted to embody them in propositions, they will be sure to take distorted, perhaps erroneous forms. In all departments of speculation, metaphysical, ethical, and theological, we meet with persons whose faith is strong, whose sentiments are fervent, and whose very reason is far-seeing, but whose creed—that is, formalized doctrine—is extravagant, or even perilously wrong. In other cases the conviction, genuine in itself, is put forth in a mutilated shape by prejudiced men to support a favourite doctrine, or by party men to get rid of a formidable objection.

The human mind is impelled by an intellectual craving,

and by the circumstances in which it is placed, to be ever generalizing, and this in respect both of material and mental phenomena. But its earliest classes and systems, even those of them made for scientific purposes, are commonly of a very crude character. Still, even such generalizations, though at the best mere approximations, at times serve valuable ends in the absence of better and until better appear. Such laws as these have been laid down, "Nature abhors a vacuum;" "Some bodies are naturally light, and others heavy;" "Combustible bodies are chemically composed of a base with phlogiston combined with it;" "The organs of the flower are transformed leaves." These were the best general statements which scientific inquirers could give at the time of their observations. They served to express, if not to explain, certain phenomena. Nature's horror of a vacuum showed how water rose in a pump. The doctrine of the natural heaviness and lightness of bodies seemed to explain how stones fell to the earth, while smoke rose in the atmosphere. The burning of brimstone was thought to be satisfactorily accounted for, when it was said that brimstone being composed of sulphurous acid and phlogiston, the combustion consisted in giving out phlogiston. The undoubted correspondence between the leaf and the stamen suggested the idea that the leaf had been transformed into a stamen. But modern science, advancing in the inductive method, has shown that none of these were correct expressions of the real laws of nature. It cannot be because of its aversion to a vacuum, that water rises in a pump, for if the vacuum extends higher than a certain number of feet, the water allows it to exist in its emptiness. Smoke rises from the earth, not because of its natural levity, but because it is buoyed up by the atmosphere. It unfortunately happens that lead, after it is burned,—that is, after it has given off, according to the phlogiston theory, one of its ingredients,—is found to be heavier than before. Stamens and pistils have never been leaves, they are merely after the same model.

These are examples from physical science. Metaphysical science, from the subtle and intertwined nature of the phenomena, can furnish far more numerous instances. In the mental sciences the general statements have commonly a genuine fact, but mixed with this there is often an alloy. The error may not influence the spontaneous action of the primitive principle, but it may tell terribly in the reflex application. It may not even exercise any prejudicial influence in certain departments of investigation, but in other walks it may work endless confusion, or land in consequences fitted to sap the very foundations of morality and religion. Take the distinction drawn, in some form, by most civilized languages, between the head and the heart. The distinction embodies a great truth, and when used in conversation or popular discourse it can conduct to no evil. But it cannot be carried out psychologically. For in each a number of very distinct faculties are included. Under the phrase 'heart,' in particular, are covered powers with wide diversities of function, such as the conscience, the emotions, and the will. The question agitated in this century, whether religion be an affair of the head or the heart, has come to be a hopelessly perplexed one, because the offices of the powers embraced under each are diverse, and run into each other; and certain of the positions taken up are, to say the least of it, perilous: as when it is said that religion resides exclusively in the heart, and persons understand that it is a matter of mere emotion, omitting understanding, will, and conscience, which have equally a part to play. Of the same description is the distinction between the reason and the understanding. It points to a reality. There is a distinction between reason in its primary, and reason in its secondary or logical exercises, and the mind can rise, always however by a process in which the logical understanding is employed, to the discovery of universal and necessary truth. But each of the divisions, the reason and the understanding, comprises powers which run into each other. This distinction is at the best confusing,* and it is often so stated as to imply that the reason, without the use of the understanding processes of abstraction and generalization, can rise to the contemplation of the true, the beautiful, and the good.

It can be shown that some of the ancient philosophers, and Kepler in modern times, had glimpses of a law of universal gravitation before the days of Newton, but none of these had been able to determine its exact nature and rule. Suppose that while science was at this stage, some person had affirmed that there was a power of attraction among all bodies, varying inversely not according to the square of the distance, but according to the distance: he would no doubt have had a truth, and a very important one; but the law thus stated, while it explained in a general way a number of the phenomena, would, when deductions were drawn from it, have issued in ever accumulating errors, and this not because no such law existed, but because its rule had been improperly apprehended and enunciated. Almost all metaphysical errors spring from this source, from the improper formalization of principles which are real laws of our constitution. When presented in this mutilated shape, even truth may lead to hideous consequences. It will be shown as we advance that there is an intuitive law of cause and effect, but this law has not always been correctly enunciated. Suppose it be put in this form, that "Everything must have a cause:" it will issue logically and necessarily in the result that the

* This distinction is examined, Part III. Book I. Chap. II. sect. v., *Supplementary*.

Intelligent Cause of this world must Himself have had a cause. This consequence can at once be avoided by a proper enunciation of the law of causation.

We may now see how it is that metaphysicians, when they go wrong, go further wrong than others. This proceeds from the fundamental nature of metaphysical principles: every error here, like a mistake in taking down the *datum* of an arithmetical or mathematical question, must issue in fearfully magnified error in the results reached. This weakness in the foundation must make the structure insecure to its topmost pinnacle. The tainting of the fountain will go with the stream in all its length. Suppose that we set out in ethical discussion, with the assumption that virtue is just a far-sighted love of pleasure; or in theology, with the dogma that justice is a modification of benevolence: it will turn out that these principles (which I believe to be wrong) will affect the whole superstructure of speculation, and lead those who adopt them to take very inadequate views of sin on the one hand, and the justice of God on the other. It should be added, that an error in the starting principle comes out in more exaggerated errors in the issue, in very proportion to the rigid consecutiveness of the deduction, and the extent to which it is carried. A mistake in the first steps of an arithmetical question, may be lessened by some counterbalancing blunder in the further calculations. It has often happened that philosophers have shrunk from following out their principles to their consequences. Locke in particular has often been saved from extreme opinions to which his theory led, but from which his sagacity and honesty recoiled, by falling into inconsequences and inconsistencies. Powerful logical minds, like Spinoza and Hegel, have, on the other hand, boldly avowed the most extravagant doctrines, as being the legitimate result of their gratuitous assumptions.

There is another circumstance to be taken into account by those who would unfold the theory of the metaphysician's extravagancies; he is not restrained as the physical investigator is by stubborn facts, nor checked as the commercial man is by stern realities, which he dare not despise. He has only to mount into a region of pure (or rather, I should say, cloudy), speculation to find himself in circumstances to cleave his way without meeting with any felt barrier. At the same time one might have reasonably expected, that when such speculators as Spinoza, Fichte, Schelling, and Hegel, felt themselves rushing headlong against all acknowledged truth, they would have suspected that there was something wrong in their assumptions, or in their method. Whenever the results reached contradict the senses or the established doctrines of physical science, whenever they lead to the denial of the distinction between good and evil, or the personality of the soul, or of the existence, the personality, and continual providence of God, it is time to review the process by which they have been gained, for they are running counter to truths which have too deep a foundation to be moved by doubtful speculations. The remark of Bacon as to physical, may be applied to metaphysical speculation, that doctrine is to be tried by fruits. "Of all signs there is none more certain or worthy than that of the fruits produced; for the fruits and effects are sureties and vouchers, as it were, for philosophy." "In the same manner as we are cautioned by religion to show our faith by our works, we may freely apply the principle to philosophy, and judge of it by its works, accounting that to be futile which is unproductive, and still more, if instead of grapes and olives it yield but the thistles and thorns of dispute and contention."

SECT. III. CONDITIONS OF THE LEGITIMACY OF THE APPEAL TO INTUITIVE PRINCIPLES.

There is scarcely occasion to lay down any rules as to the spontaneous use of the regulative principles of the mind. It is of their nature to act, and, like the physiological processes of seeing and breathing, they act all the better when no notice is taken of them. All that is necessary to call them forth is to present the appropriate objects;—in mathematics, for example, to present geometrical figures and quantities, and in moral subjects to present models and ideals of excellence. Thus are they evoked in the first instance, and thus are our intellectual and moral intuitions refined, elevated, and strengthened. Any other rules fitted to promote their right action are of a moral, rather than a speculative character. If the motive power of the mind be right, if the man be impelled by a love of truth, and swayed by a spirit of candour, then the regulative principles, if occupied about the proper objects, will of themselves perform their proper function. There is truth in the common observation that a mind sophisticated by logic and confused by metaphysics will often fall into errors from which others who follow only good sense and good feeling are happily delivered.

But if persons wish at any time to review their opinions, or answer objections, or convince others by argument, they must employ principles of some kind, and these, in the last resort, must conduct to first principles. I suppose that if man's moral nature had been pure, he would never have fallen into error; there would have been no difference among mankind in regard to questions of vital moment, and controversy would have been unknown. In such a happy condition, I believe that first principles would have been contemplated simply as a matter of intellectual curiosity, and as illustrative of the Divine wisdom. It is not necessary to prove that man is not placed in such a blessed state of things. It is scarcely possible to find three men met together whose opinions are at one, even on essential points; to err is an inherent weakness of humanity, and some have fallen into most pernicious mistakes. Every man needs, in consequence, to examine the apprehensions he has formed, and the convictions which he has been led to entertain; he has to defend what he believes to be truth when it is assailed, and he has, in a spirit of love, to endeavour to convince others of their errors when these relate to matters of great moment for this life or the life to come. In this world of ours, the review of impressions and opinions, and discussion, are matters of absolute necessity: but this implies the use of proofs, premisses, tests; and if we pursue these sufficiently far (as we must at times be constrained to do), we go beyond derivative to original principles. But are we allowed to call in a supposed fundamental principle when it suits us, or use it in the form we please, to justify an opinion to which we are determined to adhere at all hazards, or to crush our opponent? As there are logical rules to guard against abuse in derivative argument, so there may also be logical rules laid down to restrain the appeal to assumable premisses.

1. Those who appeal to first truths must be prepared to show that they are first truths. In most investigations it is not necessary ever to be going down to the foundation. In ordinary physical inquiry, for example, we may assume such laws as gravitation and chemical affinity, without being required to prove them once and and again. But in certain discussions, theological and philosophical, more especially when the controversy is with the doubter or the sceptic, it may be needful to rest

our first stones on the foundation,—in all such cases we must be sure that we have gone down to the rock. We must hold ourselves ready to prove, not indeed the truth of the first principle,—for this is impossible in the nature of things,—but that it is a first principle. We are required to show that it is self-evident; and if this be denied, we may show that we are constrained to believe it, and cannot be made to judge or decide the contradictory of it to be true; and we may confirm all this by showing that all men adhere to it. We should not stop short of this in the argument which we construct for our own conviction. An opponent has a right to insist on this in arguing with us on questions which go down to the bottom; and we have a right, in arguing with one who makes any appeal to primary principles, to demand of him to prove that what he is calling in be in fact a self-evident and necessary conviction.

2. Those who employ intuitive principles in demonstration, speculation, or discussion of any kind, must see that they accurately express them. This is done in the science of geometry, which owes much of its certainty, and the satisfaction which the mind feels in contemplating its truths, to the circumstance that it begins with announcing, in the rigid form of axioms, or postulates, all that it assumes. We should insist that the same be done in all other branches which employ first principles. The canon is, not only that they be enunciated, but that their precise rule be enunciated. It often happens that in the popular expression of material facts, a law is put in a form which gives some information, but which may not after all be absolutely correct. People often say that mountains draw the clouds, and thus foster rain, and this gives a sort of statement of certain facts; but the true account is that the cold mountain condenses the moisture in the current of air sweeping over it. It

is quite right to say that the tides are produced by the attraction of the moon, and this explains some of the facts; but then it cannot show how there is full tide not only on the side of the earth next the moon, but on the opposite side. In the expression of the phenomena of the mind, there are still more frequent instances of statements which are only approximately correct. Thus substance has been explained as that which subsists of itself, or needs nothing else in order to its existence. This account contains a truth, but is expressed in too unrestricted a form. Spinoza, proceeding on such a definition, which had been supplied him by the school of Descartes, goes on with a bristling array of forms, and much word-quibbling, to demonstrate, that there can be only one substance, of which all other things are the attributes or modes. We are at once saved from this pantheistic consequence by putting the proper limitation on the definition. It is quite true that in all discussion, theological and moral, philosophic principles are often appealed to, and may serve a proper purpose, even when not very formally or accurately expressed. This they do because the truth contained in the principle happens to be applicable. But it might have happened to be otherwise. "Every event has a cause:" this is a maxim which we are applying in our every-day reasonings and observations. But has it no limits? or is causation of the same character in regard to every event? In particular, does causation reign in the will, as it reigns in the material universe? or if it does, is causation in the will the same in kind as causation in external nature, or as causation in the intelligence? He who uses the principle of causation indiscriminately, may, before he is aware of it, land himself in the conclusion that man is as much the slave of circumstances as every spoke in the wheel, or as every link in a chain, which a strong force is dragging along. We can save ourselves from such consequences only by limiting, modifying, or explaining the doctrine of causation. We have already seen that our intuition regarding causality may be so stated as to land us in an infinite series of causes; we now see that it may be so enounced as to undermine the great moral doctrine of the essential freedom of the will. We see how important it must be to have the nature and the precise range of the law clearly and definitely settled.

The two rules now laid down may seem to some to be very hard ones; but they are very necessary ones to arrest those confused and confusing controversies which abound to such an extent in philosophy, in theology, and in other departments of investigation as well. It is always indeed to be allowed that our inquiries on most subjects may be conducted and terminated satisfactorily without our being required to go down to metaphysical principles. The farmer, the merchant, the politician, and even the physical investigator in most of his walks, may come to the right conclusion in regard to the topics which they wish to settle, without its being necessary for them to determine the nature of mathematical axioms or the law of cause and effect; on which, notwithstanding, some of these calculations regarding the seasons or the tides or the movements of the heavenly bodies, or the probable actings of men, may after all depend—only, however, in the sense of a deep foundation which it is not necessary for these parties to examine. But if any one will enter on speculations involving radical truth, he must be prepared to submit to the conditions on which they can be properly conducted. No man is bound to be a metaphysician unless he chooses, but if he insist on becoming one, he must attend to the rules of the office which he takes on himself. Every man is not under a moral obligation to throw aside other useful pursuits, and devote himself to answering such speculations as those of Spinoza, Berkeley, Hume, Fichte, or Hegel; but if he ventures into the arena, he must conform to its rules. Every friend of religion is not obliged to write a philosophic defence of it, and some who have ventured upon such a work might have been more profitably employed in some less ambitious undertaking, as in defending some of the outworks of religion, or illustrating its power by their lives; but those who claim to be philosophers must comport themselves as philosophers. It is to be regretted that multitudes dabble in metaphysics who have no capacity for grappling with its subtle truths; but the only effective mode of curbing this incompetency and quackery, is by insisting on all those who would enter the trade undergoing some sort of scientific apprenticeship or process of training. Nor are these restrictions the less necessary from the circumstance that not a few of those who possess the greatest aversion to metaphysics are all the while deep in metaphysics without their knowing it, and certainly without their being prepared to avow it, and it is necessary to lay an arrest on such by showing what the science is, and compelling them if they enter the country to conform to its laws.

There are persons who are constrained by the circumstances in which they are placed, or by what they believe to be the voice of duty, to discuss fundamental questions. There have been persons, even in the lowest walks of life, troubled, owing to a peculiar intellectual temperament (commonly not of a very healthy character), with speculative doubts, which are only to be removed by speculative arguments; but, if convinced, it must surely be by arguments built on a sure foundation. Some are placed in a position in which they are assailed by the infidel, and feel that they must meet him in the cause of truth and religion. Some, as knowing that they possess peculiar gifts, feel themselves called on to defend the very citadel of morals or of religion, or to rear a fabric of truth compacted from the very base. But if these men are not to waste their strength in a war of subtleties, they must be careful how they begin to build, lest what they rear turn out to be crazy and unstable, and a source of weakness rather than of strength. Paying attention to certain restrictions and precautions themselves, they will be in a position to insist on wild speculators, or the sceptics whom they oppose, conforming themselves to these canons of the logic of metaphysical speculation.

These then I reckon as the conditions of all argument which appeals formally to primary truth, to necessary conviction, or common sense. Persons not pretending to be philosophers, and discussing none of those topics which philosophers alone can discuss, may claim the privilege, when a sceptical objection comes in their way, or an altogether unbelievable dogma is asserted, of rejecting it at once, on the ground of spontaneous conviction, and troubling themselves no more about it. They must take care, however, in all such cases, that what they suppose to be a native conviction be not a mere prepossession of education, or prejudice of temper, and if there be ground for doubt, there is no help for it but in an appeal to the tests of intuitions, and the canons of their legitimate use. And as to those who profess to proceed philosophically, it is incumbent on them that they prove that what they assume is an original conviction, and that they generalize the spontaneous exercises, and express them in rigid formulæ. But when it is thus conducted, the argument from intuition or common sense is not an *argumentum ad populum*, and least of all an argument addressed to vulgar prejudice. It presupposes a rigid scientific process, and should not be attempted by any except those who possess the requisite retrospective powers of observation, and have disciplined themselves to the rules of the logic of first principles. When conformed to the right conditions, it is an argument strictly scientific, eminently satisfactory within its proper domain, and is in an especial sense the philosophical argument.

Such restrictions as these would, I know full well, lay an arrest at once on more than one-half of the metaphysics of this age, and of every age. This would be felt to be a discouragement by certain eager youths, full of expectations of the results to be reached by philosophic speculation, and by certain older, but not wiser men, who have mapped out the whole intellectual globe, and would feel troubled at the idea of their distribution being disturbed: but in the end there would be no loss; for the part remaining after the refining process, would be of vastly more worth, and would soon be acknowledged to be so.

When speculative philosophy is pursued in the usual unrestrained manner, the results reached are of the most unsatisfactory character, and at times are felt to be so. How often do ardent youths rush into the country opened to them, as keenly as the adventurers in the sixteenth century set out in search of El Dorado, and after spending years, and wasting the strength of manhood, they come back with a sense of emptiness and a feeling of disappointment! Even those who refuse to abandon the hope, and who cling most resolutely to the idea that they have discovered genuine gold, are now and again all but overwhelmed with a feeling of prostration and bitterness, and break out, as the Doctor in 'Faust,'—

> "I feel it, I have heaped upon my brain
> The gathered treasure of man's thought in vain."

In such there is a weariness, an aching, an *ennui* of the head, which is felt to be as deep, if not so keen, as the aching, the *ennui* of the heart ever is; and yet there may coexist with this a determination to continue the fruitless pursuit. Others have had a confession wrung from them like that of Jacobi: "In my younger years it stood thus with me in regard to philosophy: I seemed to myself to be heir to innumerable riches, and only some unimportant lawsuits and some unmeaning formalities seemed to hinder me from taking full possession of my inheritance. The suits, while pending, grew to be important. At last it appeared that I had inherited nothing but lawsuits, and that the whole bequest was in insolvent hands."

Happy are those who advance, or who can return, as fresh in spirit and as innocent as when they entered. Some, feeling as if no certainty could be reached, or as if, after unwinding the folds of the mystery, nothing wonderful or worthy has been discovered, have come to the settled conclusion that it is vain for them ever after to expect to find certainty, to reach felt assurance, or even to look for anything worth seeing, and so give themselves up to listlessness and apathy. Wandering till they have become bewildered, as if in a deep and gloomy forest, they sit down with the intention of never rising; or, like persons wearied and worn out in snowdrift, they lie down to become benumbed, and are ready to perish in cold. Still worse consequences have followed. How often does the eager youth rush on till he falls into the abyss!—

"He eagerly pursues,
Beyond the realms of dreams, that fleeting shade;
He overleaps the bounds!"

Entering into the labyrinth, to survey its wonders, he is lost in its numberless passages and its endless windings, without being ever able to find his way back to the open light and air; nay, how often has it happened that the builder of such intricacies has himself been imprisoned and entombed within them. Or, rushing eagerly to solve the sphinx riddles which Nature is propounding, and unable to find the solution, he must pay the awful penalty to that terrible Power, which insists on a reply, and crushes those who try and do not succeed! Some have entered, with lively anticipations, this temple of mystery, only to come out oppressed with doubt, or with the language of scorn and scepticism on their lips; they have seen all, they say, been in the very Holy of Holies, and found it empty, with no God dwelling between the Cherubim or uttering his voice in the Shechinah.

> "He dropped his plummet down the broad
> Deep universe, and said, 'No God,'
> Finding no bottom."

Sect. IV. Method of Investigating and Interpreting our Intuitions.

Two questions require to be answered in all metaphysical investigation. The one is, What is the nature of the intuition itself? and the other, What is the nature of the object at which it looks, and for which it is the guarantee? These two inquiries are to be prosecuted in one and the same way,—that is, in the method of induction; not with sense, but consciousness, as our informant. There is really no other manner of determining the nature of the intuitional power, its law, rule, and manner of operation; nor any other mode of ascertaining what is the kind of object or truth revealed by that power. I know of no shorthand or summary way, by logic or cogitation, of settling these two essential questions in philosophy. It might have been different if man had been conscious of the intuition as an intuition. In this case it would only have been needful to look within by the internal sense in order to find its nature.

But just as the law of gravitation is not written on the face of the sky so that the eye can see it, so neither is the law of causation printed on the soul so that consciousness can read off the inscription. The one law, like the other, is to be ascertained by an investigation of its individual acts, and this in a state of things in which the action of one property is closely interblended with that of another property; necessitating not only an observation of facts, but a very patient and discerning induction, so that we may catch the rule of the distinct agencies.

The task, so far as the second question is concerned, might have been easier if all our intuitions had been constructed so as to discover one and the same kind of truth. But as each of the senses is organized to discover its own kind of material qualities, so each of the internal perceptions reveals its peculiar object or truth, and in its own peculiar manner. As inductive inquiry into the nature of perception through the eye will not settle for us what is the nature of perception through the touch, so neither can an investigation of any one intuition settle for us the nature of the apprehension which the others, or any of the others, are fitted to furnish. The metaphysician, in conducting his delicate inquiries, must go over the intuitions one by one, asking of each what it has to say of itself, and what is the vision which it has to disclose; in this respect acting like the divine who has the proper respect for revelation, and who does not determine beforehand what the inspired record should say, but reverently asks, What saith the Scripture? A thousand errors have arisen in philosophy from omitting to look at our intuitions one by one, and from affirming of all what may be true only of some.

It is the special office of the metaphysician to go to our intuitions one by one, and ask, What does it say of itself? what does it profess to look at and discover? This latter is the inquiry which we should make when our aim is to discover whether the conviction testifies to the existence of an object or truth external to, or independent of, the mind perceiving it. To give some examples. What, we may ask, is the object attested by the mind when it is perceiving through the senses? The answer seems to be, an object external to self, extended and movable. In this exercise, and in every other intelligent exercise, consciousness testifies to the existence of a self in intelligent exercise. There are other operations in which the mind is simply imagining: even in such cases it has a knowledge; but it has no knowledge of, or belief in, an object external to the mind. If I am picturing a griffin, I am conscious of self thus engaged, but I have no intuitive conviction of the existence of a griffin, independent of my thinking of it, as I have of the existence of a pen or table when I press my hand upon it. In the interpretation of the intuition, it is essential to inquire what, if any, is the sort of object to the existence of which it testifies.

These two are different from yet another, and a third inquiry: Does, or does not, the intuition speak the truth? Is it not possible that it may deceive us? I am anxious to avoid this question for the present, and defer it till we have got an answer to the two prior ones,—What is the nature of the intuitions? and what the precise object looked at?—questions which will be settled as we examine the intuitions in order. The question as to what saith the intuition, is not the same as the question as to whether the intuition should be trusted. It is expedient to determine precisely what the witness says, before we inquire whether he does or does not speak the truth; and so we adjourn this last question to the close of our survey.

In questioning the witness, it will be necessary, when a testimony is given in favour of a reality independent of the contemplative mind, to determine very precisely what is the sort of reality. In particular the question should be put, Is the attestation in behalf of an independent thing, or merely of the quality of a thing, or of the relation between one thing and another, or what else? For example, self-consciousness seems to testify in behalf of self as an individual existence, and sense-perception seems to assert of bodily objects that they have a separate being; but when the mind contemplates thinking, or solidity, or potency, though it undoubtedly affirms of them that they are real, it does not look on them as separate entities, as this paper or as this book is. The mind declares that moral excellence is a reality, and not a figment; but it does not attribute the same sort of reality to it as it does to the man who possesses moral excellence. The mind seems to me to declare that there is a reality in space and time, but we may land ourselves in innumerable difficulties if we make rash assertions as to the kind of reality we give them. Unless we draw such distinctions, we may altogether misunderstand the testimony given, and then be tempted to charge the blunders, which our own hastiness has committed, on our mental constitution. And yet these are distinctions which are altogether lost sight of by those who juggle with the phrases 'objective' and 'subjective.' Even in our most subjective exercises, as when the mind is thinking of one of its own states, there is always an object known, namely, self; and when we say that such a thing has an objective existence, we may mean a great many different things which should be carefully distinguished.*

The meaning and importance of these cautions may best be comprehended by giving examples of the evil which has arisen from neglecting them. Kant laboured

* On Subjective and Objective, see Part III. Book I. Chap. II. sect. v., *Supplementary*.

to determine more critically than had been done before, the nature of the mind's convictions regarding space, time, and causation, and he stood up resolutely for their reality; but then it was a merely subjective reality—a reality in the mind. Time and space are represented by him as forms under which we cognize all phenomena presented to the senses, and cause and effect is a category under which events are arranged by the understanding. Now, in examining this theory, I start with inquiring, What do our native convictions say in regard to these subjects? Are they satisfied when it is said that time and space and causation have no existence out of the mind? They seem to me, on the contrary, to declare that time and space have a reality out of the mind, and independent of the mind, quite as much as the phenomena which we discover in space and time, and that cause and effect have an existence quite as much as the events which they connect. No doubt I may deny the trustworthiness of my intuitive convictions as attesting the existence of external being, but immediately after, some one, proceeding a step further in the same direction, will deny the trustworthiness of all their other testimonies, till we are landed in a scepticism which sets aside the reality, subjective as well as objective.

This is an illustration of evil arising from a refusal to listen to our convictions. Mistakes have also arisen from neglecting the distinctions between the kinds of testimony. M. Cousin finds fault, very properly, with Kant, for not allowing an objective existence to substance and causation, and other truths attested by reason. But then he does not institute a patient inquiry into the nature of the reality which the mind gives to such things as substance and cause and moral good; and he argues as if these must have the same sort of reality as the individual soul has, or as an individual acting causally has, or as a good man has; and he has thus been led to argue at once, from our idea of objective substance to God as absolute substance, from creature effect to God as the Supreme Cause, and from the idea of moral good to the existence of a good God,—a mode of argument which I cannot but regard as inconclusive and highly unsatisfactory, the more so as it operates, with other considerations, to lead him to represent God as a cause which must create.*

By steadily adhering to this method of induction, and attending to such cautions, we may surely hope to be able to ascertain something as to the original principles of the mind, and determine likewise what are the truths guaranteed by them: and this, I apprehend, is the main work which metaphysics should attempt.

In regard to systems not built upon inductive psychological proof, I confess that to me they are all very much alike; they differ only in respect of the intellectual temperament of the individual constructing them, or the influences under which he has been nurtured. The man of genius, like Schelling, will create an ingenious theory, beautiful as the golden locks of the setting sun; the man of vigorous intellect, like Hegel, will erect a fabric which looks as coherent as a palace of ice: but until they can

* See a summary of his admirable review of Kant, Prem. Sér. tom. v. leç. viii. In Prem. Sér. tom. ii. leç. vii., viii., xiv., xxii., he labours to show that the ideas of the true, the beautiful, the good, imply the existence of a God who is the true, the beautiful, the good; and in Deux. Sér. tom. i. leç. iv., v., that the finite implies the infinite, that the effect implies a cause, and the cause an effect. In these last lectures he had spoken of God as necessarily creating. In Fragments Philosophiques, Aver. de la trois. éd., he withdraws the language 'necessity of creation,' as not sufficiently reverent towards the Creator; but he adheres to the meaning, "Or en Dieu surtout la force est adéquate à la substance, et la force divine est toujours en acte; Dieu est donc essentiellement actif et créateur."

be shown to be founded on the inherent principles of the mind, or to be built up of materials thence derived, I wrap myself up in philosophic doubt, as not being sure whether they may disappear while I am gazing on them.

Nor am I to be seduced into an admiration of such imposing systems by the plea often urged in their behalf, that they furnish a gymnasium for the exercise of the intellect. I acknowledge that one of the very highest advantages of study of every description is to be found in the vigour imparted to the mind which pursues it. But whatever may have been the difficulty in the days of the schoolmen, it is not necessary now to resort to fruitless *a priori* speculation, in order to find an arena in which to exercise the intellect. Nay, I am convinced that when the research conducts to no solid results, it will weary the mind without strengthening it; the effort will be like that of one who beateth the air, and activity will always be followed by exhaustion, by dissatisfaction, and an unwillingness to make further exertion. Labour, it is true, is its own reward; but if there be no other reward, there will be the want of the needful incentive. The vigour imparted is only one of the incidental effects which follow when labour is undertaken in the hope of securing substantial fruits. Nor is it to be forgotten that these speculations, though fruitless of good, are not fruitless of evil. In the struggles thus engendered there are other powers of the mind *tried* as well as the understanding; there are often sad agonizings of the feelings, of the faith, and indeed of the whole soul, which feels as if the foundation on which it previously stood had been removed and none other supplied, and as if it had in consequence to sink for ever; or as if it were doomed to move for ever onward without reaching a termination, while all retreat has been cut off behind. In these wrestlings I fear that many wounds are inflicted, which continue long to rankle and often terminate in something worse than the dissolution of the bodily organism, for they end in the loss of faith and of peace, in cases in which they do not issue in immorality, in scepticism, or in blasphemy. Any sentiment of admiration which might be excited by the display of mental power and learning on the part of the speculators, is counteracted in my mind by more painful associations than the Quaker poet connected with the sound of the drum.

> "I hate that drum's discordant sound,
> Parading round and round and round;
> To me it talks of ravaged plains,
> And burning towns and ruined swains,
> And mangled limbs and dying groans,
> And widows' tears and orphans' moans,
> And all that Misery's hand bestows
> To fill the catalogue of human woes."

These exercises, I suspect, resemble not so much those of the gymnasium, as of the ancient gladiatorial shows, in which no doubt there were many brilliant feats performed, but in which also members were mutilated, and the heart's-blood of many a brave man shed. I fear that in not a few cases generous and courageous youths have entered the lists, to lose in the contest all creed, all religious, and in some cases, all moral principle, and with these all peace and all stability.

> "I see before me the gladiator lie,
> He leans upon his hand—his manly brow
> Consents to death, but conquers agony;
> And his drooped head sinks gradually low:
> And through his side the last drops ebbing slow
> From the big gash, fall heavy one by one,
> Like the first of a thunder-shower. And now
> The arena swims around him—he is gone."

SECT. V. WHAT EXPLANATION CAN BE GIVEN OF THE INTUITIONS OF THE MIND?

As we are about forthwith to ask the Intuitions to

give an account of themselves, it may be as well to have it settled what sort of information we may expect to draw from them.

Our intuitions are at once the clearest and the darkest objects which the mind can contemplate; constituting the intellectual sense by which we get all our original knowledge, it is found to be a painful and arduous work to turn back the eye upon itself. Truths seen by intuition shine in their own light, like the luminary of day, and any attempt to make them clearer is like "going out with a taper to see the sun," and yet when we would look steadily on them our eye is apt to be blenched. In another respect too they are like the sun—they shine the brightest when we get the first glance at them, and if we continue to gaze, they appear dim and dark to our oppressed vision. And yet it is only by reflexly looking on them as they shine, that we can expect to be able to determine their form and dimensions.

There are senses in which they cannot, there are senses in which they can be explained.

I. 1. They cannot be explained in the sense of being rendered intelligible to any one naturally without them. He who is born blind cannot be made to see colours by help of a microscope or telescope, nor could the most vivid description give him any idea of them. In like manner, if there were a human being without the intuitions, he could not be made to understand the objects which they reveal: he who does not see them when he opens his eyes, will never be enabled to behold them by any logical process of explanation or definition. If men were without the native capacity of perceiving extension, or power of discerning moral good, it would be impossible by any description or argument to convey the dimmest idea of them. This is one reason why the subject of our original perceptions has been felt to be so very mysterious. It is seen that human discussion can do nothing in clearing them up, and that if it attempt to do so, it is only "darkening counsel by words without knowledge." But all this dazzling of our eye arises not from any darkness enveloping them, but from the very brightness of the light in which they shine.

2. They cannot be explained in the sense of being resolved into simpler elements. In physical science we can gain important information regarding many objects, by resolving them into their constituents ; even there however we come to simple substances which cannot be decomposed. In mental science we can explain many phenomena by explicating the processes involved in the formation of them ; thus, in regard to the perception of distance by the eye, we can show what are the original endowments of the sense of sight, and what are the acquisitions of experience ; and in regard to reasoning, we can point out the relation of premisses and conclusion. But in the process of decomposition we must come to simple properties which admit of no analysis. The intuitive principles of the mind are the simple powers to which we owe all our original cognitions : he who would attempt to cut these atoms will find the edge of his analysis bent back and blunted, as the razor is when it is applied to the rock.

3. They cannot be explained in the sense of being referred to higher principles from which they derive their authority. Some phenomena, both material and mental, can be thus shown to hang on higher truths : the movements of the planets and of the moon up in the sky, are dependent on the law of gravitation, and on the collocation of the several bodies. We may lawfully and profitably seek out for the authority on which certain of our apprehensions or cognitions rest : we may trace the steps, for example, by which we are led to believe that Julius

Cæsar lived, or that Jesus Christ died and rose again, or those by which we come to be assured that the square of the hypothenuse of a right-angled triangle is equal to the square of the other two sides. But in all such regressions we must at last come back to something original, and having its authority in itself.

For some things we must have a foundation, but we do not seek for a foundation for everything. It was the idea that everything must lean on something else, which led the Indians to place the earth on the back of an elephant, and to make the elephant stand on a tortoise. I use this as a mere illustration. It is quite true that most truths known to us stand on other truths. But we come at last to truths which stand on nothing else. The mind does not feel on this account that the truths are less stable: it is convinced as to certain truths that they need something else to lean on; but of certain truths it sees that they bear up other truths and yet themselves need no support beyond or beneath them; and it sees that these are the truths which are the firmest and the most secure. He who would go beyond them is going further back than the beginning; he who would go further down is trying to get beneath the foundation.

II. But there are senses in which an account or an explanation can be given of them.

1. Negative definitions may be given of them. The knowledge which we have of the objects being in its very nature the simplest of all knowledge, we cannot make it simpler. But if any one mistakes in regard to the objects, and says that they possess qualities which we know do not belong them, then we can correct him. We can by reason of our intimate knowledge of the objects make an indefinite number of negative assertions regarding them. Thus, we can affirm of self perceiving that it is different from the body perceived, of extension that it

is not the same as consciousness or intelligence, of space and time that they can have no bounds, of moral excellence that it is not the same as the pleasurable, and of vice that it is not the same as the painful. These negative propositions may be made to face error from whatever quarter it makes its hostile assaults.

2. Their peculiarity may be brought out by abstraction. Not that their nature may be explained to one who is not already cognizant of them. But the native cognizance which the mind has of them is concrete, is mixed. Several intuitions are mingled in one act, or our intuitive perceptions are bound up with our derivative or experiential exercises. As long as our reflex knowledge is of this character, it is indistinct and confused, and we are ever liable to fall into error when we make affirmations regarding it; for what we assert of the whole, or of every one of the parts, may be true only of some or of one of the parts. But by analysis we can make the given intuitions stand forth separately to the view, just as by experiment in physical science we can separate the agencies of nature which usually work in combination,—separate, for example, in the exhausted receiver of an air-pump, the power which draws a body to the earth from the resistance given to it in ordinary circumstances by the atmosphere. Looking at it thus, we can distinguish and express its peculiarity. Not that this expression could convey any meaning to one without the intuition, but to one with the intuition the meaning flashes immediately on the vision. Naturally, there is never a knowledge of not-self without a co-existing knowledge of self, but by abstraction we can separate the two and look at each by itself; and when we describe the not-self as extended or in motion, or the self as conscious and intelligent, an apprehension at once starts up in the mind corresponding to the object.

3. The nature of the object intuitively known can be specified. Not indeed that it could be apprehended by one without the proper perception, but to one with the corresponding intuition its nature can be distinctly stated. Thus we can, in intelligent language, describe the extension of body as its being contained in space and occupying space, and virtue as the approvable quality of voluntary actions of intelligent beings, and the mind at once understands what is meant to be affirmed of the objects.

4. We may generalize or classify the intuitions of the mind.* Fixing by abstraction on certain common qualities, we may then, by generalization, place all those possessing them into one class. We may fix on the more marked and decided points of resemblance, with their implied differences, and this will give us the Grand Divisions. We may then divide and subdivide, according to other, and minor, but still important points of resemblance and difference, in due ordination and subordination. In this Treatise we classify the intuitions according to what they look at and discover, as

I. THE TRUE. II. THE GOOD.

I. THE TRUE.

1. Primitive Cognitions. 2. Primitive Beliefs. 3. Primitive Judgments.

The justification of this arrangement can be found only in its embracing all the phenomena, and of this the reader must judge as we proceed with the exposition.

I speak of our intuitions as looking to the true and the good, and the true and the good thus perceived have a reality, but this is not to be understood as a reality of the same sort as is possessed by individual things, which

* Locke says truly, that if we include all self-evident propositions, principles will be almost infinite (Essay, book ii. ch. vii. s. 10). Hence the need of generalizing them.

may be true or good. They have a reality, not as individual entities, but as common qualities, which should be expressed by a common epithet. But the qualities always imply individual objects, in which they inhere. And wherever the qualities of knowledge and moral excellence are to be found in the creature they are but emanations from the Creator. The streams, if we follow them, will lead us up to the Fountain. It will be seen that our intuitive convictions, whether they relate to the true or the good, all conduct us to Him who is emphatically the True and the Good.

CHAPTER III.

(SUPPLEMENTARY.)

BRIEF CRITICAL REVIEW OF OPINIONS IN REGARD TO INTUITIVE TRUTHS.

I. The Pre-Socratic Schools of Greece.—The Greek philosophers who flourished in the sixth and fifth centuries before Christ, if they did not exactly discuss, did, at least, start the question of man's native power of intuition. The Ionian School, founded by Thales, and continued by Anaximander, Anaximenes, Anaxagoras, and others, dwelling among material elements, found only the mutable and the fleeting; till at length it was laid down systematically by Heraclitus, that all things were in a state of perpetual flux, under the power of an ever-kindling and ever-extinguishing fire. Running to the opposite extreme, the Eleatic School, of which Xenophanes, Parmenides, and Zeno were the most illustrious masters, appealed altogether from sense (*αἴσθησις*) and opinion (*δόξα*) to reason (*λόγος*); fixed its attention on the abiding nature of things beneath all mutation; dived into profound, but over-subtle, and often confused and quibbling disquisitions regarding Being; and ended by making all things so fixed that change and motion became impossible. It was in the very midst of the collision of these sects that Socrates was reared. Professing to have only a practical aim in view, he yet, in putting down the opposition to that end, indulged in all the subtlety of a Greek intellect, and thus stimulated the dialectic spirit of his pupil Plato, who sought to harmonize the fleeting and the fixed.

II. Plato.—It would be altogether a mistake to suppose, as some have done, that Plato is for ever inquiring into the origin of ideas in the mind, like the metaphysicians who came after Descartes and Locke. His aim was of a character loftier and wider, but more unattainable by the cogitation of one thinker, or indeed by cogitation at all. Nor was it his object to discover the absolute, as if he had been reared in the schools of Schelling or Hegel. His grand aim was to discover the real (τὸ ὄν) and the abiding, amidst the illusions of sense and the mutations of things. And in following this end he sought prematurely to determine questions which can be settled only by a long course of patient induction, carried on by a succession of observers of the world without and the world within. But in the search he started many deep views of God, of man, and of the world, which have been established by the Bible, and by inductive mental and physical science. 1. He everywhere proceeds on the doctrine that man is possessed of a power of reason (λόγος, or νοῦς, or νόησις) above sense, or faith, or understanding (διάνοια). 2. This reason contemplates ideas (ἰδέαι, or εἴδη) suprasensible, immutable, eternal, which ideas are realities. 3. He sees that there is need of a process of thought, specially of abstraction, in order to the mind rising to these ideas. 4. The discovery of these ideas should be the especial aim of the philosopher, and the gazing on them the highest exercise of wisdom. But Plato moves above our earth like the sun, with so dazzling a light that we feel unable, or unwilling, to look too narrowly into the exact body of truth which sheds such a lustre. 1. He has given a wrong account of the reality in these eternal ideas, making them the only realities; denying reality to the objects of sense, except in so far as they partake of them, and seeming to make them independent even of the Divine Mind. 2. Under the one phase, 'idea,' he gathers an aggregate of things which require to be distinguished,—such as the true, the beautiful, the good, unity and being, natural law and moral law, the forms of objects, and even the universals fashioned arbitrarily by the mind. By heaping together and confounding all these things which should be carefully distinguished, he has given a grandeur to his views, but at the expense of clearness and accuracy. 3. He does not see that ideas exist naturally in the mind merely in the form of laws or rules. To account for them he is obliged to suppose that the soul pre-existed, and that the calling up of the ideas is a

H 2

sort of reminiscence. 4. He does not see how the mind reaches them in their abstract, general, or philosophic form. He did not observe that the mind begins with the knowledge of particular objects, and must thence rise by induction to generals. He thus laid himself open to the assaults, always acute, often just, at times captious, of Aristotle, who saw that the general existed in the individuals, and that it was from the singulars that man rose to the universals (see Metaph. i. 12.) 5. He attaches an extravagant value to the contemplation of these ideas in their abstract and general form. Overlooking the other purposes served by ideas, and their indissoluble connection with singulars,—forgetting that philosophy consists in viewing law in relation to its objects,—he represents the mind as in its highest exercise when it is gazing upon them in their essence, formless and colourless: Ἡ γὰρ ἀχρώματός τε καὶ ἀσχημάτιστος καὶ ἀναφὴς οὐσία ὄντως οὖσα ψυχῆς κυβερνήτῃ μόνῳ θεατῇ νῷ χρῆται· περὶ ἣν τὸ τῆς ἀληθοῦς ἐπιστήμης γένος τοῦτον ἔχει τὸν τόπον (Phædrus, 58). He thus prepared the way for the extravagancies of the Neoplatonist School of Plotinus and Proclus, who reckoned the mind as in its loftiest state when under an intuition or ecstasy, which looks on the One and the Good, and who found, I believe, the gazing idle and unprofitable enough.

III. Aristotle.—His views, if not so grand as those of Plato, are much more sober and definite. He has specified most of the separate characteristics of intuition, but I have not been able to find how he reconciles his several statements. 1. He has a power, or faculty, called Νοῦς, which he represents as concerned with the principles of thought and being: Ὁ νοῦς ἐστὶ περὶ τὰς ἀρχὰς τῶν νοητῶν καὶ τῶν ὄντων (Mag. Mor. i. 35). Elsewhere he shows that it cannot be φρόνησις, nor σοφία, nor ἐπιστήμη, but νοῦς, which has to do with the principles of science: Λείπεται νοῦν εἶναι τῶν ἀρχῶν (Eth. Nic. vi. 6: ed. Michelet). 2. He fixes on self-evidence and independence as tests of what he calls first truths and principles. First truths are those whose credit is not through others, but of themselves. Ἔστι δ' ἀληθῆ μὲν καὶ πρῶτα τὰ μὴ δι' ἑτέρων ἀλλὰ δι' αὑτῶν ἔχοντα τὴν πίστιν· οὐ δεῖ γὰρ ἐν ταῖς ἐπιστημονικαῖς ἀρχαῖς ἐπιζητεῖσθαι τὸ διὰ τί, ἀλλ' ἑκάστην τῶν ἀρχῶν αὐτὴν καθ' ἑαυτὴν εἶναι πιστήν (Top. i. 1: ed. Waitz). 3. He fixes on necessity as a test, and represents the truths as eternal. Thus he speaks of necessary principles, and of their being inherent in things: Εἰ οὖν ἐστιν ἡ ἀποδεικτικὴ ἐπιστήμη ἐξ ἀναγκαίων ἀρχῶν (ὃ γὰρ ἐπίσταται, οὐ δυνατὸν ἄλλως ἔχειν), τὰ δὲ καθ' αὑτὰ ὑπάρχοντα ἀναγκαῖα τοῖς πράγμασιν, κ.τ.λ. (Anal. Post. i. 6). Τὰ ἐξ ἀνάγκης ὄντα ἁπλῶς ἀΐδια, πάντα τὰ δ' ἀΐδια ἀγένητα καὶ ἄφθαρτα (Eth. Nic. vi. 3). 4. It is a favourite maxim with him that everything cannot be proven. He says that all science is not demonstrative, that the science of things immediate is undemonstrable; for as all demonstration is from things prior, we must, at last, arrive at things immediate which are not demonstrable: Ἡμεῖςδέ φαμεν οὔτε πᾶσαν ἐπιστήμην ἀποδεικτικὴν εἶναι, ἀλλὰ τὴν τῶν ἀμέσων ἀναπόδεικτον. καὶ τοῦθ' ὅτι ἀναγκαῖον, φανερόν· εἰ γὰρ ἀνάγκη μὲν ἐπίστασθαι τὰ πρότερα καὶ ἐξ ὧν ἡ ἀπόδειξις, ἵσταται δέ ποτε τὰ ἄμεσα, ταῦτ' ἀναπόδεικτα ἀνάγκη εἶναι (Anal. Post. i. 3); see also i. 22, where he says there must be principles of demonstration, τῶν ἀποδείξεων ὅτι ἀνάγκη ἀρχὰς εἶναι. He speaks of science and demonstration carrying us to intuition, νοῦς (i. 23). 5. He draws the distinction between two classes of truths. We believe all things, either through syllogism or from induction, ἅπαντα γὰρ πιστεύομεν ἢ διὰ συλλογισμοῦ ἢ ἐξ ἐπαγωγῆς (Anal. Prior. ii. 23). To nature, the syllogism is the prior and the more known; but to us, that which is through induction is the more palpable: Φύσει μὲν οὖν πρότερος καὶ γνωριμώτερος ὁ διὰ τοῦ μέσου συλλογισμὸς, ἡμῖν δ' ἐναργέστερος ὁ διὰ τῆς ἐπαγωγῆς (ib.). In explaining this, he says that he calls 'things prior and more knowable to us' those which are nearer to sense, and 'things prior and more knowable simply' those which are more remote; but those things which are universal, belong to the most remote, and those which are singular, to the nearest: Λέγω δὲ πρὸς ἡμᾶς μὲν πρότερα καὶ γνωριμώτερα τὰ ἐγγύτερον τῆς αἰσθήσεως, ἁπλῶς δὲ πρότερα καὶ γνωριμώτερα τὰ ποῤῥώτερον. ἔστι δὲ ποῤῥωτάτω μὲν τὰ καθόλου μάλιστα, ἐγγυτάτω δὲ τὰ καθ' ἕκαστα" (Anal. Post. i. 2). But the question is started, How does the human mind, which must begin with the singulars, as better known to it, reach the universal? He seems to say, in the following passage, we reach universal truth through induction: Μανθάνομεν ἢ ἐπαγωγῇ ἢ ἀποδείξει. ἔστι δ' ἡ μὲν ἀπόδειξις ἐκ τῶν καθόλου, ἡ δ' ἐπαγωγὴ ἐκ τῶν κατὰ μέρος. ἀδύνατον δὲ τὰ καθόλου θεωρῆσαι μὴ δι' ἐπαγωγῆς· ἐπεὶ καὶ τὰ ἐξ ἀφαιρέσεως λεγόμενα ἔσται δι' ἐπαγωγῆς γνώριμα ποιεῖν, ὅτι ὑπάρχει ἑκάστῳ γένει ἔνια, καὶ εἰ μὴ χωριστά ἐστιν, ᾗ τοιονδὶ ἕκαστον. ἐπαχθῆναι δὲ μὴ ἔχοντας αἴσθησιν ἀδύνατον. τῶν γὰρ καθ' ἕκαστον ἡ αἴσθησις· οὐ γὰρ ἐνδέχεται λαβεῖν αὐτῶν τὴν ἐπιστήμην. οὔτε γὰρ ἐκ τῶν καθόλου ἄνευ ἐπαγωγῆς, οὔτε δι' ἐπαγωγῆς ἄνευ τῆς αἰσθήσεως (*ib.* i. 18; cf. Eth. Nic. vi. 3). All these are important principles. But how does he reconcile them? How in particular does he reconcile his doctrine, that universals are gained by induction, with his statement as to the mind having a νοῦς which looks at principles? There are passages in his Metaphysics which show that such questions had been before his mind. The question is put whether first principles are universal, or are as singulars of things; and the further and most important question, whether they subsist in capacity or in energy, that is, whether they exist virtually or in act: Πότερον αἱ ἀρχαὶ καθόλου εἰσὶν ἢ ὡς τὰ καθ' ἕκαστα τῶν πραγμάτων, καὶ δυνάμει ἢ ἐνεργείᾳ (Metaph. ii. 2. 10: ed. Bonitz). In another passage he seems to answer, that those things which are predicated of individuals are first principles rather than the genera, but adds that it would not be easy to express how one should conceive these first principles: Ἐκ μὲν οὖν τούτων μᾶλλον φαίνεται τὰ ἐπὶ τῶν ἀτόμων κατηγορούμενα ἀρχαὶ εἶναι τῶν γενῶν. πάλιν δὲ πῶς αὖ δεῖ ταύτας ἀρχὰς ὑπολαβεῖν οὐ ῥᾴδιον εἰπεῖν. For this statement he gives reasons, which lead him to the conclusion that the universals which are predicated of individuals are principles in the ratio of their universality, and that the very highest generalizations must be emphatically principles: Τὴν μὲν γὰρ ἀρχὴν δεῖ καὶ τὴν αἰτίαν εἶναι παρὰ τὰ πράγματα ὧν ἀρχή, καὶ δύνασθαι εἶναι χωριζομένην αὐτῶν· τοιοῦτον δέ τι παρὰ τὸ καθ' ἕκαστον εἶναι διὰ τί ἄν τις ὑπολάβοι, πλὴν ὅτι καθόλου κατηγορεῖται καὶ κατὰ πάντων; ἀλλὰ μήν, εἰ διὰ τοῦτο, τὰ μᾶλλον καθόλου μᾶλλον θετέον ἀρχάς. ὥστε ἀρχαὶ τὰ πρῶτ' ἂν εἴησαν γένη (ii. 3. 15). There are points of connection not brought out in this statement. But we are not rashly to charge Aristotle with an inconsistency. I believe that his statement as to first truths and syllogism, and his statement as to the universality of induction, are both true. But he has not drawn the distinction between first principles as forms in the mind, and as individual convictions, and as laws got by induction; nor has he seen how the self-evidence and necessity, being in the singulars, goes up into the universals when (but only when) the induction is properly formed.

IV. Descartes seized on a large body of important truth in regard to innate ideas. 1. He saw that they were of the nature of powers or faculties ready to operate, but needing to be called forth. "Lorsque je dis que quelque idée est née avec nous, ou qu'elle est naturellement empreinte en nos âmes, je n'entends pas qu'elle se présente toujours à notre pensée, car ainsi il n'y en aurait aucune; mais j'entends seulement que nous avons en nous-mêmes la faculté de la produire" (Trois Objec. Rép. Obj. 10). See other passages to the same effect, quoted by Mr. Veitch, Trans. of Med., etc., pp. 207–208. 2. He had a glimpse, but confused, of the test of self-evidence, which he unhappily represents as clearness. "Toutes les choses que nous concevons clairement et distinctement sont vraies de la façon dont nous les concevons" (Méd. Abrégé). He thus explains clearness and distinctness: "J'appelle claire celle qui est présente et manifeste à un esprit attentif; de même que nous disons voir clairement les objets, lorsqu'étant présents à nos yeux ils agissent assez fort sur eux, et qu'ils sont disposés à les regarder; et distincte, celle qui est tellement précise et différente de toutes les autres, qu'elle ne comprend en soi que ce qui paroît manifestement à celui qui la considère comme il faut" (Prin. Phil. i. 45). 3. He sees that they assume the shape of common notions. 4. These are represented as eternal truths of intelligence. "Lorsque nous pensons qu'on ne sauroit faire quelque chose de rien, nous ne croyons point que cette proposition soit une chose qui existe ou la propriété de quelque chose, mais nous la prenons pour une certaine vérité éternelle qui a son siége en notre pensée, et que l'on nomme une notion commune ou une maxime; tout de même quand on dit qu'il est impossible qu'une même chose soit et ne soit pas en même temps, que ce qui a été fait ne peut n'être pas fait, que celui qui pense ne peut manquer d'être ou d'exister pendant qu'il pense, et quantité d'autres semblables, ce sont seulement des vérités, et non pas des choses qui soient hors de notre pensée, et il y en a un si grand nombre de telles qu'il seroit malaisé de les dénombrer" (Prin. Phil. i. 49). 5. He discovers that they come forth into consciousness; hence he calls them innate ideas, and defines idea: "Cette forme de chacune de nos pensées par la perception immédiate de laquelle nous avons connaissance de ces mêmes pensées" (Rép. aux Deux Object.). But there is confusion throughout, in the view which he takes and in his mode of expression. 1. He gives no account of the relation between the faculty on the one hand, and the idea or common notion on the other. He does not see that abstraction and generalization are necessary in order to reach the abstract and general idea. 2. The test of self-evidence is not well expressed; in this respect he is inferior to Locke. The clearness and distinctness of an idea is, to say the least of it, a very ambiguous phrase, for in some senses of the word we may have a very clear idea of an imaginary object, or a distinct idea of a falsehood. 3. That there is confusion in his view is evident from the circumstance that he often states that these truths are not equally admitted by all, because they are opposed to the prejudices of some. He speaks of persons "qui ont imprimé de longue main des opinions en leur créance, qui étaient contraires à quelques-unes de ces vérités" (Prin. i. 50). 4. He expects far too much from a bare contemplation of the principles or causes of things. "Mais l'ordre que j'ai tenu en ceci a été tel: premièrement, j'ai tâché de trouver en général les principes ou premières causes de tout ce qui est ou qui peut être dans le monde, sans rien considérer pour cet effet que Dieu seul qui l'a créé, ni les tirer d'ailleurs que de certaines semences de vérités qui sont naturellement en nos âmes. Après cela, j'ai examiné quels étaient les premiers et les plus ordinaires effets qu'on pouvait déduire de ces causes; et il me semble que par là j'ai trouvé des cieux, des astres, une terre, et même sur la terre de l'eau, de l'air, etc." (Méth. P. vi.).

V. LOCKE has, in his account of the Human Understanding, both a sensational or rather an experiential element, and a rational element. Eagerly bent on establishing his favourite position that all our ideas are derived from sensation and reflection, he has not blended these elements very successfully, nor been at much pains to show their consistency. In France they took the sensational element, and overlooked the other. The Arians and Socinians of Britain seized eagerly on the rational element. In his unmeasured condemnation of innate ideas in the First Book of his Essay, he seems to deny truths which he openly defends or incidentally allows in other parts of the work. 1. He gives a high place to reason. Thus, in replying to Stillingfleet, he says:—"Reason, as standing for true and clear principles, and also as standing for clear and fair deductions from those principles, I have not wholly omitted; as is manifest from what I have said of self-evident propositions, intuitive knowledge, and demonstration, in other parts of my Essay." Speaking of self-evident propositions:—"Whether they come in view of the mind earlier or later, this is true of them, that they are all known by their native evidence, are wholly independent, receive no light, nor are capable of any proof one from another" (see Rogers's Essays, Locke, p. 47). 2. He gives an important place to intuition. 3. He fixes on self-evidence as the mark of intuition. "Sometimes the mind perceives the agreement or disagreement of two ideas immediately by themselves, without the intervention of any other; and this I think we may call intuitive knowledge. From this the mind is at no pains of proving or examining, but perceives the truth, as the eye doth light, only by being directed towards it." "This kind of knowledge is the clearest and most certain that human frailty is capable of. This part of knowledge is irresistible, and, like bright sunshine, forces itself immediately to be perceived as soon as ever the mind turns its view that way, and leaves no room for hesitation, doubt, or examination, but the mind is presently filled with the clear light of it." "He that demands a greater certainty than this, demands he knows not what, and shows only that he has a mind to be a sceptic without being able to be so" (Essay, bk. iv. ch.

ii. sect. 1; see also book iv. chap. xvii. sect. 4). Among truths known intuitively, "we have an intuitive knowledge of our own existence" (bk. iv. ch. iii. sect. 21); and "man knows by an intuitive certainty that bare nothing can no more produce any real Being than it can be equal to two right-angles" (bk. iv. ch. x. sect. 3). 4. He is obliged at times to appeal to necessity of conception. Thus, in arguing with Stillingfleet:—"The idea of beginning to be, is necessarily connected with the idea of some operation; and the idea of operation with the idea of something operating, which we call a cause." "The idea of a right-angled triangle necessarily carries with it an equality of its angles to two right ones; nor can we conceive this relation, this connection of these two ideas, to be possibly mutable" (Essay, bk. iv. ch. iii. sect. 29). He speaks of certain and universal knowledge as having "necessary connection," "necessary co-existence," "necessary dependence" (see Webb on the Intellectualism of Locke, P. iii.) 5. He sees that intuitive general maxims are all derived from particulars. This follows from his general maxim that the mind begins with particulars. "The ideas first in the mind, 'tis evident, are those of particular things, from which by slow degrees the understanding proceeds to some few general ones" (bk. iv. ch. vii. sect. 9). "In particulars our knowledge begins, and so spreads itself by degrees to generals" (bk. iv. ch. vii. sect. 11). Following out this view, he speaks of the general propositions being "not innate but collected from a preceding acquaintance and reflection on particular instances. These when observing men have made them, unobserving men when they are proposed to them cannot refuse their assent to" (bk. i. ch. ii. sect. 21). 6. He saw clearly—what Kant never saw—that the mind rises to universal propositions by looking at things, and the nature of things. "Had they examined the ways whereby men come to the knowledge of many universal truths, they would have found them to result in the minds of men from the being of things themselves when duly considered, and that they were discovered by the application of those faculties which were fitted by nature to receive and judge of them when duly employed about them (bk. i. ch. iv. sect. 25).

But, on the other hand, Locke has omitted or controverted certain great truths. 1. He imagines that when he has disproved innate ideas in the sense of phantasms, and general notions, he has therefore disproved them in every sense. 2. He does not see that the intuition which he acknowledges, must have a rule, law, or principle, which may be described as innate, inasmuch as it is in the mind prior to all experience. 3. Misled by his theory of the mind looking at ideas and not at things, he represents intuition as concerned solely with the comparison of ideas. This was noticed by the Bishop of ——, in a letter dated Johnstoun, October 26, 1697, to Locke's friend, Mr. Molyneux:—"To me it seems that, according to Mr. Locke, I cannot be said to know anything except there be two ideas in my mind, and all the knowledge I have must be concerning the relation these two ideas have to one another, and that I can be certain of nothing else, which in my opinion excludes all certainty of sense and of single ideas, all certainty of consciousness, such as willing, conceiving, believing, knowing, etc., and, as he confesses, all certainty of faith, and, lastly, all certainty of remembrance of which I have formerly demonstrated as soon as I have forgot or do not actually think of the demonstration" (Letters between Locke and Molyneux). Reid refers to Locke's notion that belief or knowledge consists in a perception of the agreement or disagreement of ideas, and characterizes it "as one of the main pillars of modern scepticism." "I say a sensation exists, and I think I understand clearly what I mean. But you want to make the thing clearer, and for that end tell me that there is an agreement between the idea of that sensation and the idea of existence. To speak freely, this conveys to me no light, but darkness. I can conceive no otherwise of it than as an odd and obscure circumlocution. I conclude then that the belief which accompanies sensation and memory is a simple act of the mind which cannot be defined" (Works, p. 107). 4. He does not see the peculiar nature of intuitive maxims. He perceives that they are got by generalization—the great truth overlooked by the special supporters of innate ideas; but he fails to observe that they are the generalization of primitive cognitions and truths, which carry with them self-evidence and necessity.

VI. Leibnitz had profound but, in some respects, extravagant views of necessary truths. 1. He sees that they have a place in the mind, as habitudes, dispositions, aptitudes, faculties. "Les connaissances ou les vérités, en tant qu'elles sont en nous, quand même on n'y pense point, sont des habitudes ou des dispositions" (Nouv. Essais, Opera, p. 213: ed. Erdmann). At the same place he calls them 'aptitudes.' "Lorsqu'on dit que les notions innées sont implicitement dans l'esprit, cela doit signifier seulement, qu'il a la faculté de les connaître" (p. 212). 2. "Leibnitz has the honour of first explicitly enouncing the criterion of necessity, and Kant of first fully applying it to the phenomena. In nothing has Kant been more successful than in this under consideration." So says Hamilton (Reid's Works, p. 323). The remark seems correct; but it should be added that Aristotle, as has been shown, expressly fixed on necessity, while others appealed to it; even Locke speaks of knowledge as "irresistible," and of "necessary relations." Leibnitz draws more decidedly than had been done before, the distinction between necessary and eternal truths and truths of experience (p. 209). 3. Because of the natural faculty and "preformation," the ideas tend to come into consciousness in a special form. "Il y a toujours une disposition particulière à l'action, et à une action plutôt qu'à l'autre" (p. 223). He illustrates this by supposing that in the marble there might be veins which marked out a particular figure, say that of Hercules preferably to others. "Mais s'il y avoit des veines dans la pierre, qui marquassent la figure d'Hercule préférablement à d'autres figures, cette pierre y seroit plus déterminée, et Hercule y seroit comme inné en quelque façon" (p. 196). 4. He represents the intellect itself as a source of ideas. To the maxim "*Nihil est in intellectu quod non fuerit in sensu*," he adds, "*nisi ipse intellectus*." The expression is not very explicit. He explains it:—" Or l'âme renferme l'être, la substance, l'un, le même, la cause, la perception, le raisonnement, et quantité d'autres notions." But he is surely wrong in identifying these with Locke's ideas of reflection (p. 223). 5. He sees that there is need of more than spontaneity, that there is need of some intellectual process, in order to discover the general truth. "Les maximes innées ne paroissent que par l'attention qu'on leur donne" (p. 213). But,—1. He separates necessary truth from things, and making them altogether mental, he led the way to that subjective tendency which was carried so far by Kant. 2. He does not distinguish between the necessary principle as a disposition unconsciously in the mind, and a general maxim discovered by a process. 3. He does not see that the general maxim is reached by generalizing the individual necessary truths.

VII. BUFFIER's principal treatise is on 'Premières Vérités.' He saw:—1. That there was in the mind an original law, which he characterizes as a 'disposition.' 2. He speaks of it as coming forth in common and uniform jndgments among all men or the greater part. 3. He sees that it does not thus come forth till mature age, and till men come to the use of reason. These three points are all brought out in the following sentence. "J'entends ici par le SENS COMMUN, la disposition que la nature a mise dans tous les hommes, ou manifestement dans la plupart d'entre eux, pour leur faire porter, quand ils ont atteint l'usage de la raison, un jugement commun et uniforme sur des objets différents du sentiment intime de leur propre perception : jugement qui n'est point la conséquence d'aucun principe antérieur" (p. i. c. v.). 4. He specifies several important practical characteristics of first truths. "(1.) Le premier de ces caractères est qu'elles soient si claires, que quand on entreprend de les prouver ou de les attaquer, on ne le puisse faire que par des propositions qui manifestement ne sont ni plus claires ni plus certaines. (2.) D'être si universellement reçues parmi les hommes en tout temps, en tous lieux, et par toutes sortes d'esprits, que ceux qui les attaquent se trouvent, dans le genre humain, être manifestement moins d'un contre cent, ou même contre mille. (3.) D'être si fortement imprimées dans nous, que nous y conformions notre conduite, malgré les raffinements de ceux qui imaginent des opinions contraires, et qui eux-mêmes agissent conformément, non à leurs opinions imaginées, mais aux premières vérités universellement reçues" (p. i. c. vii.). It does not appear however that (1) he fixed explicitly on their deeper qualities of self-evidence and necessity, nor (2) showed the relation between their individual and general form.

VII. Reid's great merit lies in establishing certain principles of Common Sense, such as those of substance and quality, cause and effect, and moral good, as against the scepticism of Hume. He does not profess to give an exhaustive account of these principles, nor to enter minutely into their distinctive character and mode of operation, but in conducting his proper work, he has mentioned nearly all their distinctive qualities. 1. He represents them as being in the nature of man: thus he speaks of "an original principle of our constitution" (p. 121), and calls them "original and natural judgments," as "part of that furniture which Nature hath given to the human understanding," as "the inspiration of the Almighty" and "a part of our constitution" (p. 209, Works: Hamilton's edition). 2. He represents the mind as having a sense or perception of them; and on the one hand avoids the error of Locke, who regards intuition as concerned solely with a comparison of ideas, and he does not on the other hand fall into that of Kant, who looks on them as mere forms in the mind. 3. He follows Locke in fixing on self-evidence as a decisive test. "We ascribe to reason two offices, or two degrees. The first is to judge of things self-evident; the second, to draw conclusions that are not self-evident from those that are. The first of these is the province, and the sole province, of common sense, and therefore it coincides with reason in its whole extent, and is only another name for one branch or one degree of reason" (p. 425: see also p. 422). 4. He specifies necessity as a mark. "By the constitution of our nature we are under a necessity of assent to them" (p. 130). He speaks of a certain truth "being a necessary truth, and therefore no object of sense." "It is not that things which begin to exist commonly have a cause, or even that they always in fact have a cause, but that they must have a cause and cannot begin to exist without a cause" (p. 455: see also pp. 521, 456). Yet he has not a steady apprehension of necessity as a test, for he says:—"I resolve for my own part always to pay a great regard to the dictates of common sense, and not to depart from them without absolute necessity" (p. 113), as if necessity did not preclude our departing from them. 5. He characterizes them as universal; thus he appeals to the "universal consent of mankind; not of philosophers only, but of the rude and unlearned vulgar" (p. 456).

His positive errors on this subject are not many, but he has not seen the full truth, and he has fallen into several oversights. 1. By neglecting a rigid use of tests, he has described some truths as first principles, into which there enters an experiential element. Thus, for example, "that there is life and intelligence in our fellow-men," "that certain features of the countenance, sounds of the voice, and gestures of the body, indicate certain thoughts and dispositions of the mind" (p. 448), and that "there is a certain regard due to human testimony in matters of fact, and even to human authority in matters of opinion" (450); and "that in the phenomena of Nature, what is to be will probably be like to what has been in similar circumstances" (451). A rigid application of the tests of self-evidence and necessity, would have shown that these were not first principles. 2. He is not careful to distinguish between the Spontaneous and Reflex use of common sense. He uses legitimately the argument from common sense against Hume, but in philosophy we must use the reflex principle carefully expressed, whereas Reid often appeals in a loose way to the spontaneous conviction. And here I may take the opportunity of stating my conviction (and this notwithstanding Sir W. Hamilton's defence of it in Note A) that the phrase 'common-sense' is an unfortunate, because a loose and ambiguous one. Common sense (besides its use by Aristotle, see Hamilton's Note A) has two meanings in ordinary discourse. It may signify, *first*, that unacquired, unbought, untaught sagacity, which certain men have by nature, and which other men never could acquire, even though they were subjected to the process mentioned by Solomon (Prov. xxvii. 22), and brayed in a mortar. Or it may signify the *commu-*

nis sensus, or the perceptions and judgments which are common to all men. It is only in this latter sense that the argument from common sense is a philosophic one; that is, only on the condition that the appeal be to convictions which are in all men; and further, that there has been a systematic exposition of them. Reid did make a most legitimate use of the argument from common sense, appealing to convictions in all men, and bringing out to view, and expressing with greater or less accuracy, the principles involved in these convictions. But then he has also taken advantage of the first meaning of the phrase; he represents the strength of these original judgments as *good sense* (p. 209): he appeals from philosophy to common sense; and in order to counteract the impression left by the high intellectual abilities of Hume, he showed that those who opposed Hume were not such fools after all, but had the good sense and shrewdness of mankind on their side (see p. 127, etc., with foot-notes of Hamilton). This has led many to suppose that the argument of Reid and Beattie is altogether an address to the vulgar. In this way, what seemed at the time a very dexterous use of a two-edged sword, has turned against those who employed it, and injustice has been done to the Scottish School of philosophers, who do make a proper use of the argument from common sense. 3. He does not see how to reconcile the doctrine (of Locke) that all maxims appear in consciousness as particulars, with his own doctrine of there being principles in the constitution of the mind, and there coming forth in general propositions.

IX. KANT has, next to Locke, exercised the greatest influence on modern speculation. As a general rule, the one dwells upon and magnifies the truths which the other overlooks. Kant is a reaction against Locke. He carries out, in his own logical way, certain principles which had grown up in the schools of Descartes, Leibnitz, and Wolf. 1. He sees more clearly, and explains more fully than ever had been done before, that the *a priori* principles are in the mind in the character of forms, or rules, prior to their being called forth or exercised. Thus, speaking of our intuition of space, he says it must be ready *a priori* in the mind, that is, before any perception of objects. "Die Form derselben muss zu ihnen insgesammt im Gemüthe *a priori* bereit liegen und daher abgesondert von aller Empfindung können betrachtet werden" (Werke, bd. ii. p. 32: ed. Rosenkranz). The mind has not only Intuitions of Space and Time to impose on phenomena or presentations, it has Categories of Quantity, Quality, Relation, Modality, to impose on its cognitions; and Ideas of Substance,

Totality of Phenomena, and Deity, to impose on the judgments reached by the Categories. 2. He maintains that the forms of the sensibility, and the categories of the understanding, have all a reference to objects of experience, real or possible; this, in fact, is their use; without this they would be meaningless. The ideas of pure reason do, however, refer to the comparisons of the understanding, and not to objects, and fruitless speculation arises from supposing that they refer to objects; and there may, also, be an undue use of the forms of sense and the categories of the understanding, but in themselves they refer to objects of possible experience (Kr. d. r. Vern., Trans. Dial.). 3. He proposes in his great work, the Kritik of Pure Reason, to give an inventory, in systematic order, of the *a priori* principles in the mind. "Denn es ist nichts als das Inventarium aller unserer Besitze durch reine Vernunft, systematisch geordnet" (Vorrede zu erst. Auf.). He seeks for an organon, which would be a compendium of the principles according to which *a priori* cognitions would be obtained. "Ein Organon der reinen Vernunft würde ein Inbegriff derjenigen Principien seyn, nach denen alle reine Erkentnisse *a priori* können erworben und wirklich zu Stande gebracht werden" (Einleit.). 4. He uses systematically the tests of Necessity and Universality, meaning by Universality the Universality of the Truth (see *supra*, p. 43, foot-note).

But, on the other hand, he has fallen into the grossest misapprehensions regarding the nature of the *a priori* principles of reason. 1. He maintains that the mind can have no intuition of things. All that it can know are mere presentations or phenomena. It is all true that the Forms of Sense and the Categories relate to objects of possible experience, but then experience does not give us a knowledge of things. "Es sind demnach die Gegenstände der Erfahrung niemals an sich selbst." Speaking even of self-consciousness he says, it does not know self as it exists: "Und selbst ist die innere und sinnliche Anschauung unseres Gemüths (als Gegenstandes des Bewusstseyns) ... auch nicht das eigentliche Selbst, so wie es an sich existirt" (Bd. ii. p. 389). He thus separates the intuitions of the mind altogether from things. 2. He makes our *a priori* Intuitions impose on phenomena the forms of Space and Time, which have no existence out of the mind. The categories are frameworks for binding conceptions into judgments. The ideas of pure reason reduce the judgments to unity, but have no reference to objects; and if we suppose them to have, we are landed in illusion and contradictions. By this system he makes much ideal which we are naturally led to regard as real, and thus prepared the way for Fichte, who made the whole ideal. 3. His Method of discovering the *a priori* principles of the mind is not the Inductive, but the Critical. Reason is called to undertake the task of self-examination, which may secure its righteous claims, not in an arbitrary way, but according to its own eternal and unchangeable laws. "Eine Aufforderung an die Vernunft, das beschwerlichste aller ihrer Geschäfte, nämlich das der Selbsterkenntniss aufs Neue zu übernehmen und einen Gerichtshof einzusetzen, der sie bei ihren gerechten Ansprüchen sichere, dagegen aber alle grundlose Anmaassungen nicht durch Machtsprüche sondern nach ihren ewigen und unwandelbaren Gesetzen" (Vor. z. erst. Auf.). Reason was thus set on criticizing itself according to laws of its own, and a succession of speculators set out each with what he alleged to be the laws of reason, but no two of them agreed as to what the laws of reason were, or what the standard by which to test them, and conclusions were reached which were evidently most irrational.

X. Dugald Stewart delighted to look on our intuitions under the aspect of "Fundamental Laws of Human Belief" (Elem. vol. ii. ch. i.). 1. He sees that they are of the nature of laws in the mind. 2. He sees that they are natural, original, and fundamental. 3. He sees that they are involved in the faculties. Hence he calls them "elements of reason" (Elem. vol. ii. p. 49: Ham. edit.); he would identify them with the exercise of our reasoning powers, and speaks of them as *component elements*, without which the faculty of reasoning is inconceivable and impossible (p. 39). It may be added that while he never formally appeals to necessity, he is obliged to use it incidentally. Thus "every man is impressed with an irresistible conviction that all his sensations, thoughts, and volitions belong to one and the same being" (Elem. vol. i. p. 47); and "we are impressed with an irresistible conviction of our personal identity" (Essays, p. 59). Speaking of causes, in the metaphysical meaning of the word, he says, the "word cause expresses something which is supposed to be necessarily connected with the change" (Elem. vol. i. p. 97). In looking on them as "fundamental laws," and in avoiding the ambiguity of the phrase "common sense," he has gone beyond Reid, but otherwise he has not thrown much light on them. He is in great confusion from not discovering how it is that "the elements of reason" may become general maxims, axioms, or principles.

XI. Dr. Thomas Brown has demonstrated, with great ingenuity, that our belief in the invariableness of cause and effect cannot be had from experience (Cause and Effect, part iii. sect. 3). He has also shown that the belief in our personal identity is intuitive (Lect. 13). When he comes to our intuitions, he speaks of them as "principles of thought;" as "primary universal intuitions of direct belief;" as "being felt intuitively, universally, immediately, irresistibly;" as "an internal, never-ceasing voice from the Creator and Preserver of our being;" as "omnipotent, like their Author;" and "such that it is impossible for us to doubt them" (Lect. 13). These are fine expressions, but his view of them is meagre after all, and a retrogression from the Scottish School. He makes no inquiry into their nature, laws, or tests.

XII. M. Cousin has given throughout all his philosophical works, clear and beautiful expositions of the elements of reason. 1. It is a favourite doctrine that reason looks at truths, eternal, universal, and absolute; truths, not to the individual or the race, but to all intelligences. 2. He uses, most successfully, the tests of necessity and universality, in order to distinguish the truths of reason from other truths. 3. He has distinguished between the spontaneous and reflective form of the truths of reasons (see *supra*, p. 62). 4. He has shown that primitive truths are all at first individual. "C'est un fait qu'il ne faut pas oublier, et qu'on oublie beaucoup trop souvent, que nos jugements sont d'abord des jugements particuliers et déterminés, et que c'est sous cette forme d'un jugement particulier et déterminé que font leur première apparition toutes les vérités universelles et nécessaires" (ser. ii. t. iii. leç. 19; see also ser. i. t. i. progr.; t. ii. progr. leç. ii.–iv., xi.). But on the other hand, he has given an exaggerated account of the power of human reason, and has not seen that induction is necessary in order to the discovery of necessary truth in its general form. 1. He uses unhappy and unguarded language in speaking of reason. His favourite epithet as applied to it is 'impersonal;' language which has a correct meaning inasmuch as the truth is not to the person but to all intelligences, but is often so employed as, without his intending it, to come very close to those pantheistic systems which identify the Divine and human reason (see ser. ii. leç. v.). 2. His reduction of the ideas of reason to three is full of confusion. The first idea is supposed to be unity, substance, cause, perfect, infinite, eternal; the second, multiple, quality, effect, imperfect, finite, bounded; and the third, the relation of the other two. It is to confound the things which manifestly differ, to make unity, cause, good, infinite indentical. The business of the metaphysician should be to observe each of these carefully, and bring out their peculiarities and their differences. 3. He does not see how it is that the general maxim is formed out of the particulars. He says that abstraction, "saisit immédiatement ce que le premier objet soumis à son observation renferme de général" (ser. i. t. i. leç. xi.). He does not see that in order to the formation of the general law there is need of a process, often delicate and laborious, of observation, abstraction, and generalization.

XIII. Sir William Hamilton's Note A, appended to his edition of Reid's Works, is the most important contribution made in this century to the science of first truths. 1. He has there specified nearly every important character of our intuitive convictions, and attached to them an appropriate nomenclature. 2. He has shown that the argument from common sense is one strictly scientific and eminently philosophic. 3. He has with unsurpassed erudition brought testimonies in behalf of the principles of common sense from the writings of the eminent thinkers of all ages and countries. But on the other hand:—1. He fails to draw the distinction between common sense as an aggregate of laws in the mind, as convictions in consciousness, and as generalized maxims. Thus the confusion of the spontaneous cognition and its generalized form appears in such passages as the following:—"The primitive cognitions seem to leap ready from the womb of reason, like Pallas from the head of Jupiter; sometimes the mind places them at the commencement of its operations in order to have a point of support and a fixed basis without which the operations would be impossible; sometimes they form in a certain sort the crowning, the consummation of all the intellectual operations" (Metaphysics, Lect. 38). 2. He does not properly appreciate the circumstance that intuitive convictions all look to singulars, and that there is need of induction to reach the general truth. He supposes that the general truth is revealed at once to consciousness. "Philosophy is the development and application of the constitutive and normal truths which consciousness immediately reveals." "Philosophy is thus wholly dependent on consciousness" (Reid's Works, p. 746). It is true that philosophy is dependent on consciousness, but it is dependent also on abstraction and generalization. He calls ultimate, primary, and universal principles, facts of consciousness (Metaphysics, Lect. 15). 3. His method is not the Inductive, but that of Critical Analysis introduced by Kant (Met. Lect. 29). 4. He fails to observe that the mind in intuition looks at objects. He makes the mind's conviction in regard to such objects as space, substance, cause, and infinity, to be impotencies, and their laws to be laws of thought and not of things (Append. to Discussions on Phil.). The error of such views will come out as we advance. I have endeavoured to expose it in the appendix to 'Method of Divine Government,' in an article in the 'North British Review,' for August, 1857, and an article in the 'Dublin University Magazine,' for August, 1859.

XIV. Dr. Whewell has done great service at once to the physical sciences and to metaphysics, by showing, in his 'Philosophy of the Inductive Sciences,'—1. That the former proceed upon and imply principles not got from experience; that geometry and arithmetic depend on first truths regarding space, time, and number; and mechanical science on intuitions regarding force, matter, etc. 2. He has exhibited these principles in instructive forms, announcing them in their deeper and wider character under the designation of fundamental ideas, and then presenting them under the name of conceptions in the more specific shapes in which they become available in the particular sciences: thus, in mechanical science the fundamental idea of cause becomes the conception of force. But then he has injured his great work:—1. By following the Kantian doctrine of forms, and supposing that the mental ideas "impose" and "superinduce" on the objects something not in the objects, whereas they merely enable us to arrive at what is in the objects. 2. He also fails to show that the ideas or maxims in the general form in which alone they are available in science, are got by induction. 3. The phraseology which he employs is unfortunate, it is 'fundamental ideas' and 'conceptions.' The word 'idea' has been used in so many different senses by different writers, by Plato, Descartes, Locke, Kant, and Hegel, that it is perhaps expedient to abandon it altogether in strict philosophic writing; it is certainly not expedient to use it, as Whewell does, in a new application. The word 'conception' stands in classical English both for the phantasm, or image, and the logical notion—certain later metaphysicians would restrict it to the logical notion; and there is no propriety in using it to signify an *a priori* law. 4. He has damaged the general acceptance of his principles, which seem to me to be as true as they are often profound, by making a number of truths *a priori* which are evidently got from experience: thus he makes the law of action and reaction, and the laws of motion generally, self-evident and necessary.

PART SECOND.

PARTICULAR EXAMINATION OF THE INTUITIONS.

BOOK I.

PRIMITIVE COGNITIONS.

CHAPTER I.

BODY AND SPIRIT.

SECT. I. THE MIND BEGINS ITS INTELLIGENT ACTS WITH KNOWLEDGE. THE SIMPLE COGNITIVE POWERS.

IT is a favourite position in the views expounded in this treatise, that the mind begins its acts of intelligence with knowledge. This is not the common representation. According to a very ancient doctrine, the mind has, prior to the acquisition of knowledge, a stock of ideas out of itself, or in itself, at which it looks, and its primary exercises consist in contemplating or in forming these ideas. This view, with no pretensions to precision in the statement of it, was a prevalent one in ancient Greece, in the scholastic ages, and in the earlier stages of modern philosophy. It seems to me to be the view which was habitually entertained by Descartes and Locke. In later times, the mind was supposed to commence with impressions of some kind. This view may be regarded as introduced formally into philosophy by Hume, who opens his 'Treatise on Human Nature' by declaring that all the perceptions of the mind are impressions and ideas; that impressions come first, and that ideas are the faint images of them. This view has evidently a materialistic tendency. Literally, an impression can be produced only on a material substance, and it is not easy to determine precisely what is meant by the phrase when it is used metaphorically. This impression theory is the one adopted by the French Sensational School, and by the physiologists of this country. In Germany the influence exercised by Kant's Kritik of Pure Reason has made the general account to be that the mind starts with presentations, and not with things, with phenomena in the sense of appearances, which 'phenomena' are but modifications of Hume's 'impressions,' and of the 'ideas' of the ancients. Now it appears to me that all these accounts, consciousness being witness, are imperfect, and by their defects erroneous. The mind is not conscious of these impressions preceding the knowledge which it has immediately of self, and the objects falling under the notice of the senses. Nor can it be legitimately shown how the mind can ever rise from ideas, impressions, phenomena, to the knowledge of things. The followers of Locke have always felt the difficulty of showing how the mind from mere ideas could reach external realities. Hume designedly represented the original exercises of the mind as being mere impressions, in order to undermine the very foundations of knowledge. Though Kant acknowledged a reality beneath the presentations, beyond the phenomena, those who followed out his views found the reality disappearing more and more, till at length it vanished altogether, leaving only a concatenated series of mental forms.

There is no effectual or consistent way of avoiding these consequences but by falling back on the natural system, and maintaining that the mind in its intelligent acts starts with knowledge. But let not the statement be misunderstood. I do not mean that the mind commences with abstract knowledge, or general knowledge, or indeed with systematized knowledge of any description. It acquires first a knowledge of individual things as they are presented to it and to its knowing faculties, and it is out of this that all its arranged knowledge is formed by a subsequent exercise of the understanding. From the concrete the mind fashions the abstract, by separating in thought a part from the whole, a quality from the object. Starting with the particular, the mind reaches the general by observing the points of agreement. From premisses involving knowledge, it can arrive at other propositions also containing knowledge. It seems clear to me, that if the mind had not knowledge in the foundation, it never could have knowledge in the superstructure reared; but finding knowledge in its first intelligent exercises, it can thence, by the processes of abstraction, generalization, and reasoning, reach further and higher knowledge.

The mind is endowed with at least two simple cognitive powers,—sense-perception and self-consciousness. Both are cognitive in their nature, and look on and reveal to us existing things; the one, material objects presented to us through the bodily senses, and the other, self in a particular state or exercise. It is altogether inadequate language to represent these faculties as giving us an idea, or an impression, or an apprehension, or a notion, or a conception, or looking on unknown appearances, they give us knowledge of objects under aspects presented to us. No other language is equal to express the full mental action of which we are conscious.

In this Book it is my aim to seek out, to analyze, and expose to the view the convictions that are involved in the exercise of these two powers. I shall begin with our cognitions in their more concrete form, and then dwell more specially on the cognitions discovered by abstraction to be involved in these.

SECT. II. OUR INTUITIVE COGNITIONS OF BODY.

We are following the plainest dictates of consciousness, we avoid a thousand difficulties, and we get a solid ground on which to rest and to build, when we maintain that the mind in its first exercises acquires knowledge; not indeed scientific or arranged, not of qualities of objects and classes of objects, but still knowledge—the knowledge of things presenting themselves, and as they present themselves; which knowledge, individual and concrete, is the foundation of all other knowledge, abstract, general, and deductive. In particular, the mind is so constituted as to attain a knowledge of body, or of material objects.

It is through the bodily organism that the intelligence of man attains its knowledge of all material objects beyond. This is true of the infant mind; it is true also of the mature mind. We may assert something more than this regarding the organism. It is not only the medium through which we know all bodily objects beyond itself, it is itself an object primarily known; nay, I am inclined to think that, along with the objects immediately affecting it, it is the only object originally known. Intuitively man seems to know nothing beyond his own organism, and objects immediately affecting it; in all further knowledge there is a process of inference proceeding on a gathered experience. This theory seems to me to explain all the facts, and it delivers us from many perplexities.

Let us go over the senses one by one, with a view of determining what seems to be the original information supplied by each. In the sense of smell, the objects immediately perceived are the nostrils as affected; it is only by experience that we know that there is an object beyond, from which the smell proceeds, and it is only by science that we know that odorous particles have proceeded from that object. In hearing, our primary perceptions seem to be of the ear as affected; that there is a sounding body we learn by further observation, and that there are vibrations between it and the ear we are told by scientific research. In taste, it is originally the palate as affected by what we feel by another sense to be a tangible body, which body science tells us must be in a liquid state. In touch proper, there is a sensation of a particular part of the frame as affected by we know not what, but which we may discover by experiential observation. It is the same with all the impressions we have by the sense of temperature, the sense of titillation, the sense of shuddering, the sense of the creeping of the flesh, the sense of lightness or of weight, and the like organic affections, usually but improperly attributed to touch. In regard to all these senses, it seems highly probable that our original and primitive perceptions are simply of the organism as affected by something unknown, so far as intuition is concerned. But there are other two senses which furnish, I am inclined to think, a new and further kind of information. The sense of touch, when the phrase is used in a loose sense, is a complex one, embracing a considerable number and variety of senses, which have not been scientifically classified, and which, perhaps, cannot be so till we have a more thorough physiology of the nerves. Certain it is that there is a locomotive energy and a muscular sense entirely different from feeling, or such affections as those of heat and cold. The soul of man instinctively wills to move the arm; an action is produced in a motor nerve, which sets in motion a muscle, with probably an attached set of bones, and the intimation of such a movement having taken place is conveyed to the brain by a sensor nerve. As the result of this complex physiological process, we come to know that there is something beyond our organism; we know an object out of our organism hindering the movement of the organ and resisting our energy.* It is more difficult to determine what is the original perception by sight. It must certainly be of a coloured surface affecting the felt organism. The boy born blind, when his sight was restored by an operation by Cheselden, felt as if every object "touched his eyes, as what he felt did his skin." I think it probable that the coloured surface perceived as affecting the living organism, is seen as in the direction of the felt and localized sentient organ, neither behind it, nor at the side, but at what distance we know not till other senses and a gathered experience come to our aid. Such seems to be our original knowledge, received through the various senses as inlets.

But we are not to understand that the mind receives sensations and information only from one sense at a time. In order to have a full view of the actual state of things, we must remember that man, at every instant of his waking existence, is getting organic feelings and perceptions from a number of these sources ; say at one and the same time from the sense of heat, from the sense of taste in

* The following is the account given by Müller (trans. by Baly, p. 1080):—"First, the child governs the movements of its limbs, and thus perceives that they are instruments subject to the use and government of its internal 'self,' while the resistance which it meets with around is not subject to its will, and therefore gives it the idea of an absolute exterior. Secondly, the child will perceive a difference in the sensations produced according as two parts of its own body touch each other, or as one part of its body only meets with resistance from without. In the first instance, where one arm, for example, touches the other, the resistance is offered by a part of the child's own body, and the limb thus giving the resistance becomes the subject of sensation as well as the other. The two limbs are in this case external objects of perception, and percipient at the same time. In the second instance, the resisting body will be represented to the mind as something external and foreign to the living body, and not subject to the internal self. Thus will arise in the mind of the child the idea of a resistance which one part of its own body can offer to other parts of its body, and at the same time the idea of a resistance offered to its body by an absolute exterior. In this way is gained the idea of an external world as the cause of sensations."

the mouth, from the sense of hearing, the sense of sight—suppose of a portion of our own body and of the walls of the apartment in which we sit, and from the muscular sense—say of the chair on which we sit, or the floor on which we stand. Our whole conscious state at any given time is thus a very complex, or rather, a concrete one. There is in it at all times a sense of the living body as extended, and, I may add, as ours. This is a sense which human beings, infant and mature, carry with them every instant of their waking existence, perhaps in a low state even in their times of sleep. "This consciousness of our own corporeal existence is the standard by which we estimate in our sense of touch the extension of all resisting bodies."* Along with this there will always be in our waking moments a sense of something extra-organic but affecting the organism, such as the surface before the eye, or the object which supports us. But the vividness of the impression made, or some decisive act of the will in order to accomplish a desired end, will at times centre the mind's regards in a special manner on some one of the objects made known by the senses. Thus, a violent pain in an organ will absorb the whole attention on itself; or a vivid colour will draw out the mind towards the coloured object. By these concentrations of intelligence we obtain a more special acquaintance with the nature of the objects presenting themselves. It is thus only that the special senses fulfil their full function, and impart information abiding with us beyond the moment when the action takes place.

Such seems to be our original stock of knowledge acquired by sense. It is as yet within very narrow limits, within our frames, and a sphere immediately in contact.†

* Müller's Physiology, translated by Baly, p. 1081.

† "We perceive and can perceive nothing but what is relative to the organ." (Hamilton, foot-note to Reid, p. 247).

We reach a wider knowledge by remembering what we have thus obtained, by subjecting it to processes of abstraction and generalization, and drawing inferences from it. Our information is especially enlarged and consolidated, by combining the information got from several of the senses, which are all intended to assist each other. In particular, the two intellectual senses *par excellence*, sight and the muscular sense, are fitted to aid each other and all the other senses. By sight we know merely a coloured surface; by the muscular sense we may come to know that the object with a superficies has three dimensions and is impenetrable,—we may know the object to be the same by our seeing upon it the hand which feels the pressure. By sight we know not how far the coloured surface is from our organism; by inferences founded on gathered information from the muscular sense, we come to know how far it is from us, whether an inch or many feet or yards. By the muscular sense we know solid objects only as pressing themselves immediately on our organism; by sight we see objects—which sight does not declare to be solid but which a combined experience declares must be solid—thousands or millions of miles away. By inferences from various senses united, we know that this taste is from a certain kind of food, that this smell is from a rose or lily, that this sound is from a human voice or a musical instrument. Thus our knowledge, commencing with the organism and objects affecting it, may extend to objects at a great distance, and clothe them with qualities which are not perceived as immediately belonging to them. We know that this blue surface seen indistinctly is a bay of the ocean fifty miles off, and that this brilliant spark up in the blue concave, is a solid body, radiating light hundreds of millions of miles away.

Let us analyse what is involved in this intuitive knowledge.

I. We know the object as existing or having being. This is a necessary conviction, attached to, or rather, composing an essential part of our concrete cognition of every material object presented to us, be it our own frame, or of things external to our frame; whether this hard table or stone, or this yielding water, or even this vapoury mist, or this fleeting cloud. We look on each of the objects thus presented to us, in our organism or beyond it, as having an existence, a being, a reality. Every one understands these phrases; they cannot be made simpler or more intelligible by an explanation. We understand them because they express a mental fact which every one has experienced. We may talk of what we contemplate in sense-perception being nothing but an impression, an appearance, an idea, but we can never be made to give our assent to any such statements. However ingenious the arguments which may be adduced in favour of the objects of our sense-perceptions being mere illusions, we find that after listening to them, and allowing to them all the weight that is possible, we still look upon bodies as realities next time they present themselves. The reason, is we know them to be realities, by a native cognition which can never be overcome.

II. In our primitive cognitions, we know objects as having an existence independent of the contemplative mind. We know the object as separate from ourselves. We do not create it when we perceive it, nor does it cease to exist because we have ceased to contemplate it. All this is involved in our very cognition of the object, and he who would deny this is setting aside our very primitive knowledge, and he who would argue against this, will never be able to convince us in fact, because he is opposing a fundamental conviction which will work whenever the object is presented.*

* The convictions referred to in these paragraphs, set aside at once

III. We know the object as having an abiding existence. This is a truth which requires to be stated with not a few explanations and cautions. I can merely give a hint of what is meant, and reserve the fuller discussion of it till I come to speak of substance, in the next chapter. I have already affirmed that every material object has an existence abiding, in this sense, that our contemplation did not create it, nor will it cease to exist because our attention is not directed towards it. But this is not all: we apprehend that this thing has an abiding being in itself. Our intuition indeed does not say, as to this being, how or when it came to be there, nor whether nor in what circumstances it may cease; for information on such topics we must go to other quarters. But when the question is started, we must decide that this thing had a being prior to our perceiving it, unless indeed it so happened that it was produced by a power capable of doing so at the very time our senses alighted on it, and that it will continue to exist after we have ceased to regard it, unless indeed something interpose to destroy it. But enough for the present of this somewhat difficult discussion.

IV. In our primitive cognition of body there is involved a knowledge of outness or externality.* We

the doctrine of Kaut, that the mind in the intuition of sense, takes cognizance of phenomena in the sense of appearances. They should also modify the doctrine of Hamilton. "Our knowledge of qualities or phenomena is necessarily relative, for these exist only as they exist in relation to our faculties." (Foot-note to Reid, p. 323.) It is a truism that we can know objects merely as our faculties enable us to know them; but the question is, What is the nature and extent of the knowledge which our faculties furnish? I admit that whatever external objects we know, we know in a relation to us. But I hold that man and his faculties are so constituted as to know things (with being) exercising qualities, and to know qualities as existing separate from and independent of our cognition of them.

* "Perception involves in every instance the notion of externality, or outness" (D. Stewart, Essays, p. 419).

know the object perceived, be it the organism or the object affecting the organism, as not in the mind, as out of the mind. In regard to some of the objects perceived by us we may be in doubt as to whether they are in the organism or beyond it, but we are always sure that they are extra-mental. This is a conviction from which we can never be driven by any power of will or force of circumstances. It is at the foundation of the judgments to be afterwards specified as to the distinctions between the self and the not-self, the *ego* and the *non-ego*.*

V. In all our knowledge through the senses we know the object as extended. I am inclined to think that this knowledge in the concrete is involved even in such perceptions as those of smell, taste, hearing, and feeling, and the allied affections of temperature and titillation. In all these we intuitively know the organism as out of the mind, as extended, and as localized. At every waking moment we have sensations from more than one sense, and we must know the organs affected as out of each other and in different places.† It is acknowledged that the primitive

* The convictions spoken of in these paragraphs set aside all forms of idealism in sense-perception. Berkeley says that, so far as matter is concerned, "*esse est percipi.*" I hold, that according to our intuitive conviction, the thing which we perceive must exist before we can perceive it, and that we perceive it as an extended thing independent and out of the contemplative mind. Fichte represents the external thing as a creation or projection of the perceiving mind. But the mind in knowing the self as perceiving, knows that it is an external thing that is perceived, and cannot be made to think otherwise. Professor Ferrier bases his fabric of demonstrated idealism on the proposition, the object of knowledge "always is, and must be, the object with the addition of oneself,—object *plus* subject,—thing, or thought, *mecum*" (Inst. of Metaph. prop. ii.). If this proposition professes to be a statement of fact, I deny that the fact of consciousness is properly stated. If it professes to be a first truth, I deny that it ought to be assumed in this particular form. No doubt we always know self at the same time that we know an external object by sense-perception, but we know the external object as separate from and independent of self. We might as well deny that we know the object at all, as deny that we know it to have an existence distinct from self.

† Hamilton says, "An extension is apprehended in the apprehension

knowledge got in this way is very bare and limited, and without those perceived relationships and distinctions which become associated with it in our future life. But imperfect though it be, it must ever involve the occupation of space. The other two senses furnish more express information, the eye giving a coloured surface of a defined form, and the muscular sense extension in three dimensions. It should be noticed that in our knowledge of extra-organic objects, whether by the eye or the muscular sense, we know them as situated in a certain place in reference to our organism, which we have already so far localized and distributed in space, and which henceforth we use as a centre for direction and distance.

VI. We know the objects as affecting us. I have already said that we know them as independent of us. This is an important truth. But it is equally true and equally important that these objects are made known to us as somehow having an influence on us. The organic object is capable of affecting our minds, and the extra-organic object affects the organism which affects the mind. Upon this cognition are founded certain judgments as to the relations of the object known to the knowing mind. In particular,

VII. In certain, if not in all, of our original cognitions through the senses we know the objects as exercising potency or property. This is denied in theory by many who are yet found to admit it inadvertently when they tell us that we can know matter only by its properties: for what, I ask, are properties but powers to act in a certain way? But still it is dogmatically asserted, that whatever we may know about material objects, we can

of the reciprocal externality of all sensations" (Appendix to Reid, p. 885). Again, "In the consciousness of sensations relatively localized and reciprocally external, we have a veritable apprehension and consequently an immediate perception of the affected organism, as extended, divided, figured, etc." (*ib.* p. 884).

never know that they have power; we cannot see power, they say, nor hear power, nor touch power. In opposition to these confident assertions, I lay down the very opposite dogma, that we cannot see body, or touch, or even hear, or taste, or smell body, except as affecting us, that is, having a power in reference to us. When an extra-organic body resists our muscular energy,* what is it doing but affecting our organism in a certain way? The very coloured surface revealed through sight, is known to us as affecting, that is, having an influence over, our organism. But there is more than this,—the organism is known as having power to affect the cognitive self. The muscular effort resisted, the visual organs impressed by the coloured surface, are known as producing an effect on the mind. The organs affected in smell, in taste, in temperature, in hearing, in feeling, are all known as rousing the mind into cognitive activity. It might be further maintained, even in regard to those senses which do not immediately reveal anything extra-organic, that they seem to point to some unknown cause of the affection known; but it is better to postpone the discussion of this question till it can be discussed fully. But in regard to the two senses which reveal objects beyond the bodily frame, and in regard to all the senses so far as they make known our frame to us, there is an intuitive conviction of potency wrapped up in all our cognitions.

But it will be vehemently urged that it is most pre-

* Locke says that impenetrability, or, as he prefers calling it, as having less of a negative meaning, solidity, seems the "idea most intimately connected with and essential to body, so as nowhere else to be found or imagined, but only in matter;" and he adds, we "find it inseparably inherent in body wherever or however modified;" and in explaining this, he says of bodies, that "they do by an unsurmountable force hinder the approach of the parts of our hands that press them" (Essay, ii. iv. 1).

posterous to assert that we know all this *by the senses.* Upon this I remark that the phrase *by the senses* is ambiguous. If by senses be meant the mere bodily organism,—the eye, the ears, the nerves, and the brain,—I affirm that we know, and can know, nothing by this mere bodily part; that so far from knowing potency or extension, we do not know even colour, or taste, or smell. But if by the senses be meant the mind exercised in sense-perception, summoned into activity by the organism, and contemplating cognitively the external world, then I maintain that we do know, and this intuitively, external objects as influencing us—that is, exercising powers in reference to us. I ask those who would doubt of this doctrine, of what it is that they suppose the mind to be cognizant in sense-perception. If they say, a mere sensation or impression in the mind, I reply that this is not consistent with the revelation of consciousness, which announces plainly that what we know is something extra-mental. If they say, with Kant, a mere phenomenon in the sense of appearance, then I reply that this too is inconsistent with consciousness, which declares that we know the thing. But if we know the thing, we must know something about it. If they say they know it as having extension and form, I grasp at the admission, and ask them to consider how high the knowledge thus allowed, involving at one and the same time space, and an object occupying space, and so much of space. Surely those who acknowledge this much may be prepared to confess further that the mind which in perception is capable of knowing an object as occupying space, is also capable of knowing the same object as exercising power in regard to us.* We have only to

* "C'est la raison, et la raison seule, qui connaît, et connaît le monde; et elle ne le connaît d'abord qu'à titre de cause; il n'est d'abord pour nous que la cause des phénomènes sensitifs que nous ne pouvons nous rapporter à nous-mêmes; et nous ne rechercherions pas cette

examine the state of mind involved in all our cognitions of matter, to discover that there is involved in it a knowledge both of extension and of property.

Such seem to be some of the principal of our cognitions through the senses; and I have sought to evolve them by an analysis proceeding on a careful observation of their nature.

Sect. III. Some Distinctions to be Attended to in Regard to our Cognition of Body.

It is a fundamental position with the author of this treatise that we ought to look on all our primitive cognitions as guaranteeing a reality. In particular we are to look on each of our sense-perceptions as pointing to a corresponding extra-mental object. But in order to be able to maintain this doctrine with even the appearance of plausibility, it is necessary to attend to certain distinctions.

cause, par conséquent nous ne la trouverions pas, si notre raison n'était pourvue du principe de causalité, si nous pouvions supposer qu'un phénomène peut commencer à apparaître sur le théâtre de la conscience, du temps ou de l'espace, sans qu'il ait une cause. Donc le principe de causalité, je ne crains pas de le dire, est le père du monde extérieur, loin qu'il soit possible de l'en tirer, et de le faire venir de la sensation." So says M. Cousin in criticizing Locke (Deux. Ser. tom. iii. leç. 19). This is not far from the truth. There is reason or intelligence involved in our knowledge of the external world, and there is causality in this knowledge. The mind knows the external thing as a cause—it must know it in other characters as well, in particular it must know it as extended—still, it knows it as a cause. But except in the mode of development, this doctrine does not differ so much from that of Locke as Cousin imagines. Locke derives the materials of all our ideas from sensation and experience. He derives our idea of cause from both these sources. But then the mind, in the formation of its ideas, proceeds intelligently, reasonably. There is intelligence, according to Locke, in sensation, and in comparing certain ideas the mind perceives their agreement immediately by intuition. Locke's account of the full phenomenon does not seem to me satisfactory, or very congruously wrought out; but it is quite as near the truth as that of Cousin, who calls sensation the chronological condition, and reason the logical principle (See this distinction examined, *infra*, Part III. Bk. I. Ch. II. sect. v.).

I. There is the DISTINCTION BETWEEN OUR ORIGINAL AND ACQUIRED PERCEPTIONS. In standing up for the trustworthiness of our perceptions, I always mean our original perceptions, proceeding from the primitive principles of the mind, and having the sanction of Him who gave us our constitution. The perceptions acquired by inference, or other intellectual processes grounded on experience, will have a corresponding reality only when these processes have been validly conducted.

I have endeavoured in last Section to give an approximately correct account of what seem to be our original perceptions through the various senses. But to our primitive stock we add others, and in doing so we employ rules derived from the generalizations of experience, and deductive reasoning in applying them to given cases. It has been all but universally acknowledged, since the days of Berkeley, that the perception of distance is not an original endowment of the sense of sight in human beings, but that we come to determine it by a gathered observation. As the result of experience, we lay down such rules as these: that an object with whose form we are familiar,—such as a watch,—if seen with a faint colour and outline, and with a smaller disc in comparison with other known objects in the field of view, must be more distant than when seen with a better defined figure and a more vivid colour and a fuller form. We lay it down as another rule, that when a number of objects intervene between us and a scene on which we are looking,—say a mountain,—it must be at a considerable distance. Such rules formed by us are found approximately correct, and useful in ordinary cases, and at every instant at which our eyes are open they conduct us to a knowledge which carries us far beyond our primitive perceptions. But then it is to be noticed that error may creep into our acquired perceptions. We may reckon a rule as universal which has many exceptions, and may make an application of it to a wrong case. It will not be difficult to show that all the supposed deception of the senses is to be traced to the wrong inferences which we draw in our acquired perceptions.

Almost all forms of idealism—the system which supposes certain of our supposed cognitions to be creations of the mind, and all forms of scepticism—the system which would set aside all our cognitions, plead the deceitfulness of the senses. Our senses are not to be trusted in some things, says the idealist, and we are to determine by reason when they are to be trusted. Our senses delude us in some things, says the sceptic, and we may therefore distrust them in all. It is of vast moment to stop these errors at the point at which they flow out, by showing that the senses, meaning our original perceptions through the senses, can all be trusted in regard to the special testimony which they furnish.

But how, it is asked, does the stick in the water, felt to be straight by the sense of touch, seem crooked to the sense of sight? The answer is, that the knowledge of the shape of an object does not primarily fall under the sense of sight, and that when we determine whether a stick is or is not straight, by the sense of sight, it is by a process of inference in which we have laid down the rule that objects that give a certain figure before the eye are crooked, a rule correct enough for common cases, but not applicable to cases in which the rays of light are refracted in passing from one medium to another. Why does a boy seem a man, and a man a giant in a mist, whereas if you clear away the mist, both are instantly reduced to their proper dimensions? An answer can easily be given. We have laid down the rule that an object seen so dimly must be distant; but an object appearing of such dimensions at a distance must be large: and the

phenomenon is felt to be a deception only by those who are not accustomed to move in the mist. Why does a mountain, viewed across an arm of the sea, seem near, while the same mountain, seen at an equal distance beyond an undulated country studded with houses and trees, will seem very remote? The answer is not that the eye has deceived us, but that we have made a mistaken application of a rule usually correct, that an object must be near when few objects intervene between us and it; and it is to be noticed that those who are accustomed to look across sheets of water, commit no such mistakes, for they have acquired other means of measuring distance. Again, we have found it true in cases so many, that we cannot number them, that when we are at rest and the image of an object, say a carriage, passes across the vision, the object must be in motion. That rule is accurate in all cases similar to those from which it was derived; but it fails the landsman when, feeling as if he were at rest in the ship, he infers that the shore is moving away from the vessel. In all such cases we see that it is not the senses, that is, the natural and original perceptions of the senses having the authority of God, which deceive us, but rules formed by ourselves, and illegitimately applied. It may be observed that the same experience which enables us to gather the rules, may enable us to ascertain the limits of the rules, and the exceptions. It is only the landsman who is deceived into the thought that the shore is moving; the seaman has modified the rule, or rather, he realizes the idea that he himself is moving, and he is not deceived for one instant.

Supposing this to be the correct account, we may stand up for the trustworthiness of all our intuitive perceptions, at least when the organism and the mind are in a healthy state. Even in cases in which the organism is diseased, the error lies commonly, perhaps always, in a wrong inference.* When our visual organs are distempered, we may seem to see a solid figure before us which touch tells us has no reality ; but the fact is, all that we intuitively see is a coloured surface, whether in or out of the organism, whether solid or aerial, we know not intuitively. We hear a sound which we interpret as coming from a voice where no living being can be, but the interpretation is our own : all that our nature declares is, that there is an affection of our auditory organs. The visions, the imaginary sounds, touches, and smells, felt by persons whose organs are diseased, or excited by strong mental fancy within—just as they would be by an object without, are, after all, inferences from what are in themselves mere organic affections. In the greater number of such cases, there is a means of detecting the error occasioned by disease in one of the organs, by other organs not distempered. At the same time I am not inclined to deny that there may be cases in which the brain is so disorganized, and the mind so deranged, that the person is given up for life to hopeless delusion. We are now within the

* Aristotle had an apprehension of what I am convinced will turn out to be the true account of these seeming errors of the senses. (See his Treatise on the Soul, b. iii., c. i., iii., vi.) He says the perception, by a sense, of things peculiar to that sense, is true, or involves the smallest amount of error. But when such objects are perceived in their accidents (that is, as to things not falling peculiarly under that sense), there is room for falsehood ; when, for instance, something is said to be white there is no falsehood, but when the object is said to be this or that (if the white thing is said to be Cleon), (cf. iii., i. 7), there may be falsehood. 'Η *αἴσθησις τῶν μὲν ἰδίων ἀληθῆς ἐστὶν ἢ ὅτι ὀλιχίστον ἔχουσα τὸ ψεῦδος. δεύτερον δὲ τοῦ συμβεβηκέναι ταῦτα· καὶ ἐνταῦθα ἤδη ἐνδέχεται διαψεύδεσθαι· ὅτι μὲν γὰρ λευκὸν, οὐ ψεύδεται, εἴ δε τοῦτο τὸ λευκὸν ἢ ἄλλο τι ψεύδεται* (iii., iii., 12 : ed. Trendelenburg). 'Αλλ' *ὥσπερ τὸ ὁρᾶν τοῦ ἰδίου ἀληθές, εἰ δ' ἄνθρωπος τὸ λευκὸν ἢ μὴ, οὐκ ἀληθὲς αἰεί* (*ib.* vi. 7). Aristotle saw that the difficulties might be cleared up, by attending to what each sense testifies, and separating the associated imaginations and opinions or judgments. The full explanation, however, could not be given till Berkeley led men to distinguish between the original and acquired perceptions of the senses, by showing that the knowledge of distance by the eye, is an acquisition.

range of phenomena which carry us into the deepest mysteries of our world, and have a connection with man's liability to disease, and the existence of sin.

II. There is the DISTINCTION BETWEEN SENSATION AND PERCEPTION. It may be laid down as a general fact, that every given state of man's mind is concrete; that is, in the one act there are elements which may be separated at other times, or which may be separated by analysis. Thus in purely mental action, there may at one and the same moment be an exercise of the intelligence, of feeling, and of will; in one act we may comprehend that our friend is in distress, may feel grieved in consequence, and resolve to take steps to relieve him. In like manner all the mental affections excited by the action of the bodily senses are concrete. What is thus mixed up in one concrete act, can be separated by analysis, and ought for important ends to be so separated: indeed the separation is often made for us naturally, for we have now one portion, and now another of the combined state. In particular, it is of great moment in philosophy to distinguish between the sensations and perceptions which are always mixed up together.

Perception is the knowledge of the object presenting itself to the senses, whether in the organism or beyond it. Sensation is the feeling associated,—the feeling of the organism. These two always coexist.* There is never the knowledge without an organic feeling, never a feeling of the organism without a cognitive apprehension of it. These sensations differ widely from each other, as our consciousness testifies; some of them being pleasant, some painful; others indifferent as to pleasure

* Reid represents the sensation being "followed by a perception of the object;" on which Hamilton remarks, "that sensation proper precedes perception proper is a false assumption; they are simultaneous elements of the same indivisible energy" (Reid's Works, p. 186: see also p. 853).

and pain, but still with a feeling. Some we call exciting, others dull; some we designate as warm, others as cold; and for most of them we have no name whatever,—indeed they so run into each other that it would be difficult to discriminate them by a specific nomenclature. The perceptions, again, are as numerous and varied as the knowledge we have by all the senses. Now these two ever mix themselves up with each other. The sensation of the odour mingles with the apprehension of the nostrils; the flavour of the food is joined with the recognition of the palate; the agreeableness or disagreeableness of the sound comes in with the knowledge of the ear as affected; and the organ which we know as feeling has an associated sensation. There is an organic sensation conjoined even with the knowledge we have of the extra-organic object affecting our muscular sense or our visual organism. This sensation may be little noticed because the attention is fixed on the object; still it is always there, as we may discover by a careful introspection of the combined mental affection.

But this leads me to notice that in the concrete mental state sometimes the perception or the knowledge is the more prominent, whereas at other times the sensation is the predominant. There is a difference indeed of the senses in this respect. Thus in the senses of taste, smell, touch proper, and the allied senses of temperature, titillation, shuddering, and flesh-creeping, the sensation is the prevailing element. These may be regarded as the lower and the more animal senses, in which the attention is largely absorbed in self. In hearing, so far as the original perceptions are concerned, the sensation is still the predominant affection; but as we come to know the sounding bodies, our attention is often directed almost exclusively to the object. Thus as we are listening to a person speaking we lose sight of the hearing ear, and think only of what is said. Still, when the sounds are unpleasant, or when they are peculiarly pleasant, as in music, it is the sensation that absorbs the attention. In the muscular sense it is the resisting object that is most noticed. In sight the colour is largely (but not exclusively, as will be shown forthwith) a sensational, whereas the spread-out surface is the perceptive element. In many of our acts of vision there is a nice balancing of the two, the colour and the form being alike noticed; in others the colour, by its gorgeousness, absorbs the whole mental energy; while in a third class the colour-sensation is lost sight of, and we are conscious of scarcely anything more than the form. And here I am tempted to remark that in the lower forms, both of nature and of the fine arts, it is the colour which is the more striking characteristic; and children, and persons low in the scale of intelligence, feel a peculiar delight in such objects. As we rise, in nature to the common herbaceous plants, and in art to flower-painting, there is often a union of the beauty, both of colour and of form. When we mount to the highest plants, as to the trees of the forest, and to the animal creation and the human form, and in art to historical painting, varied colouring disappears, that higher minds may gaze with undivided attention on objective forms characterized by high proportions, or full of life or suggestive of character.

It should not be omitted that the mind can at any time fix its attention more specially on one of these, and then the other will very much disappear from the field of view. Sometimes this is done for us spontaneously, by the vividness of the sensation on the one hand, or by the interest which collects around the external object on the other. Sometimes the concentration is effected by a strong act of will, fixing the mind's regards on one or other in order to gain a special end. Thus we may yield ourselves entirely to a luscious strain of music, or we may be absorbed in thought about some object, so as scarcely to notice the sounds. Under ear-ache we may have the whole energy of the mind concentred on the pain, and be able to attend to nothing else; or we may be so interested in a discourse or a topic of thought as scarcely to feel the torture.

But while the two ever coexist,—sometimes with the one prevailing and sometimes with the other predominant, and sometimes with the two nicely balanced, it is of importance to distinguish them. Every man of sense draws the distinction between the music and the musical instrument, between the ear-ache and his ear. The metaphysician should also draw the distinction,—indeed it is essential that he do so. The two were given for different ends. Our perceptions are the main means of supplying us with knowledge, whereas our sensations are meant to increase our enjoyment, to stimulate to exertion, to give warning, or perhaps to inflict penalties. We must beware, both philosophically and practically, of confounding our sensations and our perceptions, our feelings and our cognitions. In the confounding of the two we have another circumstance leading men to charge their senses with deception. This will appear more fully when we come to notice another set of distinctions.

III. There are Distinctions between the Objects Known. There is the distinction between the organic object and the object beyond the organism. There is the more delicate distinction between the objects immediately known as extra-organic and objects inferred as affecting the organism but themselves unknown. Let me explain these distinctions.

We have seen that in some of the senses the proper object of perception is the organism itself. In two others it is beyond the organism. Let us consider these two classes in order.

In the first class all that we know immediately is the organism as affected. But if affected, it must be affected by something. It is in one state this instant, and it will be in another state the next. The intuitive conviction of causation—to be afterwards discussed—constrains us to look for an agent to produce the effect. And where is this agent to be found? In the organism, or beyond the organism? I am certain, in regard to some of our organic affections, that intuition says nothing on this special point. This is the case with our sense of smell, our taste and touch, and sense of temperature,—and I think also, though with some hesitation, of the sense of hearing. The intuitive conviction of cause and effect does indeed intimate that there must be a cause, but as to where that cause is to be found we must trust to experience, which tells us that the cause is in some cases to be found in the organism itself, and in other cases in an agent beyond,—such as odorous particles, sapid bodies, heat, undulations from a sounding body, or a solid object applied to our nerves of touch. In all cases the affection of sense and the conviction of cause combined are sufficient to prompt us to look round for an agent. The senses act as monitors, and most important monitors they are, of powers working in our bodily frames, and in the physical universe around us. I believe that every one of our senses gives us intimation of powers,—such as floating particles, light, and heat, which are among the most powerful agencics conducting the processes of the material world. Still these are unknown to our senses, and we become aware of their existence merely as causes of known effects. As to what odours, sounds, flavours, heat, and, we may add, light and colours are, our intuitions are silent, and their nature is to be determined by observation,—indeed can be determined only by elaborate scientific research. It should be added, that while science has ascertained much about them, it has not, in its latest advances, been able to settle what is the exact nature of such agents as heat, light, and colour.

Let us turn now to the other class of senses, which give us a knowledge of extra-organic objects. By the muscular sense we know an object as extended in three dimensions, and as resisting our effort. We have thus a knowledge of objects extended, and exercising dynamic energy beyond the little world of self.

The sense of sight presents peculiar difficulties in this connection. It seems to me clearly to look at an extended surface, not part of our organism, but affecting it. But what are we to make of colour? It is the greatest difficulty which the metaphysician meets with in the investigation of the senses. The mind knows the perceived object to be in its nature extended; but do we also know it as in its very nature coloured? If so, is there colour in the object as there is extension? The following is the solution which I am inclined to offer of this difficult subject. The sense of colour may be regarded as intermediate between those senses in which we perceive an extra-organic object, and those other senses which reveal merely the organism as affected, but whether by agents within or beyond the organism we know not. In the sense of colour, we primarily know only the organism as affected, but we are intuitively led, at the same time, to look on what thus affects our organism as not in the organism, but as in the extended surface in which it is seen. But beyond this, that is beyond colour being an extra-organic cause of an organic affection, we know nothing of its nature by intuition. If this account be correct, we see that our sense of colour is different, on the one hand, from our knowledge of our sensations of heat, or smell, or taste, for we do not know whether these are within or beyond the frame, while we do know that colour is out of ourselves in a surface; and different, too, on the other hand, from the knowledge of the extended surface and the impenetrability which are revealed directly by the sight and muscular sense, whereas we do not know what colour is. Hence arises, if I do not mistake, that peculiar conviction regarding colour which has so puzzled metaphysicians. The sense of colour combines, in closest union, the sensation and the perception, the organic affection and the extra-organic. I confess I have always fondly clung to the idea that, sooner or later, colour will be found by physical investigation to have a reality, I do not say of what kind, in every material object.*

By help of such distinctions as these, we may defend the validity of all our native convictions through the senses. In doing so, it will be observed that we stand up for the trustworthiness of our original, but not necessarily of our acquired perceptions; that we stand up for a reality corresponding to our perceptions proper, but not therefore to our associated sensations; and that we stand up for a reality, be it organic, or extra-organic, or both, corresponding to each particular sense as for itself, but not a reality for any one sense of precisely the same kind as the reality for the others. The senses can be supposed to deceive us, when the organism and mind are in a sound state, only when we overlook one or other or all of these distinctions.

* I have, in 'Typical Forms and Special Ends,' by J. M'Cosh and Geo. Dickie (p. 165, 2nd ed.), pointed to a number of phenomena, which seem to show that colour is a reality in the object, which reality is made known to us by means of the reflection of the beam by the colour. When the undivided beam falls on the green leaves of a plant, the green beam is reflected and reaches our eye, and the red is absorbed, not to be lost, but to come out in russet bark, or red flower, or berry.

SECT. IV. THE QUALITIES OF MATTER KNOWN BY INTUITION.

The distinctions unfolded in last Section seem to be the all-important ones, in order to enable us to defend the trustworthiness of our sense-perceptions. I have not, in that Section, made mention of the famous distinction between the Primary and Secondary Qualities of Matter, because, so far as it is fitted to clear up and establish the validity of the senses, it is embraced in those which we have drawn, and which are fitted, in my opinion, to bring out the whole truth in a fuller and more distinct manner. But it will be necessary, for other philosophic ends, to draw a distinction between the qualities of matter which are primitively known, and others which may become known by induction or scientific research. The qualities of matter known to intuition may be divided into three classes:—those which relate to space; those which one body exercises in reference to another; those which body exercises in reference to the sensitive and perceiving mind. Let it be observed, in regard to all of these, that the quality in the body always relates to something else, so passive and dependent is body on something out of itself.

I. There are the Qualities of Matter by which it occupies Space and is contained in Space, that is, Extension. We have this knowledge, I believe, through each of our senses; for in each of our senses we know the corresponding organs as extended and out of each other, and through two of the senses we know objects beyond our bodily frame as extended. Hamilton represents extension as a necessary constituent of our notion of Matter, and evolves it from "two catholic conditions of matter; (I.) the occupying space, and (II.) the being contained in space. Of these, the former affords (A) Trinal Extension, explicated again into (I.) Divisibility, (II.) Size, containing under it Density or Rarity, (III.) Figure, and (B) Ultimate Incompressibility; while the latter gives (A) Mobility, and (B) Situation. Neglecting subordination, we have thus eight proximate attributes; 1, Extension; 2, Divisibility; 3, Size; 4, Density or Rarity; 5, Figure; 6, Incompressibility absolute; 7, Mobility; 8, Situation."*

II. The Qualities which one body exercises in reference to another; in other words, the Properties or Forces of matter. I have expended much labour in vain if I have not shown, in previous Sections, that here we have a necessary conviction. In the visual and locomotive senses, we know an extra-organic object as affecting us and our organism. All this seems to be involved in our perception, and to be a native conviction of the mind, to which it is ever prompted, and from which it can never be delivered. Not only so, we are ever led to look for a producing cause, even of our purely organic affections in the ear and palate and nostrils. A knowledge of power, and a conviction of power being in exercise, is thus involved in our very perceptions through the senses.

Adhering to these views, we must set aside at once two opposite doctrines which have had the support each of a number of eminent metaphysicians or metaphysical speculators. The one is that matter is known as possessing no other quality than extension. This error originated with Descartes,† and has prevailed extensively among those metaphysicians who have felt his influence. But the view is opposed to that intuition which represents all matter as having and exercising energy. On the other side, there are speculators who maintain that all the phenomena of matter can be explained by suppo-

* Hamilton's Reid, Note D, p. 848.

† "L'espace ou le lieu intérieur et le corps qui est compris en cet espace, ne sont différents aussi que par notre pensée. Car, en effet la même étendue en longueur, largeur et profondeur qui constitue l'espace constitue le corps" (Des. Med. p. ii. 10).

sing it to possess potency. This mistake sprang from Leibnitz, who supposed that the universe of matter (and of mind) was composed of monads having power, and to which the mind imparted the relation of space.* But the dynamical theory of body, so far as it denies the existence of space, and body as occupying space, is utterly inconsistent with that fundamental conviction, of which the mind can never be shorn, which declares that the matter which has force must be extended, and that the force exercised is a force in a body in one part of space, over another body in a different part of space.

III. There is the influence, that is, power, which the bodily organs have over the mind. I feel that I must speak with great caution on this topic. Neither physiology nor psychology has been able to throw any light on the particular way in which body affects mind. The theories which have been introduced,—such as that of Occasional Causes by the disciples of Descartes, and of Pre-established Harmony by Leibnitz, and of impressions by modern physiologists,—have only increased, instead of removing the difficulties. We cannot say whether the organism affects the knowing mind immediately or mediately. We cannot say whether it has power in itself, or whether the power may not lie in some other agent working in the organ. We cannot say whether the power lies exclusively in the organ, or, as is more probable, in the organ and mind combined. Scientific research has thrown no light on these mysteries, and intuition should not pretend to settle these questions. Still intuition seems to me to say, that connected with the organism

* Leibnitz held that bodies are endowed with some sort of active force. "Les corps sont doués de quelque force active." This force may be called life. "C'est une réalité immatérielle, indivisible et indestructible: il en met partout dans le corps croyant qu'il n'y a point de partie de la masse où il n'y ait un corps organisé, doué de quelque perception ou d'une manière d'âme (Op. p. 694: ed. Erdmann). That he looked upon space as a relation will come out below.

there is power of some kind to call forth mental action.

Such seem to be the qualities of matter which we know by intuition. But even in regard to these, experience is ever adding to our knowledge, which we arrange and systematize by induction and science. Whatever other qualities of matter—if there be such—may become known to us, are discovered by experience. I have put the qualification *if there be such*, because in fact we do not know whether all the other qualities of body be not modifications of those we have named. We are made aware of such agents as heat, light, electricity, magnetism, but it is an unsettled question whether they are bodies or (as is more probable) affections of body, implying forces of a peculiar character. These are questions which can be determined only by physical science, proceeding in the method of induction.

SECT. V. OUR INTUITIVE COGNITION OF SELF OR OF SPIRIT.

It is very probable (though it can never be positively proven) that the first knowledge acquired by the mind is of our own bodily frame, through the sensitive organism —a view which does not imply that, apart altogether from such perceptions, the spirit would not have operated. But whatever may be the theory formed on this speculative subject, it is certain that whenever or however the mind is aroused into an act of intelligence, there is always involved in the exercise a knowledge of self. Coexisting with every intelligent act of mind there is always a self-consciousness. But let it be carefully observed that this knowledge is not of an abstract being or substance, or of an *ego*, or of an essence, but of the concrete self in the particular state in which it may be, with the particular thoughts, sensations, or purposes, which it may be entertaining at the time. Let us observe, and seek to evolve, what is involved in the cognition of self.

I. We know self as having being, existence. The knowledge we have in self-consciousness, which is associated with every intelligent act, is not of an impression, as Hume would say, nor of a mere quality or attribute, as certain of the Scottish metaphysicians* would affirm, nor of a phenomenon, in the sense of appearance, as Kant† supposes, but of a thing or reality. In affirming this, we are bringing out and expressing what is embraced in our primitive cognition. No account which falls short of this can be regarded as a full exhibition of the facts falling under our eye when we look within. If any man main-

* The Scottish School generally maintains that we do not know mind and body, but only the qualities of them. Reid indeed says, "Every man is conscious of a thinking principle, or mind, in himself" (Works, p. 217). Campbell, in his 'Philosophy of Rhetoric,' speaks of consciousness being concerned with "the existence of mind itself, and its actual feelings, etc." (b. i. c. v. p. ii.). But this language is not free from ambiguity. Reid says that "sensation suggests to us both a faculty and a mind, and not only suggests the notion of them, but creates a belief of their existence;" and he defends the use of the word 'suggest,' which I reckon a very unfortunate one in such an application (Works, pp. 110-111). This view is carried out and elaborated by D. Stewart: "It is not matter or body which I perceive by my senses, but only extension, figure, colour, and certain other qualities, which the constitution of my nature leads me to refer to something which is extended, figured, and coloured. The case is precisely similar with respect to mind. We are not immediately conscious of its existence, but we are conscious of sensation, thought, and volition, operations which imply the existence of something which feels, thinks, and wills" (Elem. vol. i. p. 46). See also vol. ii. p. 41, and Phil. Essays, p. 58.

† Kant holds that the inner sense gives no intuition of the soul as an object. "Der innere Sinn, vermittelst dessen das Gemüth sich selbst, oder seinen inneren Zustand anschaut, giebt zwar keine Anschauung von der Seele selbst, als einem Object" (Kr. d. r. V. p. 34). He speaks of the subject envisaging itself, not as it is, but as it appears: "Da es denn sich selbst anschaut, nicht wie es sich unmittelbar selbstthätig vorstellen würde, sondern nach der Art wie es von innem afficirt wird, folglich wie es sich erscheint, nicht wie es ist" (Zw. Aufg. p. 718). He says that by the inner sense we know the subject self as phenomenon, and not as it is in itself: "Was die innere Anschauung betrifft,

tains that all that we can discover is a mere idea, impression, phenomenon, or quality of an unknown thing, I ask him for his evidence, and he must, in replying, call in the internal sense, and I can then show him that this sense, or cognitive power (for it is not a sense except in an abusive application of the term), declares that we know a something, or thing with a positive existence.

This is a knowledge which cannot be explained, nor defined in the sense of being resolved into anything simpler or founded on anything deeper. It is a simple element implied in every intelligent act, and not derived from any other act or exercise. It is a basis on which other knowledge may be reared, and not a superstructure standing on another foundation.

As it is a primitive, so it is a necessary conviction. We cannot by any other supposed knowledge undermine or set aside this fundamental knowledge. We cannot be made by any process of speculation or ratiocination to believe that we have not being. The process of reasoning which would set aside this cognition can plead no principle stronger than the conviction which we have in favour of the reality of self.

In saying that we know self as possessed of being, we do not mean to affirm that we know all about self, or about our spiritual nature. There are mysteries about self, and about everything else we know, sufficient to awe every truly wise man into humility. All that is meant is, that, whatever may be unknown, we always know

unser eigenes Subject nur als Erscheinung, nicht aber nach dem, was es an sich selbst ist, erkennen" (*ib.* p. 850). Mr. Mansel has done great service to philosophy by maintaining so clearly and resolutely, in his 'Prolegomena Logica,' and the article on 'Metaphysics' in the 'Encyclopædia Britannica,' that we intuitively know self. "I am immediately conscious of myself seeing and hearing, willing and thinking" (Prol. Log. p. 129). Hamilton speaks of our being conscious every moment of our existence, and of the *ego* as a "self-subsistent entity" (Metaph. Lect. 19).

being whenever we know any of the objects presented to us from within or from without. This subject will be resumed in a more special manner in next Chapter.

II. We know self as not depending for its existence on our observation of it. Of course we can know self only when we know self; our knowledge of self exists not till we have the knowledge, and it exists only so long as we have the knowledge. But when we come to know self, we know it as already existing, and we do not look on its continued existence as depending on our recognition of it.

III. We know self as being in itself an abiding existence. Not that we are to stretch this conviction so far as to believe in the self-existence of mind, or in its eternal existence. We believe certainly in the permanence of mind independent of our cognition of it, and amidst all the shiftings and variations of its states. Yet this does not imply that there never was a time when self was non-existing. For aught this conviction says, there may have been a time when self came into existence—another conviction assures us that when it did, it must have had a cause. It must be added that this conviction does not go the length of assuring us that mind must exist for ever, or that it must exist after the dissolution of the body. It does indeed seem to say that, if it shall cease to exist, it must be in virtue of some cause adequate to destroy it; and it helps to produce and strengthen the feeling which the dying man cherishes when he looks on the soul as likely to abide when the body is dead. But as to whether the dissolution of the bodily frame is a sufficient cause of the decease of the soul,—as to whether it may abide when the bodily frame is disorganized,—this is a question to be settled not altogether by intuition, but by a number of other considerations, and more particularly by the conviction that God will call us into judgment at last, and is most definitely settled, after all, by the inspired declarations of the Word of God. But it is pleasant to observe that there is an original conviction altogether in unison with this derivative belief, a conviction leading us to look on self as permanent unless there be a cause working adequate to its dissolution.

According to the views presented under these heads, the existence of self is a position to be assumed, and not to be proven. It does not need proof, and no proof should be offered; no mediate evidence could possibly be clearer than the truth which it is brought to support. It has been keenly disputed how we are to understand the "Cogito, ergo sum," of Descartes. Are we to regard it as a process of reasoning? If it be so, it is either a *petitio principii,* or its conclusiveness may be doubted. If the *cogito* be understood as embracing *ego,* that is, be understood as *ego cogito,* then the *ego* is evidently involved in it, is in fact assumed. If it means anything short of this, then it might be difficult to establish the accuracy of the inference; thus, if the *cogito* does not embrace the *ego,* it is not clear that the conclusion follows.* Or are we to regard the statement as a sort of primitive judgment, not implying mediate reasoning or a middle term?† Taken in this sense, I would reckon that the connection between thought and existence is involved in our knowledge of self as existing, rather than that the knowledge of self issues from the perception of the connection between thought and personal existence. Or are we to look on the expression as simply a mode of

* Kant has a powerful criticism of the "Cogito, ergo sum," considered as an argument, in his Paralogismen d. r. Vern. in the Kritik.

† In answering the objections of Gassendi, Descartes says: "Cum advertimus nos esse res cogitantes, prima quædam notio est quæ et nullo syllogismo concluditur; neque etiam quis dicit 'Ego cogito, ergo sum, sive existo,' existentiam ex cogitatione per syllogismum deducit, sed tanquam rem per se notam simplici mentis intuitu agnoscit." See the subject discussed by Cousin, Prem. Sér. tom. i. leç. vi.

stating an assumption? In this case the word *ergo*, the usual symbol of reasoning, comes in awkwardly; and besides, the truth to be assumed is not the complex judgment, *cogito, ergo sum*, but the fact revealed at once to consciousness of *ego cogitans*.* This primitive cognition may be the ground of a number of judgments, but it is to reverse the order of things entirely to make any one of these judgments the ground of the cognitions.

The cognitions which have been unfolded in this Chapter, form, when memory begins to be exercised, the ground of our recognition of our personal identity, and lead us to believe in a self which abideth amid all changes of thought and mood and feeling. This subject will be resumed by us under the head of Primitive Judgments.

IV. We know self as exercising potency. We have seen that we know it as having being; we know it further as having active being. We know it as acting, we know it as being acted on, we know it as the source of action.† Even in sense-perception we know it as being acted on from without,—nay, we know it as itself acting in producing the result. So far as we know objects acting on it, we know it as capable of being influenced,—in other words, as having a capacity of a particular description. So far as we know it acting in producing changes in itself or other things, we know it

* "C'est par une même perception de notre âme que nous éprouvons le sentiment intime et de notre pensée et de notre existence" (Buffier, Prem. Vér. p. i. c. i.).

† Sir W. Hamilton admits all I am pleading for. "I know myself as a force in energy, the not-self as a counter-force in energy" (Note D, p. 666, of Ap. to Reid). And again: "We have a perception proper, of the secundo-primary quality, of resistance in an extra-organic force as an immediate cognition" (p. 883). Is this statement an essential part of his doctrine, or an incidental admission? If part of his system, it should modify the view he has given elsewhere of our conviction of power as being a mere impotency (see Appendix to Discuss.). If it be inadvertent, it is a proof that truth will come out of honest men, in spite of the errors of their system.

as a potency, as having power. When we recollect, when we fondly dwell on a particular scene, when we fix the thoughts on a particular object, we are exercising power, and by consciousness we know that we are doing so. When in consequence of coming to know of events bearing upon us personally,—say of some blessing about to descend, or calamity about to befall,—we rejoice or grieve, we experience an effect. This conscious potency is especially felt in all exercises of the will, whether it be directed to the mental action which we wish to stay or quicken, or the bodily organism which we purpose to move. I demur, indeed, to the view maintained by some philosophers of eminence, that our idea of power is obtained exclusively from the consciousness of the power of will over the muscles. But I am persuaded that our most vivid conviction of power is derived from the influence of the will both on bodily and mental action,* and that the influence of the will on the organism is what enables us to connect mental with bodily action.

But here it will be necessary to offer an explanation to save ourselves from obvious difficulties, which many have not seen their way to overcome. We shall find, under another head, that while we believe intuitively that every effect has a cause, we do not know by intuition what the cause is apart from experience; and that while we are convinced that the cause produces the effect, it is only by experience we know what the effect is. It follows that we do not know intuitively what or how many

* This is substantially the view of Locke, who says, "Bodies by our senses do not afford us so clear and distinct an idea of active power as we have from reflection on the operations of our own mind." In deriving our idea of Power from Sensation and Reflection, he supposes the mind to be actively and intelligently exercised. "Whatever change is observed, the mind must collect a power somewhere to make that change" (Essay, ii. xxi. 4). But Locke has omitted to inquire what it is in the mind which insists that *it must collect a cause wherever there is a change.*

powers must concur to produce a given effect. This qualification will be found to have a great significance imparted to it by the circumstance to be afterwards noticed, that in order to most creature effects there is need of a concurrence of causes, or of a concause. When I will to move my arm, I know that the will is one of the elements in producing the effect, but I do not know, till physiology tells me, how many others must co-operate. It follows that one of the elements of a complex cause may act and no effect follow, because one part of the concause is absent. I may will to take a cheerful view of everything, and yet not be able owing to the rise of gloomy thoughts. I may will to move my arm and yet the arm may not move, because paralysis has cut off the concurrence of the organism. This subject will again come before us under various aspects.

V. We know the knowing mind to be different from the material object known, whether this be the organism as affected or the object affecting it. Not that we know by intuition wherein the difference lies; not that we are in a position to say whether they may not, after all, have points of resemblance, and a mutual dependence, and a reciprocal influence,—on these points our only guide is a gathered experience. But in every act in which we know a bodily object, we know it to be different from self, and self to be different from it. This is a conviction which we can never lose, and of which no sophistry can deprive us. We carry it with us at all times, and wherever we go. It makes it impossible for any man to confound himself with the universe, or the universe with him. Man may mistake one external object for another, but it is not possible that he should mistake an external object for himself, or identify himself with any other object. This conviction is thus a means, as shall be shown later in the treatise, of delivering us from the more common forms of idealism, and from every form of pantheism.

VI. We know self in every one of its states, as these pass before self-consciousness. And herein lies an important difference between the knowledge we have of mind and the greater portion of the knowledge we have acquired of the material universe. The knowledge which we have of matter by intuition is extremely limited. What we thus know, indeed, is supremely valuable, as the ground on which we erect all our other information; still it is in itself very narrow, being confined to an acquaintance with our organism as extended and as exercising an influence on the mind, and to objects immediately in contact with it. Most even of the knowledge which we have of our organism, and of objects in contact with it, is derivative; and there is a process of inference in all that we know of objects at a distance,—of sun, moon, stars, of hills, rivers, valleys,—and of the persons and countenances and conversations of our friends. But in regard to our own minds, we know all the individual facts directly and intuitively. We gaze at once on the mind thinking, imagining, feeling, resolving. In this view it may be safely said that we know more of certain of the states and of the action of mind than we know of the whole material universe, even in this age of advanced science. It should be added, in order to save the remark from appearing to some incredibly extravagant, that while we thus know spontaneously so much about the workings of the mind, the majority of men think far more about their objective than their subjective knowledge. It should be further added, that while we are ever growing, more than people who have not thought on the subject imagine, in the knowledge of our mental affections, yet there are greater difficulties in adding to our original stock in the mental than in the material world.

It is the office of psychology, as a science, to observe wherein the states of mind which fall under consciousness agree and wherein they differ, and to endeavour to arrange and classify them. In conducting this its work, all the facts are discovered by consciousness as an intuitive faculty. Our sensations, our perceptions, our elaborated thoughts, our moral cognitions, our emotions, our wishes, our volitions, and all our necessary convictions, are under our immediate view. But it is to be carefully observed that the classification is a work of discursive, and not of intuitive thought. We know our thoughts and feelings, but not as thoughts or feelings. As to how we are to arrange them, and as to what is the best classification of our mental states, this is a question not for intuition, but for mental science, looking to the facts which consciousness makes known. We are conscious, not of faculties, but merely of individual energies, which we compare and arrange under certain heads as faculties. It is important to state here once more that we are conscious of the intuitions of the mind as individual energies, and not as abstract forms or general laws.

CHAPTER II.

ANALYSIS OF OUR PRIMITIVE COGNITIONS.

SECT. I. (*Preliminary.*) ON THE NATURE OF ABSTRACTION AND GENERALIZATION.

As abstraction and generalization perform so important a part in the formation of the *a priori* notions and maxims out of the concrete and individual convictions, it will be necessary to explain the nature of these processes, the more so as a defective account has often been given of them.

It is very generally acknowledged that man's mind begins with the concrete, and thence reaches the abstract, that is, that it first knows or contemplates an object with the qualities presenting themselves, and that it afterwards learns to consider the object apart from any particular quality, or the quality apart from the object. The statement now made, does not imply that man's primary knowledge is complex. The complex is not the same as the concrete. In complex knowledge man has mingled several cognitions which are simple; but to man the concrete is the simple. His primary knowledge is of objects with certain qualities which he may subsequently be able to separate and distinguish. Thus by the eye he gets a knowledge of the bodies before him as at one and the same time extended and coloured. By the muscular sense, or locomotive energy, he knows objects as extended, movable, and resisting energy. It is a curious circumstance that when the memory recalls an object, it always presents it in the concrete, that is, with qualities which can be separated. We cannot even imagine an object except in the concrete; we cannot picture to ourselves an extended surface without giving it colour of some kind, and we cannot imagine a colour except on an extended surface.

With this primary knowledge and these representations in possession, the mind proceeds to abstract, and is urged to do so by a native intellectual impulse. It can separate in thought the qualities from the object, or one quality from another, say the colour from the form.

Abstraction may be considered in a wider or in a narrower sense. It may be regarded, in an extended sense, as that operation of mind, in which, to use the language of Whately, "we draw off and contemplate separately any part of an object presented to the mind, disregarding the rest" (Logic Anal. Out.). In this more general sense the parts may exist separately as well as the whole; thus, having seen a judge with his wig, we can not only separate in thought the wig from the judge, but the wig can in fact be separated from the wearer. In a narrower sense, abstraction is that operation of mind in which we contemplate the quality of an object separately from the object. "An abstract name," says Mr. Mill (Logic, b. i. c. ii.), "is a name which stands for an attribute of a thing." In this sense the part separated in thought cannot be separated from the object in fact. Colour may be thought of (not seen or imagined) apart from an extended body, but cannot exist apart from a coloured object.

It is a very common impression that our abstractions are in no sense realities. I wish at this early stage of the investigations to be prosecuted in this treatise, to set myself against this view, which has sometimes been positively expressed, but is far more frequently underlying and implied in statements and arguments without being formally announced. I lay down a very different position, that if the concrete be real, and the abstraction be properly made, the abstract thing, that is, the thing contemplated in the abstraction, will also be real. I may never have seen a bird without wings, but I can consider the wings apart from the bird, and I am sure that the wings have as real an existence as the bird itself. This will be admitted at once in regard to all such cases as this, in which I can in fact separate the pinions from the body of the fowl. But I go a step further, and maintain, that even in cases in which the part abstracted cannot be separated in reality from the whole, still it is to be considered as real. It may not have, or be capable of having, an independent reality, but still it has a reality. I can think of gravitation apart from a given body, or from the chemical affinity of that body; and in doing so I do not suppose that it can exist apart from body; still the gravitation has an existence just as much as the body has, it has not a reality independent of the body, but it has a reality in the body, as a quality of it. The same remark might be applied to, and will hold good of, any other abstraction. No doubt if the original concrete object be imaginary, the abstraction formed from it may be the same; I can separate in thought the beauty of Venus from Venus herself; and of course, as Venus is ideal, so also is her beauty. But when the object is real, and I abstract or separately contemplate what has been known in the real, then, as the concrete object is real, so is also the part or quality abstracted real; not that it may be a reality capable of subsisting in itself, but still a reality in the object as a quality of it.

I reckon it of the utmost moment to make this remark. The view here presented saves us on the one hand from an extreme Realism, which would attribute an independent reality to every quality abstracted, which would for example represent beauty as a separate thing, like a beautiful scene in nature, and on the other hand, from what is more important in our present inquiry, from regarding it as a nonentity, or at the utmost as a mere form or creation of the mind.* We are ever hearing the phrase repeated a

* "Concreta vere res sint, abstracta non sunt res sed rerum modi; modi autem nihil aliud sunt quam relationes rei ad intellectum seu apparendi facultates" (Leibnitz de Stilo Philos.: Nizolii Op. p. 63). In this as in other matters, Leibnitz introduced a *subjective* tendency, which came forth in full manifestation only in a later age.

"mere abstraction;" and the language is applied to such objects as space, time, beauty, and even truth and moral good. In opposition to such views, I maintain that abstraction is not necessarily concerned about fictions or illusions. Abstractions are not, as they have often been represented, the attenuated ghosts of departed quantities; they may rather be represented as the very skeleton of the body, not capable of action alone, but still an important existence in the body, acting with its covering of flesh and skin. Abstraction is not only a lofty intellectual exercise, it is in a sense a cognitive act, and when the concrete object looked at is real, it will give us, if properly conducted, a reality in the part separated. As to whether this part is or is not capable of a separate existence, this depends on the nature of the original concrete cognition.

Generalization is dependent on abstraction, and arises out of it. In generalization we contemplate an indefinite number of objects as possessing a common attribute or attributes. A general notion is a notion of these objects. This expressed in language is a common term, which therefore stands for an indefinite number of objects, for all that possess the common quality or qualities.

As abstractions are formed out of concretes, so generalizations are formed out of individuals or singulars. It has been very generally allowed by philosophers that the mind begins with the knowledge of individual objects or scenes presented to it. Among these objects it may, by its comparative faculty, discover resemblances. In some cases the comparison is preceded by an abstraction of the qualities in respect of which the objects are alike; in other cases it may be perceived at once that there is a resemblance, and the abstraction of the points of resemblance may follow. In all cases, both the discovery of resemblance and abstraction are needful to generalization, in which we put in a class, and usually call by a common name, the objects thought to resemble each other in certain respects, and so far as they resemble each other.

I am prepared to lay down in regard to generalization a proposition similar to that which I am inclined to enforce in regard to abstraction. When the individuals are real, the generalization has also a reality; that is, there is a reality in the class. True, I may constitute a class from imaginary individuals,—say a class of griffins, or a class of mermaids, or a class of ghosts. In such a case the general is as unreal as the singular. But if my generalization is from real objects; if it is a generalization made of objects in nature, say of marbles, or reptiles, or cruciferous plants, or even of objects of human workmanship, such as chairs, or houses, or churches, then the intellectual product has also a reality involved. I do not mean to say that the general exists, or can exist, as an individual thing, like the singulars which it embraces,—that the class crocodile has the same sort of existence as the individual crocodile,—but I maintain that it has a reality in the common attributes possessed by the objects.

In abstraction, the reality may be simply that of an attribute in an individual object. In generalization, it is the possession of a common attribute by an indefinite number of objects. The composition of marble is a fact quite as much, though not exactly of the same sort, as the limestone itself. The possession of cold blood, and of the three heart-compartments, is a reality quite as much as the individual crocodile is. The possession of four cross petals is a real thing, just as a particular wild mustard-plant is. The structure and adaptation to a practical use of chair, house, and church, are not fictitious any more than this chair, or this house, or this church is. This account preserves us on the one hand from an extravagant realism, which would give to the universal the same sort of reality as the singular; and on the other, from an extreme conceptualism or nominalism, which would place the reality solely in the conception of the mind, or in the name. The class has a reality, but it is simply in the possession of common qualities by an indefinite number of objects.

According to this view, abstraction and generalization are processes of a very high order; they are, in fact, essential to philosophy, quite as much so, indeed, as Plato and the Schoolmen supposed; without them we can never reach the truths on which the higher forms of wisdom gaze. They always pre-suppose, indeed, that something has been given them; but, acting upon this, they turn it to most important purposes, and if they start with realities and are properly conducted, they are ever in the region of realities, and of realities of the highest kind. We shall see as we advance that all philosophic notions and maxims are the results of these processes, some of them being abstractions, and others being also of the nature of generalizations.

SECT. II. ON BEING.

But what can be said of Being? Verily, little can be said of it. The mistake of metaphysicians lies in their saying too much; and they have made assertions which have, and can have, no meaning, and landed themselves in self-created mysteries or in contradictions. So little can be affirmed of Being, not because of the complexity of the idea, but because of its simplicity; we can find nothing simpler into which to resolve it. We have come to ultimate truth, and there is really no deeper foundation on which to rest it. There is no light behind in which to show it in vivid outline.

In the concrete every one has the cognition of Being, just as every man has a skeleton in his frame. But the common mind is apt to turn away from the abstract idea, as it does from an anatomical preparation; or rather, it feels as if such attenuated notions belong to the regions of ghosts, where

> "Entity and quiddity,
> The ghosts of defunct bodies, fly."

All that the metaphysician can do is to appeal to the perception which all men form, to separate this from the others with which it is joined, and make it stand out singly and simply, that it may shine and be seen in its own light, and with this the mind will be satisfied:—

> "Who thinks of asking if the sun is light,
> Observing that it lightens?"

Those who attempt anything more, and to peer into the object, will find that the light darkens as they gaze upon it. "When I burned in desire to question them further, they made themselves—air, into which they vanished."

I allow that the abstract notion of Being is one which the mind is not inclined spontaneously to fashion. As to many other abstractions, it is led naturally to form them; they are framed for it, or it is compelled by the circumstances in which it is placed to frame them. Thus I see a man with a black coat one day, and with a grey coat the next, and I cannot but separate the colour from the object. But in such high abstractions as Being, that which we contemplate is never, in fact, separated from any one thing. Still Being is an abstraction which we are constrained to make for philosophic purposes, and it was, in fact, formed so early as the age of the speculators of the Eleatic School. It is the one thing to be found objectively in all our knowledge. Hence in all our abstractions it is that which remains; in the ascending process of generalization it is the *summum genus*. This does not prove that Being can exist apart from a special mode of existence, or the exercise of some quality. Nor does it prove that we can know Being separate from a concrete existence. I hold the one as well as the other of these to be impossible. But in all knowledge we know what we know as having existence, which is Being.

I cannot give my adhesion to the opinion of those who speak so strongly of man being incapacitated to know Being. I have already intimated my dissent from the Kantian doctrine that we do not know things, but appearances; and even from the theory of those Scottish metaphysicians who affirm that we do not know things, but qualities. What we know is the thing manifesting itself to us,—is the thing exercising particular qualities. But then it is confidently asserted that we do not know the "thing in itself." The language, I rather think, is unmeaning; but if it has a meaning, it is incorrect. I do not believe that there is any such thing in existence as Being in itself, or that man can even so much as imagine it: and if this be so, it is clear that we cannot know it, and desirable that we should not suppose that we know it. Of this I am sure, that those Neo-Platonists who professed to be able to rise to the discovery of Being in itself (which could only be the abstract idea of Being), and to be employed in gazing on it, had miserably bare and most unprofitable matter of meditation, whether for intellectual, or moral, or religious ends. But if any mean to deny that we can know Being as it is, I maintain in opposition to them, and I appeal to consciousness to confirm me when I say, that we immediately know Being in every act of cognition. But then we are told that we cannot know the mystery of Being.* I am under a strong impression that speculators have attached a much greater amount of mystery to this simple subject than really belongs to it. Of this I am sure, that much of the obscurity which has collected around it has sprung from the confused discussions of metaphysicians, who have laboured to explain what needs no explanation to our intelligence, or to get a basis on which to build what stands securely on its own foundation. I do indeed most fully admit that there may be much about Being which we do not know; much about Being generally, much about every individual Being, unknown to us and unknowable in this world. Still I do affirm that we know so much of Being, and that any further knowledge conveyed to us would not set aside our present knowledge, but would simply enlarge it.

Sect. III. On Substance.

All that the metaphysician can do in regard to sub-

* Kant everywhere speaks of our not knowing the "Ding an sich." See in the Kritik of Pure Reason (Antin. d. r. V. Abs. vi.). M. Cousin allows to Kant that we have not a consciousness of our proper nature, otherwise, he says, that the abysses and mysteries of existence would all be known; but to save himself from the Kantian consequences, he calls in reason to give us a conviction of self and personal identity:—"Nul de nous n'a conscience de sa propre nature, sans quoi les abîmes de l'existence seraient faciles à sonder, les mystères de l'âme nous seraient parfaitement connus." "L'identité personnelle est une conviction de la raison" (sér. ii. leç. xviii.). It were surely both simpler and wiser to suppose that there is intelligence in consciousness, and that this intelligent consciousness knows self.

stance is to show that our cognition of it is original and fundamental, and to evolve what is contained in the cognition. He should not attempt to prove how it is so and so (the διότι of Aristotle), but he may show that it is so and so (the ὅτι of Aristotle). He could not give the dimmest idea of it to one who had not already the knowledge, but he may separate it by analysis from the other cognitions with which it is combined, and make it stand out fully to the view. He may so weigh and measure it as to show its extent and boundary, and deliver it from those crudities in which speculators have incrusted it. The following is the best analysis I am able to furnish.

I. In all knowledge of substance there is involved BEING OR EXISTENCE, not of being in the abstract, but of something in being. This we have seen is an essential element in our cognition, both of mind and body. The mind starts with knowledge, and with the knowledge of things as having being. This is the foundation, the necessary foundation, of all other exercises. If the mind did not begin with knowledge, it could not end with knowledge. In particular, if it had not knowledge in the concrete, it never could get knowledge in the abstract. If there were not a knowledge of things in the premisses with which we set out, there never could be such a knowledge in the conclusion. But having knowledge, obtained by intuition, to set out with, we find that when we proceed legitimately—that is, according to the laws of thought—in our discursive exercises, we have always reality in the conclusion.

II. In all knowledge of substance there is involved ACTIVE POWER. We cannot know self, or the mind that knows, except as active, that is, exerting power, or as being affected. Nor can we know material objects except as exercising or suffering an influence—that is a certain kind of power. They become known to us as having a power either upon ourselves or upon other objects, and we express this when we say that we know matter by its properties.

This is a doctrine which has been opposed by a large school of metaphysicians that have felt directly or indirectly the influence of Descartes, who represented extension as the essence of matter. This oversight has marred their whole speculations, and landed them in innumerable difficulties. For not finding power in our original cognitions, they have either with the sceptic Hume denied that we have any such cognition, or they have with Kant made it a form which the mind imposes on objects. Still a large amount of authority can be pleaded in behalf of the doctrine, that power is involved in our idea of substance. It is the expressed view of Locke. It is maintained by Leibnitz with all the ingenuity of his speculative genius. Even Kant acknowledges (though from the subjective character which he ascribes to our intuitive convictions, he can turn it to no profitable account) that cause is involved in our idea of substance.* It has been incidentally admitted by many who have theoretically denied it.

III. There is involved in our knowledge of substance a conviction of its having A PERMANENCE.† This proposition must be very guardedly stated. By being loosely and inaccurately announced, it has led to very erroneous and

* Locke says that "powers make a great part of our complex ideas of substances" (Essay ii. xxiii. 7–10). Leibnitz says, "Jusqu'ici rien n'a mieux marqué la substance que la puissance d'agir" (Op. p. 460). The language of Kant is, "Diese Causalität führt auf den Begriff der Handlung, diese auf den Begriff der Kraft und dadurch auf den Begriff der Substanz." "Wo Handlung mithin Thätigkeit und Kraft ist, da ist auch Substanz" (Werke, pp. 172, 173). "Die Substanz in Raume kennen wir nur durch Kräfte" (p. 218). See also Abrici System der Logik, Th. i. 5, where are some profound views of power.

† Speaking of such qualities as hardness, Reid says:—"They were real qualities before they were perceived by touch, and continue to be so when they are not perceived; for if any man will affirm that dia-

dangerous doctrines. But there is a truth here, if we could only properly apprehend and express it. A substance is not a spectre which appeared when we began to see it, and which may cease to exist when we have ceased to view it. This conviction is at the basis of the belief in the abiding nature of every existing thing, amid all the changes which it may undergo. However a piece of matter may be beat or cut mechanically, we do not believe it to be destroyed. However it may be evaporated or decomposed by heat or chemical processes, we are not convinced that it is annihilated. When the moisture on the earth disappears, we do not therefore conclude that it has vanished into nothing; we look for it in a new form, and our expectation is gratified when we discover it in the vapour of the atmosphere or the cloud. When fuel is put on the fire it gradually disappears from the view, but we inquire for it elsewhere, and find it in the ashes and in the smoke. Our conviction of the abiding nature of self is still more deeply rooted and fixed. We believe in its continuance amid all the changes of thought and sensation, mood and feeling, lethargy and activity.

But while there is all this in our apprehension of substance, there is not more than this, and the errors have arisen from supposing that there is more. In particular, our conviction does not require us to believe either in the necessary existence of every substance or in its indestructibility. Our intuition does not say whether it has or has not been created, whether it does or does

monds were not hard till they were handled, who would reason with him?" "Our sensations suggest to us a sentient being or mind to which they belong, a sentient being which hath a permanent existence, although the sensations are transient and of short duration, a being which is still the same while its sensations and other operations are varied ten thousand ways" (Reid's Works, pp. 120, 122). The word *suggest*, taken from Berkeley and from Locke, was appropriate enough as used by idealists, but comes awkwardly from Reid. The word should have been *know*.

not need the Divine power to maintain and uphold it, whether it may or may not be destroyed. It does not entitle us to affirm that matter must ever have existed, or must, if formed, have been fashioned out of pre-existing materials. Nor does it say how long it has existed, or how long it will exist. An analogous intuitive conviction—that of cause—says that if produced, it must have been produced by a cause; that if destroyed, it must be by a power independent of itself. Hence we cannot assert positively, when we see a substance, say a piece of burned coal, disappearing from our view, that it must still exist, for in the operation of combustion there may have been a power to destroy it; all that we can affirm is, that the substance did not vanish of itself. All that our intuition guarantees is, that in itself substance has permanence, and that if destroyed, it must be by something *ab extra*.

By this limitation we are saved at once from certain pernicious consequences which were drawn from the doctrine of Descartes. According to him, a substance is that which subsists of itself, which has no need of anything from without in order to its existence.* Proceeding on this definition, Spinoza laboured to show that there was and could be only one substance, of which everything is an attribute or a mode. The school of Descartes sought to save themselves from this pantheistic consequence by various devices. It is not to our present purpose to inquire whether these were or were not successful, as in accordance with the principles of Descartes. To me it appears that we must amend the definition of Descartes,

* "Per substantiam nihil aliud intelligere possumus, quam rem quæ ita existit, ut nulla alia re indigeat ad existendum. Et quidem substantia quæ nulla plane re indigeat, unica tantum potest intellige, nempe Deus. Alias vero omnes non nisi ope concursus Dei existere posse percipimus" (Prin. Phil., p. i. 51). He speaks of created substances "quod sint res quæ solo Dei concursu egent ad existendum" (ib. 52).

and reject the definition of Spinoza, and then all the conclusions founded on them must fall to the ground.

"I understand," says Spinoza, "by substance, that which is in itself, and conceived by itself; that is to say, that of which the concept can be formed without having need of the concept of any other thing."* There is a whole aggregate of things jumbled in this definition. That which is in itself is one thing, that which is conceived by itself is another thing, which is not even necessarily the same as that which is given as an explanation, viz. that of which a concept can be formed without having need of the concept of any other thing. I object to our conviction in regard to substance being called a concept, a phrase denoting an abstract or general notion formed by a discursive process of the understanding; the conviction is an intuition. The intuition says of every substance that it is a thing or reality, but it does not say whence the reality proceeded. It says that substance has power, but it does not say whence that power. No doubt a substance is a thing known (not merely conceived) in itself, but the same may be said of space and time, and everything apprehended intuitively. Having removed this definition out of the way, as not the expression of our intuitive knowledge, we leave the whole pantheism of Spinoza without a foundation. I am certain that our native conviction as to substance gives no countenance to pantheism of any kind. Our intuition says that substance has being, but it does not say whether it is dependent or independent being. It says that it has power, but it does not say that it is underived, or whence it is derived. It says that it has permanence, but does not say that it has not been created, and that it cannot be destroyed.

* "Per substantiam intelligo id quod in se est et per se concipitur; hoc est id cujus conceptus non indiget conceptu alterius rei a quo formari debeat" (Ethices p. i. def. 3: ed. Bruder).

According to the account now given, self or spirit must be a substance. We know it as having being, we know it as having power and permanence. While it has all these, it is to be studiously noticed that we do not know it to have all, or indeed any, of these independently. For aught our intuition says, it may be dependent for all of these on the creative power or concurrent power of God. Not only so, it may, for anything our intuition intimates, be dependent for some of these on its association with the bodily organism in this present state of things. If we wish to settle these questions, we must look to other circumstances and considerations.

Many metaphysicians have felt greater difficulty in allowing that matter is a substance. But explaining substance as has been done in this Section, it is entitled to be so regarded. It too has being, power, and endurance. We can deny this only by refusing to follow our native convictions. But in standing up for the substantial nature of body, it is still more necessary than in the case of spirit, to bear in mind the qualifications under which we make the statement. We cannot affirm of matter that it has derived its characteristics from no source independent of itself. Nor can we declare of it that it can subsist of itself, and independent of the co-operating power of mind, that is, the Divine Mind. We are stretching intuition altogether beyond its province, if we make it pronounce oracular decisions on any such questions.

But are mind and matter different substances? I reply that there are certain positions on this subject which can be defended against all opposition. First, in the cognition of the knowing mind, which ever co-exists with our cognition of matter, we always know the two to be different. When we look at these hills we have ever an accompanying cognition of self as looking at the hills, and we know the hills to be different from self, and self to be different from the hills. Secondly, we know that the very things by which substance is characterized—existence, potency, and permanence—are not the same in the case of mind and body. Thus the being of mind is not the same with that of matter, nor are the powers of mind the same with those of matter, nor does the permanence of body depend on human beings observing it, nor can it be shown that the permanence of mind depends on the permanence of the bodily frame. With these proofs or presumptions in our favour, we may surely throw the *onus probandi* of proving that they are the same substance on our opponents. But, thirdly, all attempts to resolve mind into matter, or matter into mind, have utterly failed. If we deny that matter has an existence independent of the contemplative mind, we are trampling on one of the intuitions of our nature. Those who resolve mind into matter always overlook the very essential qualities of the knowing, the conscious, the thinking, the moral, the responsible soul. We are thus entitled, from all we can know of substance, to declare them to be different substances. As to whether they may not, after all, have some unity in the view of higher intelligences, who take a deeper view of substance, this is a question which we need not start, for we cannot settle it, and the unity is one which we can never discover nor comprehend. It is enough for us that they are different substances in all the characteristics of substance known to us.

Sir W. Hamilton* remarks that the word 'substance' (*substantia*) may be "viewed as derived from *subsistendo*, and as meaning *ens per se subsistens* (οὐσία, in Greek); or it may be viewed as the basis of attributes, in which sense it may be regarded as derived from *substando*, and *id quod substat accidentibus;* like the Greek, ὑπόστασις,

* Metaph., Lect. 8., where are admirable definitions of terms.

ὑποκείμενον. In either case it will, however, signify the same thing, viewed in a different aspect." With this latter statement I cannot concur. In the first of these senses there is such a thing as a substance, and its characteristics can be specified. But I can see no evidence whatever for the existence of any such thing as a substance in the other sense, that is, as a *substratum* lying in and beyond, or standing under, all that comes under our immediate knowledge.* There is no topic on which there has been a greater amount of unintelligible language employed than on this. We know, it is said, only qualities,

* "If any one will examine himself concerning his notion of pure substance in general, he will find that he has no other ideá of it at all, but only a supposition of he knows not what support of such qualities which are capable of producing simple ideas in us; which qualities are commonly called accidents" (Locke, Essay ii. xxiii. 23). His view is thus fully expounded in his 'Letter to Stillingfleet:'—"Your Lordship well expresses it,—*We find that we can have no true conception of any modes or accidents, but we must conceive a substratum or subject wherein they are; i.e.* that they cannot exist or subsist of themselves. Hence the mind perceives their necessary connection with inherence or being supported; which being a relative idea, superadded to the red colour in a cherry, or to thinking in a man, the mind frames the correlative idea of a support. For I never denied that the mind could frame to itself ideas of relation, but have showed the quite contrary in my chapters about relation. But because a relation cannot be founded on nothing, or be the relation of nothing, and the thing here related as a supporter or support is not represented to the mind by any clear and distinct idea, therefore the obscure, indistinct, vague idea of thing or something is all that is left to be the positive idea which has the relation of a support or substratum to modes or accidents; and that general undetermined idea of something is by the abstraction of the mind derived also from the simple ideas of Sensation and Reflection; and thus the mind, from the positive simple ideas got by sensation or reflection, comes to the general relative idea of substance; which without these positive simple ideas it could never have." I have quoted this passage because it lets us see fully what Locke's precise theory is, and what are its defects. The mind gets all its ideas from sensation and reflection, but in comparing ideas it discovers necessary relations. Among these is substance, of which the idea is very obscure. Still the mind is led to suppose that there is such a thing acting as a support or *substratum.*

but we are constrained by reason, or by common sense, to believe in a something in which they inhere. Or qualities, it is said, fall under sense, while substance is known by νοῦς, or reason. Others, proceeding on these admissions, maintain that qualities alone being known, we may doubt whether there is such a thing as substance, and may certainly affirm that we can never know it. Now in opposition to all this style of thinking and writing, which has prevailed to so great an extent since the days of Locke, I maintain that we never know qualities without also knowing substance. Qualities, as qualities distinct from substances, are as much unknown to us as substance distinct from qualities. We shall show in next Section that we know both in one concrete act. We know qualities as qualities of a real thing, having being and power and permanence.

Sect. IV. On Mode, Quality, Property, Essence.

Two great truths press themselves on the reflecting mind when it contemplates this world of ours. One of these, the more obvious, is the mutability of all mundane objects. Nothing seems to be enduring, all appears to be fluctuating. This has been a favourite view of poets, to whom it has furnished a succession of kaleidoscope pictures; moralists and divines have dwelt upon it, in order to allure us to seek for something more stable than this world can furnish; and even libertines have turned it to their own use, and exhorted us to catch the enjoyment while it passes, to shoot the bird on the wing: "Let us eat and drink, for to-morrow we die." Philosophies have been built on this doctrine of the fluctuation of all things. Heraclitus of Ephesus taught that all things are in a perpetual flux; that we cannot enter the same stream twice; whereon Cratylus rebuked him, and showed that we cannot do so once.* But there is another truth

* Aristotle, Met. iii. v. 6.

which has a no less important, indeed a deeper place in the nature of things. In the midst of all these mutations objects have, after all, a permanence. Ever changing, they are yet all the while ever the same. Persons of deeper thought, or at least more addicted to abstraction, looking beneath the changing surface, dwell on this permanence, which they discover to be like the fixed mountain—while the changes are merely like the colours that pass over its surface; and some have so magnified it as to make it set aside the mutability. The Eleatics carried their doctrine so far as to maintain the oneness and unchangeableness of all being. The founder of the school, Xenophanes, identified this immutable oneness with the Divine Being. His disciple, Parmenides, degenerating in religious faith, though superior to the master in logical power, narrowed this unity into metaphysical being. Zeno, who followed, showed his subtlety by pointing out the difficulties in which they are involved who maintain the existence of multiplicity and motion. The expansive mind of Plato wrestled with both these extremes, and sought by his doctrine of supra-sensible ideas, and an exuberance of subtleties, to establish a doctrine of being not inconsistent with multiplicity and change. In modern times Descartes and Spinoza have magnified the importance of Substance quite as much as the Eleatics did Being, while the great mass of physicists, and all the speculators of the Sensational School never get deeper than the fleeting and the phenomenal.

The wise, and the only proper course, is to assume both, to assume both as first truths. No attempt should be made to support either by mediate proof; each carries with it its own evidence. Neither can be set aside by any sophistical reasoning founded on the other. It is the business of philosophy not to attempt to discard either, but rather to give the proper account of each, when they will be seen not to be inconsistent. The doctrine of the permanence of objects is founded on being and substance. We must take a view of the other truth in this Section.

Every substance, we have seen, is known as having being, power, and endurance. But every terrestrial substance is at the same time known as changing. Self changes as we look in upon it; the material world changes as we look out upon it. No attempt should be made to explain *how* the two can co-exist, the permanent and the changeable. For mind and body are known at one and the same time as both. The one is quite as much known, and therefore quite as conceivable ever afterwards, as the other; and there can be no difficulty (whatever metaphysicians may ingeniously urge in opposition) in conceiving of their compatibility, since they were ever known to exist together. It is one of the permanent characters, both of mind and body, that they are ever known as changing. Their liability to change is an element in their very nature. Now the appropriate term to express the given state of any one substance is MODE; or if we wish a convenient change of phraseology, *Modification*, *State*, or *Condition*.

From this account we see in what sense it is that substance implies mode, and mode implies substance. Mode implies substance, not only inasmuch as a state must be the state of something, but inasmuch as mode is the state of a substance liable to change, and so capable of manifesting itself in more than one phase. Substance implies mode, inasmuch as it must always be in a certain state, and is liable to be in different states. The maxim is more than a verbal one, more than a truism, more than an identical (analytic) judgment involved in the terms; it is a judgment affirming a truth intuitively discovered by the mind when looking at the things (a synthetic judgment *a priori.*)

Every object is known not only as having being, but is known as having a certain being or nature. That which is thus manifested to us may be something common to this one thing with other things, or it may be something peculiar to the thing itself. Every particular substance known, is known as at least having being and potency and an abiding nature, and is known also as possessing peculiar or distinguishing attributes. That by which the object is thus known to us as in itself, or as acting, may be called a quality of the substance. Sir W. Hamilton speaks of the qualities of substance as "its aptitudes and manners of existence and of action."*

But let us properly understand the relation of the two, substance and quality. The two are ever known in one concrete act. Thus when at a given moment we know self as rejoicing, we do not know the self as separate, or the rejoicing as separate, but we grasp the self and the rejoicing at once. But then it is necessary for many purposes to distinguish between them, and we do so by analysis; indeed, the analysis is in a sense done for us naturally. For while self is rejoicing to-day, it may be grieving to-morrow. To express the distinction it is needful to have a nomenclature, and so we distinguish between the substance and the quality. Not that the substance can ever exist without the quality, or the quality without the substance. On the contrary, the one implies the other. The substance must always have at least the qualities by which all substance is characterized, and it may have many others. The qualities must always be qualities of a thing having these characteristics. The maxim that the substance implies the quality, is thus a proposition of the same character as that the substance implies the mode.

The word 'substance' may be used either as an abstract

* Metaph., Lect. viii.

or a general term. As an abstract term it designates the thing as having the characteristics of substance, which I believe to be existence, potency, and continuance. As a general term it denotes all those things which have the characteristics of substance. Quality, too, may be employed as an abstract or a general term. As an abstract term it denotes *that* in any given substance by which it acts or manifests itself. As a general term it denotes all the manifestations or actions of a substance. Some of these qualities are found in all substance: such are the characteristics of substance of which I have so often spoken. Others are peculiar to certain substances, or manifest themselves in certain substances at certain times. Particular qualities are known by us intuitively to be in mind or matter. Thus we know consciousness, personality, thought, and will, as in mind; while we know extension and incompressibility as being in matter; these may appropriately be styled Essential Qualities of spirit and body. Other qualities are discovered by experience. Both mind and body may have qualities which can never be known by us. As to the qualities which become known to us by experience, and the qualities concealed from us, we can never know whether any of them are, or are not, essential either to body or mind.

If this view be correct, we see that a wrong account is often given of substance and qualities, and the relation between them. Thus it is very common to say that substance is a thing behind the qualities or underneath them, acting as a substratum, basis, ground, or support. All such language is in its very nature metaphorical; the analogy is of the most distant kind, and may have a misleading character. The substance is the very thing itself, considered in a certain aspect, and the qualities are its action or manifestation. Again, it is frequently said that qualities are known, whereas substance cannot be known, or if known, known only by some deeper or more transcendental principle of the mind. Now I hold that we never know quality except as the quality of a substance, and that we know both equally in one undivided act. This a somewhat less mystical or mysterious account than that commonly given by metaphysicians, but is, as it appears to me, in strict accordance with the revelations of consciousness.

I have said that the term 'quality' expresses all in the substance by which it acts or manifests itself. That in substance which acts, is power, and in all substance (we have seen) is power. The term PROPERTY, which signifies peculiar quality, might, I think, in accordance with a usage to which it has of late been approximating more and more, be appropriated to express the powers of any given substance, as the power of thinking or feeling in mind, or of gravity or chemical affinity in body. To vary the phraseology, the word *Faculty* may be employed when we speak of mental powers, and *Force* when we speak of material powers. It is the business of science to determine by observation and generalization, the powers or properties of mind and body.

Another phrase with the ideas involved in it requires to be explained here, and that is ESSENCE. It is a very mystical word, and a whole aggregate of foolish speculation has clustered round it. Still it may have a meaning. As applied logically to classes of objects, it has a signification which can be precisely fixed; it denotes the common quality or qualities which are found in all the members of the class. Thus the possession of four limbs is the essence of the class quadruped. It is to be remembered that when the class is one of what some logicians call Kinds, it is impossible to specify all the common qualities which go to constitute it. Thus we cannot tell all the attributes which go to make up such natural classes as those of metal, dog, or rose. All that we can do is to specify some of the more marked, which are signs of others. But for such logical purposes the phrase 'common attribute' or 'differentia' is the better, and is more frequently employed. It is in metaphysics that the word 'essence' is supposed to have a place. Thus the question is often put, What is the essence of mind? or What is the essence of body? or What is the essence of this individual mind, or of this piece of clay or chalk? Now we can answer such a question as this, only when we are allowed to draw distinctions and offer explanations. *First*, we may allowably conceive that every one object, and every class of objects, has an aggregate of things which go to constitute it, and we may with perfect propriety refer to such an essence as possibly or probably existing,* but always on the distinct condition forthwith to be specified more formally, that we do not speak of the essence as something which can be known by us in all its totality. *Secondly*, there are some things which we know to belong to the essence of certain objects; thus we know that being, power, and permanence, are essential to all substance, and that certain qualities belong to mind, and certain qualities, such as extension and incompressibility, to body. But we must ever guard against the idea that there may not be other qualities also essential to these objects. For, *Thirdly*, the essence of a thing, at least in its totality, must always be unknown to man. How many things are united in body or mind, or in any individual mind or material object, this can never be ascertained by human observation or ingenuity. In this sense it is proper in us to speak of the essence of things

* Locke, 'Letter to Stillingfleet,' takes Essences "to be in everything that *internal constitution*, or frame, or modification of the *Substance*, which God, in his wisdom and good pleasure, thinks fit to give to every particular creature when he gives it a being; and such essences I grant there are in all things that exist."

as being unknown to man; meaning thereby, not that we cannot know the substance, which I maintain we do know, or that we cannot know some of the qualities which go to make up the essence, but merely that we cannot know what precisely constitutes the essence in its entireness. But, *Fourthly*, we are not warranted to maintain that there must be something lying further in than the qualities we know, and that this one thing is entitled to be regarded as the essence of the object. We have no ground whatever for believing that there must be, or that there is, something more internal or central than the substance and quality which we know. True, there are probably occult qualities, even in those objects with which we are most intimately acquainted, but we are not therefore warranted to conclude that what is concealed must differ in nature or in kind from what is revealed, or that it is in any way more necessary to the existence or the continuance of the object. I have a shrewd suspicion that there is a vast amount of unmeaning talk in the language which is employed on this special subject by metaphysicians, who would see something which the vulgar cannot discern, whereas they should be contented with pointing to what all men perceive. It is quite conceivable, and perfectly possible, that though we should know all about any given terrestrial or material object, we should after all not fall in with anything more mysterious or deep than those wonders which come every day under our notice in the world without, or the world within us.

Sect. V. On Personality.

Our perception of personality is closely connected with our knowledge of being, but there is more in personality than in being. We know material objects as having existence, but we have a special apprehension in regard to self beyond what we have in regard to material objects.* Like every other simple perception, it cannot be defined, but it may be brought out to separate view by abstraction; and consciousness (with memory) will recognize it as one of the cognitions which it had seen before in company with others. We express this conviction when we say we are persons. The abstract idea is one not likely to be spontaneously formed. The infant, the child, the savage, are not in the habit of making any such analysis of consciousness, nor are the great body of mankind at the trouble of asserting their own existence. Such a proposition, with its subject and predicate, will be formed only after philosophy has taken a shape,—probably only after sophistry and scepticism have been attacking our original convictions. It is only the metaphysician who will ever take the trouble of affirming that he exists, and the wise metaphysician will refrain from going further and trying to prove that he exists.

Yet it is a conviction which the mind ever carries with it; it is one of the high characteristics of humanity. Inanimate matter is without it. The brute shows that he is tending towards it, yet can have it only in an incipient degree. It is the very essence of the man's individuality,

* "This self-personality, like all other simple and immediate presentations, is indefinable; but it is so, because it is superior to definition. It can be analyzed into no simpler elements, for it is itself the simplest of all; it can be made no clearer by description or comparison, for it is revealed to us in all the clearness of an original intuition, of which description and comparison can furnish only faint and partial resemblances" (Mansel, 'Prolegomena Logica,' p. 129; see also Art. Met. in Encyc. Brit. p. 618, 619, etc.). It was the greatest of all the oversights of Kant that he did not give personality a place among the intuitions of the mind, to which it was entitled quite as much as space and time. Held in by no primary belief in personality, those who came after, such as Fichte, Schelling, and Hegel, wandered out into a wide waste of Pantheism. Taking with them no belief in the personality of self, they never could reach personality in God.

and is one of the main elements in his sense of independence, in his sense of freedom, in his sense of responsibility. As possessing it, man feels that he is independent of physical nature; independent of all creature intelligences; independent, in a sense, of God, against whom, alas! he may rebel, and to whom he must for certain give an account. It is a conviction to be used and not abused. It would certainly be abused were it to seduce man to isolate himself from the objects around him, to try to become independent of the provisions made to aid his weakness in physical nature, or to separate himself from his brothers or sisters of humanity; and still more were it to tempt him to rebel against God. It is properly used when, under the guidance of moral law, it is leading him, not to be ever floating on with the stream, but at times to be standing up in the midst of it and acting as a rampart in its current, or as a martyr seeking to stem the tide of corruption, or Prometheus-like, rising up, not against the true God, but against the false gods who rule in Olympus. Powers hostile to the progress of humanity have sought to subdue this principle. Absolutism would crush it, and make man live for some dominant end, political or ecclesiastical. Pantheism would dissipate it till man became relaxed and lost all individuality, as he moves listlessly in a hot and hazy atmosphere. It is this conviction which makes man feel that he is not a mere bubble on the surface of being, blown up in one chance agitation, and about to be absorbed in another. It keeps man from being lost,—lost in physical nature, lost in the crowd of human beings, or lost in the ocean of being; he is, after and amidst all, *a person.* As such he has a part to perform, an end to serve, a work to do, a destiny to work out, and an account to render.

Sect. VI. On Extension.

The knowledge of extension is involved in every exercise of sense-perception, even as the knowledge of personality is implied in every exercise of self-consciousness. We certainly cannot exercise the senses of sight and muscular energy,—we cannot, I believe, perceive through any of the senses,—without knowing the object, be it the organism or something affecting the organism, as possessing extension—always along with other qualities. This, then, is historically the origin of our idea of extension or space,—that is, we have a perception of it in every cognition of body. But in this primitive knowledge we do not apprehend it as distinct from body. It is an extended and a coloured surface, which we know through the eye; it is an extended body capable of resisting us, which we know through the muscular sense and locomotive energy; it is a set of organs localized and out of each other, that we know by the other senses. But by an easy intellectual act we can separate the extension from the impenetrability and the associated sensations. We are greatly aided in our apprehensions of empty space by certain exercises of sense-perception. For we have experience ever presenting itself of two bodies seen or felt, with nothing between obvious to the senses. True, scientific research shows that the interval is not a pure vacuum, that there is air, or ether, between the bodies; still it is in our apprehension a void,—that is, a space, with no perceived body to fill it. We are thus led to an apprehension of space as different from body occupying space. We are not to look on the extension thus reached as an illusion, a nonentity, or as nothing. If we know, as I maintain we do, body in space, the space must have an existence (I do not say what sort of existence), just as much as the body has.

But when we separately contemplate the extension, we are contemplating a reality just as verily as when we perceive the body. It will not do to dismiss space summarily by describing it as a mere abstraction; in order to our apprehension of it there is need of abstraction, but it is an abstraction of a real part from a real whole.

To this cognition of space, and to every apprehension of it, there is attached a number of intuitive beliefs. It is the business of the metaphysician to unfold these in an inductive manner, and point out and determine their nature and laws as precisely as possible. This falls to be done in another Book of this Treatise, to which therefore I adjourn the further discussion of space, as it embraces a larger faith than it does of a cognitive element in our apprehension of it.

Sect. VII. On Number.

We seem to derive our knowledge of number from our cognition of being, and especially from our cognition of self as a person. We know self as one object; we also know other and external objects as singulars. Already then have we number in the concrete, involved in this our primary knowledge.* Every object known, and especially self, is known as *one*. Every other object known, is known as another *one*. If we know self as *one*, then the external object which is known as different from self, is known as a second *one*. The mind can now think of one object, and of one object + another object, or of two, and of one object + another object + another ob-

* Aristotle places number among the sensibles perceived by the common sense (De An. ii. 6; iii. 1). He says each sense perceives unity: ἑκάστη γὰρ ἓν αἰσθάνεται αἴσθησις (iii. 1. 5 : ed. Trend.). Descartes makes number perceived by us in all perceptions of body (Prin. p. i. 69). Locke says of Unity or One, "Every object our senses are employed about, every idea in our understandings, every thought of our minds, brings this idea along with it" (Essay ii. xvi. 1). Buffier says that the knowledge that *I exist, I am, I think*, is in a sense the same as, or at least includes this, I am *one* (Prem. Vér. p. ii. 10).

ject, or of three. It can then, by a process of abstraction, separate the numbers from the objects, in order to their separate consideration. Not that it supposes for one instant that numbers can exist apart from objects, but it can separately contemplate them. *One* cannot exist apart from one object, or *two* from two objects, but the mind can think about the *one* or the *two* apart from the peculiarity of the objects. Its judgments and its conclusions in all such cases, if conducted according to the laws of thought, will apply to objects; that is, all its judgments regarding one, two, or a thousand, will apply to a corresponding number of objects. Having obtained in this way a knowledge of numbers in the concrete, and numbers in the abstract, the mind is prepared to discover relations among numbers in a manner to be afterwards specified in the book on Primitive Judgments.

But before leaving our present topic, it may be proper to state that the mind has no such conviction of the existence of numbers separate from the objects numbered, as it has of space, distinct from the objects in space, or as it has of time, distinct from the events which happen in time; nor has it any intuitive belief as to the necessary infinity of objects or of numbers. True, it can set no limit to the number of objects, but it is not compelled to believe that there can be no limits, as it is constrained to believe that there can be no bounds to space or to time.

Sect. VIII. On Motion.

Our perception of motion is, as it appears to me, intuitive. But it supposes more than sense, or sense-perception, in the narrow sense of the term. It is probable that we have an apprehension of change of place, from the movement of our intuitively localized organs,—say from a member of the body being moved by the locomotive energy, as when I lift my arm; this perception will be especially apt to arise when we move the hand along organs to which a place has been given. Or we may apprehend an extra-organic body by the touch or muscular sense, and by the same sense feel our hand or some other extra-organic body passing over it. We may also get the perception by the sense of sight. The child touching another part of the body by its hand, will see the image of its hand moving to perform the act. Besides, the "image of our own body occupies, in nearly all pictures on our retina, regularly some determinate space in the upper, middle, or lower part of the field of vision;" it remains constant while the other images are seen moving.* There is more here however than immediate cognition. There is a brief exercise of memory; we must, at the same time that we perceive the body as now in one place, remember that it was formerly in another place. There is an exercise too of comparison in noticing the relation between the object in respect of the place in which it has been, and the place in which it now is. And upon our discovering change of any kind in the motion, the intuition of cause comes in to declare that there must have been active power at work. This is one of those cases which will come before us more and more frequently as we advance, in which cognitions, beliefs, and judgments mingle together; and yet the act can scarcely be described as complex, except in this sense, that on other occasions some of the parts can exist separately or in other combinations. The circumstance that these other elements conjoin in our conviction as to motion, will bring the subject before us in other parts of the Treatise.

* (Müller's Physiology: trans. by Baly, p. 1083.) Aristotle places motion, like number, among the common sensibles, Descartes among the properties perceived in every perception of body (see places in last note), and Locke among the primary qualities of bodies, which are always in them (ii. viii. 22). See some profound observations on motion in 'Logische Untersuchungen v. Trendelenburg,' b. i. iv.

Sect. IX. On Power.

I have been labouring to show, in the last Chapter and in this, that power is involved in our knowledge of substance. We can never know either self, or bodies beyond self, except as exercising influence or potency. Not that we are to suppose that we have thus by intuition an abstract or a general idea of power: all that we have is a knowledge of a given substance acting. This seems the only doctrine in accordance with the revelations of consciousness. It is involved in the common statement that we cannot know substance except by its properties; for what are properties but powers acting when the needful conditions are supplied? I reckon it as an oversight in a great body of metaphysicians that they have been afraid to ascribe our apprehension of power to intuition. In consequence of this neglect, some never get the idea of power, but merely of succession, within the bare limits of experience, which can never entitle us to argue that the world must have proceeded from Divine Power; others have been obliged to find cause, not in any perception of the mind as it looks on things, but in some form imposed by the mind on objects; while a considerable number hesitate and vacillate in their account, representing it now as an original conviction, and now as an acquisition of experience.

Wherever there is power in act, there is an effect. But the discovery of the relation between cause and effect cannot be discovered, except by an exercise of judgment. The discussion of the nature of our conviction of Power will be resumed under the head of Primitive Judgments.

Sect. X. (*Supplementary.*) The various Kinds of Power known by Experience.

We are led by the cognitive nature of the mind to look on substance as necessarily possessing potency, but it is after all by experience that we have to determine the nature of the power exercised by any particular substance. Experience shows us that all potency is not of the same description. The precise nature of the power residing in any one substance is to be ascertained by a generalization of its individual operations. Though it does not fall within our precise province, yet it may help to clear up some important metaphysical questions, if we particularize some of the kinds of potency made known by experience.

I. Force in Inanimate Objects.—In order to the exercise of this potency there is need of two or more bodies in a particular relation to each other. A simple body existing alone in the universe, and in a state of isolation, that is, in no relation to any other body, could exercise no active power whatever. Indeed, the power of a body seems to be a power to influence some other body, or some other substance. It seems also to be a law of the action of bodies that when any one body acts on another, that other acts on it. In all bodily causation there is thus mutual action; and experience seems to show that the action of each of the bodies is equal to that of the other. It is the aim of the physical sciences to determine the nature and measure of this reciprocal operation.

According to this account there is need, in order to material action, of two or more bodies. When these bodies are in such a relation as suits their several properties, action takes place, and an effect is produced. It follows that cause—meaning by cause the invariable and unconditional cause, that which of itself will produce the effect, and ever produce the effect—must always be more or less complex; it always implies two or more bodies in a particular relation to each other. The effect will always be found to be of the same complex character, will always be found to consist of the bodies which acted as a cause, being in some way changed. To illustrate what I mean:—Let us suppose that we have two material substances to experiment with, salt and water. Place the two out of relation to each other, and no effect will be produced. Bring them into contact, and action will commence. The salt acts on the water, and the water on the salt. The cause, properly speaking, of this action is not the salt alone, or the water alone, but the salt and water in a particular relation. This is the true cause, productive and necessary; the cause which, wherever it exists, will tend to produce the same effect, and in fact produce it, except when counteracted by other forces. The effect is also dual, and it is to be found in the very substances which acted as the cause; it is not to be found in the salt, or in the water, or in a third substance, but in the salt and water in a new and different state. This is the invariable effect which will be for ever produced by the same cause.

Such seems to be the nature of material causation and effectuation. In all cases the cause is dual, or plural, as is also the effect; and the bodies which acted as the cause are the bodies acted on in the effect. I am persuaded that the well-known law of action and reaction proceeds on this circumstance, which is also intimately connected with the polar action of substances. In the common statements as to cause and effect there is only one of the elements of the complex cause or complex effect mentioned, the other being omitted because it does not seem needful to express it. Thus we speak of the salt as the cause, making the water of a particular taste as the effect. But there is an omission in all such statements, which require to be completed by calling in the missing part, when we profess to give a thoroughly accurate and philosophic account of the process. There are cases in which the complexity of the cause or of the effect is not so evident as in the example I have given. Thus, if a picture were to fall upon a table and break it, we would say in loose language that the fall of the picture was the cause of the breaking of the table. But when the full cause is spread out, it is seen to be the picture falling with a particular force, and striking the table in a particular direction, while the effect consists not in the breaking of the table merely, but also in the picture losing a portion of its momentum. We have but to reflect for a very little to see and be prepared to acknowledge that in all gravitating action, in all chemical, in all magnetic and electric, there is the co-operation of two or more bodies, and that the cause consists of the bodies in one state and the effects of the same bodies in a different state.*

II. VITAL POWER.—The attempts which have been made to determine wherein life consists cannot be said to have as yet been crowned with anything like success. There is every reason to think that there is a vital power so far different from the mechanical or chemical, but science has not yet ascertained its nature and its laws. So far as we have glimpses of its mode of operation, it seems to involve a complexity of agents. One part of the cell acts on another, or one cell acts on another, or it acts on external matter, and whatever acts is being acted on.

A curious question is here started, What is the nature of the power involved in vegetable and animal reproduction? This

* This subject is illustrated, 'Method of Divine Government,' b. ii. c. i.

is a subject still involved in great mystery, but there are obvious and well-ascertained facts which go to establish a general doctrine.

First, there is a duality in all vital reproduction. In certain portions of the vegetable kingdom, the reproductive powers are in different organs, in others they are on different plants. In the animal creation the reproductive organs are commonly in different individuals, which must therefore pair in order to the production of young. This is an example in a higher scale, and in a more patent form, of that duality in causation which we traced already in inanimate creation, and which makes all physical creation so dependent on arrangements which have been made by the Creator of all things.

Secondly, there is a positive and adequate power in the dual parentage to produce the offspring as an effect. No living creature can proceed except from a parent of its own kind, no vegetable or animal can spring from a vegetable or animal inferior to itself in the order of beings. This is one of the best established generalizations of natural history, and it has not been shaken by any of the attempts which have been made to find exceptions to it, certainly not by the analogies which have been urged against it, derived from objects totally different. The whole of the true analogies of Nature, that is, those derived from objects really correlated, show that every substance or aggregate of substances producing an effect, as it must have power to produce the effect, so it must have power to produce an effect of that particular kind; indeed we cannot conceive that a cause should produce an effect of a higher nature than itself. The parents seem to be endowed with a power to produce an offspring "after their kind," that is, of the same species and no other. There is no power on the part of an inferior plant to produce a higher, on the part of a vegetable to produce an animal, or on the part of an inferior animal to produce a higher. In particular, human beings with intelligences, and such only,—certainly not apes or monkeys,—can have an offspring possessed of reasonable and responsible souls.

This doctrine brings reproduction under laws analogous to those laws of causation which reign in other departments of Nature. The particular mode of the operation of the power has not been and may never be fully determined, but that there is power required, special in kind and adequate in amount, seems to be established on amply sufficient evidence. This doctrine opens to us a glimpse of the deep foundation which the law that the offspring must be of the same species as the parent, has in the very constitution of things, and in the nature of the power that operates in the universe.

III. Reciprocal Action of Mind and Body.—That the two have been so constituted as that the bodily organism acts on mind, while mind is also capable of operating on the organism, this seems to me to be the most satisfactory as it is certainly the simplest account which can be given of the connection. But let us properly understand what, on such a supposition, is the precise cause. It is a complex one in every case; it is the mind and the body in a particular relation to each other. The coexistence of the two is necessary to any effect being produced, and the effect is the result of the two operating and co-operating. Thus in all perception through the senses there is a cerebral power and there is mental power, and without both there will be no result, no object perceived. There seems also to be a duality in the effect: there is certainly a mental effect, for the mind now perceives; and the cerebral mass, in the very act of producing mental action, may undergo a change; thus there seems to be a fatigue and exhaustion produced in the organism by the very act of perceiving an immense number of objects within a brief time, as when we travel a great distance by railway, and this can be accounted for by supposing that the organism is affected by the action which has taken place.

There is a similar duality of power in all those cases in which the action begins from the mind, as when we will to move the arm, and the arm moves. Here the concurrence of two factors is necessary in order to the result: there is a volition, and a nicely adjusted organism in a healthy state; and if either were wanting, the effect would not follow. Possibly, as there is a duality in the cause, there may also be a duality in the effect, and the next mental state may be so far modified by the joint bodily and mental exertion; but I have to add, that it is just as possible that we may have here come into the region of pure mental causation, in which, as we shall see forthwith, there is no such complexity.

In a vast amount of the results of which we are conscious, the concurrence and co-operation both of mental and cerebral potency are required in order to action. Thus it has been proven that a healthy state of the brain is requisite in order to our remembering or even imagining sensible objects; for in certain derangements of the brain the person cannot image an object with a figure. In all such cases the main cause is to be found in the mind; still the body has a part to play, and if it does not co-operate, the effect is not produced. In all those actions in which there is the active operation of the bodily organism, in order to a mental effect, it seems probable that the mental act, or rather the joint act, produces also an effect on the bodily organism which has been in action. In all mental emotion there seems to be involved the active co-operation of a bodily organism, and there is always a reaction on the organism, often in wearying and deranging it, at least when the feeling, say fear or sorrow, is excited by the contemplation of evil. Even in the exercises of the intellect there seems to be a concurrence of organic agency necessary, and there is always a lassitude following long and continuous intellectual efforts. I have sometimes thought that a certain organic state is necessary in order to our very volitions; and hence our incapacity to form a fixed purpose in certain states of the body, and the weariness which follows a long stretch of attention, even when this has been accompanied with no bodily exertions.

I am aware that the account now given of the reciprocal action of mind and body, is exposed to a great amount of questioning. Thus, it will be asked, How does mind act on body, and body on mind? To this I reply by a counter-question, What is meant by 'How'? If nothing more be meant than simply the occurrence of the facts, then I answer that psychological and physiological research has discovered some of the facts, and may possibly detect more, and may very probably never be able to discover the whole. If something more than this be intended, then I ask, What is intended? If it be expected that we find out some mysterious bond between mind and body, I answer that there is no reason to think that there is any such bond, and that if there did exist such a bond, and we could discover it, it would only increase instead of lessening the mystery. The most reasonable and the most simple view is that spirit and body have been so constituted, that is, have had such a nature imparted to them, that they mutually influence each other, and co-operate to produce a joint result.

IV. Mental Action.—We are not to suppose that purely mental is in every respect the same as material action. There is a sense in which every given body is inert and passive, it is active only so far as it is acted on. In this respect there is a wide difference between material and mental power. Material causation implies the presence of two or more bodies, whereas mental causation requires the presence of only one—the self-acting mind. I can think, feel, will, without requiring any external object (always perhaps excepting the organism, in the subordinate sense already referred to) to co-operate with me. The oldest definition of mind handed down to us, embodies a great truth when it describes it as that which moves itself. It can set a train of thought a-going, and modify an existing train by a power within itself. This is one of the prerogatives of mind, eminently characterizing it, and at once distinguishing it from sluggish and passive matter.

But while there is self-acting power within the mind itself, there is a sort of duality or plurality even in mental action. What is the cause of any given state, say of the grief I may be feeling at this present time? I have just heard of the death of a particular individual known to me, and the intelligence apprehended is, no doubt, part of the cause; but it is not the whole of it, for the same news may have been comprehended by another person without producing any such effect. In the unconditional cause there must be included not only the immediate intelligence as apprehended by me, but the affection which I acquired in former years for the individual, and even my original susceptibility of friendship and of grief; the concurrence of all these is necessary in order to this particular state under which I am now labouring. Even here, too, we may discover a kind of duality in the effect, for the result of my cherishing grief at this time is to deepen my affection for my friend, and even to increase my original capacity for affection and sorrow.

V. Causation in the Will.—We have seen that mental action differs widely from material. And we are not to suppose that every mental action is the same in kind as every other. Every faculty of the mind indeed has its own rule and mode of operation, which it is the office of psychological science to ascertain. In particular, causation in the will may differ from causation in other mental action.

I am prepared indeed to maintain that our volitions are not absolutely beyond the law of causation. If I rightly interpret my intuition on the subject of causation, it leads me to look for a cause of our very volitions as well as of our intellectual acts. Besides, as a matter of fact, there have been predictions of voluntary acts, say of crimes, as accurate as of physical events, such as births or deaths. On such grounds as these I am inclined to say that causation must have some sort of place in the will as in all other creature-action. But causation in regard to the will may be of a totally different character from causation in acts of intelligence or feeling.

While our intuition seems to me to say that causation has a place even in voluntary acts, it does not say what is the nature of that causation; this is to be determined by an inductive inquiry into the operations of our voluntary acts. And here we are once met by the fact that man has free will. This fact cannot set aside the other fact that our volitions are caused; but as both are facts, the one must be so stated as to be seen not to be inconsistent with the other. And when we contemplate our volitions by the light of consciousness, we discover at once that causation does not operate in the will as it does in the material universe, or even in our intellectual and emotional actions. Here, I believe, lies the key which is to explain the enigma of the consistency of man's free will and the Divine Sovereignty. We may not be able to find the key, but we can tell the place where it lies.

VI. Divine Causation.—I shrink from entering minutely into the consideration of the action of causation within the Divine Mind. It is evidently a subject which stretches far beyond human discussion or comprehension. But it appears very evident that we are led to look on God as a Substance, having power in himself and the cause of effects produced. Indeed it is from the effects in the universe, and proceeding on an intuitive principle, that we argue that there is a cause above the world. The nature of the causation is in every case to be determined by an inductive investigation of facts, and not by *a priori* speculation. Such an inquiry will soon convince us that causation in the acts of God is not of the same kind as causation in the operations of created objects. In particular there is no need, as in physical nature, of any co-operation in order to the Divine workmanship. "He spake, and it was done: he commanded, and it stood fast." "He said, Let there be light: and there was light." Not only so, but in the original operation of God in the universe, there must have been the exercise of a power, to which we see nothing similar in the actions of any created object. Man cannot create anything absolutely new; he cannot create a new power or property: he can merely modify the old powers; and even this, so far as the external world is concerned, he can do simply by using the power laid up for him in the brain; and all the changes which take place, fall out according to the agencies of Nature. But it is different with God, who must at first have created all things out of nothing; that is, there was a power to create in him, and this power he chose in his infinite wisdom and goodness to exert.

Metaphysicians have often used very absurd language about man's incapacity so much as to conceive of creation. It is quite true that man himself can perform nothing similar to creation, but still he can conceive of it. He can suppose that there was a time when there was no created object, and he can then conceive a world springing into being. He cannot indeed believe that this world started into being without a producing cause, but he is not compelled to believe that it was effected in the same manner as we form a new object, that is, out of pre-existing matter. When I am led, as I am led on good evidence, to look on this world as being produced by God, I can conceive it caused by an immediate exercise of his power. I am not necessarily led to believe that it must have been formed out of Himself or out of any pre-existing substance; it may have been made not out of Himself, but by Himself, by the power that is in Him. Nor am I led to look upon the forces now in the world as existing in some other form in God: to suppose this is to forget that the mode of the operation of causation varies in the case of every order of beings, and to insist that the power exercised by God must be exerted in the same way as creature potency. The mode of the operation of causation when God creates, is quite as accordant with our intuitive belief as the manner in which the forces operate in the mental or material world.

And here I take occasion to remark that the pantheistic doctrine which maintains that the world must have been drawn out of the Divine Substance, of which therefore it participates, receives no sanction whatever from the primary beliefs of the mind. It is simply a rash and unfounded inference from certain experiential facts which are true of the creature, but may have no application to the Creator. Whatever evidence it may profess to advance, it cannot plead intuition; and I may have occasion to show elsewhere that there are intuitions directly opposed to it, especially that intuition which I have of self as a separate intelligence.

There is another and a kindred topic which here opens to the view, but from the minute discussion of which I draw back. I am led to believe that God is a substance, and an unchanging substance, unchanging in the character of His voluntary acts. We have proof that He is a Being of essential holiness, benevolence, and truth, and we further believe that He never will or can do an unrighteous act. On what ground do we cling to this belief? It seems to be founded on the conviction that there may be, that there is, an unchanging substance possessed of moral excellence which never can and never will be defiled by sin, and are we not thus, and this lawfully and properly, carrying up the law of substance and cause to the Divine Being, and making it guarantee for us the eternal righteousness of God?

BOOK II.

PRIMITIVE BELIEFS.

CHAPTER I.

THEIR GENERAL NATURE.

OUR primary cognitions and beliefs are very intimately connected, and they run almost insensibly into each other. Yet they may be distinguished. The word 'cognition,' when we find it needful to separate it from faith, might be confined in strictness to those mental energies in which the mind looks on an object now present,—say on a body perceived by the senses, or on self in a particular state, or on a representation in the mind; and then 'faith' would be applied to all those exercises in which we believe—we can only use a synonymous word when we describe a simple mode of mind—in the existence of an object not now before us, and under immediate inspection.

Philosophers have drawn the distinction between Presentative and Representative Knowledge. In the former the object is present at the time,—we perceive it, we feel it, we are conscious of it as now and here and under our inspection. In Representative Knowledge there is an object now present, representing an absent object. Thus I may have an image or conception of Venice, with its decaying beauty, and this is now present, and under the eye of consciousness; but it represents something absent and distant, of the existence of which I am at the same time convinced. When I was actually in Venice, and gazed on its churches and palaces rising out of the waters, there would be no propriety in saying that I believed in the existence of the city,—the correct phrase is that I knew it to exist. I know, too, that I have at this moment an idea of Venice; but as Venice itself is not before me, the proper expression of my conviction is that I believe in its existence. I maintain that whenever we have passed beyond Presentative Knowledge, and are assured of the reality of an absent object, there faith—it may be in a very simple form, but still real faith—has entered as an element. So far as I am conscious of an imaging of the past, or a judging of it, or a reasoning about it, my mental state is cognition; but so far as I am convinced of the existence of the absent object, my state of mind is belief.*

* The distinction between Presentative and Representative Knowledge is drawn by Hamilton in his edition of Reid, Note B. The view given by me in the text seems to be in accordance with such language as the following, used by him in Metaph. Lect. 12: "Properly speaking, we know only the actual and the present, and all real knowledge is an immediate knowledge. What is said to be mediately known is in truth not known to be, but only believed to be." Speaking of memory, he says: "It is not a knowledge of the past at all, but a knowledge of the present and a belief of the past." Consistently or inconsistently, he says that "belief always precedes knowledge" (Lect. 3). Speaking of the external world, he says: "We believe it to exist, only because we are immediately cognizant of it as existing" (Reid, p. 750). With this I concur. But I cannot agree with what follows, where he seems to found our knowledge on a belief, and represents our knowing that we know as founded on a belief prior to or deeper than, knowledge. "If asked indeed, How do we know that we know it? . . . how do we know that this object is not a mere mode of mind illusively presented to us as a mode of matter? then indeed we must reply that we do not (?) in propriety *know* that what we are compelled to perceive as not-self is not a perception of self, and that we can only on reflection believe such to be the case, in reliance on the original necessity of so believing imposed on us by our nature."

In such examples the faith is of a low order, and need not be distinguished from knowledge, except for the purposes of rigid science; but still faith is there, and there in its essential character; and he who would know what faith is, must view it in these lower forms, "which exist more simple in their elements," as well as in the higher, just as he who would know the nature of the plant or animal must study it in the lichen or zoophyte. These are the incipient movements of a mental power which is capable of rising to the greatest heights of earth, and looking up to the heaven above, which can call before it all time, and go forth even into the eternity beyond. Already do we see how it joins on to cognition, and mingles with it. Faith, as the telescope, shows objects which unaided sense cannot discern, but still there is personal knowledge, an eye to guarantee the accuracy of the vision. We have immediate knowledge always with us, we have self in a particular state or exercise; but rising from this, we believe in an object which is absent,—in the loftier energies of faith we believe in objects which we have never seen, and which we never can see in this world.

According to this account we are said to know ourselves, and the objects presented to the senses and the representations (always however as presentations) in the mind, but to believe in objects which we have seen in time past, but which are not now present, and in objects which we have never seen, and very specially in objects which we can never fully know, such as an Infinite God. The mind seems to begin not with faith, but with cognition. It sets out with the knowledge of an external object presented to it, and with a knowledge of self contemplating that object. I cannot, then, agree with those who maintain that faith—I mean natural faith—must precede knowledge. I hold that knowledge, psychologically considered, appears first, and then faith. But around our original cognition there grows and clusters a body of primitive beliefs which go out far beyond our personal knowledge. Knowledge is, after all, the root; but from this stable and more earthly ground there spring beliefs which mount in living power and in lovely form and colour toward the sky.*

The two differ psychologically, and there are important philosophic ends to be served by distinguishing between them; but after all it is more important to fix our attention on their points of agreement and coincidence. The belief has a basis of cognition, the cognition has a superstructure of beliefs. In a sense we know space, for it is present to us; certainly body occupying space is ever before the senses, but when we look on space as having no bounds, we are beyond the territory of cognition, we are in the region of faith. The one conviction, equally with the other, carries within itself its authority and validity. No man is entitled to restrict himself to cognitions, and refuse to attend or to yield to the beliefs which he is also led to entertain by the very constitution of his mind. No man can do so, in fact. Every man must act upon his native beliefs as well as upon his cognitions. He requires no external consideration to lead him to trust in the one any more than in the other, for each has its sufficiency in itself. He

* There were profound discussions in the scholastic ages as to the separate provinces of faith and knowledge or reason, but it was in regard to matters of religion, and specially of revelation, including Church authority. Anselm gave the first, or deeper place, to faith, and Abelard to knowledge. But there was confusion in the controversy, owing to its not being determined psychologically what is the precise difference of knowledge and faith, and of reason and faith. In every exercise of mind about the great objects and truths of religion, there must be both cognitive and faith (psychological) elements embraced, and reason always comprises faith when it refers to the existence of objects. The relation of faith and reason will fall to be discussed in the last Chapter of this Volume.

who would weakly give up his native faiths because assaults are made on them, and doggedly resolve to yield to nothing but immediate cognitions, will find that the sceptic who has driven him from the beliefs will go on to attack the cognitions likewise, and that he can defend the cognitions only on grounds which might have enabled him to stand by his credences likewise. On the other hand, I grieve over the attempts, for the last age or two, of a school of thinkers who labour to prove that the understanding or the speculative reason leads to scepticism and nihilism, and then appeal to faith to save us from the abyss before us. I have no toleration for those who tell us with a sigh, too often of affectation, that they are very sorry that knowledge or reason leads to contradictions and insoluble doubts, from which they are longing to be delivered by some mysterious faith. It is time to put an end to this worse than civil strife, to this setting of one part of the soul against another. I do not believe that the understanding, or the reason, or any other power of the mind, lands us in scepticism. Each cognitive faculty conducts in its own way to its own truths. The intelligence and the faith are not conflicting, but conspiring elements. I am sure that the criticism which has attacked the knowledge, would, if followed out, be no less formidable in its assaults on the belief. In these pages I am endeavouring to show how they concur and co-operate, being almost always associated in one concrete act, which we analyze merely for scientific ends.*

* Kant laboured to demonstrate that the Speculative Reason lands us in contradictions, and was not given us in order to reach objective truth; but then he called in a Practical Reason, which guaranteed a moral law, a God, and immortality. See the 'Methodenlehre' in the 'Kritik.' Jacobi admitted, far too readily, to Kant and Fichte, that speculation and philosophy led to scepticism, but he fell back on Faith (*Glaube*) or Sentiment (*Gefühl*), which he represented as a Revelation (*Offenbarung*). See his 'David Hume: Ueber den Glauben,' and 'Jacobi an Fichte.' He has given views of intuition and of faith as true

But while we must yield to our intuitive beliefs as well as perceptions, we are not therefore to suppose that our faiths are beyond inspection and above examination. They are liable to be tried, and should at times be tried, by the very same tests as our cognitions. We are not to allow ourselves, without examination and without review, to yield to whatever may suggest itself to our own minds, or be recommended to us by others, as a primitive belief. We must try the spirits, whether they are of God. In nothing is man so apt to run into excess and extravagance, into folly and error, as yielding to plausible beliefs. The tendency of faith is upwards, but it needs weights and plummets to hold it down, lest it mount into a region of thin air, and there burst and dissolve. Fortunately we have a ready means at hand of trying our constitutional beliefs, and determining for us when

as they are beautiful; but he has not unfolded the precise nature of faith, nor seen its relation to the understanding. Even Fichte, after trying to show that knowledge (*Wissen*) leads to an absolute idealism, in which we know not whether our very thought may not be a dream, resorts to Faith (*Glaube*), and allows an appeal to the Heart (*Herz*) (Bestimmung des Menschen, Buch iii. Glaube). Sir W. Hamilton maintains that "all that we know is phenomenal of the unknown" (Discuss. p. 644, 2nd ed.), and that "the knowledge of Nothing is the principle or result of all true philosophy" (p. 609), but delights to recognize a faith which looks beyond; of which faith, however, he gives no account. "We are warned," he says, "from recognizing the domain of our knowledge as necessarily co-extensive with the horizon of our faith." And he adds, "And by a wonderful revelation, we are thus, in the very consciousness of our inability to conceive aught above the relative and finite, inspired with a belief in the existence of something unconditioned, beyond the sphere of all comprehensive reality" (p. 15). Ever since the days of Schleiermacher, there has been a body of theologians who in the very same spirit admit that the existence of God cannot be established by human intelligence, and who call in a God-consciousness, or a faith, to reveal God to us. I admit that intuition and faith have their part to act, but so also has the understanding. (See *infra*, Part III. Book II. Chap. V.) For an account of the German systems, see Michelet, 'Entwickelungsgeschichte;' Chalybäus, Hist. Entwick. d. Specul. Philos. von Kant bis Hegel; Willm, Hist. Phil. Allemande, and Morell's limpidly clear 'History of Speculative Philosophy.'

they should be disallowed, and when they should be allowed to flow out freely. Are they self-evident? Are they necessary, so necessary that we cannot believe the opposite? Are they universal? These three questions, searchingly asked and honestly answered, will settle for us whether we ought or whether we ought not to follow a belief proffered to our acceptance. We are at liberty to employ a belief in argument, appeal, and speculation, only under the same conditions as a cognition; that is, having shown that it is a constitutional one, we must further determine more accurately its nature and law, its extent and limits. Thus, and thus only, can we hope on the one hand to be kept from mistaking our own fancies, misapprehensions, wishes, or prejudices, for primitive and heaven-born beliefs, and on the other hand be justified in appealing to the faiths which have the sanction of our constitution, and the God who gave us our constitution, and in using them as a basis on which to rear a fabric of philosophical, or ethical, or theological truths.

CHAPTER II.

TIME AND SPACE.

Of space in the concrete we have an immediate knowledge; that is, by the senses, certainly by some of them, such as the touch and the sight, most probably by all of them, we know bodies, say our own bodily organism as extended, that is, as occupying space. By abstraction we can fix our attention on the space as distinct from associated qualities, and by inward reflection we can gather what are the convictions attached. These convictions pass beyond knowledge proper, and become beliefs, that is, convictions in regard to something which we do not immediately know, nay, which we may never be able to know.

With time, also, we have an immediate acquaintance. In sense-perception and self-consciousness we know a particular object or mental state as now present. Our consciousness is continuous; speedily does immediate consciousness slide into memory; the present becomes past, and is remembered as past. The child's organism is now in a state of pain; immediately after the pain is gone, but the pain of the past is remembered, and remembered as being past. Already, then, there is the idea of time always in the concrete. We remember something as having been under our consciousness in the past. By abstraction we can then think of the time as different from the event remembered in time; and by introspection we can ascertain the nature of the attached convictions. Many of these are of the nature of faiths going far beyond what is, or ever can be, immediately known.

Space and time mingle with all our perceptions. Yet after all we can say little about them; all that we can do as metaphysicians is to analyze and express our original convictions. It belongs to the mathematician to evolve deductively what is involved in certain of them. In unfolding the necessary convictions we may make the following affirmations.

I. Time and space have a reality independent of the percipient mind, and out of the percipient mind. The intelligence does not create them, it discovers them, and it discovers them as having an existence independent of the mind contemplating them, as having this existence whether the mind contemplates them or no, and an existence out of and beyond the mind as it thinks of them. He who denies this is in the very act setting aside one of the clearest of native principles, and has left himself no stand-point from which he can repel any proposal suggested to himself or offered by another, to set aside any other conviction, or all other convictions. If some one affirm that space has no objective existence, he leaves it competent for any other coming after him, to maintain that the objects perceived in space have no reality. He who allows that time may have no reality except in the contemplative mind, will find himself greatly troubled to answer the sceptic, when he insists that the events in time are quite as unreal as the time is in which they are perceived as having occurred. There is only one sure and consistent mode of avoiding these troublesome and dangerous consequences, and that is by standing up for the veracity of all our fundamental perceptions, and, among others, of our convictions regarding the reality of space and time.

According to Kant, space and time are the forms given by the mind to the phenomena which are presented through the senses, and are not to be considered as having anything more than a subjective existence. It is one of the most fatal heresies—that is, dogmas opposed to the revelations of consciousness—ever introduced into philosophy, and it lies at the basis of all the aberrations in the school of speculation which followed. For those who were taught that the mind could create the space and time, soon learned to suppose that the mind could also create the objects and events cognized as in space and time, till the whole external universe became ideal, and all reality was supposed to lie in a series of connected mental forms. He who would arrest the stream, must seek to stop it at the place whence it flowed out; otherwise all his efforts will be ineffectual.*

* Dr. Thomas Brown, in an article on Villers, 'Philosophie de Kant,' in No. 2 (1803) of the 'Edinburgh Review,' dwells on this.

II. Space and time are continuous, that is, they extend out, flow on, without break, separation, or interruption. In this respect they are different from matter or body, which may be broken into parts, and the parts separated from each other. But there can be no gaps in space, no cessation in time.

This is one of several circumstances which has made space and time to be classed together. Yet while they may be grouped under one head, they are not identical, and they have their points of difference. In particular, space has three dimensions,—length, breadth, and depth;

"The truth of space and of the world being to our reasoning scepticism the same, we cannot deny space and admit the reality of sensible objects." D. Stewart, after affirming that the idea of space "is manifestly accompanied with an irresistible conviction that space is necessarily existent, and that its annihilation is impossible," adds, "to call this proposition in question, is to open a door to universal scepticism" (Disser. p. 597). In our day we find the greatest opponent of the Dialectic of Hegel who has appeared, taking the same view. "Hiernach sind Raum und Zeit etwas Subjectives und zwar nach Kant etwas nur Subjectives. Wenn dies folgt, so verflüchtet sich damit die ganze Weltansicht in Erscheinung, und Erscheinung ist vom Scheine nicht weit entfernt. Wenn Raum und Zeit nur und ausschliessend Subjectives sind, so drängt sich allenthalben diese Zuthat ein. Wie die Luftschicht zwischen dem Auge und dem Gegenstande, wirft sie auf alles eine fremde Trübung; denn alles erscheint in Raum und Zeit, die nur aus uns geboren sind. Wir erkennen nun nichts an sich; denn die Verstandesbegriffe haben (nach Kant) nur Anwendung durch diese Formen der Anschauung und die Vernunftbegriffe suchen wieder nur eine Einheit für die Verstandeserkenntniss. Wie wollen wir uns von dem Zauberkreise lösen, da er vielmehr unser eigenstes Wesen est?" (Trendelenburg, 'Logische Untersuchungen,' b. i. v.). Sir W. Hamilton agrees with Kant as to the *a priori* idea of space, and to avoid the difficulties calls in an *a posteriori* notion:—"We have a twofold cognition of space; (*a*) an *a priori* or *native* imagination of it in general, as a necessary condition of the possibility of thought; and (*b*) under that an *a posteriori* or *adventitious* percept of it, in particular as contingently apprehended in this or that complexus of sensations" (Reid's Works, p. 882). "In this I venture a step beyond Reid and Stewart, no less than beyond Kant" (p. 126). A simpler and a more natural account of the relations between *a priori* and *a posteriori* would bring these two notions to a unity.

that is, we may contemplate it as extending along any given line, as spreading out in a surface, or as going out in all directions. Time again has only succession, or priority and posteriority. We often apply to time language derived from space, and we represent time as a line, and speak of it as being only in one direction. But it is to be remembered that such language is used metaphorically, and has no literal meaning as applied to time. Still it points to a truth, and specifies a difference between space and time.* But in regard to their extension or flow, both are continuous, and spread out or run on without a possible division.

But it will be urged, that the question is often discussed as to whether space and time are infinitely divisible, and that certain mathematicians maintain that they have demonstrated the infinite divisibility of space. In looking at this question, it is desirable first of all to have it settled in what sense extension is capable of division. We cannot divide space in the sense in which we divide matter. In dividing body we separate one part of it from another, so as to leave a space between. We can thus divide an apple, and keep one part of it in our hand, and put the other in our mouth. But we cannot thus separate or isolate space apart from space. In the sense of separation, we cannot with propriety speak of the infinite divisibility of space, for it is not divisible at all,

* It has been asked why the mind gives three dimensions to space and only one to time. Those who regard space and time as the creation of the mind, may amuse themselves with answering this question. There is profound sense in the following remarks of Sir J. Herschel, in his 'Review of Whewell' (Essays, p. 202):—"The reason, we conceive, why we apprehend things without us, is that they *are* without us. We take it for granted that they exist in space, because they *do* so exist, and because such their existence is a matter of direct perception, which can neither be explained in words nor contravened in imagination; because, in short, space is a *reality*." "That which has parts, proportions, and susceptibilities of exact measurement, must be a 'thing.'"

either finitely or infinitely. The same remark holds good of time. The mind declares that the separation of space from space, or of time from time, is impossible in the nature of things.*

There may however be relations discovered both in space and time. We can conceive of less or more of extension, and of proportions between the less and the more; the one may be twice or ten times as much as the other. All this we are allowed, nay necessitated, to think. The science which treats of quantity, that is, mathematics, has specially to do with their relations. There may be little or no impropriety in calling these proportions parts, provided we do not misunderstand the language we employ, or understand it as implying that between two spaces there can be an interval in which there is no space. What is meant by the infinite division of space seems to be, that fixing our thoughts on any given section or proportion of space, say the thousandth part of an inch, we are at liberty to conceive of the half of it, and again of the half of the quotient, and so on indefinitely as far as may serve our purpose or we may choose. Some of these subjects will be resumed when we come to consider those primitive judgments which relate to quantity.

But before leaving the subject immediately before us, it is of importance to have it noticed that our convictions say nothing whatever on (what is a very different matter from the divisibility of space, though the two have often been confounded) the infinite divisibility of matter. This latter is a question which can be settled by nothing but experience; experience at this present stage of science says nothing whatever on the subject, and I suspect will never be able to settle it on one side or other. There might be limits to man's capacity of dividing body which

* This view is developed with great acuteness in Gillespie's 'Necessary Existence of Deity' (Exam. Antith. Refut. p. iii.).

would not be limits to other beings, and whether there could be any limits to a Being of Infinite Power is a question which it transcends our faculties to answer, and which therefore we should not attempt to answer.

But the difficulty has been started, are space and time made up of parts? and if so, are infinite time and space made up of parts? To this I reply, first and decisively, that we cannot conceive them as made up of partitions, or separable parts, as an apple or an orange is, or as the earth is, or the sun is. But then, secondly, we can conceive proportion in space and time, and if we take any of these proportional sections, and divide it into two, thought will compel us to say that the two must make up the whole. In this sense the parts make up the whole, that is, the subsections make up the section. If the question be extended beyond this, and it be asked, Is infinite space made up of parts? I answer, that as we can have no adequate notion of infinite space, so we cannot be expected to answer all the questions which may be put regarding it. It is certain that neither infinite space nor finite space is made up of separable parts. We can speak intelligibly of proportions in finite space, and determine their relations to each other and the whole. I tremble to speak of the proportions of infinite space, lest I be using language which has or can have no proper meaning, and the signification attached to which by me or others might be altogether inapplicable to such a subject. Still there are propositions which we might intelligibly use. It is self-evident that any proportion of space must be less than infinite space. And if infinite space can be conceived as having proportions, and we could conceive all these proportions, then these proportions would be equal to the whole. But as we cannot adequately conceive the whole, so neither can we conceive of the proportions of the whole. We are in a region dark and pathless and directionless, and we may as well draw back at once, for nothing is to be gained by advancing.* We are on the verge of another subject, to which we must turn.

III. Space and time have and can have no limits. Nor is this a mere negative proposition, as some have declared it to be; it is a positive affirmation that to whatever point we go, in reality or in imagination, there must be a space and time beyond. Nor is it, as it has been represented, an impotency of mind. It is not a mere incapacity to conceive that when we go a certain length back or forward in time, or out into space, there time and space should cease. It is a conviction of a positive kind, that beyond these points, or beyond any other space conceivable, there must still be time and space. This, as will be shown more fully forthwith, is a truth self-evident, necessary, universal. If we were carried out to the utmost point to which the furthest-seeing telescope can reach, or beyond this as far as imagination can range, we should confidently stretch forth our hand into an outer region, believing that there must be space into which it might enter, and that if it were hindered, it must be by body occupying space.

There is more than this embraced in our native conviction. We are constrained to believe, as to the space and time which we know in part, and which we are constrained to regard as beyond our power of imagination, that they are such that no addition could be made to them. This is a further and a most important element in our conviction. We intuitively know space and time: with this we start. Looking to the space and time which we

* "Non igitur respondere curabimus iis, qui quærunt an si daretur linea infinita, ejus media pars esset etiam infinita; vel an numerus infinitus sit par anve impar; et talia; quia de iis nulli videntur debere cogitare nisi qui mentem suam infinitam esse arbitrantur" (Descartes, Prin. p. i. 26).

thus know, we are constrained to regard them as ever going beyond our image of them. But we do more, we are convinced that they are such in their very nature, that no further space and time could be added to them. Join these elements together, and so far as I can discover by reflection on the operations of my own mind, we have the conception and belief which the mind of man is able to attain as to the infinity of space and time.

But we are already in the heart of the subject of the infinite, to which a separate Section must be allotted. In this Section we have yet to take up certain difficulties which press on us when we contemplate space and time. We may have occasion to show, at a later part of this work, that our very cognitions often land us in mysteries, that is, in propositions to which we must assent, but which have bearings which we cannot comprehend. To a still greater extent is it of the nature of faith ever to be going out into darkness. For the truths believed in may not be fully comprehended in themselves, and their relations may be altogether beyond our ken. It should be frankly acknowledged that we are landed in mysteries which the human intellect cannot explicate, whenever we inquire beyond the narrow limits within which our convictions restrain us. But it is of all courses the most foolish and suicidal to urge the difficulties connected with space and time as a reason for setting aside our intuitive convictions respecting them, say in regard to their reality. Doubtless we are landed in some perplexities by allowing that they are real, but we are landed in more hopeless difficulties and in far more serious consequences, when we deny their reality; and there is this important difference between the cases, that in the one the difficulties arise from the nature of the subject, whereas in the other they are created by our own unwarranted affirmations and speculations.

But what *are* space and time? is the question that will be pressed on us. To this I reply, that it is true of them, as of the objects of every other intuitive conviction, that we cannot explain them except by referring to our original perception. All that has been attempted in this Section is to bring out clearly what is involved in the perception.

But it will be asked, Are they substances, are they modes, or are they relations? To this I reply, that these questions relate not so much to the nature of space or time as the classification of them, and that they are not to be classified with substances, modes, or relations.* We cannot call them substances, for we do not know that they have power or action. Nor can we call them modes, for we have no intuitive knowledge of any substance in which they inhere. And they are certainly more than relations of one thing to another, for we know no two or more things which by their relation could yield space and time. They are not then to be arranged with such cognitions as these. They seem indeed to be entitled to be put in a class by themselves, and resemble substances, modes, relations, only in that they are existences, entities, realities.

Certain mystical divines and philosophers are accustomed to speak of space and time as having no reality to

* Leibnitz held space and time to be relations given to objects by the mind. "Je tenois l'Espace pour quelque de PUREMENT RELATIF, comme le Temps; pour un ORDRE DE COEXISTENCES, comme le Temps est un ORDRE DE SUCCESSIONS" (Op. p. 752. See also pp. 756, 769, 461). He speaks of space and time as being "rapports," and as "idéal." Leibnitz thus prepared the way for the more systematic doctrine of Kant. Samuel Clarke argues powerfully that space and time are realities, but makes them attributes, properties, or modes, of an eternal substance (see his Letters to Leibnitz). D. Stewart, with his usual wisdom, says that "space is neither a *substance*, nor an *accident*, nor a *relation*;" adding, "But it does not follow from this that it is nothing objective" (Dissert. p. 596).

the Divine mind. It follows, I think, that if they have no reality to the God who knows all truth, they can, properly speaking, have no reality at all. If our convictions testify (as I have endeavoured to show) that they have a reality, it follows, I think, that they have a reality to the Divine mind. Again, there are some who talk of an Eternal Now :—

> "Nothing is there to come, and nothing past,
> But an Eternal Now does ever last."

These verses of Cowley embody, as definitely as can be done, a view which has often been floating in the statements of divines in speaking of God and Eternity and Time. But the language has either no meaning, or if it has, it lands us in hopeless contradictions.

It would have been very different if divines had contented themselves with stating that they do not know how space and time stand related to the Divine mind. We are here in the midst of a mystery, which we have no faculties to clear up. We know that space and time exist; we know on sufficient evidence that God exists: but we have no means of knowing how space and time stand related to God. The view taken by Sir Isaac Newton,—"Deus durat semper et adest ubique, et, existendo semper et ubique, durationem et spatium constituit,"*—is certainly a grand one, but I doubt much whether human intelligence can dictatorially affirm that it is as true as it is sublime.

It is by placing the subject beyond the human faculties that we are able to meet an objection urged with great logical power by Kant, and usually thought to be insuperable.† If space and time be real and infinite, then we have two infinites; and if God be also infinite, our difficulties are increased. For it is absurd, if not

* Scholium at close of Phil. Nat. Prin. Math.

† Kr. d. r. Vern., Die transcen. Aesthet.

contradictory, to suppose that there can be two infinite things—that God can be infinite while space and time are also infinites. Now to this I might without the possibility of a positive refutation, urge that there may, for aught we know, be nothing inconsistent in supposing that there are two things, as space and time, the one unbounded and the other without beginning or end, and that there can even be nothing contradictory in supposing that space and time on the one hand, and God on the other, may have infinite attributes. They could be held as contradictory only in the supposition that the existence of unbounded space and unending time were, in the nature of things, inconsistent with the existence of an infinite God; which it may safely be said can never be proven. As to how they could subsist together, is a question we are not obliged to answer, for we must believe many separate truths, each on its evidence, without being able to trace a connection, or being able so much as to say that there is a *how* between them. But I plant myself on far firmer ground, when I maintain, secondly, that while I believe that space and time are infinite, and that God is infinite, I am not necessarily obliged to hold that the infinity of space and time is independent of the infinity of God. Who will venture to affirm that the statement we have quoted from the great Newton may not be true? Who will venture to affirm that space and time, being dependent on God, may not stand in a relation to God, which is altogether indefinable and utterly inconceivable by us? True we are constrained to believe that space and time have an existence independent of us, but we are not compelled to believe that they have an existence independent of everything else, and least of all independent of God. In such a subject, where we have no light from intuition or from experience to guide us, true wisdom shows itself in refusing to assert or dogmatize, or even to speculate; and when it has observed this rule for itself, it is the better able to rebuke doubt and scepticism, when they would bring forth their difficulties from regions which are beyond the reach of human knowledge.

CHAPTER III.

THE INFINITE.

The subject now opening before us is a profound one in itself, and has exercised the profoundest minds ever since thought began the attempt to solve the problems of the universe. All that I profess to do is to endeavour to discover by induction what is the mind's conviction in regard to infinity. *A priori* cogitation is not to be tolerated in its proffered determinations of what our idea of Infinity should be or must be. Logical dissection and division, instead of aiding, may only lead us into hopeless difficulties. Lofty generalizations embracing all other objects, may have no application to an object which from its very nature must be *sui generis.*

This belief, like every other, will be found to grow out of a cognition, and to have an apprehension or conception as a body round which it gathers. Yet it should be admitted as

Preliminary, *that we cannot form an adequate idea or conception of an infinite object.** It is a favourite position of certain British philosophers, that the mind of man can form no conception of the infinite, or that the

* I regard this truth as established by Locke (Essay ii. xvii). Sir W. Hamilton has overthrown those gigantic systems which proceed on an opposite view (see his 'Philosophy of the Unconditioned'). At the

conception is at best negative. There is a great truth, but we shall show that there is also a fatal oversight, in this statement.

First, it may be admitted that the mind can form no apprehension of the infinite, in the sense of image or phantasm. In saying so, I do not mean merely that we cannot construct a mental picture of the infinite as an attribute. Of no quality can the mind fashion a picture; it cannot have a mental representation of transparency, apart from a transparent substance, and just as little can it picture to itself infinity apart from an infinite duration, or infinite extension, or an infinite God. But it is not in this sense simply that the mind cannot apprehend the infinite, it cannot have before it an apprehension of an infinite object, say of an infinite space, or an infinite God. For to image a thing in our mind is to give it an extent and a boundary. When we would image unlimited space, we swell out an immense volume, but it has after all a boundary, commonly a spherical one. When we would picture unlimited time, we let out an immense line behind and before, but the rope is after all cut at both ends. When we would represent to ourselves almighty power, we call up some given act of God, say creating or annihilating the universe; but after all, the work has a measure, and may be finished. In the sense of image, then, the mind cannot have any proper apprehension of infinity as an attribute, or of an infinite object.

But apprehension may be considered as an act of the understanding as well as a mere act of the phantasy. We can conceive, we can think about much, which we cannot image. We can meditate and reason about such

same time I do not think that either Locke or Hamilton has given a full exposition of the mind's intuitive conviction respecting infinity. Mr. Calderwood opposes the views of Hamilton, but is obliged to admit that we have not an adequate conception of the infinite (see 'Philosophy of the Infinite').

things as law, government, duty, religion, while yet we can form no mental picture of them. The grand question in this discussion is, Can we form an intellectual notion of an infinite object, say of an infinite God? And I feel constrained to admit and maintain that human intelligence can form no proper or adequate conception of an infinite existence. By what process can it be supposed to construct such a conception? Certainly not by abstraction, for abstraction separates, takes away, diminishes. It is just as certain that it cannot compass this end by generalization, for generalization merely groups objects by attributes known, and unless we have infinity first in the individual, we cannot have it in the general. Nor can we reach it by addition, multiplication, composition; these will give the enlarged, but not the unlimited: a distance of a quintillion of quintillions of years, or ages, has as distinct a boundary as an ell or an inch. Nor can the understanding attain it by a process of ratiocination, for unless the infinite were in the premiss, no canon of reasoning would justify its having a place in the conclusion. If the intelligence does not find the infinite in the perception with which it sets out, it never could fashion it by cutting or carving, by construction or supraposition.

But it may be said that we have an apprehension, or conception, or perception of the infinite by intuition. I am about to show that we have a conviction in regard to infinity of a very deep and positive character. But I am at present arguing that this does not take the shape of an adequate mental representation or logical notion. What is its nature is to be determined solely by a process of inward observation, and this I am now endeavouring to conduct.

I. We have an intuitive belief in regard to the infinity of certain objects. Let me endeavour to unfold it. I have allowed that we cannot have an idea of infinite space or time, in the sense of imaging, picturing, or representing them. Stretch itself as it may, the imaging power of the mind can never go beyond an expansion, with a boundary, commonly a globe or sphere of which self is the centre, and duration stretching along like a line, but with a beginning and an end. In respect then of the mental picture or representation, the apprehension is merely of the very large or the very long, but still of the finite, of what might be called the indefinite, but not the infinite. But any account of our conviction as to infinity which goes no further, leaves out the main, the peculiar element. The sailor is not led by any native instinct to believe that the ocean has no bottom, simply because in letting down the sounding-line he has not reached the ground. When the astronomer has gauged space as far as his telescope can penetrate, he finds that there are still stars and clusters of stars, but he is not necessitated to believe that there must be star after star on and for ever. The geologist in going down from layer to layer still finds signs of the existence of a previous earth, but he is not obliged to conclude that there must have been stratum before stratum from all eternity. But man is constrained to believe that whatever be the point of space or time to which his eye or his thoughts may reach, there must be a space and time beyond. Whence this belief of the mind on space and time being presented to it? Whence this necessity of thought or belief? This is the very phenomenon to be accounted for; and yet the British school of metaphysicians can scarcely be said to have contemplated it seriously or steadfastly with the view of unfolding the depth of meaning embraced in it.* It implies that to whatever point

* Locke was prevented by the defects of his theory and his antipathy to innate ideas from developing all that is in our conviction of infi-

of space or time we might go in our persons or in our fancy, there would still be a space and a time beyond. I can easily, in imagination, go out as far as the rim of the earth, or as the moon, or as the sun, or as the nearest star, or as the furthest star seen by the eye, or as the remotest star discovered as a speck in a nebulous cloud of light by the telescope, but when there, I must believe that space still goes on, and that if I were carried ten thousand million times further there would still be space. I can represent to myself the instant of time when man was created, and beyond this the time when the lion or the worm, or the palm or the lichen, were created, or when the earth or the angels were created; but though this period were multiplied by itself millions

nity. Yet, while he maintains that our idea of the infinite is negative, he admits "that it has something of positive in all those things we apply to it, inasmuch as the mind comprehends so much of the object" (Essay ii. xvii. 15). He even admits, though rather incidentally, that the mind has a necessary conviction as to the existence of an infinite. Thus, speaking of space, he says the mind "must necessarily conclude it, by the very Nature and *Idea* of each part of it, to be actually infinite" (4). Again, "I think it unavoidable for every considering rational creature that will but examine his own, or any other existence, to have the notion of an eternal wise Being who had no beginning; and such an *Idea* of infinite duration I am sure I have" (17). It is to be regretted that Locke never unfolded all that is contained in these "necessary" and "unavoidable" mental processes. Hamilton represents the notion of infinity as an "impotency" of the mind, an impotency to conceive that space and time should have bounds. I am endeavouring to show in these paragraphs that there is more than this. Hamilton admits that we have a belief in the infinite. "The sphere of our belief is much more extensive than the sphere of our knowledge; and therefore when I deny that the Infinite can by us be *known*, I am far from denying that by us it is, must, and ought to be believed. This I have indeed anxiously evinced both by reason and authority" (Metaph. vol. ii. App. p. 530). Handing us over in this way to belief, he has nowhere explained the psychological nature of this belief, or of belief in general. Must not a belief in a thing of which we have no conception be a belief in *zero?* He maintains that our conceptions as to the infinite land us in contradictions. "We are altogether unable to conceive space as bounded, as finite; that is, as a whole beyond which there

of billions of trillions of times, I not only cannot believe that duration did then begin, I am constrained to believe that it did not and could not then commence. This intuitive belief, accompanied as it is with a stringent necessity of feeling, is the very peculiarity of the mind's conviction in regard to infinity, as it is one of the grandest characteristics of human intelligence. It should be added that it is a power which ever impresses man with his powerlessness.

This conviction has the characters and can bear the tests of intuition. It is self-evident. Indeed, if it did not shine in its own light, it could never be seen in any other which we might hold up to it. It can stand the test of necessity. It is necessary, we must believe it

is no further space." "On the other hand, we are equally powerless to realize in thought the possibility of the opposite contradictory. We cannot conceive space infinite, or without bound" (Metaph. Lect. 38). I may be permitted to quote the criticism I have offered on this seeming contradiction in a review of Hamilton in Dub. Univ. Mag., Aug. 1859. "The seeming contradiction here arises from the double sense in which the word 'conceive' is used. In the second of these counter-propositions the word is used in the sense of imaging, or representing in consciousness, as when the mind's eye pictures a fish or a mermaid. In this signification we cannot have an idea or notion of the infinite. But the thinking, judging, believing power of the mind is not the same as the imaging power. The mind can think of the class fish, or even of the imaginary class mermaid, while it cannot picture the class. Now, in the first of the opposed propositions, the word 'conceive' is taken in the sense of thinking, deciding, being convinced. We picture space as bounded, but we cannot think, judge, or believe it to be bounded. When thus explained, all appearance of contradiction disappears; indeed, all the contradictions which the Kantians, Hegelians, and Hamiltonians are so fond of discovering between our intuitive convictions will vanish, if we but carefully inquire into the nature of the convictions. Both propositions, when rightly understood, are true, and there is no contradiction. They stand thus:—'We cannot image space as without bounds;' 'we cannot think that it has bounds, or believe that it has no bounds.' The former may well be represented as a creature impotency; the latter is most assuredly a creature potency, is one of the most elevated and elevating convictions of which the mind is possessed, and is a conviction of which it can never be shorn."

when our intelligence is directed towards it. We cannot be made to believe otherwise, or that there is a limit to immensity and duration. It is, when properly understood, universal. The image, it is true, of space or time, formed by the boy or savage, may be very contracted. The widest space of which he has had any experience may be the glorious dome spread over his head in the sky, and his imagination may be able to go very little beyond the visible heavens or the distant hills which bound his view, still he is sure that beyond there must be something, an "outer infinite," and perhaps he will be eager to know what is beyond his horizon. His idea of time, as a positive picture, may extend no further than the date of the oldest story which his grandfather has told him; but he is sure that at that point duration did not begin, and he may be interested to know what happened before.

"Heaven lies about us in our infancy.

. . . .

Hence in a season of calm weather,
  Though inland far we be,
Our souls have sight of that immortal sea
    Which brought us hither,
  Can in a moment travel thither,
And see the children sport upon the shore,
And hear the mighty waters rolling evermore."

But this is not all that is contained in our conviction. We are constrained to believe, in regard to the objects which we look upon as infinite, that they are incapable of augmentation. Here, as in every apprehension which we have of infinity, the imaging power of the mind fails and must fail; still we have an image and an intellectual conception—say, an image with a notion of extension, or duration, or Deity. Or we represent to ourselves the Divine Being, with certain attributes,—say, as wise or as good,—and our belief as to Him and these attributes is, that he cannot be wiser or better. This aspect may be appropriately designated as the Perfect. This is the conviction of the Perfect, of which many profound philosophers make so much, but not more, as I think, than they are entitled to do; though they have not, as it appears to me, always given the correct account of the nature and of the genesis of the notion.* We think of God as having all his attributes such that no addition could be made to them: and we call such attributes His perfections. In regard, indeed, to the moral perfections of Deity, it is this expressive word Perfect, rather than infinite, which expresses the conviction which we are led to entertain in regard, for example, to the wisdom, or benevolence, or righteousness of God.

This, too, seems a native conviction of the mind. It needs, indeed, a certain matter provided for it, and to which it may adhere. In a positive shape it springs up late, and grows slowly in all minds to which it is not externally given by education, out of the Bible or otherwise. Still it is there in the mind as a tendency, placing

* In musing on divine things, the thought occurred to Anselm that it might be possible to find a single argument which would of itself prove that there is a God, and that he is the Supreme Good. Man, he says, is able to form a conception of something than which nothing greater can be conceived; and this conception, he argues, implies the existence of a corresponding being (Proslogion). A similar argument occurred to Descartes. He found in himself the idea of a Perfect being; and he argues that in this idea the existence of the Being is comprised, as the equality of the three angles to two right-angles is comprised in the idea of a triangle (Méth. p. 4, etc.). Leibnitz acknowledges that the argument is valid, provided he is allowed to supply a missing link, and to show that it is possible that God should exist (Op. p. 273). It may be doubted whether these arguments for the Divine existence, derived from the mere idea of the Perfect, are valid, independent of external facts. But these eminent men are right in saying that the mind has some conception and conviction as to the perfect; and these combine, with the observation of traces of design, to enable us to construct an argument for the Divine existence. In our day, M. Cousin maintains that the mind has the idea of the perfect, which he employs in his theistic argument, Ser. ii. t. ii.

before every man some sort of "Idea" in the Platonic sense; a model, or *beau idéal*, which he is ever prompted to strive after, while he is made to feel that he has not reached it. It is this impulse, I apprehend, which makes even the heathens speak of their gods, or at least their supreme God, as ineffably good and immortal;—their actual conceptions of his excellence and duration may be extremely inadequate, still they will not allow that there could be any increase made to his attributes; and, under fostering circumstances, the conviction will come out in a more decided form. When the object is brought under our notice we see that it is perfect, that it must be perfect, and that it cannot be otherwise. The faith is universal, but the conception takes the form which may be given it by the education or the intellectual strength and growth of the individual.

But it will be urged that these two views or sides of infinity are inconsistent. According to the one, infinity is something to which something can be ever added; whereas, according to the other, it is something to which nothing can be added. But in this, as in every other case of apparent or alleged contradiction among our original perceptions, the inconsistency vanishes on a careful inspection of the precise nature of the convictions. The infinite is something beyond *our* image or notion; but it is not something beyond the infinite itself. It is something which admits of no increase, but that something is not the imperfect notion we form, and which we know to be imperfect. The two are not contradictory, but the one is supplementary to the other. They cannot however be represented as the complement the one of the other; for while they make up such an apprehension as the finite mind of man can form, they do not make up the infinite itself, which is confessedly far beyond. The first of these views tends to humble us, as showing how far our creature impotency is below Creator Power. The other has rather a tendency to elevate us, by showing a perfect exemplar, which is indeed far above us, but to which we may ever look up. The Perfect shines above us like the sun in the heavens, distant and unapproachable, dazzling and blinding as we would gaze on it, but still our eye is ever turned up towards it, and we feel that it is a blessed thing that there is such a light, and that we are permitted to walk in it and rejoice in it.

II. We believe in infinite space and time, and in the possibility of infinite substance or being. After what has been already said of space and time we need not dwell on the first of these positions. But in believing in the infinity of extension and duration, we believe that there may possibly be infinite substance dwelling in them. I am not satisfied that our intuitive convictions go beyond this, or that they of themselves, apart from auxiliary considerations, guarantee the existence of infinite substance. I am sure they do not give any authority to the doctrine held by so many of the ancient Greek philosophers, that material substance is eternal: we can easily believe matter to have been brought into existence at some point in time by a power adequate to produce it. It does not appear to me that we are constrained by our convictions on this special subject, taken apart from all other evidence, to believe in the existence of an eternal or omnipresent God. Herein I have always thought that the argument *a priori*, or intuitive, in behalf of the Divine existence fails. There is a link wanting which shows that the proof is not apodictic or demonstrative, that it is not founded on truths which are self-evident throughout, as is, for example, the proposition that the opposite angles made by the intersection of two straight lines are equal. We have, and can have, no demonstrative evidence of other truths to which the mind cleaves most resolutely,—as, for example, that we ever had a sister, or brother, or friend, or that we were ever favoured to sit under the shelter of a father's wisdom, or the dews of a mother's tenderness. There is need of other considerations, and particularly of an experiential element, in the form of certain obvious facts, to prove the existence of a Being dwelling in infinite time and space, and possessed of infinite power and goodness. I may have occasion to show that when the patent facts and the native convictions are brought together, the certainty is of the very highest order short of demonstration, which it falls beneath only so far as not absolutely to preclude the possibility of doubt when the fool is determined to say in his heart, "There is no God." It would be premature and out of place to bring forward in array these combined considerations at this stage of our inquiries, and to show how the order and adaptation in nature are evidence of a designing and planning mind,—how these effects in nature evoke the intuition which demands that there be a cause,—how our convictions of moral obligation imply a law, the embodiment of the nature of a lawgiver,—and how all these unite to establish the existence of a living Being intelligent and holy. But it is to our present purpose to show how these individually, and in their union and co-operation, fall in with, and exactly suit, our intuition regarding time and space.

For I think it may be admitted that there is an emptiness, if I may so speak, about pure space and time. We know not, in fact, of a space or time without a substantial existence in them. I do indeed maintain, on the ground of irradicable conviction, that we must believe them to be independent of ourselves contemplating them, or of material objects placed in them. But the mind has a difficulty in conceiving of them as altogether separate and independent entities. It is from this cause, I am convinced, that so many philosophers represent them as mere relations of things rather than things, or as forms given to objects by the mind, or as mere conditions of existence. These are very incorrect representations; still the very fact that they have been advanced is an evidence of the difficulty which the mind experiences in grasping the realities of empty space and time, which do look as if they were voids to be filled up. Independent of us, they scarcely look as if they were independent of a substantial existence. I am not prepared to affirm with S. Clarke, that they are modes of substance, but I have little to say against another statement of the same author, that "they are immediate and necessary consequences of the existence of God, and that without them his Eternity and Ubiquity would be taken away;" or the statement of Newton, that "God constitutes time and space." The mind feels as if there were something a-wanting, till it learns of ONE to occupy the vacuum; but it is met and gratified in every one of its intellectual and moral intuitions when it is brought to know Him who inhabiteth eternity and immensity, and filleth them with living and life-giving fulness.

III. We look on infinity as an attribute of some object supposed to exist. Infinity is not to be regarded as a substance, or a distinct entity; we do not reckon it as an independent something, but we attribute it to something which has existence. It is the more necessary to make this remark from the circumstance that metaphysicians are very much tempted to give an independent being to abstractions, and often write about the infinite in such a way as to make their readers look upon them as separate entities. I stand up for the reality of infinity, but I claim for it a reality simply as an attribute. It is regarded intuitively as an attribute of expansion and duration. But the mind is not satisfied that it has got the whole truth till it looks on it as an attribute of God, and of his glorious perfections.

IV. We have a conception of the objects which we believe to be infinite. I have admitted that this notion is not adequate; in short, it is not a notion of infinity. Still the mind has a notion in regard to the infinite. On this, as a basis, the belief stands; round this, as a body, the belief gathers, as the atmosphere does round the earth. First, there must always be a notion of an existing thing, say space or time; or, as far more conceivable, a living and an intelligent God. The mind labours to heighten, deepen, widen, this notion on every side. Still it is within limits: but it can inquire what is beyond. It can do more: it can look out on what is beyond. It can do yet more: it knows that there is something beyond, and perceives somewhat of it. It perceives, for example, that far as it has gone in space, there is a space beyond; far as it has gone in time, there is a time beyond; much as it has conceived of God, there is, after all, more of the Divine perfections. There is thus a clear conception of an object; there is thus, too, a conception of this same object being beyond, and still further. The belief attaches to this conception, and declares that this thing conceived, this thing conceived as still beyond, is a reality, and that it is such that it cannot be increased. My readers must consult their own consciousness as to whether the account now given of the nature and genesis of our conviction is the correct one.

This notion, with its adhering belief, is a mental phenomenon which we have a word to express. We can subject it to logical processes; it comes in, like all our perceptions, in the concrete,—it is something, say space, time, or Deity, we apprehend as infinite; but we can abstract the infinite from the object regarded as infinite, and form the abstract idea of infinity. We can generalize it, and use it as a predicate; thus we can talk of space and time and God as being infinite. We can utter judgments regarding it, as that the infinite God is in every given place; there is no place of which we may not say, "Surely the Lord is in this place." We can even reason about it; thus we can infer that this puny effort of man, set against the recorded will of God, shall most certainly be frustrated by His Infinite power. Keeping within the limits prescribed by the nature of the convictions, man can speak about the infinite and be intelligible, he can legitimately employ it in argument, and he can muse upon it and find it to be among the most ennobling and precious of themes.*

* It should be carefully observed that according to this account, infinite is not a separate or an independently existing thing, but the attribute of a thing,—very possibly an attribute of an attribute of an existing thing. It is of something, say of space, or of the attribute of something, say of the power of God, that we predicate that they are infinite. This certainly implies that no space can be added to infinite space, but does not imply that space, because it is infinite, must contain all existence, must comprise, say wisdom and goodness. It implies that God cannot be more righteous than he is, but does not involve that his righteousness or even that his being must embrace all being. Mr. Mansel, in the 'Limits of Religious Thought Examined,' 3rd ed. p. 46, quotes the language of Hegel: "What kind of an Absolute Being is that which does not contain in itself all that is actual, even evil included?" and refers to Schelling, Schleiermacher, and Parker, as holding similar views. I am sure that the mind is not shut up into any such doctrine by its native convictions. Against such a view the artillery of Hamilton and Mansel tells with irresistible power. They have shown most conclusively that such a notion involves inextricable confusion and hopeless contradictions. I freely abandon such a conception to them, to tear it to pieces with their remorseless logic. But I decidedly demur to the statement of Mr. Mansel, "that which is conceived as absolute and infinite must be conceived as containing within itself the sum, not only of all actual, but of all possible modes of being." I have nothing here to say as to the absolute, but I do affirm that we have a conception as to the infinite, the perfect—I do not say *of* the infinite, the perfect—which does not imply this consequence, and that we can both think and speak of infinity without falling into contradictions. But Mr. Mansel says (p. 335) that my view (as partially expounded in Ap-

And yet it is true all the while that the notion is engulfed in mystery; it is but a small lamp of light hanging in (to us) circumambient darkness. It is of all things the most preposterous in certain speculators to set out with the idea of the infinite without a previous induction of its nature, and thence proceed, consecutively or deductively, to draw out a body of philosophy or theology. Such men have lost themselves in attempting to voyage an "unreal, vast, unbounded deep of horrible confusion;" and yet they would seek to pilot others, only to conduct them into darker gloom and more inextricable straits, and, in the end, bottomless abysses. The account we have given of the conception and belief, shows how narrow the limits within which man can make intelligible assertions; how strait the road in which he must walk, if he would not lose himself in wilderness and bog. He who passes these bounds is talking without a meaning; he who would start with the notion of the absolute, and thence construct a system embracing God, the world, and man, will without fail land himself in helpless and hope-

pendix to 'Method of Divine Government,' and in an Article on "Intuitionalism and the Limits to Religious Thought" in the 'North British Review' for February, 1859), differs from that of Sir W. Hamilton rather in language than in substance, and that it is not opposed to any principle of the 'Philosophy of the Conditioned.' I rejoice to believe this, as I would rather agree with Sir W. Hamilton and Mr. Mansel than with any metaphysicians of the past or present age. But whether I agree with them or not, I must hold it to be quite possible to muse and reason about the attribute 'infinite,' as it is in fact conceived and believed in by the mind, without falling into the difficulties in which the German supporters of the absolute have involved themselves, and that we can think of God and write about God as infinite, without being compelled by any logical necessity to look upon Him as embracing all existence, or to reckon it impossible or inconceivable that He should create a world and living agents different from Himself. We cannot conceive that God's power should be increased, but we can conceive it exercised in creating beings possessed of power. We cannot conceive His goodness to be enlarged, but we can, without a contradiction, conceive Him creating other beings also good. Nor are we by this con-

less contradictions—the necessary consequent, and the appropriate punishment, of his folly and presumption.*

The nature of man's conviction in regard to infinity, is fitted to impress us, at one and the same time, with the strength and the weakness of human intelligence, which is powerful in that it can apprehend so much, but feeble in that it can apprehend no more. The idea entertained is felt to be inadequate, but this is one of its excellencies, that it is felt to be inadequate; for it would indeed be lamentably deficient if it did not acknowledge of itself that it falls infinitely beneath the magnitude of the object. The mind is led by an inward tendency to stretch its ideas wider and wider, but is made to know at the most extreme point which it has reached that there is something further on. It is thus impelled to be ever striving after something which it has not yet reached, and to look beyond the limits of time into eternity beyond, in which there is the prospect of a noble occupation in beholding, through ages which can come to no end, and a space which has no bounds, the manifestations of a might and an excellence of which we can never know all, but of which we may ever know more. It is an idea which would ever allure us up towards a God of

ception shut up to the conclusion that the creature-power or creature-excellence might be added to the Divine power and goodness, and thus make it greater. To all quibbles proceeding in this line, I say that for aught I know it may not be possible they should be added, or that if added they should increase the Divine perfections; and no reply could be given, drawn either from intuition or experience, the only lights to which I can allow an appeal.

* It is at this point that Sir W. Hamilton has done such unspeakable service to Philosophy in his 'Philosophy of the Unconditioned,' and Mr. Mansel to Theology, in his 'Limits of Religious Thought,' by dispelling and scattering for ever the Philosophy of the Absolute, and the Theology which issued from that dark thunder-cloud, bulking so large to the eye, and sending forth terrific lightnings, with bellowing sounds and dreadful tempests, which brooded so long over Germany, and has been hovering on our shores and those of the United States of America.

infinite perfection, and yet make us feel more and more impressively the higher we ascend, that we are, after all, infinitely beneath Him. Man's capacity to form such an idea is a proof that he was formed by an infinite God, and in the image of an infinite God; his incapacity in spite of all his efforts to form a higher idea, is fitted to show us how wide the space and how impassable the gulf which separates man as finite from God the infinite.

They are in error who conclude that they cannot know an Infinite God, but they are equally in error who suppose that they can reach a perfect knowledge of Him. There is a sense in which he may be described as the unknown God, for no human intellect can come to know all the attributes of God, or even know all about any one of his perfections; but there is a sense in which he is emphatically the known God, inasmuch as he has been pleased to manifest and reveal himself, and every human being is required to attain a clear and positive, though at the same time a necessarily inadequate knowledge of him. It is true, on the one hand, that the invisible things of God from the creation of the world are clearly seen, being understood from the things which are made, even his eternal power and Godhead; but it is equally true, on the other, that we cannot by searching find out God, that we cannot find out the Almighty unto perfection. The wide finite, with its horizon ever widening as we ascend, should call forth our admiration, our adoration, and our love; the wider infinite, which is round about, and into which we can only gaze as we often gaze into the deep sky, should impress us with a feeling of awe in reference to Him who fills it all, and a feeling of humility in reference to ourselves who can know so little.

He who dwells in infinity is at once a God who reveals and a God who conceals himself. We can know, but we can know only in part. The knowledge which we can attain is the clearest, and yet the obscurest of all our knowledge. A child, a savage, can acquire a certain acquaintance with Him, while neither sage nor angel can rise to a full comprehension of Him. God may be truly described as the Being of whom we know the most, inasmuch as His works are ever pressing themselves upon our attention, and we behold more of His ways than of the ways of any other; and yet He is the Being of whom we know the least, inasmuch as we know comparatively less of His whole nature than we do of ourselves, or of our fellow-men, or of any object falling under our senses. They who know the least of Him have in this the most valuable of all knowledge; they who know the most, know but little after all of His glorious perfections. Let us prize what knowledge we have, but feel meanwhile that our knowledge is comparative ignorance. They who know little of Him may feel as if they knew much; they who know much will always feel that they know little. The most limited knowledge of Him should be felt to be precious, but this mainly as an encouragement to seek knowledge higher and yet higher, without limit and without end. They who in earth or heaven know the most, know that they know little after all; but they know that they may know more and more of Him throughout eternal ages.

CHAPTER IV.

THE EXTENT, TESTS, AND POWER OF OUR NATIVE BELIEFS.

THE above are some of the principal—I will not venture to say that they are the whole—of our native beliefs. As they grow upon our native convictions, so they attach themselves to our primitive judgments, in most of which there is more or less of the faith-element, that is, belief in the existence of an object not directly known. There is belief, for instance, involved in the judgment that this effect has a cause, which cause may be unknown. There is belief, too, exercised in certain of our moral judgments, as when we believe in the integrity of a good man, or trust in the Word of God, even when His Providence seems in opposition. But these are topics which will fall to be discussed specially in subsequent Books.

It is scarcely necessary to remark that faith is an affection of mind, not limited to our primary convictions. Faith collects round our observational knowledge and even around the conclusions reached by inference. We believe—the course of Nature being unchanged by its Author—that the seed cast into the ground in spring will yield a return in autumn, that the sun will rise to-morrow as he has done to-day, and that the planet Saturn a year hence will be found in the very place calculated for us by the astronomer. We exercise faith, every one of us, in listening to the testimony of credible witnesses, and faith is in one of its liveliest forms when it becomes trust in the ability, the excellence, and the love of a fellow-creature. Our highest faiths are those in which there is a mixture of the observational and intuitional elements, the observational supplying the object, and the intuitional imparting to them a profundity and a power as resting on an immovable foundation and going out into the vast and unbounded. In particular, when God has been revealed, faith ever clusters round Him as its appropriate object.

There are canons whereby to try the trustworthiness of our belief. First, so far as our intuitive beliefs are concerned, these are the general tests of intuition. Take our belief in the infinite. We have to ask, Is the truth believed in self-evident, or does it lean on something else? Is it necessary? Can we believe that space and time and the Being dwelling in them have limits? Is it universal, that is, do men ever practically believe that they can come to the verge of time and space? Such queries as these will settle for us at once what beliefs are original and fundamental. We should put these questions to every belief that may suggest itself to our own minds. We are entitled to put them to every belief which may be pressed on us by others. Then, secondly, as to our derivative or observational beliefs, there are the ordinary rules of evidence as enunciated in works of special or applied logic, or as stated in books on the particular departments of knowledge, or, more frequently, as caught up by common experience, and incorporated into the good sense of mankind. In no such case are we to believe without proof being supplied, and we are entitled and required to examine the evidence. Thirdly, as to mixed cases in which our faith proceeds partly on intuition, and partly on observation; our business is carefully to separate the two, and to judge each by its appropriate tests. In the use of such rules as these, while led to yield to the faith sanctioned by our rational nature, we shall at the same time be saved from those extravagant credences which are recommended to us by unauthorized authority, by mysticism which has confused itself, by superstition, by bigotry, by fanaticism, by pride, or by passion.

Looked at under one aspect, faith might be considered as so far a weakness cleaving to man, for where he has faith, other and higher beings may have immediate knowledge. But when contemplated under other aspects, it is an element of vast strength. In heaven, much of what is faith here, will be brightened into sight, but even in heaven faith abideth. Our faiths widen indefinitely the sphere of our convictions, they surround our solid cognitions with an atmosphere in which it is bracing and exhilarating to walk, which no doubt has its mists and clouds, but has also a kindling and irradiating capacity, and may be warmed into the fervour, and reflect the very light of heaven in a thousand varied colours. He who would tear off from the mind its proper beliefs, would in the very act be shearing it of one of its principal glories.

What a power even in our earthly faiths, as when men sow in the assurance that they will reap after a long season, and labour in the confidence of a reward at a far distance! What an efficacy in the trust which the child reposes in the parent, which the scholar puts in his master, which the soldier places in his General, and which the lover commits to the person beloved! These are among the chief potencies which have been moving mankind to good, or, alas! to evil. By the sharpness of its vision it discovers an outlet where sense thought that the way was shut in and closed. Difficulties give way as it advances, and impossibilities to prudence speedily become accomplishments before the might and energy of faith. To it we owe the greatest achievements which mankind have effected in art, in travel, in conquest; setting out in search of the unseen, they have made it seen and palpable. It was thus that Columbus persevered till the long hoped-for country burst on his view; it is always thus that men discover new lands and new worlds outside those previously known.

But faith has ever a tendency to go out with strong pinions into infinity, which it feels to be its proper element. It has a telescopic power, whereby it looks on vast and remote objects, and beholds them as near and at hand. There is a constancy in its course and a steadiness in its progress, because its eye is fixed on a pole-star far above our earth. How lofty its mien as it moves on, looking upward and onward, and not downward and backward, with an eye kindled by the brilliancy of the object at which it looks! Hence its power, a power drawn from the attraction of the world above. No element in all nature so potent. The lightning cannot move with the same velocity; light does not travel so quick from the sun to the earth, as faith does from earth to heaven. It heaves up, as by an irresistible hydrostatic pressure, the load which would press on the bosom. It glows like the heat, it burns like the fire, and obstacles are consumed before its devouring progress. Persecution coming like the wind to extinguish it, only fans it into a brighter flame.

The proper object of faith is, after all, the Divine Being. Time and space and infinity seem empty and dead and cold, till faith fills them with the Divine presence, quickens them with the Divine life, and warms them with the Divine love. When thus grounded, how stable! firmer than sense can ever be, for the objects at which it looks are more abiding. "The things which are seen are temporal, but the things which are unseen are eternal." When thus fixed, the soul is at rest, as secure in Him to whom it adheres. When thus directed, all its acts, even the meanest, become noble, being sanctified by the Divine end which they contemplate. All doubts are now decided on the right side by eternity being cast into the scale. When thus associated, its might is irresistible. It carries with it, and this according to the measure of it, the power of God. It is, no doubt, weak in that it leans, but it is strong in that it leans on the arm of the Omnipotent. It is a creature impotency which makes us lay hold of the Creator's power.

BOOK III.

PRIMITIVE JUDGMENTS.

CHAPTER I.

THEIR GENERAL NATURE, AND A CLASSIFICATION OF THEM.

THE mind of man has a set of Simple Cognitive—called by Sir William Hamilton Presentative—Powers, such as Sense-Perception and Self-Consciousness, by which it knows objects before it. From these we obtain our Primitive Cognitions. It has also a set of Reproductive Powers, such as the Memory and the Imagination, by which it recalls the past in old forms or in new dispositions. Out of them arise many of our Faiths, as in the existence of objects which fell under our notice in *time* past, and in an *infinity* surpassing our utmost powers of imagination. But the mind has also a Power of Comparison, by which it perceives Relations and forms Judgments.

Our Primitive Judgments are formed from our Primitive Cognitions and Primitive Beliefs. On comparing two or more objects known or believed in,* we discover

* A judgment is usually defined as a comparison of two notions. Upon which Mr. J. S. Mill remarks, that "propositions (except where the mind itself is the subject treated of) are not assertions respecting our ideas of things, but assertions respecting things themselves," adding, "My belief has not reference to the ideas, it has reference to the

that they bear a necessary relation to each other. The necessity of the relation arises from the nature of the things. We discover that objects have a certain relation because of the nature of the objects, as these become known to us, or as we have been led to believe them to be; and whenever we are led to discover a necessary relation, it is because we have such an acquaintance as to observe that there is a relation implied in their very nature. It should be added, that because of our limited and imperfect acquaintance with things, there may be many necessary relations which are altogether unknown to us, even among objects which are so far known.

In accepting this account, we are saved from the extravagant positions taken up by many metaphysicians as to the *a priori* judgments of the mind, which they represent as fashioned by a power of reason independent of things, whereas they are formed on the contemplation of things, and of the nature of things so far as apprehended. Such questions as the following are often put by ingenious minds :—How is it that two straight lines cannot enclose a space? How is it that time appears like a line stretching behind and before, whereas the analogous thing, space, extends in three dimensions? The proper reply is, that all this follows from the very nature of space and time. And if the question be put, How do we know that two straight lines cannot enclose a space, and

things" (Logic, i. v. 1). There is force in the criticism, yet it does not give the exact truth. In propositions about extra-mental objects, we are not comparing the two notions as states of mind; so far as logicians have proceeded on this view, they have fallen into confusion and error. But still, while it is true that our predications are made, not in regard to our notions, but of things, it is in regard to things apprehended, or of which we have a notion, as Mr. Mill admits: "In order to believe that gold is yellow, I must indeed have the idea of gold and the idea of yellow, and something having reference to those ideas must take place in my mind."

that time has length without breadth? the answer is, that all this is involved in our primary knowledge of space and time. No other answer can be given; no other answer should be attempted. Our primitive judgments proceed on our primitive cognitions and beliefs, which again are founded on the nature of things, as we are constituted to discover it.

It will be necessary at this place to examine a very common representation that the mind begins with judgments, rather than the knowledge of individual things, and that there is judgment or comparison in all knowledge. According to Locke, knowledge is nothing but the perception of the connection and agreement, or disagreement and repugnancy, of any two ideas. Sir W. Hamilton and Mr. Mansel maintain that in every cognitive act there is judgment. In opposition to Locke, I hold that the mind does not commence with ideas and the comparison of ideas, but with the knowledge of things, of which it can ever after form ideas, and which it is able to compare. I reckon it impossible for the mind, from mere ideas not comprising knowledge, or from the comparison of such ideas, ever to rise to knowledge, to the knowledge of things. The system of Locke is at this point involved in difficulties from which it cannot be delivered by those who hold, as he did, that man can reach a knowledge of objects. The only consistent issue of such a doctrine is an idealism which maintains that the mind can never get beyond its own circle or globe, and is there engaged for ever in the contemplation and comparison of its own ideas, in regard to which it never can be certain whether they have any external reality corresponding to them. If the view of Hamilton and Mansel were slightly modified, or were otherwise expressed, I am not sure that I should widely dissent from it. I acknowledge that every intuitive cognition may furnish the matter and supply the ground for a judgment. Thus, out of the knowledge of a stone as before me, I can form the judgment "This stone is now present," by an analysis of the concrete cognition. The knowledge of self as thinking enables me, as I distinguish between the *ego* and the particular thought, and observe the relation of the two, to affirm, "I think." Nay, I believe that every primary cognition may entitle me, by an easy abstraction and comparison, to frame a number of primary judgments. Thus, the cognition of the stone enables me to say, "This stone exists;" "This stone is here;" and if the perception be by the eye, "This stone is extended;" and if it be by the muscular sense, "This stone resists pressure;" while the cognition of self as perceiving the stone, enables me to affirm, "I perceive the stone;" "I exist;" "I perceive." The two, indeed—our primary cognitions and beliefs on the one hand, and our primary judgments on the other—are intimately connected. Every cognition furnishes the materials of a judgment; and a judgment possible, I do not say actual, is involved in every cognition. As the relation is implied in the nature of the individual objects, and the judgment proceeds on the knowledge of the nature of the objects, so the two, in fact, may be all but simultaneous, and it may scarcely be necessary to distinguish them, except for rigidly exact philosophic purposes.* Still it is the cognition which comes first, and

* According to Locke, "Perception is the first operation of all our intellectual faculties, and the inlet of all knowledge into our minds" (Essay, ii. x. 15). According to the view I take, perception *is* knowledge. According to Locke, "Knowledge is nothing but the Perception of the Connection and Agreement, or Disagreement and Repugnancy of any of our ideas" (iv. i. 1). Hamilton says,—"Consciousness is primarily a judgment or affirmation of existence. Again, consciousness is not merely the affirmation of naked existence, but the affirmation of a certain qualified or determinate existence" (Metaph. Lect. 24. See also Notes to Reid's Works, pp. 243, 275). Mr. Mansel says,—

forms the basis on which the judgments are founded; in the case of the primitive judgments, directly founded. It should be frankly admitted that what is given in primary cognition, is in itself of the vaguest and most valueless character till abstraction and comparison are brought to bear upon it. Still our cognitions and beliefs furnish the materials of all that the discursive understanding weaves into such rich and often complicated forms.

It is to be carefully observed that our primitive cognitions and beliefs being of realities, all the intellectual processes properly founded on them must relate to realities also. If what we proceed on be unreal, that which we reach by a logical process may also be unreal. If space and time, for example, have, as some suppose, no reality independent of the contemplative mind, then all the relations of space and time as unfolded in mathematical demonstrations, must also be regarded as unreal in the same sense. On the other hand, if space and time have (as I maintain) an existence irrespective of the mind thinking about them, then all the necessary relations drawn from our knowledge may also be regarded as having a reality independent of the mind reflecting on them. Not that they are to be supposed to have an existence as individuals, or independent of the things related: they have precisely such a reality as we are intuitively led to believe them to have; that is, they exist as necessary relations of the separate things.

"It may be laid down as a general Canon of Psychology, that every act of consciousness, intuitive or discursive, is comprised in a conviction of the presence of its object, either internally in the mind, or externally in space. The result of every such act may thus be generally stated in the proposition, 'This is here.'" To this statement I have scarcely any objection to take, the more especially as he goes on to distinguish between such a psychological judgment and a logical one. "The former is the judgment of a relation between the conscious subject and the immediate object of consciousness. The latter is the judgment of a relation which two objects of thought bear to each other" (Proleg. Logica, ch. ii.). I prefer saying that what he calls a psychological judgment is a cognition, which may be explicated into a judgment, which judgment will be a logical one.

It may be as well to announce here generally, what will be shown specially at every stage as we advance, that all the primitive judgments of the mind are individual. The mind does not in its spontaneous operations declare that it is impossible for the same thing to be and not to be, but upon being satisfied that a certain thing exists, it at once sets aside the thought or assertion that it does not exist. It does not affirm in a general proposition that no two lines can enclose a space; but it says, these two lines cannot enclose a space: and it would say the same of every other two lines. It does not metaphysically announce that every quality implies a substance, that every effect must have a cause, but it declares of this property contemplated that it implies a substance, and of this given effect that it must have had a cause. It is out of these individual judgments that the general maxim is obtained by a process of generalization. But then it is to be observed that it is not a generalization of an outward experience,—which must always be limited, and never can furnish ground for a necessary and universal proposition, but of inward and immediate judgments of the mind, which carry in them the conviction of necessity, which necessity therefore will attach itself to the general maxim, on the condition of our having properly performed the process of generalization.

It is necessary for our purposes to classify the primary judgments pronounced by the mind; but this is by no means an easy task. An arrangement may however serve very important ends, even though it be not thoroughly exhaustive, and altogether unobjectionable. The following is to be regarded simply as the best which I have been able to draw out, and may be accepted as a provisional one till a better be furnished.* The mind

* Locke speaks of relations as being infinite, and mentions only a few. He specifies Cause and Effect, Time, Place, Identity and Diversity, Pro-

seems capable of noticing intuitively at least the following relations :—

Those of (I.) Identity and Difference; (II.) Whole and Parts; (III.) Space; (IV.) Time; (V.) Quantity; (VI.) Resemblance; (VII.) Active Property; (VIII.) Cause and Effect.

CHAPTER II.

RELATIONS INTUITIVELY OBSERVED BY THE MIND.

Sect. I. Relation of Identity.

We have seen that every object known by us is known as having being; I do not say an independent being, but a separate and individual being. This being continuing in the object constitutes its identity. This identity every object has as long as it exists, and this whether the identity does or does not become known to us or to any other created being. An object has identity not because the identity is known to us; but an object having continued being, and therefore identity, intelligent beings may come to discover it. We are so constituted as to be able to know being,—that is, that the object known to us possesses being,—and we look on the object as retaining that being as long as it exists. We are prepared to

portion, and Moral Relations (Essay, ii. xxviii.). Hume mentions Resemblance, Identity, Space and Time, Quantity, Degree, Contrariety, Cause and Effect. Kant's Categories are :—(I.) Quantity; containing Unity, Plurality, Totality; (II.) Quality; containing Reality, Negation, Limitation; (III.) Relation; comprising Inherence and Subsistence, Causality and Dependence, Community of Agent and Patient; (IV.) Modality; under which are Possibility and Impossibility, Existence and Non-Existence, Necessity and Contingence. Dr. Brown arranges them as those of—(I.) Co-existence; embracing Position, Resemblance or Difference, Proportion, Degree, Comprehension; (II.) Succession; containing Causal and Casual Priority.

decide then that if we ever fall in with this object again, it will have retained its identity. We may fall in with the same object again without discovering it to be the same, because of a defect of memory, or because the object was disguised in a crowd. But in regard to certain objects, we cannot avoid observing the sameness, and cannot be deceived in pronouncing them the same.

So far as self is concerned, we discover the identity intuitively as we look on the objects presented in self-consciousness and memory. We have an immediate knowledge of self in every exercise of consciousness. We have a recollection of self in some particular state in every exercise of memory. The mind has thus before it, at every waking moment, a knowledge of a present self; and in every exercise of memory it has a past self; and in looking at and comparing the two, it at once proclaim sthe identity. It will be observed that here, as in every other case, the judgment throws us back on cognition and belief; the necessary facts on which the mind pronounces the necessary judgment, are furnished in the exercise of consciousness and memory.

In regard to objects external to the mind we have no such intuitive means of discovering an identity. Our original perceptions do not extend even to the identity of our bodily frame. Every particle of matter in the body may be changed in seven years, as physiologists tell us, in perfect accordance with our intuitive perceptions. We may be without a body in the state between death and the resurrection, and may receive an entirely new and spiritual body in heaven, and yet retain all the while our identity and feeling of identity. And in the case of extra-organic objects there is always a possibility of doubt as to whether what we perceive now is the same object as fell under our notice at some previous time. The infant, prompted by his instinct as to the

R 2

continuance of being, and making a wrong application of it, will often be inclined to discover identity where there is only resemblance, and will be apt, for example, to look on every man he meets with as his father. As he advances in life he will be led to pay more regard to differences. As to when there is a sufficient amount of resemblance to denote a sameness, this is to be determined solely by the laws of experiential evidence. In some cases, as when we recognize our friends and familiar objects, there is moral certainty; in other cases there is probability, less or greater, according to the proof which is perceived or can be adduced.*

The intuitive judgments are always individual, and are pronounced on the objects being presented. When generalized, they take the form of such metaphysical maxims as these:—"It is impossible for the same thing to be and not to be at the same time." "Everything preserves its identity as long as it exists." "We are sure that we are the same beings as we were since consciousness began, and must continue the same as long as consciousness exists."

The above are judgments pronounced on individual

* These views determine the light in which we should look on as 'pretty' a controversy as ever raged in metaphysics or out of it, as to whether two things in every respect alike—say two drops of water—would or would not be identical. Leibnitz held that each thing differed from every other by an internal principle of distinction, and that no individuals could be alike in every respect; and that if they were, they could have no principle of individuation (Op. p. 277). Kant criticized this view, and urged that even though they were in every respect alike, they would differ as being in different parts of space (Werke, Bd. ii. p. 217). The common representation was that they would differ numerically. I am not sure that any of these accounts is correct. It is quite conceivable that there might be two things in every respect alike, except in their individual being. It is not their existence in different parts of space which constitutes their diffrence, but as different in their being they exist in different parts of space. They have a distinct being, not because they are numerically different, but they are numerically distinct because they have a distinct being.

objects contemplated. Under the same head there fall to be placed predications which the mind makes at once and intuitively in regard to relations which have been previously perceived and sanctioned by the mind. Suppose that, on the ground of experience, we become convinced that no reptile is warm-blooded; the mind, on the bare contemplation of the notions, will at once and intuitively declare that no warm-blooded animal can be a reptile. In all such cases it is presupposed that there is a previously discovered relation. It is possible that the mind may have been deceived, and that the relation does not exist in fact; and in this case the judgment pronounced according to the law of identity would also be wrong as a matter of fact. Thus if a proposition were given that 'no mammal is warm-blooded,' the mind would pronounce that no 'warm-blooded animal can be a mammal.' The error, however, would lie not in the law of thought, but in the original proposition furnished.

This is the proper place to explain the famous distinction drawn by Kant between Analytic and Synthetic Judgments. Analytic Judgments are those in which the predicate is involved in the very notion which constitutes the subject; as when we say that 'an island is surrounded with water,' 'a king has authority to rule,' 'the moral law should be obeyed.' All such judgments are said, in the nomenclature of the Kantian school, to be *a priori*. We have come to entertain certain apprehensions in regard to island, king, and moral law, and now we pronounce a set of judgments on the bare contemplation of these, and involved in them by the law of identity. The judgments involved in the general law of identity, the analytic judgments of Kant, are represented by Sir W. Hamilton as capable of being resolved into three specific laws. "1. The Law, Principle, or Axiom of *Identity*, which, in regard to the same thing, immediately or directly enjoins the affirmation of it with itself, and mediately or indirectly prohibits its negation: (A is A). 2. The Law, etc., of *Contradiction* (properly *Non-Contradiction*), which in regard to contradictories explicitly enjoining their reciprocal negation, implicitly prohibits their reciprocal affirmation: (A is not A). In other words, contradictories are thought as existences incompatible at the same time, as at once mutually exclusive. 3. The Law, etc., of *Excluded Middle* or *Third*, which declares that whilst contradictories are only two, everything, if explicitly thought, must be thought as of these, either the one or the other: (A is either B or not B). In different terms:—Affirmation and Negation of the same thing, in the same respect, have no conceivable medium; whilst anything actually may, and virtually must, be either affirmed or denied of anything. In other words:—Every predicate is true or false of every subject; or contradictories are thought as impossible, but at the same time one or other as necessary."* These laws have a great importance in Formal Logic. Being carried out and applied in special forms, they show what may be drawn from any proposition or set of propositions given, and they keep thought consistent with itself.

Synthetic (as distinguished from Analytic) Judgments are those in which the predicate affirms or denies something more than is embraced in the subject: as when we say 'gold is yellow,' 'body gravitates,' 'sin will be punished.' Some of these judgments are *a posteriori*; that is, we reach them by experience. Others of them are said to be *a priori*; that is, the mind, on the bare contemplation of the notions, at once pronounces the agreement or disagreement. As examples, there are the

* Metaph. vol. ii. append. ii.

mathematical axioms, such as that two straight lines cannot enclose a space; and metaphysical principles, such as that every effect must have a cause. In this Section, I have given Sir W. Hamilton's analysis of Identical or Analytic Judgments. In the remaining Sections, I am to endeavour to unfold the Synthetic Judgments *a priori*.

Sect. II. Relation of Whole and Parts.

It is a fundamental principle of this treatise that the mind begins with the concrete,—a truth which should always go along with the other, which has, however, been more frequently noticed, that it begins with the individual. Being thus furnished with the concrete in its primary knowledge and beliefs,—and we may add, imaginations,—the mind can consider a part of the concrete whole separate from the other parts. In doing so, it is much aided by the circumstance that the concrete whole seldom comes round in all its entireness. The child sees a man with a hat to-day and without his hat to-morrow, and is thus the better enabled to form a notion of the hat apart from the man that wore it.

In all abstraction there is judgment or comparison; that is, we discover a relation between two objects contemplated. We contemplate a concrete whole, and we contemplate a part, and observe a relation of the part as a part of the whole. It should be admitted that, without any exercise of comparison, we are capable of imaging a part of a whole, in cases where the part can be separated; thus, having seen a man on horseback, I can easily picture to myself the man separately or the horse separately, without thinking of any relation between them; but in such processes there is no exercise of abstraction. Abstraction is eminently an intellectual operation. In it we contemplate a part as part of a whole, say a quality as a quality of a substance; for example, transparency as a quality of ice, or of some other substance. In all such exercises there is involved a Correlative Power. This power may be called Comprehension, inasmuch as it contemplates the whole in its relation to the parts; or Abstraction, inasmuch as it contemplates the part as part of a whole; and the Faculty of Analysis and Synthesis, inasmuch as it contemplates the two in correlation,—the parts and the whole. There is, if I do not mistake, intuition involved in every exercise of this power. The operations of the intuition are always singular, but they may be generalized, and being so, they will give us the following as involved in Abstraction.

1. The Abstract implies the Concrete. This arises from the very nature of abstraction. When an object is before it in the concrete, the mind can separate a quality from the object, and one quality from another. It can distinguish, for example, between a man taken as a whole, and any one quality of his, such as bodily strength; and distinguish between any one quality and another, as between his bodily strength and intellectual power, between his intellectual faculties and his feelings, and between any one feeling, such as joy, and any other feeling, such as sorrow. But we are not to suppose that, while we can thus distinguish between a whole and its parts, between an object and its qualities, between one quality and another, therefore the part can exist independent of the whole, or the quality of its object. Every abstracted quality implies some concrete object from which it has been separated in thought.

2. When the Concrete is Real, the Abstract is also Real. In this respect there is a truth in the now exploded doctrine of realism. Abstraction, if it proceeds on a reality and is properly conducted, ever conducts to

realities. It is thus a most important intellectual exercise for the discovery of truth, enabling us to discover the permanent amidst the fleeting, the real amidst the phenomenal. As I look on a piece of magnetized iron, I know it to be a real existence, and I think of it as having a certain form, and of its attracting certain objects, and I must believe that this figure is a reality quite as much as the iron which has the form, and that the attractive power is not a mere fiction, any more than the iron of which it is a property. But it is to be carefully observed that this abstract thing, while it has an existence, has not necessarily an independent existence. We have already seen that when it is a quality it must always be the quality of a substance. Beauty is certainly reality, but it has no existence apart from a beautiful person or scene, of whom or of which it is an attribute.

A philosopher, says Kant, was asked, What is the weight of smoke? and he answered,—Substract the weight of the ashes from the weight of the fuel burned, and we have the weight of smoke. At the basis of this judgment is the intuitive maxim that the whole is equal to the sum of its parts. The individual intuitive judgments which the mind pronounces on looking at whole and parts may perhaps be all generalized into two principles. (1.) The parts make up the whole. (2.) The whole is equal to the sum of its parts. From the first of these we may derive the rules, that the abstract part is involved in the concrete whole, and that the abstract, as part of a real concrete thing, is also a real. From the first we have the rule that the parts are less than the whole, and from the second the maxim that the whole is greater than the parts. It is of importance to have such maxims as these accurately enunciated in mathematical demonstration and logical and metaphysical science. Spontaneously, however, the mind does not form any such maxims, which are merely the generalized expression of its individual judgments.

Still the maxim is underlying many of our thoughts in all departments of investigation. Thus, in Natural History it urges us to seek for a classification in which all the members of any subdivision will make up the whole. It impels the chemist to look out for all the elements which go to constitute the compound substance. In psychology and metaphysics it prompts us to analyze a concrete mental state into parts, and insists that in the synthesis the parts be equal to the whole. In logic it demands, as a rule of division, that the members make up the class, and is involved in all those processes in which we infer (in subalternation) that what is true of all must be true of some; or (in disjunctive division) that what is true of one of two alternatives (A and B), and is not true of one (A), must be true of the other (B). In most of such cases the more prominent elements are got from experience; in some of them, other intuitions act the more important part; but in all of them there are intuitions of whole and parts underlying the mental processes,—unconsciously and covertly, no doubt, but still capable of being brought out to view for scientific purposes.

Sect. III. Relations of Space.

I have endeavoured to show that the mind in sense-perception has a knowledge of objects as occupying space, and that round these original cognitions there gather certain native beliefs. Upon the contemplation of the objects thus apprehended, the mind is led at once and necessarily to pronounce certain judgments. They may be arranged as follows:—

1. There are all the mathematical axioms which relate to limited extension, such as, "The shortest distance between any two points is a straight line;" "Two straight

lines cannot enclose a space;" "Two straight lines which when produced the shortest possible distance are not nearer each other, will not, if produced ever so far, approach nearer each other;" "All right-angles are equal to one another." Under the same head are to be placed the postulates involved in the definitions and in the propositions founded on them, such as the following, put in the form of maxims:—"A straight line may be drawn from any one point to any other point;" "A straight line may be produced to any length in a straight line;" "There may be such a figure as a circle, that is, a plane figure such that all straight lines drawn from a certain point within the figure are equal to one another;" and that "A circle may be described from any centre at any distance from that centre." I shall have occasion, in speaking of the application of the principles laid down in this treatise to mathematics, to return to axioms, and shall then show that the intuitive judgments pronounced by the mind in regard to the relations of space are all individual, and that the form assumed by them in the axioms of geometry is the result of the generalization, not indeed of an outward experience, but of the individual decisions of the mind.

2. There are certain axioms in regard to motion, such as that "All motion is in space;" "All motion is from one part of space to another;" "All motion is by an object in space;" "A body in passing from one part of space to another must pass through the whole intermediate space."

3. There are the primitive truths which arise from the relation of objects to space, such as "That body occupies space;" "That body is contained in space;" "That body occupies a certain portion of space;" and thus "That body has a defined figure." But what, it may be asked, do our intuitive convictions say as to the relation of mind

and space? I am inclined to think that our intuition declares of spirit, that it must be in space. It is clear, too, that so far as mind acts on body, it must act on body as in space, say in making that body move in space. But beyond this, I am persuaded that we have no means of knowing the relations which mind and space bear to each other. As to whether spirit does or does not occupy space, this is a subject on which intuition seems to say nothing, and I suspect that experience says as little.

4. There are certain metaphysical judgments as to space, such as "Space is continuous;" "Space cannot be divided in the sense of its parts being separated;" and all those derived from the infinity of space, such as that "Space has no limits;" "Any line may be infinitely prolonged in space."

Sect. IV. The Relations of Time.

The apprehension of time is given in every exercise of memory; we remember the event as having happened in time past. Round this primary conviction there collect a number of beliefs. When time thus apprehended is contemplated by us, we are led, from the very nature of the object, to make certain affirmations and denials. It declares that "Time is continuous;" that "Time cannot be divided into separable parts;" and that "Time has no limits." The mind also declares of every event that it happens in time.

Sect. V. The Relations of Quantity.

These are equivalent to the relations of proportion referred to by Locke, and the relations of proportion and degree mentioned by Brown; they are the relations of less and more. The mind, in discovering them, proceeds upon the knowledge previously acquired of objects as being singulars, that is, units; it is upon a succession of units coming before it that the judgment is pronounced. It also very frequently proceeds on other relations which have been previously discovered; on perceiving, for instance, that objects resemble each other in respect of space, time, and property, we may notice that they have less or more of the common thing in respect of which they agree.

It is to this intuition I refer the power which the mind has of discovering the relation of simple numbers. A very high authority on this subject has given a somewhat different account. Dr. Whewell refers our conception of number to the sense of successiveness, or, as I would render it, the faculty which discovers the relations of Time. "The conception of number appears to require the exercise of the sense of succession. At first sight indeed we seem to apprehend number without any act of memory, or any reference to time; for example, we look at a horse, and see that his legs are four, and this we seem to do at once without reckoning them. But it is not difficult to see that this seeming instantaneousness of the perception of small numbers is an illusion. This resembles the many other cases in which we perform short and easy acts so rapidly and familiarly that we are unconscious of them, as in the acts of seeing, and articulating our words. And this is the more manifest since we begin our acquaintance with number by counting even the smallest numbers. Children, and very rude savages, must use an effort to reckon even their five fingers, and find a difficulty in going further. And persons have been known who were able by habit, or by peculiar natural aptitude, to count by dozens as rapidly as common persons can by units. We may conclude therefore that when we appear to catch a small number by a single glance of the eye, we do, in fact, count the units of it in a regular though very brief succession. To count requires an act of memory; of this we are sensible when we count very slowly, as when we reckon the strokes of a church clock, for in such a case we may forget in the intervals of the strokes, and *miscount.* Now it will not be doubted that the nature of the process in counting is the same, whether we count fast or slow. There is no definite speed of reckoning at which the faculties which it requires are changed, and therefore memory, which is requisite in some cases, must be so in all." I entirely concur with this statement. I am convinced that the perception of the relations of time, is presupposed in our discerning the relations of number. But there may be more required. Dr. Whewell appends a foot-note, "If any one holds number to be apprehended by a direct act of intuition, as space and time are, this view will not disturb the other doctrines delivered in the text."* I believe that one, or unity, is involved in our primary cognition of objects. Not that I think it necessary to call in a special intuition in order to our being able to count or number; but I believe that, besides the exercise of memory, and the discovery of the relations of the succession in time, there must be the general power of discovering the relations of quantity: we must be able, not only to go over the units, but further, to discover the relations of the units and of their combinations.

To this faculty I refer all those operations in which we discover equality, or difference, or proportions of any kind, in numbers. The mental capacity is greatly aided, and its intuitive perceptions are put in a position to act more readily and extensively, through the divisions and notations by tens in our modern arithmetic; every ten, every hundred, every thousand, and so on, comes to be regarded as a unit, and the judgments in regard to units are made to reach numbers indefinitely large. These

* 'Philosophy of Inductive Sciences,' II. ix. 4.

numerical judgments admit of an application to extension in space. Fixing on a certain length, superficies or solid, as a unit, we form judgments which embrace lines or surfaces or solids never actually measured. I am persuaded that, even in its common and practical operations,—as, for example, in the measurement of distance by the eye,—the mind fixes on some known and familiar length as its standard, and estimates larger space by this. Ever since Descartes conceived the method of expressing curve lines and surfaces by means of equations, mathematics may be said to be concerned with quantity as their *summum genus*. The judgments as intuitive are all individual, but they can be generalized, when they will assume such forms as the "Common Notions," so far as they relate to quantity, prefixed by Euclid to his Elements. "Things which are equal to the same are equal to one another." "If equals be added to equals, the wholes are equal." "If equals be taken from equals, the remainders are equal." "If equals be added to unequals, the wholes are unequal." "If equals be taken from unequals, the remainders are unequal." "Things which are double the same thing are equal to one another." "Things which are half the same thing are equal to one another."

SECT. VI. THE RELATIONS OF RESEMBLANCE.

It has been generally acknowledged that man's primary knowledge is of individual objects: not that he as yet knows them to be individual; it is only after he has been able to form general notions that he draws the distinction, and finds that what he first knew was singular. What is meant is, that the boy does not begin with a notion of man, or woman, or humanity in general, but with a knowledge of a particular man, say his father, or a particular woman, say his mother; and it is only as other men and other women come under his notice, and he observes their points of agreement, that he is able to rise to the general notion of man, or woman, or humankind.

In the mental processes involved in generalization, the most important part is the observational one. When we discover, for example, the resemblances of plants, and proceed to group them into species, genera, and orders, the operation is one of induction and comparison. There is no necessity of thought involved in the law that roses have five petals, or that fishes are cold-blooded, or indeed in any of the laws of natural history. Still there are laws of thought which have a place in the generalizing process.

1. The universal implies the singular. The mind pronounces this judgment when it looks at the nature of the individuals and the generals. The universal is not something independent of the singulars, prior to the singulars, or above the singulars. A general notion is the notion of an indefinite number of objects possessing a common attribute or attributes. It is clear, therefore, that the general proceeds on and presupposes individuals. If there were no individuals, there would be no general; and if the individuals were to cease, the general would likewise cease. If there were no individual roses, there would be no such thing as a class of plants called roses.

2. When the singulars are real, the universal is also real; always, of course, on the supposition that the generalization has been properly made. There exists, we shall suppose, in nature, a number of objects possessing common attributes, we have observed their points of resemblance, and put them in a class: has, or has not, the class an existence? In reply, I say that the genus has an existence and a reality as well as the individual objects. An indefinite number of animals chew the cud, and are called ruminant; the class ruminant has an existence

quite as much as the individual animals. But let us observe what sort of reality the class has; it is a reality merely in the individuals, and in the possession of common qualities by these individuals.

3. Whatever is predicated of a class may be predicated of all the members of the class; and *vice versâ*, whatever is predicated of all the members of a class may be predicated of the class. This is a self-evident and necessary proposition. It is pronounced by the mind in an individual form whenever it contemplates the relation of a class and the members of the class; thus, if the general maxim be discovered or allowed, that all reptiles are cold-blooded, and the further fact be given or ascertained that the crocodile is a reptile, the conclusion is pronounced that the crocodile is cold-blooded.

We shall discover, when we come to apply these general principles, that the laws mentioned in this Section play an important part in Logic, and have a place in the Notion, in the Judgment, and in Reasoning.

Sect. VII. Relations of Active Property.

I have been striving to prove that we cannot know either self or body acting on self, except as possessing property. On looking at the properties of objects, the mind at once pronounces certain decisions. These, like all our other intuitive judgments, have a reference, in the first instance, to the individual case presented, but may be made universal by a process of generalization. Thus, the mind declares, "this property implies a substance," "this substance will exercise a property." The abstract truths will seldom be formally enunciated, but, as regulative principles, they underlie our common thoughts, and we proceed on them, even when entirely unaware of their nature or of their existence. Every action or manifestation we intuitively regard as the action or exhibition of a something having a substantial being. On falling in with a new substance, say an aerolite just dropped from the heavens, we know not indeed what its properties are, but we are sure that it has properties, and we make an attempt to discover them.

Sect. VIII. Relation of Cause and Effect.

All our primitive judgments carry us back to primitive cognitions and beliefs, that is, they are pronounced by the mind as it looks to objects intuitively known or necessarily believed in. The judgment which affirms that the cause must produce its effect, and that the effect has resulted from a cause, proceeds from and is grounded on a cognition which has already passed under our notice, the intuitive knowledge of substance exercising power. It will appear, as we advance, that those who overlook or deny the mind's primary knowledge of power, can give no adequate or satisfactory account of the nature or meaning of the causal judgment.

It will be needful to show here, first of all, that the judgment is not derived from the generalizations of outward experience. As we do so, it will be necessary to state, though it will not be necessary to dwell on it after the enunciations which have been so often repeated, that our conviction is not of a general truth, but relates solely to individual facts presented to or contemplated by the mind. Our original judgment is not that every cause has an effect, and that every effect has a cause, propositions which will not be admitted and cannot be understood till the words 'cause' and 'effect,' terms very abstract and general, be explained,—but it is that this thing having power, may produce an effect, and that this thing apprehended as a new thing or as having been changed must have had a cause.

In proceeding to prove that the mental conviction, thus

understood, is not derived from experience, I am disposed to admit at once that observation might, without any original intuition, lead to a loose general belief in cause and effect. On seeing two events in frequent juxtaposition, we might be disposed when we see the one to think of the other by the ordinary law of association, and when we see the one to expect the other, as the result of a process of generalization. This I freely admit; but I maintain, at the same time, that the intuitive conviction is, in fact, one powerful means of making us associate cause and effect so naturally in our minds, and to generalize our experience of causation. Any experiential conviction would necessarily want certain essential elements ever found in our conviction regarding causation.

First, it would not, as being the result of generalization, operate at so early a period of life as our belief in cause and effect evidently does. The causal belief is as strong in infancy as in mature life or in old-age, is as strong among savages as in civilized countries in which scientific observation has made the greatest advances. True, savage nations have not a belief in the uniformity of nature, which is a result (as shall be shown further on) of observation; they discover events which are thought to have no cause in nature, but then they seek for a cause beyond nature. Now, if the conviction of causation were like the belief in the uniformity of nature, a principle derived from induction,—which must necessarily be a large induction,—it would be difficult to account for its existence and its invariable operation in the earliest stages of individual life and of society. I admit that all this merely proves that there is a native instinct or inclination prompting us to rise from an effect to a cause, and by no means justifies us in standing up for a necessary conviction.

Secondly, it would scarcely account for the universality

of the belief among men brought up in such various countries and situations, attached to such different sects and creeds, and under the influence of all kinds of whim and caprice. This can be most satisfactorily explained by supposing that there is a native principle at work, inclining and guiding all men. Such a consideration, I allow, does not show that the conviction is a fundamental one, nor would I urge it as in itself a positive proof of the existence even of a native instinct: still it is a strong presumption. Indeed the theory which supposes that there is some original impulse or inclination, is the only one which can give a full explanation of all the beliefs which man cherishes, and the judgments which he ever pronounces.

Thirdly, it would not account for the fundamental and necessary character of the judgment. This is the conclusive circumstance, of which the others are to be regarded as merely corroborations. No possible length or uniformity could or should give this necessity of conviction to the judgment. We might have seen A and B, this stone and that stone, this star and that star, this man and that man together, a thousand, or a million, or a billion of times, and without our ever having seen them separate, but this would not and ought not to necessitate us to believe that they have been for ever together, and shall be for ever together, and must be for ever together. No doubt, it would lead us, when we fell in with the one to look for the other, and we would wonder if the one presented itself without the other; still, it is possible for us to conceive, and, on evidence being produced, to believe, that there may be the one without the other. It was long supposed that all metals are comparatively heavy, but while every one was astonished at the fact, no one was prepared to deny it, when it was shown by Davy that potassium floated on water. Down to a very recent date civilized men had never seen a black swan, yet no naturalist was ever so presumptuous as to affirm that there never could be such an animal; and when black swans were discovered in Australia, scientific men, no doubt, wondered, but never went so far as to deny the fact. A very wide and uniform experience would justify a general expectation, but not a necessary conviction; and this experience is liable to be disturbed at any time by a new occurrence inconsistent with what has been previously known to us. But the belief in the connection between cause and effect is of a totally different character. We can believe that two things which have been united since creation began, may never be united again while creation lasts; but we never can be made to believe, or rather, think, judge, or decide (for this is the right expression) that a change can take place without a cause. We can believe that night and day might henceforth be disconnected, and that from and after this day or some other day there would only be perpetual day or perpetual night on the earth; but we could never be made to decide that, the causes which produced day and night being the same, there ever could be any other effect than day or night. We could believe, on sufficient evidence, that the sun might not rise on our earth to-morrow, but we never could be made to judge that, the sun and earth and all other things necessary to the sun rising on our earth abiding as they are, the luminary of day should not run his round as usual. We see at once that there is a difference between the judgment of the mind in the two cases; in the case in which we have before us a mere conjunction sanctioned by a wide and invariable induction, and that in which we have an effect, and connect it with its cause. The one belief can be overcome, and should be overcome at any time by a new and inconsistent fact coming under our observation; whereas, in regard to the other, we are confident that it never can be modified or set aside, and we feel that it ought not to be overborne.

It is to be carefully noticed that while we have a native and necessary conviction, it does not announce what effect any given cause must produce, or what is the cause of any given effect. On an effect presenting itself to our notice, we believe that it must have a cause, but what the cause is, is to be determined, after all, by observation. On discovering a new substance, say a metal, we anticipate that it will act in some particular way on the needful conditions being supplied; but how it will act, chemically or magnetically, or in reference to any other agent, we cannot predict beforehand. It is of the utmost moment that we ever take this view of the intuitive principle when we would use it in speculation, and that we should distinctly know what it cannot do, as well as what it can do. It is meant to be a regulative principle underlying and guiding our inquiries, but it is not intended to supersede experience. On the contrary, it is when an effect or a cause is presented, that the intuitive principle begins to operate, and constrains us to look for a cause or an effect. And as to what the precise cause or effect may be, even this is not announced by the conviction, but is to be discovered by experience; that is, having discovered that a substance has operated in a certain way in time past, we are sure that it will so operate again; and having found that a particular effect has proceeded from a certain cause, we are sure, on the same effect presenting itself, that it must have come from the same cause. It thus appears that intuition and experience combine, each meanwhile having its own province, in all the judgments which we pronounce as to the mode of the operation of any given cause, or the cause of any given effect. It is our special business, in what remains of this Section, to determine in an inductive manner what is involved in our conviction of cause and effect, and the relation between them.

I. Cause implies a Substance with Potency. This doctrine was explicitly stated and defended by Leibnitz, and has been incidentally admitted by many who have not been prepared to adhere to the general view.* We never know of a causal influence being exercised, except by an object having being and substantial existence. We decide, and must decide, that every effect proceeds from one or more substances having potency. If a tree is felled to the ground, if the salt we saw dry a minute ago is now melted, if a limb of man or animal is broken, we not only look for a cause, but we look for a cause in something that had being and property, say in the wind blowing on the tree, or in water mingling with the salt, or in a blow being inflicted by a stick, or other hard substance, on the limb. When we discover effects produced by light, heat, electricity, or similar agents, whose precise nature has not been discovered, we regard them either as separate substances, or if this seems (as it does) highly improbable, we regard them as properties or affections of substances. If this world be an effect, we look for its cause in a Being possessed of power.

And this, I may remark in passing, seems to be the reason why we do not place Time and Space under the law of causation. Causes operate and effects take place in time and space, but we are not led to look on duration and place producing effects, or being themselves affected by any agents. We talk, indeed, of time effecting mighty changes, say in elevating or abrading the earth's surface, or in revolutionizing society, and changing men's opinions and sentiments; but the language is elliptical, and it means, when the steps are fully un-

* See *supra*, pp. 147, 166.

folded, that powers residing in substances produce effects when time is allowed them. So far as we know, or can know, of time or space, we look on them as unchanged and unchangeable, though it would be presumptuous in us to affirm that they can in no way be affected or influenced by the Divine Power.

II. Power residing in substance is exercised when the needful conditions are supplied. All creature power is conditioned and limited: it is a power to produce a certain particular effect. Commonly, if not invariably, there is need, as has been shown in treating of Power, of the concurrence of two or more agencies in order to action, and there will be operation only when there is co-operation. The very power of God is in a sense qualified, it is guided by that which should ever direct it, by His Will, which is holy and benevolent. But confining our attention to creature power, mental or material, it has always a rule, or defined mode of action, and can act only in a particular way, and to a certain extent. That which is necessary to the exercise of power in a substance may be called the conditions, and it is only on the conditions being supplied that power is exercised. A magnet has a power of attracting iron, but it is only when iron is within reach that the property is active.

There is a sense, and an important sense, in which power may be said to be in the substance, to be inherent in the substance, to constitute, indeed, an element in the nature of the substance. In this sense the power of the substance is always the same; that is, the same substance will always act in the same way on the conditions being supplied. Allotropism may seem an exception, but it is so only in appearance; for when phosphorus produces one effect in one state, and another effect in another state, it is because of some change produced by heat, or electricity, or some other agent; and that the power continues the same, is evident from the circumstance that when the substance is brought back from its allotropic state, it exercises the same power as it did at first, a clear proof that in the allotropic state it was simply put under new conditions. It appears from these statements that there may be perfect propriety in speaking of latent power, that is, of a power not in action because the conditions needful to its operation are not supplied. Nay, it is possible, I do not say probable, that there are properties both of mind and matter which are usually occult, and only appear in action on rare occasions. Nay, some have supposed that the soul has capacities which are altogether dormant here (like the capacity of the dumb to learn languages if only they had hearing), and are to be awakened into life only on the conditions needful to their exercise being presented in the world to come.

III. There must be an adequacy or sufficiency of power to produce the effect. We not only look for a cause, but for a competent cause. Experience, it is true, and experience alone, can tell us what is a sufficient cause, as it alone can inform us what is the cause. Still there seems to be an inherent conviction of the mind which leads us, in looking for a cause, to make the cause equal to the work which it accomplishes. Powers differ in kind, and they differ in degree. There is need, for instance, of more than human power to create a substance out of nothing. There is need of more than the power residing in material substance to produce thought and emotion and will. The ant which carries a seed of grain, is not competent, like man, to carry a sack of corn; and the strength of man is inadequate to raise a weight which can be lifted with ease by a steam-engine. The lily can reproduce a lily after its kind, but cannot produce a pine or an oak. These facts, I am aware, can be known only by observation. But underneath all our experiential knowledge there is a necessary principle which constrains us, when we discover an effect, to look not only for a cause, but a cause with the kind of power which is fitted to produce the kind of effect, and to proportion the extent of the power to the extent of the effect. This original principle is the source of a number of most important derivative ones; as, when we have found a substance exercising a certain sort of power, we anticipate that it will always exercise the same sort of power, and when we have found it exercising a certain amount of force, we expect that it will always be fit for the same, —of course, always on the necessary conditions being furnished. Thus, having found that our minds can follow a train of reasoning, we are sure that they will always be able to do so,—of course, on the supposition that the bodily organism needful to mental operation in man is not in a state of derangement. The amount of force which drives a ball a certain distance to-day, we are sure will drive it to the same distance to-morrow. If a definite weight of oxygen has been ascertained chemically to unite with a certain definite weight of hydrogen, we are sure it will ever do so; and if we find the very same amount of oxygen not drawing to it the same amount of hydrogen, we argue that there must have been some change in the conditions of the oxygen. It is acknowledged that in such judgments there is and must be an experiential element, which in spontaneous thought is ever the more prominent,—it is ever the one about which the mind is most anxious, as being the only doubtful one; still there is also a necessary principle, which is overlooked only because it is indisputable and invariable. Rising from earthly to heavenly things, we look on God, who has produced works in which are traces of such large power and admirable wisdom, as a Being possessed of power and wisdom corresponding to the effects we discover, and as capable, whenever he may see fit, of producing works distinguished by the same lofty characteristics.

IV. There is a necessary relation between the cause and the effect, arising from the necessity of the cause to produce the effect when the conditions are furnished. The principles laid down in preceding Sections seem to me to establish this truth, and so to clear up the subject round which the discussions regarding causation have chiefly turned since the days of Hume. Perverting and turning to his own purposes the views regarding sensation which had been maintained by Locke and other metaphysicians, the great sceptic represents the mind as starting with impressions; and it seems to me certain that, were there nothing beyond this in the original intuitions of the mind, it would be impossible to show how it could ever reach the knowledge of realities. Many of the opponents of Hume have not seen, or, at least, have not adopted the proper method of meeting him. Kant supposes the mind to start with phenomena, and not with things; and when he subsequently calls in a category of cause and effect, it is avowed that it cannot apply to things, but simply to phenomena. Dr. Thomas Brown saw clearly that our belief in cause and effect is intuitive, and so far his views are sound, and most eloquently and forcibly illustrated; but, supposing the mind to start with mere sensations, and not with the knowledge of things, and things possessing power, he never reached adequate views of the relation between the cause and the effect. Differing widely from Hume as to the nature of the mental principle which leads us to believe in the connection between cause and effect, he regards the objective connection as merely invariable antecedence and consequence. In sustaining this tenet he wastes an immense amount of ingenuity in showing that there is nothing, no link of any kind, between the cause and the effect. True I say, and I maintain that, except in the way of loose metaphor, no one ever asserted that there was. But in all this argument he blinks the main question,—and yet it is ever, as appears from chance expressions, pressing itself on him,—which is not as to what is between the cause and effect, but what is there in the cause to produce the effect. If he had supposed the mind to begin with the cognition of self and of body exercising power, he would have found more in the relation than the mere invariability of the succession : he would have discovered a power in the substance or substances acting as the cause, and that the invariableness, so far from being the primary circumstance, was a necessary consequence of this.

The invariability then carries us back to a more important circumstance, to the power which is intuitively known to be in substance. When the substances have the conditions furnished, they act, and effects must follow. The acting substances in the relation needful to their action is thus the true cause, the unconditional cause (to use a phrase of Mr. J. S. Mill's), the invariable cause ever followed by its proper and peculiar effects. This view however lends no sanction whatever to the rash statements of M. Cousin, who speaks about its being necessary for God to create. True, creation must follow if he put forth the volition, but then he has a will to exert or withhold the creating act. Creation must spring into being if he will it, but to will it is an element (always along with power) in that cause of which a created object is the effect. The same remark holds good, within certain limitations, of the acts of man : when he wills it, certain effects follow, as when he wills to lift the arm, the arm must move if the organs be in a healthy condition; but in this and all similar cases, while the effect is necessary, it is on the presupposition of a cause in which will and free will is an essential element. In other cases the effects follow from a power in substance, acting, so far as man can know, without any exercise of will. When I hear of the death of a friend, and a torrent of grief flows into my bosom, or when a spark falls on gunpowder, and an explosion follows, there is no exercise of creature will, (though there may possibly be a concurrence of the Divine Will necessary to all creature action); but whether there be or be not room for free will in the cause or substances acting, there is a necessary connection between these substances acting (with or without free will) and their proper effect. The mind, in contemplating the relation between cause and effect, declares the relation to be necessary, and cannot be made to believe otherwise, and decides that it is a necessity arising from the power intuitively known as in the substance. It is to reverse the proper order of things to resolve the necessity into the invariableness: the invariableness is the result of a necessity arising from the potency of substance.

V. An effect is known as either a new substance, or as a change in a previously existing substance. The production of a new substance, or even of a new power, property, or capacity in an old substance, is altogether beyond human power; it is probably beyond all creature power. It seems to be the special prerogative of God to create out of nothing. A large induction seems to inform us that, in creating substances, he imparted to them all their qualities and properties; and man can as little add to the powers in the substances, as he can add to the substances in the universe. Another kind of effect, and the one which alone falls under our common observation, consists in a previously existing substance being put in a new state: this is the only effect which can be produced by any modification of physical action, as by mechanical or chemical action; nay, it is the only effect which can be produced by mental action or human action of any description. Taking advantage of natural powers, we may find a body in one condition and put it in another; or, accommodating ourselves to mental laws, we may produce changes in our own state of mind: but here our power terminates. We are informed of all this by an enlarged experience rather than by intuition; but our primary conviction seems to say, that as every cause is found in a substance, so every effect is also in a substance, which may, as induction shows, be either a totally new substance, or a substance undergoing some modification.

From this doctrine of causation, there follow several corollaries of no little consequence in the settlement of speculative questions.

1. When the effect is real, that is, a real thing or substance, the cause must also be real, that is, a real thing or substance produced or changed. No doubt, it is quite possible for man, endowed as he is with the power of imagination as well as cognition, to conjure up a fanciful effect, say to fancy that some mysterious power is exercising a malign influence upon him, and in such a case the cause must be as imaginary as the effect (though even here the intuitive law of causation will constrain him to seek for producing power in some human or angelic being, in some star or animal); but if the effect be a thing in actual existence, the cause must also be in actual existence. Taking this view with us, we see how those metaphysicians who suppose that the mind primitively knows only phenomena, can never satisfactorily go beyond a phenomenology, or reach a God who has any other sort of existence than the phenomena, and the mental laws which bind them. But if the world be a reality, if mind be a real thing, and body a real thing, and

the heavens and earth be real things, and if they be effects of power which must of necessity be supra-mundane, then the constitutional laws of the mind insist that the cause must also be real, and is to be found in a Being possessed of the adequate and competent power.

2. The mind is not necessitated to seek for an endless series of causes. As the doctrine of causation is sometimes stated, it might appear as if we were required, in following the chain of cause and effect, to go back *ad infinitum*. It is said, in a loose way, that every object must have a cause; and then, as this cause must also have a cause, it might seem as if we were compelled to go on for ever from one link to another. In particular, it might appear as if we could never legitimately argue from the law of causation in favour of this world being caused; for, if the law of cause and effect be universal, then we must seek for a cause, not only of the world, but of the Being who made the world; and if it be not universal, then it is conceivable that this world may be one of the things which are not caused. This is an objection urged with great confidence by Kant; and a large school of metaphysicians seem to think that it is fatal to any argument in favour of the Divine existence derived from human intelligence, as in every such argument the law of causation must enter as an element. Kant endeavours to escape from the dismal consequences in which he felt himself being engulfed, by declaring that the law of cause and effect, which thus required an infinite *regressus*, was a law of thought and not of things, and by calling in a moral argument (which argument has again been assailed by the very objections which Kant directed against the speculative argument—for if our intelligence be a delusion, why may not our moral convictions also be so?); while a large body of thinkers have appealed to some sort of mysterious faith which will not submit to

be examined or even expressed. But, with all deference to these bold asseverations, I maintain that if only this Cosmos can be shown to bear marks of being an effect, the argument from causation can carry us up to a supramundane cause, while it does not require us to go back to a cause of that cause. All inquiry into causation conducts us to substance; but it does not compel us to go on further, or to go on for ever. The law of causality does insist that the world, as an effect, must have a cause in a Being possessing power; and if, in inquiring into the nature of that Being, we find reason to believe that He or it must be an effect, it would insist on us going on to look out for a further cause. But if, on the other hand, we find no signs of that Being who made the world being an effect, our intuition regarding causation would be entirely satisfied in looking on that Being as uncaused, as self-existent, as having power in Himself. It thus appears that this difficulty, which has puzzled so many, has arisen entirely from a misapprehension and perversion of the law of causation, commencing with Hume, and presented in a new form by Kant. It is removed at once by an inductive investigation of our cognition of power, and of our judgment regarding causation.*

* It is a circumstance worthy of being noted that the powerful mind of Kant, in his chase after an Unconditioned, represented by him as ideal, finds a *progressus* or a *regressus* of some kind or other in time, in space, in matter, in cause, in the possible or actual, but admits fully and explicitly that in regard to substance the reason has no ground to proceed regressively with conditions. In regard to causality we have a series of causes which go back unendingly, the unconditioned being the absolute totality of the series. But in substance there is no such *regressus*. "Was die Kategorien des realen Verhältnisses unter den Erscheinungen anlangt, so schickt sich die Kategorie der Substanz mit ihren Accidenzen nicht zu einer transscendentalen Idee, d. i. die Vernunft hat keinen Grund, in Ansehung ihrer, regressiv auf Bedingungen zu gehen." (Kr. d. r. Vern., p. 328.) We have only to connect this doctrine of substance, not necessarily calling, according to the principles of reason, for a *regressus*, with his admission that substance

3. By observing and classifying the effects, we may obtain a knowledge of the substances from which the effects proceed. Powers residing in substances differ in kind and in degree in different substances. The power of creation differs from the power of simply producing changes in what already exists. Power in spiritual beings differs from power in inanimate creation. Even when the power is the same in kind, it may differ in degree in different individuals. Now it is by a careful observation and generalization of its actings, and of the effects that follow, that we are enabled to gather our chief knowledge of substance. In conducting such an investigation in a scientific manner, we put in one class, and usually designate by a common name, the acts which are alike in their main features, and argue legitimately that there is a faculty in the substance to produce these effects. It is thus from a classification of the actings of natural substances that we seek to rise to a knowledge of the properties general and specific of body. It is thus that we observe and generalize the acts of the mind, and so endeavour to ascertain its faculties. It is thus, that from a careful generalization of the acts of God, the theologian attempts to give something like—he should profess to do no more—a systematic account of his Attributes. All this does not imply, though some are ever telling us that it does, that we are dividing the unity of the soul, or the unity of God. In proceeding in this inductive manner we are taking the only plan available to us of becoming acquainted with those powers or attributes which constitute an essential element in the human soul and in the Divine Mind.

involves power (see *supra*, p. 166 foot-note) to be able to maintain, and this without falling into any contradiction, that the effects seen in nature of a power above nature, argue a substance having power, for which we are not required to seek for a cause.

4. By combined intuition and experience we may often be enabled to argue that effects of a particular description imply causes of a particular kind and degree. Intuition insists that not only there be a cause of the effect, but that the cause be sufficient. Experience then comes in to give us information as to certain effects coming from certain causes or substances, and not coming from certain others. We do not expect inanimate objects to produce the effects that flow from the plant, nor the plant to accomplish what is done by the animal, nor body to effect what can be done by mind. A very wide induction informs us that order and adaptation come from a being capable of contemplating means and end, and are not to be looked for from material forces operating blindly and unintelligently. All this may not, it is true, be intuitive or apodictic, but it is the result of a large and uniform observation, and it connects itself with a primary conviction which demands an adequacy in the cause, and is satisfied when it is directed to a Supreme Intelligence, the source of all the system and utility to be found in the universe.

5. The intuitive conviction gives no sanction whatever to the maxims that like can only act on like, or like only proceed from like, or that the effect must resemble the cause. All these proceed from narrow views of cause, making that universal which holds good only in certain cases. Like things do influence each other, but unlike things also exercise a mutual affection, as when acid acts on an alkali. The offspring of plants and animals do resemble their parents; but there are effects which are in no way like their cause, as when the sun's heat makes the ice to melt. By laying down such maxims, philosophers landed themselves in innumerable difficulties; they could not allow that body could influence mind, or mind body, or conceive how it was possible for

the physical universe to proceed from a spiritual God; and they helped, with other Cartesian principles, to shut up Spinoza into a pantheism which would admit of only one substance. But such maxims have no foundation in intuition, and they are contradicted by experience. The maxim is not, the cause and effect must be alike, but that the cause must be competent to produce the effect.

6. It is not a sufficiently accurate expression of the principle of causation when it is said that like causes in like circumstances will produce like effects. When the law is announced in this vague form, we lose ourselves in determining what amount of resemblance there must be in the causes and in the effects, and in estimating the relative importance of the causes and of the circumstances. A philosophical account of the cause must specify the likeness necessary, and embrace the circumstances. We must therefore bring in substance and the power in substance acting according to a rule. Every created substance is endowed with power of a certain kind and amount, which will act, on the needful conditions being supplied; and the correct statement is, that the same substances, acting in the same relation, will always produce the same effects.

7. Our intuitive conviction is not of the uniformity or continuance of the course of nature. This is the vague shape in which the principle appears in the works of Reid and Stewart. "God," says the former, "hath implanted in human minds an original principle, by which we believe and expect the continuance of the course of nature, and the continuance of those connections which we have observed in time past" (Works, p. 198). "We attend to every conjunction of things which presents itself, and expect the continuance of that conjunction." This is far too loose a form in which to present the maxim; indeed it is altogether incorrect, and may land

us, if logically followed out, in very serious consequences. Instead of having a belief in the permanence or continuance of the course of things, the great body of mankind—nearly all in the earlier and simpler ages of society, and almost all who live beyond the pale of the countries in which physical science is cultivated—look upon this world as liable to constant interferences on the part of supernatural agencies, in cases in which they do not regard events as being produced by chance or caprice. It is vain, therefore, to speak of the belief in the uniformity of nature as a self-evident, a necessary, or a universal principle.*

Besides, if we have an intuitive belief in the permanence of nature, it will be impossible to prove that nature was created, or that there can be any miracles or interference with the agencies of nature by a supernatural power; for no evidence adduced in behalf of creation or divine interposition could ever be so strong as the necessary belief in direct opposition to it. But the fact is, that all such maxims as that the course of things is uni-

* Mr. J. S. Mill is successful in showing (Logic, bk. iii. ch. xvi.) that man's belief in the uniformity of nature is the result of experience, that it is entertained only by the educated and civilized few, and that even among such it has been of slow growth. But Mr. Mill has fallen into a glaring 'fallacy of confusion' in confounding our belief in causation with our belief in the uniformity of nature. The distinction was before him, at least for an instant, when, speaking of the irregularities of nature, he says: "Such phenomena were commonly, in that early stage of human knowledge, ascribed to the direct intervention of the will of some supernatural being, and therefore still to a cause. This shows the strong tendency of the human mind to ascribe every phenomenon to some cause or other." It is of this *tendency* that I affirm that it is native, and irresistible. He tells us that one "accustomed to abstraction and analysis, who will fairly exert his faculties for the purpose, will, when his imagination has once learned to entertain the notion, find no difficulty in conceiving that in some one, for instance, of the many firmaments into which sidereal astronomy now divides the universe, events may succeed one another at random, without any fixed law; nor can anything in our experience, or in our mental nature, constitute a sufficient or indeed any reason for believing that this is

form, and that like may be expected in like circumstances, are the result, not of any fundamental principle of intelligence, but of experience; and the same experience which determines how far they are true must determine also how they are to be understood, how they are modified, and what are the exceptions to them. Natural science proves that while the usual rule is that all plants and animals proceed from parents of the same kind, there must yet have been a time or times when new species appeared on the earth by a supernatural power, or at least a power not at work in the present processes of nature. The world as a whole bears marks of being an effect, and there must have been a time when it was produced by a power above itself. In the inspired writings we have evidence of works being done by Moses and the Prophets, by Jesus and the Apostles, surpassing the power of man or of physical nature. All this is inconsistent with a belief in the absolute uniformity of the course of nature, but it is quite in harmony with the intuitive conviction. If the world be an effect, we seek for

nowhere the case." I have remarked on this elsewhere (Method of Divine Government, p. 528). "This statement about fixed laws is ambiguous. If by fixed law be meant simply order and uniformity among physical events, the statement is true. But if meant to signify an event without a cause, material or mental, the statement is contradicted by our 'mental nature,' which impels us to seek for a cause of every event. He is right in affirming that 'experience' cannot authorize such a belief; but it is just as certain that our 'mental nature' constrains us to entertain it: and surely if there be laws in physical nature, there may also be trustworthy laws in our mental nature." There is the same confusion of two different things in the following passage. "The uniformity in the succession of events, otherwise called the law of causation, must be received not as the law of the universe, but of that portion of it only which is within the range of our means of sure observation, with a reasonable degree of extension to adjacent cases." I freely admit all this in regard to the order observable everywhere in our Cosmos; there may or may not be a similar uniformity in the regions of space beyond. But our mental nature will not allow us to think, judge, or believe (these, and not 'conceive,' which is ambiguous, are the proper phrases), that in this our world, or in any other world, there can be an event without a cause.

a cause above the world; if the new species of animated beings cannot have been produced by natural agencies, we call in a supernatural cause; if the miracles of Scripture cannot be accounted for by human power, we call in Divine Power; and we feel, meanwhile, that so far from our native convictions being violated, they are gratified to the full when they learn of the events, otherwise inexplicable, being referred to causes adequate to produce them. It thus appears that those difficulties which have been propounded so pompously about the impossibility of proving that there can have been a cause above nature producing the effects in nature, or of establishing a miraculous interposition with the course of things, all proceed on defective and erroneous views of causation, and at once disappear when the nature of our conviction is inductively investigated and correctly expressed.*

* It is not to my present purpose to enter on the subject of miracles, but it does fall in with the topics discussed in the text to remark, that there is nothing in a miracle opposed to any intuition of the mind,—certainly nothing opposed to our intuition as to cause. Hume, the sceptic, takes all sorts of objections to miracles, and the evidence by which they are supported, but he does not maintain that a miracle is impossible. It is "experience," according to him, "which assures us of the laws of nature" (Essay on Miracles); and I hold that the same experience shows us effects in nature which constrain us, according to the intuitive law of causation, to argue a Power above nature, which Power is an adequate cause of any miracle which may be attested by proper evidence. Dr. Thomas Brown has shown very satisfactorily that a miracle, with the Divine Power as its cause, is not inconsistent with our intuitive belief in causation (Cause and Effect, note E). Ever since Fichte published his 'Versuch einer Kritik aller Offenbarung,' there have been persons in Germany who represent it as impossible for God to perform a miracle. This may be a necessary consequence of those false assumptions regarding our knowing only self, which landed Fichte in an incongruous pantheism, in which he at one time represents the *Ego* as the All-including God, as the "moral order;" and at another time represents God as the All, and absorbing the *Ego*. But it can plead in its behalf no principle in the constitution of man's mind,—no principle either natural or necessary. The result at which we have arrived is, that the question of the occurrence of miracles is to be determined by the ordinary laws of evidence.

BOOK IV.

MORAL CONVICTIONS.

CHAPTER I.

GENERAL VIEW OF THE MOTIVE AND MORAL POWERS.

SECT. I. THE APPETENCIES, THE WILL, AND THE CONSCIENCE.

THE relation between the innate principles, or the fundamental laws of the mind, on the one hand, and the faculties of the mind on the other, has seldom been properly understood. The former seem to me to be the rules of the operation of the latter. I have in the first three Books endeavoured to unfold the main primary principles regulating those faculties which have been called the Understanding, or the Intellectual or Gnostic or Cognitive Powers; or, better still, the Cognitive and Contemplative, so as to embrace the Imagination, which can scarcely be called a Cognitive but is certainly a Contemplative Power. But in all classifications of the powers of the mind which have the least pretensions to completeness, there has been a recognition of another class, under the name of the Will, or the Feelings, or the Erective or Motive Powers; they may perhaps be best designated as the Motive and Moral Powers, so as to embrace unequivocally the functions of the conscience.

I am in this Chapter to take a glance at this class of powers, and afterwards seek to ascertain the fundamental principles involved in them. They are at least three in number, the Appetencies,—including the Emotions,—the Will, and the Conscience.

I. There are the native Appetencies of the Mind leading to Emotions. Man is so constituted that he is capable of being swayed in will, and so in action, by certain motives, that is, by the contemplation of certain objects or ends, while others do not influence him. It would serve many important ends to have a classification of these, that is, of the springs of human will and action. To endeavour to give a complete and exhaustive list of these, that is, of the categories of man's moral nature, would, I am aware, be quite as bold an effort as that so often made to determine the categories of the understanding. Such a classification would at the best be very imperfect in the first instance. But, even though only provisionally correct, it might accomplish some useful purposes. In the absence of any arrangement sanctioned by metaphysicians generally, it must suffice to mention here some of the principal motives which very obviously sway the will and impel to action.

1. Mankind are evidently inclined, involuntarily and voluntarily, to exercise every native power,—the senses, the memory, the imagination, the power of language, the various rational powers, such as abstraction, comparison, causality, the emotional, voluntary, and moral capacities. A vast portion of human activity proceeds from no higher and from no lower source than this. As the lamb frisks, and the colt gambols, and as the child is in perpetual rotation, so man's internal powers are for ever impelling him to exertion, independent altogether of any external object, or even of any further internal ends to be gained.

2. Whatever is contemplated as capable of securing pleasure is felt to be desirable, and whatever is apprehended as likely to inflict pain is avoided. This is so very obvious a swaying power with human beings that it has been noticed, and commonly greatly exaggerated, in every account which has been given of man's active and moral nature. The mistake of the vulgar, and especially of the sensational systems, is that they have represented pleasure and pain as the sole contemplated ends by which man is or can be swayed. It is our object in these paragraphs to show that man can be influenced by other motives better and worse.

3. There are certain appetencies in man, bodily and mental, which crave for gratification, and this independent of the pleasure to be secured by their indulgence. Of this description are the appetites of hunger, thirst, and sex, and the mental tendencies to seek for knowledge, esteem, society, power, property. These appetencies may connect themselves with the other two classes already specified, but still they are different. They will tend to act as natural inclinations, but still they look towards particular external objects. We may come to gratify them for the sake of the pleasure, but in the first instance we seek the objects for their own sakes, and it is in seeking the objects we obtain gratification. They operate to some extent in the breasts of all, and they come to exercise a fearfully controlling and grasping power over the minds of multitudes.

4. Man is impelled by an inward principle, more or less powerful in the case of different individuals, and varying widely in the objects desired, to seek for the beautiful in inanimate or in animate objects, in grand or lovely scenes in nature, in statues, paintings, buildings, fine composition in prose or poetry, and in the countenances or forms of man or woman.

5. It is not to be omitted that the moral power in man is not only (as I hope to show) a knowing and judging faculty, it has a prompting energy, and leads us, when a corrupt will does not interfere, to such acts as the worship of God and beneficence to man, done because they are right.

6. Whatever is felt to be appetible for ourselves we may wish that others should enjoy, while we may desire that they should be preserved from all that is unappetible, such as restraint and pain and sin. Man is so constituted as to be stirred to desire and prompted to action by the contemplation of other beings to whom he is related, such as God when he knows Him, and his fellow-men, more especially certain of his fellow-men, such as his countrymen and kindred, and those who have bestowed favours upon him. I must ever set myself against the miserably degrading doctrine of those who represent man as utterly selfish in his constitution, and capable of being swayed by no other considerations than those which promise pleasurable gratifications to be realized by himself. He may, by a hardening process of sin, make himself thus selfish, but in his original nature he is capable of being swayed by a great number and variety of other motives, and among others by attachments to man as man, or to particular men or women, and by sympathy for persons in trouble.

In whatever way we may classify them, these, or such as these, are the motives by which man is naturally swayed. Upon these native and primary principles of action, others, acquired and secondary, come to be grafted. Thus money, not originally desired for its own sake, may come to be coveted as fitted to gratify the love of property, the love of power, or the love of pleasure. Or a particular fellow-man, at first indifferent, comes to be avoided, because he seems inclined to thwart us in some of our favourite ends, such as the acquisition of wealth or of fame. It is a peculiarity of our nature that these secondary principles may become primary ones, and prompt us to seek, for their own sakes, objects which were at first coveted solely because they tended to promote further ends.

The appetencies, native and acquired, stir up Emotion, which is called forth by an apprehension of objects as fitted to gratify or to disappoint these appetencies. Let us call whatever accords with them the Appetible, and whatever runs counter to them the Inappetible; then the law is that the appetible, when in prospect, calls forth hope, and when realized, joy; whereas the inappetible, when in prospect, excites fear, and when realized, sorrow. It is always to be taken into account that the emotive susceptibility is naturally stronger in some minds than in others, is stronger at one period of life, or even one day or hour, than another; but making due allowance for this variable element, the intensity of feeling is determined by the strength of the motive principle, its native strength or its acquired strength, and by the extent of the appetible or inappetible embraced within the mental apprehension of the object or end fitted to gratify or disappoint the appetency. There are thus three elements determining the emotion, and these varying in the case of different individuals, and of the same individual at different times. There is the emotional susceptibility, depending largely on the state of the brain or particular organs of it. There is the mental appetency, natural or acquired. There is the mental apprehension of an object or event as tending to content or gratify the appetence. By these elements we can explain all the feelings and much of the activity of humanity. We have here the key to unlock a door through which we may see what rules the passions of men and women, often so very capricious, and apparently contradictory. This deep affection, long cherished, or this burst of sudden anger or joy or grief, reveals to the observant eye the deep moving principle of the inner soul.

It should be observed that while the mind is impelled by such appetencies towards certain objects, it has not necessarily before it the general principle by which it is actuated, nor indeed a general idea of any description. It contemplates an individual object as about to give it pleasure, or about to add to its power or fame, and it at once longs for it without generalizing its aim. Here, as in other cases which have passed under our notice, the mind is actuated by principles which are not before the consciousness as principles.

The emotions stirred up by these appetencies are characterized by two marked features; one is a drawing towards the object that is appetible, and a drawing away from what is inappetible; and the other is a lively excitement—whence the name emotions. Thus, in fear we have an apprehension of some evil as about to befall us or those in whom we feel an interest, and we shrink from the object; whereas, in hope, we have an idea of an event as about to bring good, and we, as it were, reach toward it. While thus longing or shrinking, the mind is all the while in a quickened and moved state.

II. There is the WILL. The powers I have been speaking of rush on to their ends instinctively and blindly. The native power goes on to action, the appetite claims indulgence, the dominant passion embraces its object, each according to its nature. But these activities and propensities are often inconsistent the one with the other. The intellect would set out on high pursuits, but is opposed by some grovelling appetite, or the man would wish to acquire fame, but, in doing so, finds that he cannot accumulate property as he might otherwise do. Is man condemned to be the slave of these appetencies? yielding to the one which happens to assail him, or obeying the strongest when they are competing or clashing. It is probable that this is the condition of the brute creatures, and would be the state of man did he not possesss a higher power. That power is the Will.

Properly speaking, the will does not furnish incitements, inducement, or motives; these come from the appetencies which we have just been considering. It is the province of the Will, seated above them, to sanction or restrain them when they present themselves, and to decide among them when they are competing with each other for the mastery. We have seen that the characteristic property of emotion is attachment or repugnance, with associated excitement. The distinguishing quality of will is choice or rejection. Inducements being held out, the mind, in the exercise of will, sanctions or refuses; it assumes a number of forms, in all of which there is the element of choice. If the object is present, we positively choose it or adopt it; if the object is absent, we wish for it; if it is to be obtained by some exertion on our part, we form a resolution to take the steps necessary to procure it.

III. There is the Conscience. It is the special function of this power to say when a particular appetency should be allowed and when it should be restrained; in doing so, it addresses itself to the will. The conscience thus claims to be above, not only our natural appetencies, but above the will, which ought to yield as soon as the decision of conscience is given; not that it can set itself altogether above nature, not that it should set itself above nature; it is its office to sit in judgment on appetencies which are natural or may be acquired, and it works through free will as an essential element of our nature. But, as Bishop Butler has shown, it is of the nature of our constitution that it pronounces judgments for the will and upon the appetencies. Let us endeavour to unfold the nature of this moral power. It will be seen that, though not identical with, it is so far analogous to the intellectual powers.

1. The conscience is of the nature of a cognitive power. It is analogous in this respect to the faculties of sense and self-consciousness. Not that it makes known any individual object, as the senses do when they show this table or that chair, or as self-consciousness does, when it discloses self in a particular state, say as musing or as hoping: it reveals to us merely certain qualities of objects otherwise known, that is, known by perception and self-consciousness; it lets us know, for example, of certain voluntary states of ourselves or of others, that they are good or that they are evil. Making known no new substance or independent existence, it does reveal to us a quality of all souls possessed of intelligence and free will; it was this property of the conscience that was seized by Shaftesbury and by Francis Hutcheson, when they called this power the moral sense. The phrase was adopted by them, I suspect, to make their system tally with that of Locke, who admitted an external and internal sense, to which they now added a moral sense. It was, in some respects, an unfortunate phrase, as it seemed to degrade the moral power in man to the rank of a bodily faculty, or to make it dependent on bodily organization. But it is fitted to bring out one feature of man's nature, that by which he is able to detect a certain quality in the acts of all intelligent beings.*

2. There are beliefs involved in the exercise of the moral power. These beliefs are very closely connected

* See some valuable remarks in note F, appended to Mansel's 'Prolegomena Logica.' "It appears that a power of discerning right and wrong in individual acts must be allowed as the presentative basis, without which no system of Moral Philosophy is possible." See also Art. Metaph. in Encyc. Brit.

with the cognitions, from which indeed it is scarcely necessary to distinguish them, except for certain purposes of philosophic accuracy. The phrase moral cognitions might be confined to those mental exercises in which the action which we pronounce good or bad is our own, falling immediately under consciousness, and we pronounce it to be good or bad, whereas our moral beliefs extend much further, and refer to acts not immediately under the introspective power, as when we believe that benevolence is good everywhere, and that God is good and has been good and shall be good to all eternity. I am inclined to regard our moral cognitions as the basis of our moral beliefs. We seem first to have a necessary conviction in regard to the moral nature of our own actions, and thence we arise to convictions which look to moral qualities, which, being apprehended by us, we declare to be good or evil, wherever they are to be found, and whoever may be the possessor.

3. Judgments are involved in the exercise of this moral power. These proceed on our original cognitions and beliefs. Discerning in certain agents moral qualities, we can discover relations involved in the comparison of these qualities one with another, and with other objects and qualities. Our moral, like our intellectual cognitions and beliefs, furnish matter for innumerable judgments. Thus, in looking at the relation in which man stands to God, we affirm that we ought to obey the Divine commands. Or, looking to a certain deed and to the painful consequences to which it has led, we say the sin merits the suffering. It is the special office of ethical science to generalize and express the cognitions, beliefs, and judgments of the moral power, and to derive rules from them by which to judge of actions.

4. Our apprehension of moral good and evil is accompanied with appetency and emotion. The conscience, in

fact, partakes of the nature both of a cognitive and a motive power; it knows certain qualities in objects, and, as it recognizes them, it looks on them as appetible or inappetible, and is moved towards them or away from them. Hence the conscience is not only a judge, it is a spring of action, and prompts us, if we would but obey it, to seek certain ends, and carefully to avoid others.

Sect. II. (*Supplementary.*) On the Beautiful.

A reference is here made to this subject mainly with the view of showing that, while the appreciation of beauty is a native feeling, it is not to be regarded as a necessary principle. We are certainly led by strong natural inclination to contemplate certain objects with special feelings of attachment and admiration. The science which seeks to catch and formalize these feelings, and to judge by the rules thence drawn of objects in nature and in art, has been called Æsthetics, but might perhaps be more appropriately termed Kalology, or Kallisophy, that is, the science of the Fair or Lovely. It may be doubted however whether we have any such necessary convictions in regard to beauty as we have in regard to certain fundamental intellectual truths and moral qualities. Our knowledge and belief regarding objects presented to sense and consciousness amount to this, that they have an existence independent of the mind contemplating them, and that they would and must have the same existence to all minds endowed with the capacity of becoming acquainted with them. Again, in pronouncing certain judgments, the mind declares not only that there is a relation, but that the relation is necessary. But, in looking on an attractive object, while led to delight in it as lovely, we are not constrained to believe that it must be beautiful, independent of our feeling regarding it, and that it must appear beautiful to all beings. I must believe that the sun exists as an extended body, independent of the structure of my eye or mind, and that it would be apprehended as an extended body by any inhabitant of Mars or Jupiter endowed with the capacity to perceive the object I must believe that ingratitude is a sin, not only on the earth, but everywhere, in the planet Saturn or the star Sirius, in heaven or in hell, and that all beings endowed with moral capacity must see it in the same light; but I am not necessitated to believe that the objects which appear beautiful to me, or to all men, have a beauty independent of the mind that contemplates them, and that all other minds, or even that all minds endowed with the sense of beauty, must view them in precisely the same light. We find, in fact, that the music which is felt by some to be so pleasant and exciting, has no charms whatever to others. We could easily enough believe, if evidence were furnished to us, that the colours which appear so lovely to our eyes, have no attraction whatever to the inhabitants of another planet. Not only so, we can conceive that the very order and proportions which awaken so deep an interest in our minds, might be contemplated with no feeling of admiration by beings endowed with a different mental constitution.

At the same time it should be acknowledged that there seem to be qualities which must have an excellence altogether independent of the mind which views them. It is an opinion which goes as far back as the time of Plato, and has ever since been widely entertained, that beauty of forms consists in some sort of proportion or harmony,* which may admit of a mathematical expression; and later and more scientific research is altogether in its favour. It is now established that complementary colours, that is, colours which when combined make up the full beam, are felt to be beautiful when seen simultaneously; that is, the mind is made to delight in the unities of nature. At the basis of music there are certain fixed ratios; and in poetry of every description there are measures and correspondencies. Pythagoras has often been ridiculed for his doctrine of the music of the spheres; and probably his views were sufficiently mystical and fanciful, but the latest science shows that there is a harmony in all nature,—in its forms, its forces, and its motions. The higher unorganized, and all organized objects, take definite forms which are often regulated by mathematical laws. The forces of nature can be estimated in numbers, and light and heat seem to go in undulations, or at least by intervals, while the movements of the great bodies in nature are periodical.† Such facts as these seem to show that, at the basis of beauty, there may very probably be principles which are necessary, eternal, and altogether independent of the individual mind, or even of the general mind of humanity. But over them all the mind seems to spread a colour and a lustre which we can-

* See fine Platonic speculations in M'Vicar, 'On the Beautiful, the Picturesque, the Sublime,' and the 'Philosophy of the Beautiful;' and in Blackie's 'Beauty, with Plato's Doctrine of the Beautiful;' as well as in Ruskin's 'Modern Painters,' vol. ii.

† The harmonies in nature, in respect of Colour, Number, Form, etc., are illustrated in 'Typical Forms and Special Ends in Creation.'

not regard as necessary, and which may not be universal; or which, if universal, can have become so only by the appointment of the one God, who Himself delights, and would also lead us to delight in the unity and harmony which run through all his works. It is quite possible that, so far as there are eternal principles lying at the basis of certain forms of beauty, they may only be modifications of the eternal principles of truth.

Other kinds of beauty ally themselves more closely with the morally good. There is a beauty in all truly virtuous and beneficent actions of the creature, and, above all, of the Great Creator. Whatever seems to proceed from love or from kindness, such as peace and plenty and diffused happiness, is apt to collect a feeling of loveliness around it. The question is started, May not the principles which underlie these forms of beauty be modifications of the eternal principles of right and wrong?

In the pages of all writers who have meditated profoundly on this subject, will be found such utterances as these:—"The beautiful is always true;" "The beautiful is ever good." Alas! the only exception to this last maxim is to be found in certain human beings, in which guilt has destroyed the holy, but left as yet, and for a time, the lovely, which however will in due time lose its lustre. But there is truth involved in these maxims, and I have sometimes thought that it lies in this, that at the basis of beauty there are eternal principles, modifications of the true and the good, over which the mind casts a colour and a clothing. The God who made us hath given us a nature which throws a halo and a radiance round certain kinds of everlasting verities and moral qualities, with the view of rendering them attractive, and gathering our affections about them.

CHAPTER II.

CONVICTIONS INVOLVED IN THE EXERCISES OF CONSCIENCE.

SECT. I. CONVICTIONS AS TO THE NATURE OF MORAL GOOD.

STILL deeper interests are involved in our being able to show that there is an immutable and eternal morality than even in our proving that there is immutable and eternal truth. But after having laboured at such length to demonstrate that there are native and necessary principles involved in the intellectual exercises of the mind, it will not be needful to take such pains to show that there are similar convictions of a moral character. The mind is led by its very nature and constitution to perceive that there is an indelible distinction between good and evil, just as there is an indelible distinction between truth and falsehood. It finds that every substance has potency; that the species implies the individual; but it also declares that to give every one his due is good, and must be good, and that it is wrong in children to neglect their parents, and in God's creatures to forget their Creator. Let me endeavour to bring out and express some of the principal moral convictions of the mind.

I. The moral quality is not given to the action by the mind contemplating it. It is not a colour thrown over the object by the mental eye which perceives it, but is a real quality of the object, is there prior to its being perceived, and is in the object whether it is perceived or not. It is not our perception and approbation that render a benevolent action good; but we perceive its excellence and approve of it because it is good. It follows that

II. Moral good is moral good to all intelligences so high in the scale of being as to be able to discern it. I lay down this position in order to guard against the idea that moral excellence is something depending on the peculiar constitution of man, and that it is allowable to suppose that there may be intelligent beings in other worlds to whom virtue does not appear as virtue. Such a view seems altogether inconsistent with our intuitive convictions, and would effectually undermine the foundations of morality. It is allowable to suppose that there may be beings in other worlds who see no beauty in the colours or in the shapes and proportions which we so much admire; but I cannot admit that there are any intelligent and responsible beings who look on malevolence as a virtue or justice as a sin.*

III. Moral good lays an obligation on us to attend to it. This sense, or rather, conviction of obligation, is one of the peculiarities, is indeed the chief peculiarity, of our moral perceptions. Herein do our moral convictions, whether of the nature of cognitions, beliefs, or judgments, differ from the intellectual convictions which have passed under our notice in the previous parts of this treatise. That a straight line is the shortest between two points, this I am constrained to decide when my attention is called to the subject, but I know of no duty thence arising, no affection which I should thereon cherish, no action which I ought to do. But when I am led to believe that there is a good God who made me and upholds me, the mind declares that it is and must be good to love and obey that Being, and that there is an obligation lying on me to do so. This is expressed by such phrases as δέον, *duty*, *right*, *ought*, *obligation*, the convictions embodied in which cannot be accounted for on any utilitarian hypothesis. It is shown that a particular action readily within our power will tend to promote the happiness of an individual or of society. The mind's apprehension of this is one thing, and the conviction that we ought to do it is an entirely different thing, and the two should never be confounded.

But the conscience is not only a cognitive, it is a motive power. This conviction of obligation distinguishes

* The systems which represent man's moral faculty as a mere feeling or sentiment, such as the systems of Adam Smith, of Thomas Brown, of Sir James Mackintosh, are chargeable with two defects:—First, the theory does not come up to the full mental facts, which embrace perception, or knowledge, and judgment, as well as emotion; and, as a consequence, secondly, they make it appear as if virtue might arise from the peculiar constitution or temperament of the race.

it at once from the other motive as it does from the other cognitive powers. The inducements addressed to man's sense of duty are altogether different from those addressed to the other appetencies of the mind. The love of pleasure, of fame, and of activity, do all hold out allurements to man, but none of them carries with it a binding obligation. When we follow them we have no sense of merit; when we decline them we have no sense of guilt. It is different when our moral convictions say that a particular line of conduct should be pursued. We feel now not only that we may do it, but that we should do it, and that if we neglect to do it, we are guilty of sin. Hence arises the great ethical doctrine, expounded in so masterly a manner by Bishop Butler, that the conscience is supreme; that is, supreme among the other moving powers. Just as appetite craves for food, and the love of society for social intercourse, so the conscience directs to certain conduct, but with this difference, that it declares itself superior to the others. It carries with it its authority, and asserts its claims, and is prepared to denounce us if we disregard them.

IV. The conscience points to an authority above itself. It is supreme as within the mind, but it is not absolutely supreme. It claims to be superior to all other motives, such as the love of pleasure, and even to such motives as intellectual improvement; but it seems to point to a power above the mind altogether. At the same time it does not seem to announce what is the nature of the object which it would prompt us to seek after. In this respect it is like some of our intellectual intuitions, which impel us to look round for something which they do not themselves reveal. Thus, intuitive causality constrains us when we discover an effect to look for a cause, but does not specify what the cause is. In like manner our moral faculty seems to me to point to some power, principle, or being, it says not what, above itself. It does not claim for itself that it is infallible, that it is sufficient, that it is independent. It bows to something which has authority; it acknowledges a standard which is and must be right; it looks up for sanction and guidance. It says that it ought to yield to no earthly power; but it does not affirm of itself that it can never mistake, and that there is no authority to which it should submit. On the contrary, it often finds itself in difficulty and perplexity, and feels that it should look round and up for a light, and it is sure that there is such a light. What is thus unknown to the intuition itself, but which, notwithstanding, it is ever seeking, is revealed by other processes.

V. This obligation, when we are led to believe in a Supreme Being, takes the form of law; and we believe that we are under law to God. Our moral convictions do not, so it seems to me, of themselves compel us to believe in the existence of God. I am persuaded, however, that like most of our deeper intuitions (as I hope subsequently to show) they do point upwards to God. And whenever we do, by combined intuition and the obvious facts of experience, reach God, the God who gave us all our endowments, and therefore our moral constitution, the mind traces up the obligation under which it lies to Him. The expression of this inward conviction now is not that we are under obligation to an unknown power, but under law, and under law to God. It is thus indeed we get the peculiar idea of moral government and moral law, not from sense, nor from pleasure, nor from utility, but from conscience constraining us to feel obligation, and combined intuition and experience leading us to trace up that law to God as the Being who sanctions it. Till this object is reached, our moral intuition is felt to be vague, indefinite; it is craving for something which it feels to be wanting; but when God is found, as He cannot fail to be found when we are in search of Him, then the intuition is satisfied, and ever after connects the law with the lawgiver.

VI. Moral good is perceived as having desert, as approvable and rewardable. This, too, is a peculiar idea, derived from the moral power in man, and cannot have been derived from, as it cannot be resolved into, any modification of pleasure, or pain, or sensation of any kind. We are convinced in regard to every good action that it is meritorious; we give to it our approbation, and we look for encouragement and reward. This conviction operates with other considerations in leading us to look to God as the Governor of this World, and as ready to uphold and defend the right. There are times when our expectations on this subject are disappointed, and when we see deeds of moral heroism only landing him who performs them in opprobrium and suffering. Still, even in such cases, our instincts keep firm, in spite of all appearances to the contrary; and we believe that, sooner or later, in this world or the world to come, the deeds will meet with their appropriate reward.

VII. Moral good lies in the region of the will. By this I mean that every truly virtuous act must be a voluntary one. In saying so, I do not mean to assert that every morally good act must be a volition contemplating or performing some outward deed. The will of man exists in other forms than in a resolution to act. Wherever there is choice, I hold that there is will. Whenever I adopt any particular object presented, or prefer any one object to another, there is choice. There is also the exercise of choice, and therefore of will, in all cases in which we deliberately reject any object or proposal made to us. I hold then that there is choice —not only in volition, or resolution, or the final determination to act,—there is choice in wish or in voluntary aversion. When we wish that God's name may be hallowed, that our friends may prosper and be in health, there is will. These wishes and volitions and rejections may unite themselves with any one of our feelings, and even with our intellectual exercises. Using will in this wide sense, I say that it is the region, and the exclusive region, of moral good. It is in voluntary acts that the conscience discerns a moral quality, and it is upon such acts, and no others, that it pronounces its decisions. We shall see forthwith that the will, in all its proper acts, is free; and it is upon acts which we were free to perform, but from which also we were free to abstain, that all the judgments of conscience are declared.

VIII. Moral Good is a quality of certain actions proceeding from Free Will. I have been urging that moral good is not a creation of the mind when contemplating actions or affections, but that it has an actual existence. But let us understand what is the precise nature of the reality. In order to express the reality, some are in the habit of saying that morality has an objective and not a mere subjective existence. But this language is not fitted to bring out the full truth, and may leave an erroneous impression, as if moral excellence had an existence as a separate object, like a stone or a mountain. It has an existence, but merely as a quality of free acts of intelligent beings.

IX. The moral quality of action cannot be resolved into anything simpler. The mind discerns it at once, as the eye sees a surface and the muscular sense feels pressure. If any man asks us, What is extension? we bid him exercise his bodily senses. If any man asks us, What is virtue? I bid him exercise his conscience in looking at a good action. No attempt should be made to give a positive definition of virtue. Any proffered definition will either be erroneous, or it will be a mere identical proposition. If we say that virtue consists in happiness, or in utility, or in beneficial tendency, all such accounts are utterly wrong, for they leave out the main elements, the obligation, the imperativeness of moral law, the desert, the approvableness, the rewardableness. If we introduce such phrases as the following, and say that virtue is binding, that it is right, good; we are, after all, only saying that virtue is virtue. All that can be done by moral science on this particular point is, to exhibit fully the distinctive features, so that the conscience may recognize them, to bring out the law or principle, and embody it in suitable expressions.

Sect. II. On Sin and Error.

I have been arguing that our intellectual and moral intuitions are all necessary and universal. This doctrine however must not be so stated as to imply that it is impossible for man to fall into error, or for the conscience to come to a false decision, or for human beings to commit sin.

That men do, in fact, fall into error is evident from this single circumstance, that scarcely two persons can be brought to accord in opinion, even on points of importance. In regard, indeed, to necessary truths, there are certain restrictions laid on the mind. No man who considers the subject can be made to believe that two straight lines will enclose a space. Still, even in regard to such truths, the mind has a capacity of ignorance and of error; it may refuse to consider them, and, mistaking their nature, it may make statements inconsistent with them without knowing it. Those who have gone through the demonstrations of Euclid are constrained to believe the truth of every proposition, but the truths have never so much as been presented to the minds of the great majority of mankind, and many persons might easily be persuaded that the angles of certain triangles are equal to less or to more than two right-angles. But whatever the restrictions laid on our liability to error in necessary truth, there seem to be no limits to man's exposure to mistakes in other matters. There is boundless room for them in all conclusions which are dependent on experiential evidence, especially when that evidence is of a cumulative character. In all such matters the mind may refuse to look at the evidence, or it may take only what is favourable to one side, and may arrive at most erroneous and preposterous results. This liability to error is apt to appear in all affairs in which we are under the influence of pride or party spirit, or a prejudiced and biassed disposition; in short, wherever there is moral evil swaying the will, and leading it to look on evidence in a partial spirit. If I were immediately cognizant of the heart of a good man, and could see the springs that move him to benevolence and self-sacrifice, I should be constrained to approve of him; but I may be prejudiced against him, and I shall twist and torture facts till I bring myself to believe that he is doing all this from a deep designing selfishness. The topic does not come within my proper scope, but I cannot keep from giving it as my decided conviction, that while ignorance may arise from the limited nature of our faculties and from a limited means of knowledge, positive error does in every case proceed directly or indirectly from a corrupted will, leading us to pronounce a hasty judgment without evidence, or to seek partial evidence on the side to which our inclinations lean. A thoroughly pure and candid will would, in my opinion, preserve man, even with his present limited faculties, not indeed from ignorance on many points, but from all possibility of positive mistakes.

But the question may be asked, How is the existence of sin, and of wrong decisions of the conscience, consistent with the necessity which attaches to our moral convictions? The difficulty can easily be removed so far as the existence of sin is concerned; for sin must ever proceed from the region of the will, which is free to do good, but also free to do evil. It may be necessary for the conscience to decide in a certain manner, but it is not necessary that the will should do what the conscience commands. And it is to the influence exercised by a disobedient will upon the conscience that I attribute all the errors in its decisions. In whatever way we may reconcile them, these two facts can each be established on abundant evidence: the one, that in the primitive exercises of conscience there is a conviction of necessity; the other is, that the conscience is liable to manifold perversions. Care must be taken not to state the two so as to make the one appear to be inconsistent with the other; both can be so enunciated as to make all seeming contradiction vanish. As to the exact nature of the necessity of conviction, and the ground which it covers, this is to be determined, like its existence, by an observation of the conviction itself. If we look directly and fairly at moral excellence, the mind must declare it to be good. But then first the mind may refuse to look at it at all, and secondly, it may not regard it in the right light. If we look upon the living and the true God in the proper aspect, we must acknowledge that we owe Him love and obedience; but then we may refuse to look upon Him, we may contrive to live without God, and God may not be in all our thoughts; or we may fashion to ourselves a Deity with a degraded nature, making Him one altogether like unto ourselves, and then the proper awe and affection will no longer rise in our bosoms.

It is to be taken into account that, while our decisions upon the acts presented may be intuitively certain, yet that the acts are not intuitively presented, and may be very inaccurately presented. The conscience, it is to be remembered, is a reflex faculty, judging of objects presented to it by the other powers, and the representation given it may be incorrect. The liability to deception and perversion is increased by the circumstance that the states of mind with which our voluntary acts are mixed up are of a very complicated character. There is room in this way for giving a wrong account of our actual state of mind at any given moment. I contribute a sum of money to relieve a person in distress; I may do so from a variety of motives; but I am naturally led by self-love to look on the motive as good, and then I cherish a feeling of self-approbation, in which I should by no means have been justified had I taken a searching view of the whole mental state. Again, I find a neighbour doing the very same act, and I am led by jealousy to attribute selfish motives to him, and I condemn him in a judgment in which I may be equally unwarranted. By such seductions as these the mind may become utterly perverted in the representations which it gives, and in the consequent moral judgments which it pronounces. In the case of these perversions of the conscience, as in the case of the errors of the understanding (as we have previously seen), the evil is to be traced to the will refusing to give obedience to its proper law, and conjuring up a series of deceptions to excuse and defend itself. The intuition is after all there, but it is difficult in a mind perverted by a corrupt and prejudiced will to put it in a position to act aright. In order to this, it may be needful to have a Divine Law revealed, and this applied by a teaching and quickening Spirit from above.

We are already in the heart of the subject of Sin, a topic which academic moralists studiously avoid, but which must be carefully looked at by those who would give a correct account of our moral constitution. In referring to it here, I do not profess to be able to give an explanation of the origin of sin under the government of God, whose power is Almighty, and who shows that he hates sin. This seems to be a mystery which human reason cannot clear up. The topic certainly does not fall within the scope of our present investigation. I have here simply to consider sin in its reference to our moral convictions.

I. The conscience declares that sin is a reality. It is a reality of the very same description as moral good. It is not a separate entity, like a plant or an animal, but it is a quality of certain voluntary acts. I lay down this position in opposition to those who would represent sin as a mere privation or a negation. I never can bring myself to believe that deceit and envy and malice and ungodliness and lust, are merely the absence of certain qualities; they imply the presence of real qualities in the will of those who cherish the affections and commit the deeds.

II. Sin is a quality of voluntary acts. It always resides in some mental affection or act in which there is the exercise of free will. The guilt of the sin thus always lies with him who commits it. He cannot throw the blame on any other, for he has himself given his consent to it. Others may have seduced him into it, and in that case the criminality of having tempted him lies with them; but then the sin of having yielded to the temptation and having done the wicked deed lies with himself, he can devolve it on no other.

III. Our moral convictions declare that sin is of evil desert, condemnable, punishable. This conviction is of precisely an opposite character to that which we entertain in regard to good affection and action. We declare the sin to have in itself evil desert; we condemn it in consequence, and we say of it, that it should be discouraged, nay, punished. The very ideas, so full of meaning, involved in these mental convictions, are native, original, and necessary. We cannot get them from mere sensations of pleasure or pain, or from any intellectual operation whatever; and yet we are constrained to take this view of sin wherever it is pressed fairly upon our notice. It is this conviction that stirs up and keeps alive a sense of guilt and apprehension of punishment in the breast of every sinner. It is found even among children, and among the rudest and most ignorant savages, who are urged thereby to try some means of avoiding or averting the wrath of God, and who are prepared in consequence to listen to the parent, or teacher, or missionary, when he speaks of the desert of sin, and points to a Saviour who suffered in our room and stead, and so made reconciliation for transgressors.

Sect. III. Relation of Moral Good and Happiness.

These two have a number of points of connection and correspondence. Much of moral good consists in the voluntary promotion of happiness, and the diminution of pain in a world in which there is such a liability to suffering. A very large number of human virtues, and of vices too, take their origin from man's capacity of pleasure and pain; and in a state of things in which there was no possibility of increasing felicity, or removing misery, many of this world's virtues would altogether disappear. Still the two, while they have many interesting points of affinity, are not to be identified. In particular, we are not to resolve virtue into a mere tendency to promote the pleasure of the individual or happiness of the race. There seems to me to be certain great truths which the mind perceives at once, in regard to the connection of the two.

I. The good is good altogether independent of the

pleasure it may bring. There is a good which does not immediately contemplate the production of happiness. Such, for example, are love to God, the glorifying of God, and the hallowing of His name: these have no respect, in our entertaining and cherishing them, to an augmentation of the Divine felicity. No doubt such an act or spirit may, by reflection of light, tend to brighten our own felicity; but this is an indirect effect, which follows only where we cherish the temper and perform the corresponding work in the idea that it is right. We do deeds of justice to the distant, to the departed, and the dead, who never may be conscious of what we have performed. Even in regard to services done with the view of promoting the happiness of the individual, or of the community, we are made to feel that, if happiness be good, the benevolence which leads us to seek the happiness of others is still better, is alone morally good. In all cases the conscience constrains us to decide that virtue is good, whether it does or does not contemplate the production of pleasure.

II. Our moral constitution declares that we ought to promote the happiness of all who are susceptible of happiness. The only plausible form of the utilitarian theory of morals is that elaborated by Bentham, who says that we ought to promote the greatest happiness of the greatest number. But why *ought* we to do so? Whence get we the *should*, the *obligation*, the *duty?* Why should I seek the happiness of any other being than myself? why the happiness of a great number, or of the greatest number? why the happiness even of any one individual beyond the unit of self? If the advocates of the "greatest happiness" principle will only answer this question thoroughly, they must call in a moral principle, or take refuge in a system against which our whole nature rebels, in a theory which says that we are not required to do more than look after our own gratifications. The very advocates of the greatest happiness theory are thus constrained, if they will only adhere to their view, to call in an ethical principle, and this will be found, if they examine it, to require more from man than that he should further the felicity of others.* But while it covers vastly more ground, it certainly includes this, that we are bound, as much as in us lies, to promote the welfare of

* Mr. J. S. Mill gives up Paley as an expounder of utilitarianism (Dissertations, vol. ii. p. 460), and allows, as to Bentham, "that there were large deficiencies and hiatuses in his scheme of human nature" (p. 462). To whom then are we to look, if we would examine a system which assumes such different shapes; which now takes the form of a selfish system whose principle is that every man should seek his own happiness, now the form of a benevolent system, which says that a man should promote the happiness of the greatest number? In the first of these forms it is at once set aside by an appeal to our nature, and to feelings which Mr. Mill admits to be in our nature. In the second of these forms, that taken by Bentham and Mill, there is a principle of intuitive morals surreptitiously admitted, that we should look to the happiness of others as well as our own. Mr. Mill says, "The matter in debate is what *is* right,—not whether what is right ought to be done" (p. 460). This is not a full or accurate account of the matter in debate. *One* question in debate is, Can the utilitarian theory account for our conviction as to right and wrong, merit and guilt? I hold that it cannot. The higher class of utilitarians seem to trace these convictions to the association of ideas proceeding on our feelings of pleasure and pain. Thus Mr. Mill says (vol. i. p. 137), "The idea of the pain of another is naturally painful; the idea of the pleasure of another is naturally pleasurable. From this fact in our natural constitution, all our affections, both of love and aversion, towards human beings, in so far as they are different from those we entertain towards mere inanimate objects which are pleasant or disagreeable to us, are held by the best teachers of the theory of utility to originate. In this, the unselfish part of our nature, lies a foundation, even independently of inculcation from without, for the generation of moral feelings." Let it be observed that this makes the very unselfish part of our nature stand on a selfish basis. "The idea of the pleasure of another is naturally pleasurable," that is, to ourselves. I hold that we are led to love our fellow-creatures independently of its being pleasant to ourselves; and that it is when we love them that the affection is found to be pleasant, by the appointment of the Author of our constitution, who thus prompts us to benevolence, and rewards us for cherishing it. The theory does not account for our benevolent feelings, and it fails still more when it would account for our

all who are capable of having their misery alleviated or their felicity enhanced.

III. Our moral convictions affirm that moral good should meet with happiness. They seem to declare that this is in itself appropriate and good; and when we are led to believe in the existence of a good God, we are sure that He will seek to secure this end. Experience, no doubt, shows many things in seeming opposition to this,

moral convictions. I admit that it might give some explanation of certain accompaniments, but it can give no account of the conviction of "ought," "obligation," "duty," "merit," "desert," "guilt." A *second* question in debate is, Can the utilitarian show that anything is "right"? that there is truly anything such that it "ought to be done"? Suppose some sensationalist or sceptic were to maintain, as against the utilitarian, that he was not bound to promote this happiness of the greatest number, how would the advocate of the greatest happiness principle reply to him? Consistently, he could appeal only to these personal feelings of pleasure and pain; and if he appealed to anything deeper, it must be to the very moral principle whose existence he denies. There is a *third* question in debate, which will be more easily determined after we have settled the other two. For when it is shown that man has convictions as to moral good and evil, and that these require him to do certain acts and abstain from others, we may be the better prepared to admit, as to certain of these acts, that they do not contemplate the promotion of happiness. Thus, to love God is good, and to refuse to any one his due affection and gratitude for favours seems to be evil, independently of the happiness of the creature or Creator being thereby augmented or diminished. A *fourth* question is, Does utility afford a good test and measure of virtue and vice? It is foreign to the scope of this treatise to enter on this question, but I may remark that the ultimate appeal to "ought" and "duty" being taken away, and the appeal, in the last resource, being to pleasure and pain, utilitarianism will not train men to deeds of self-sacrifice, and those who have embraced it will ever be tempted to give way on great emergencies, and to yield and equivocate when they should at all hazards resist the evil. And it has been shown again and again, that it is beyond the capacity of man to foresee the results of acts, or even to discern the tendency of certain acts done in complicated circumstances. But, omitting this, it is to my present purpose to call on my readers to notice that the theory of an independent morality, and of moral conviction, admits and embraces all that is true in utilitarianism. It affirms that we *ought* to promote the greatest happiness of the greatest number; and in regard to all questions bearing on happiness, the conscience requires us to weigh consequences and to look to long issues and results.

shows many crushed with misfortune and wrung with agony, who are far more virtuous than those who are in the enjoyment of health and prosperity. But our inward convictions guide us to the right conclusions in spite of these apparently contradictory results of outward observation. They lead us to believe that they who are thus afflicted are after all suffering no injustice, inasmuch as they have sinned against heaven, and to expect that the wicked will not be allowed to pass unpunished. And since we do not discover a full retribution in this world, they lead us to look forward to a day of judgment, in which all the inequalities and seeming incongruities of this present dispensation will be rectified in appearance as well as in reality, and the justice of God's moral government fully vindicated.

IV. Our moral convictions declare that sin merits pain as a punishment. There is as close a connection between sin and pain as there is between virtue and happiness. There may indeed be happiness, and there may be suffering, where there is neither virtue nor the opposite, as, for example, among the brute creation; but wherever there is virtue, we decide that it merits happiness, and wherever there is sin, that it deserves suffering, and we are led to anticipate that the proper consequences will follow under the government of a good and a holy God. But as the intellectual intuition of causation, while it constrains us to look for a cause, does not make known the precise cause, so our moral conviction of merit, while it leads us to look for the punishment of sin, does not specify where, or when, or how the penalty is to be inflicted: all that it intimates is that it should and shall come. This conviction keeps alive in the breasts of the wicked at least an occasional fear of punishment, even in the midst of the greatest outward prosperity, and points very emphatically, if not very distinctly, to a day of judgment and of righteous retribution. But as this instinct does not supply the object, it is quite possible that a wrong one may be presented by the baser fears of the heart, or by a degraded superstition, and the final judgment may be thought of as a petty assize, and the judge be regarded as gratifying a personal revenge, and heaven be contemplated as an elysium of sensual joys, and hell as a place of vulgar torture. Still the conviction does demand its object, and when the moral sense is refined, it feels that the account given in Scripture of a judgment day, and of a heaven of light, and a hell of darkness, is in thorough correspondence with the intuition which God has planted in our mental constitution.

But in contemplating and in harmonizing such truths as these, Natural Ethics finds itself in difficulties: it starts questions which it cannot answer; it raises doubts which it cannot dispel. We see on the one hand that God will be led to punish sin, that he "will by no means clear the guilty." But we have evidence, on the other hand, that he delights supremely in the happiness of his creatures. How then can God be just and yet the justifier of the ungodly? Intuitive Ethics conducts us to a yawning chasm, but shows no bridge across; while we are led most anxiously to long for one, and almost to expect that one will appear. It leads us to a place where we have no light, but where we are led to cry out for a light because of the very thickness of the darkness. How grateful should we be when a light is vouchsafed from heaven to show us that the gulf is spanned, and to disclose the way by which it may be crossed!

CHAPTER III.

THE FREEDOM OF THE WILL.

We have seen that conscience pronounces its decisions on acts of the will. Not only so, its judgments proceed on the supposition that the will is in the proper exercise of its full functions; in other words, that the will is free. In every act of will there is an essential freedom, of which the mind is conscious. The possession of a free will is thus one of the elements which go to constitute man a moral and responsible agent.

The will is free. In saying so, I mean to assert, not merely that it is free to act as it pleases,—indeed it may often be hindered from action, as when I will to move my arm, and it refuses to obey because of paralysis. I claim for it an anterior and a higher power, a power in the mind to choose, and, when it chooses, a consciousness that it might choose otherwise.

This truth is revealed to us by immediate consciousness, and is not to be set aside by any other truth whatever. It is a first truth equal to the highest, to no one of which will it ever yield. It cannot be set aside by any other truth whatever, nor even by any other first truth, and certainly by no derived truth. Whatever other proposition is true, this is true also, that man's will is free. If there be any other truth apparently inconsistent with it, care must be taken so to express it that it may not be truly contradictory.

It is a truth which may be expressed in words. It is so expressed when we say the mind has in itself the power of choice. But it cannot be drawn from any deeper fact, or resolved into any anterior principle. Any attempts to reduce it to simpler elements, will only perplex and confuse the whole subject. Thus, that which is free, is often supposed to be uncaused; whereas the uncaused for aught I know, might, if there could be such a thing in creation, not be free. It is from the exercise of will that we get our very idea of freedom. As we survey the external world, including even our own bodily frame, we find it bound in the chain of physical causation, in which every movement of an object is determined from without. Even our very intellectual and emotive states are under laws of association and potencies which control them. It is in the sanctuary of the will that freedom alone is to be found.

So much is clear, so very clear that any attempts to make it clearer will only darken it. The difficulties which encompass this subject do not arise from free will itself, but from its connection with other truths. First, there is the Divine Foreknowledge and the Divine Sovereignty, doctrines which recommend themselves to high reason, and which are found in the Word of God. Secondly, there is the appearance of causation in the mind, even in its voluntary acts. The attempt to reconcile these with creature freedom has engaged the subtlest and perplexed the clearest minds since men began to ask the how, the why, and the wherefore. It is my humble but decided opinion that the human understanding cannot thoroughly clear up the subject. I certainly do not profess to be able to throw light upon it. I must content myself with remarking on some of the more prevalent theories, and expounding the view which seems to me to be upon the whole the most satisfactory.

Among the speculative thinkers of the present day there are two favourite modes by which they try to extricate themselves from the difficulties which beset the subject. One was introduced by Kant, who has been followed by a long train of theologians and metaphysicians. According to this view, the mind knows only phenomena, and not things, and the law of cause and effect is a mental framework giving a form to our knowledge of phenomena. It applies therefore to phenomena, and not to things, which, for aught we know, or can know in this world, may or may not obey the law of causation. Kant acknowledges that we are led by the speculative principles of the mind to look on even the will as under the dominion of cause, but then it is quite conceivable that the thing itself may after all be free, and we are led to believe it to be free by the Practical Reason. Now I have to remark, first of all, on this theory, that it must be taken in its entirety. We are not at liberty (as some would do) to adopt it so far merely as it may suit our purpose, and refuse the very foundation on which it is built. We must, in particular, admit as a fundamental principle that we can never know things, and that causation has no respect whatever to things, but is a mere subjective principle of the mind. But I have failed in one of the main ends of this treatise if I have not succeeded in showing that the mind has knowledge of things in its primary exercises, that we know objects as having potency, and that the law of cause and effect refers to such objects. If we deny this, we are denying certain of the intuitions of the mind in certain of their clearest enunciations; and if we deny them in one of their declarations, why not in others? and if we deny one set, why not every other set? till at last we know not what to believe and what to disbelieve. Those who believe that the mind can come to the knowledge of things, and that they discover power in things, cannot resort to this theory.

A more prevalent doctrine among those who hold firmly by the freedom of the will, is that causation does not extend to the production of volitions. Thus, M. Cousin maintains that we obtain our very idea of causes from the exercise of will, which may be a cause, but cannot be an effect. The difficulties in the way of this theory arise, first, from the nature of our intuition in regard to cause, and, secondly, from certain facts which seem to show that there is causation in the will. The question is, first, whether causation reaches over our volitions, as it does over our other mental acts. A man does a malevolent or a benevolent deed: when this fact is presented, the question is, Do we, or do we not, look for a cause in the previous character and disposition of the individual, combined possibly with the circumstances in which he was placed? Do we not anticipate of the man thoroughly just, that he will ever do just acts? We are sure in regard to the good God that He will, and ever must be, good. To confirm all this we have, secondly, facts, statistical facts. Knowing that if causes keep the same, the same effects will follow, men draw out statistics of voluntary acts, which turn out to be quite as correct as statistics of the weather, or of the mortality of man. The number of thefts and murders that will be committed in a country next year, and the number of letters which will be posted, can be determined as accurately as the number of births or deaths. The facts cannot be denied, and they proceed on the principles of a sameness of causes producing a sameness of effects, which causes embrace voluntary acts.

To avoid these difficulties, I am inclined to admit that antecedent circumstances do act causally on the will. But at the same time I maintain that cause operates in a very different way upon the will from that in which it acts in other departments of nature. The mind has and must have the power of free choice: so says consciousness. But consciousness does not say, and cannot say, what antecedent circumstances of an internal character have swayed the will. These causes certainly do not operate as causes operate in physical nature, or as causes operate in our intellectual being. I have shown that cause in the mind is not of the same character as cause in physical nature. I believe that cause as operating on the will is of a different character from cause as acting in the intellectual or emotive parts of our nature. It is here, I believe,—that is, in the peculiar nature of cause as operating on the will, —that the means of clearing up this subject, and effecting a reconciliation between the seeming incongruities, are to be found.* But I do not say that man can find them, for I am convinced he cannot penetrate this region and determine the nature and mode of operation of the power which sways the will. We can point to the place where must lie the means of clearing up the mystery, but then we cannot reach that place. It is the region where operate the agencies which come between God and the will of his rational and responsible creatures. Well may we pause here, and lay our hands on our mouths, as we say in our hearts, "Once have I spoken, but I will not answer; yea, twice, but I will proceed no further."

* Some of my critics, most respected by me, such as the late Sir W. Hamilton, Dr. Fitzgerald, Bishop of Cork, Dr. Ulrici, of Halle, and Mr. Mansel, have publicly or privately taken exception to the doctrine maintained in the 'Method of Divine Government' as to there being both freedom and a peculiar sort of causation in the will. I have in that work, and now more fully in this, given the view which seems sanctioned by our constitution. But I do shrink, on so tangled a subject, from controversy, believing that I can throw no new light on it. I must ever hold most resolutely to the fundamental doctrine of the freedom of the will. But I will listen most willingly to any one who can give a better account—that is, more in accordance with our constitution—of the expectation that the thoroughly good being will continue good, and of the possibility of giving statistics in anticipation of voluntary actions.

PART THIRD.

INTUITIVE PRINCIPLES AND THE VARIOUS SCIENCES.

BOOK I.

METAPHYSICS.

CHAPTER I.

METAPHYSICS, GNOSIOLOGY, AND ONTOLOGY.

THE phrase Metaphysics is believed to have taken its rise from the title given to one of the treatises of Aristotle. There is no reason to think that the name was given to the work referred to by the author. It does not even appear that it was meant to denote the nature of the contents. Andronicus, it is said, inscribed on the manuscripts, *Τὰ μετὰ τὰ Φυσικά*, to intimate that these books were to follow the physical treatises.* In the writings of Aristotle this department is called, not Metaphysics, but the First Philosophy.

Metaphysical speculation is usually supposed, and, I believe, correctly, to have originated with the Eleatics, who flourished 450 or 500 years before our era. Separating from the physiologists, that is, physical speculators, of the Ionian School, they directed their attention to the dicta of inward reason. Going far below what they represented as the illusions of the senses, they sought to penetrate

* On the title, see Bonitz, 'Commentarius' appended to his edition of the Metaphysics. See also M'Mahon's translation of the Metaphysics, p. 1., where Clemens Alexandrinus and Philoponus are quoted as giving a different view from the common one.

the mystery of being. With them all things were one, and this incapable of motion or of change.

Metaphysics are treated, along with all other topics, by Plato, under the somewhat unfortunate name of Dialectics, which has nearly the same meaning as Speculative Philosophy has in modern times, only the former meant discussion in conversation, the latter discussion in the head or in books. According to Plato, it was the science which treated of the one Real Being (τὸ ὄν) and the Real Good. This one Real Being was not with him, as with the Eleatics, inconsistent with the existence of the many. It embraced the inquiry into the nature of the Good and the Beautiful, and expounded the Eternal Ideas which had been in or before the Divine Mind from all eternity, to the contemplation of which man's soul could rise by cogitation, because it had been formed in the Divine image, and in which the sensible universe participated, thereby having a stability in the midst of its mutability.*

According to Aristotle, the First Philosophy treats of entity so far forth as it is entity, and of quiddity or the nature of a thing, and of that which is universally inherent, so far as it is in entity. He argues that if there were not some substance (οὐσία) other than those that exist in nature, then physics would be the first science, but if there be an eternal and unmovable substance, then there must be a prior science to treat of it, and this is to be honoured as the first and highest philosophy. But the inquiry into entity is in fact an inquiry into causes, or what makes a thing to be what it is; and he shows that such an investigation conducts to four causes: (1) the Formal (τὴν οὐσίαν καὶ τό τι ἦν εἶναι); (2) the Material (τὴν ὕλην καὶ τὸ ὑποκειμένον); (3) the Effi-

* It is scarcely necessary to refer to Archer Butler's account of Plato, in Hist. of Anc. Phil., as the finest in our language.

cient (ὅθεν ἡ ἀρχὴ τῆς κινήσεως); (4) the Final (τὸ οὗ ἕνεκεν καὶ τὸ ἀγαθόν).*

From the bent of his genius, Bacon was no way addicted to metaphysics, but he allots it a separate and a most important place. He says that Physics regards what is wholly immersed in matter and movable, supposing only existence and natural necessity, whereas Metaphysics regards what is more abstracted and fixed, and supposes also mind and idea. To be more particular, he represents physics as inquiring into the efficient and material cause, and metaphysics into the formal and final.†

The two largest metaphysical treatises of Descartes are entitled 'Meditations on the First Philosophy' and 'Principles of Philosophy.' He says that the first part of philosophy is "Metaphysics, in which are contained the principles of knowledge, among which are found the explication of the principal attributes of God, of the immateriality of the soul, and of all the clear and simple notions that are in us." He represents Philosophy as a tree, of which Metaphysics is the root, Physics the trunk, and all the other sciences the branches that grow out of this trunk.‡

In the Wolfian School which proposed to systematize the scattered philosophy of Leibnitz, Metaphysics was asked to deal with three grand topics,—God, the World, and the Soul,—and should aim to construct a Rational Theology, a Rational Physics, and a Rational Psychology. Kant takes up this view of Metaphysics, but labours to show that the speculative reason cannot construct any one of these three sciences. The only available metaphysics, according to him, is a Criticism of the Reason, unfolding its *a priori* elements. He arrives at the con-

* Metaph. i. 3, 1, compared with iii. 1, v. 1, 3.

† De Augmentis, iii. 4.

‡ Prin. Phil. Epis. Auth.

clusion that all the operations of the Speculative Reason are mere subjective exercises, which imply no objective reality, and admit of no application to things; and he saves himself from scepticism by a criticism of the Practical Reason, which guarantees the existence of God, Freedom, and Immortality.*

In the schools which ramified from Kant, Metaphysics is represented as being a systematic search after the Absolute,—after Absolute Being, its nature and its method of development.

And what are we to make of Metaphysics in our own country? It is clear that she has lost, and, I suspect, for ever, the position once allowed her, when she stood at the head of all secular knowledge, and claimed to be equal, or all but equal, in rank, to theology itself. "Time was," says Kant,† "when she was the queen of all the sciences; and if we take the will for the deed, she certainly deserves, so far as regards the high importance of her object-matter, this title of honour. Now it is the fashion to heap contempt and scorn upon her, and the matron mourns, forlorn and forsaken, like Hecuba." Some seem inclined to treat her very much as they treat those *de jure* sovereigns wandering over Europe, whom no country will take as *de facto* sovereigns, that is, they give her all outward honour, but no authority. Others are prepared to set aside her claims very summarily. The multitudes who set value on nothing but what can be counted in money, never allow themselves to speak of metaphysics except with a sneer. The ever-increasing number of persons who read but who are indisposed to think, complain that philosophy is not so interesting as the new novel, or the pictorial history, which is quite as exciting and quite as untrue as the novel. The physicist who has

* See Methodenlehre, in Kr. d. r. Vern.

† Kritik, translated by Meiklejohn, p. xvii.

kept a register of the heat of the atmosphere at nine o'clock in the morning for the last five years, and the naturalist who has discovered a plant or insect distinguished from all hitherto known species by an additional spot, cannot conceal their contempt for a department of inquiry which deals with objects which cannot be seen nor handled, weighed nor measured.

In the face of all this scorn I boldly affirm that Metaphysics are not exploded, and that they never will be exploded. But if they are to keep or regain a place in this country, they must submit to lower their pretensions, and secure that the performance be in some measure equal to the profession made. In particular, they must confine themselves to a field which is open to human investigation, and which can be overtaken. Looking to the philosophies to which I have just been referring, we see that some have ascribed to it far too wide a province, allotting to it inquiries which in modern times have been happily distributed, owing to the advance in the division of labour, to a great number of sciences. The nature of things without and within us, their causes and properties and modes of operation, these are to be determined only by a great number and variety of inductive sciences, each prosecuted in its own way. Others again have allotted to it investigations which must ever be futile, either because they are meaningless, or because they are beyond the human faculties. Thus it is vain for man to seek after Being in itself, or the One in itself, because there is no such thing anywhere but in the brain of the metaphysician, who does not comprehend what sort of realities abstractions have; and as to the Absolute, if it has a signification at all, it is an object beyond the grasp of man's reason. But is there no field of inquiry left open to Metaphy sics? I believe that there is, and that in this field those who are competent for the arduous work of digging in it may find treasures of the highest value. Dugald Stewart has noticed "the extraordinary change which has gradually and insensibly taken place, since the publication of Locke's Essay, in the meaning of the word Metaphysics, a word formerly appropriated to the ontology and pneumatology of the schools, but now understood as equally applicable to all those inquiries which have for their object to trace the various branches of human knowledge to the first principles in the constitution of our nature."* This is an approximation to a proper account of the science. I am inclined to define Metaphysics as THE SCIENCE WHICH INQUIRES INTO THE ORIGINAL OR INTUITIVE CONVICTIONS OF THE MIND, WITH A VIEW OF GENERALIZING AND EXPRESSING THEM, AND ALSO OF DETERMINING WHAT ARE THE OBJECTS REVEALED BY THEM. In prosecuting the investigation, it must first be the aim of the inquirer to observe the phenomena, primarily and mainly by direct consciousness or immediate introspection, but secondarily, and often as satisfactorily, by examining the expression of the inward convictions in the conversation and writings of mankind. As he observes, he must be careful by analysis to separate the intuitions from the associated mental states, and to distinguish between one kind of intuition and another; and he must also endeavour to classify them, and to put them in rigidly exact formulæ. What he thus reaches, if the process has been properly conducted, he is entitled to regard as first, or fundamental, or philosophic principles. In this investigation he will sometimes have to look more to the subjective, and at other times more to the objective side; or, in other words, sometimes more to the knowing powers, and at other times more to the objects known. So far as the science looks at the first, it may be called Gnosiology; † so far

* Dissertation, p. 475.

† Hamilton speaks of some older treatises, which afford a name not

as it looks to the second, it may be called Ontology; which two may be regarded as subordinate departments of Metaphysics. This treatise professes to be one on Metaphysics throughout. In the Chapters which follow this, I am to single out Knowing and Being for more special consideration.

The province thus allotted to Metaphysics is quite a defined one. It is not the science of all truth, but it is the science of an important department,—it is the science of fundamental truth. It should not venture to ascertain the nature of all knowledge, Divine and human; it should be satisfied if it can find what are the original knowing powers of man. It should not pretend to settle the nature of all being, or the whole nature of any one being; but it would try to find what we can know of certain kinds of being by intuition. It should not presume to discover all causes,—which are to be discovered only partially by all the sciences,—but it should expound the nature of our original conviction regarding causation. It should not start with the Absolute, and thence derive all dependent existence; but, as I will show, it is competent to prove that our convictions, aided by obvious facts, lead us to believe in an Infinite Being. It has a field in which it is perfectly competent to discover truth. The body of truth thus reached constitutes, in a special sense, philosophy; and 'philosophical' is an epithet which may be applied to every inquiry which reaches it in the last resort, or which begins with it and uses it. It is to be valued, like all other truth, for its own sake, and because truth is the nutriment of the intellect, for which it craves, and by which, as it feeds on it, it is strengthened. The principles at which it looks are involved, as I am to show in next Book, in all the deeper sciences, in all mental

unsuitable for a nomology of cognitions, viz. Gnosiology, or Gnostologia (Met. Lect. 7).

sciences, in mathematics, and even in certain departments of physical science; and it is desirable, not only for the sake of metaphysics itself, but for their sakes, to have these principles accurately expounded, in order that other departments of knowledge may be delivered from discussions which are to them encumbrances, and have their foundations distinctly laid and firmly settled. It is a science in which progress may be made from age to age by the united action of successive labourers observing, distinguishing, arranging, and devising an appropriate nomenclature. Like every other science which has to do with facts, it must be conducted in the Inductive Method,* in which observation is the first process, and the last process, and the main process throughout; the process with which we start, and the process by which we advance all along, and at the close test all that is done; but in which, at the same time, analysis and generalization are employed as instruments, always working, however, on facts observed. It is true that metaphysics reach truth which is independent of any observation of ours, but it is truth which *we* can discover only by induction.

CHAPTER II.

GNOSIOLOGY.

Sect. I. On Knowledge.

What is Science (Ἐπιστήμη)? is the question put by Socrates in Plato's subtle dialogue of Theætetus. But

* "If ever our philosophy concerning the human mind is carried so far as to deserve the name of science, which ought never to be despaired of, it must be by observing facts, reducing them to general rules, and drawing just conclusions from them." (Reid's Works, p. 122.)

the word 'science' has two meanings. In one sense it can be defined. It is knowledge arranged, correlated, or systematized. In this sense we speak of astronomy, geology, logic, and other sciences. But the word had, at least in Greek, another signification, and meant simply knowledge; and we may suppose the question to be put, What is Knowledge? To this the reply must be, that we cannot positively define knowledge so as to make it intelligible to one who did not know it otherwise. Still we can, by analysis, separate it from other things with which it is associated,—such as sensations, emotions, and fancies,—and make it stand out distinctly to the view of those who are already conscious of it. The science which thus unfolds the nature of knowledge may be called Gnosiology, or Gnosilogy (from *γνῶσις* and *λόγος*). I prefer this to Epistemology, which would signify the science of arranged knowledge.

This science should be prosecuted in the same method as every other which has to do with facts, that is, in the Inductive. Its main office is to inquire into the nature of the knowing powers, to determine the mode of the operation of each, and the amount, and what is equally important, the kind, of knowledge which each is fitted to impart. This is what I have been doing all throughout this treatise. I am not to recapitulate the processes here. Yet it will be necessary to show, in a few sentences, how the method followed and the results reached have a bearing on Gnosiology. Commencing with sense-perception, I drew the distinction between our original and acquired perceptions, and endeavoured to ascertain what are our primary perceptions through the various senses, and also pointed out the difference between sensation and perception. Proceeding to self-consciousness, I sought to estimate the primary knowledge which we have of self as acting or exercising some property. Coming to the reproductive powers, I showed that here the faith element appears, and I pointed out the relation in which faith and cognition stand to each other, and unfolded the convictions which we have in regard to space, time, and the infinite. Looking to the objects thus made known or believed in, the mind pronounces a set of judgments, and I drew out a classification of these, and sought to unfold their nature. But the mind has not only the capacity of discovering the true, it has a power of discovering the good; and I was at pains to show wherein our moral convictions are analogous to our intellectual convictions, and wherein they differ from them.

From this statement it appears that the metaphysician, in prosecuting his pursuits, should be able to distinguish (1) between our cognitions and certain associated states; (2) between one kind of conviction and another; and (3) between our original and acquired convictions. Almost all errors, excesses, and defects in philosophy have proceeded from overlooking or mistaking these all-essential differences. Thus some confound their sensations, or their feelings, or their inferences, or even their fancies, with their primary knowledge. Some imagine that our primitive convictions must all be alike in every respect, and that what is affirmed legitimately of one may be affirmed of any other, or of all; that, for example, our primitive cognitions and moral convictions, all disclose the same sort of reality as is to be found in the perceptions of sense. Again, it is by failing to distinguish between the convictions guaranteed by our constitution and those reached by experience, that persons have been led to suppose that their senses or faculties deceive them.

In Plato's dialogue, Socrates is represented as exposing all the answers given by Theætetus, but without explicitly furnishing one of his own. He shows first, that science is not sense-perception (αἴσθησις). It is true that all knowledge is not derived from this source; but a certain portion is,—though in order to estimate it exactly, we must be careful to separate from it associated sensations, and stand up only for the positive veracity of constitutional convictions. He shows, secondly, that science is not opinion or judgment (δόξα ἀληθής). Yet, by judgment on materials supplied, we can and do reach truth, and have criteria—as will be shown in next paragraph—by which to test it. He then shows that science cannot consist in judgment with a rational process (μετὰ λόγου) accompanying it. It is admitted that no rational process can add to the force of truth, but analysis and explication can settle for us wherein lies the force of truth.

But the question is here started, Can there be a criterion of truth? The inquiry has commonly been made by those who seek for an absolute law, or for one short and easy rule, which may at once determine for us as to every given or supposable asseveration, whether it is or is not true. Now it may be confidently asserted that such a criterion is not discoverable by man, nor can he so much as know whether it is possible in the nature of things, or available to any other intelligences. But I have laboured to show that there are tests of primitive truth not very difficult of application; these tests are self-evidence and necessity, and, as auxiliary to these, catholicity. Again, of that portion of fundamental truth which may be ranked under the head of Analytic Judgments *a priori*, there are very stringent tests in the Laws of Identity, Non-Contradiction, and Excluded Middle. Some very definite rules for testing Synthetic Judgments *a priori* may be found in the maxims which have been enunciated in treating of the various classes of Primitive Judgments. As to experiential truth, there are in many departments tests quite sufficient for all practical purposes, but these are so many that they cannot be numbered. Each advanced science* and art has its own rules of evidence, quite competent to determine for it what is truth in its own department and within fields open to man's observation. But there can be no rule found by the physicist, or devised by the metaphysicist, to determine all questions, or questions beyond the range of man's observation,—as, for example, whether the Dog-star is or is not inhabited, or as to whether there are other substances in the universe besides mind and matter.

Sect. II. On the Origin of our Knowledge and Ideas.

We must now enter upon the inquiries in which Locke and five or six friends who met in his chamber in Oxford found themselves involved, and which issued twenty years afterwards in the famous 'Essay on the Human Understanding.' Starting with a far different topic, they found themselves quickly at a stand, and it came into the thoughts of Locke that before entering "upon inquiries of that nature, it was necessary to examine our own abilities, and see what objects our understandings were or were not fitted to deal with." It follows from the account given in the preceding pages that man's knowledge is derived from Four Sources.

First, we obtain knowledge from sensation, or rather, sense-perception. Such is the knowledge we have of body, and of body extended and resisting pressure, and of our organism as affcting us, or as being affected with smells, tastes, sounds, and colours.

Secondly, we obtain knowledge from self-consciousness. Such is the knowledge we have of self, and of its

* It is scarcely necessary to say, that we have admirable rules and tests, in regard to the Inductive Sciences, in Mill's 'Logic,' and in regard to the Social Sciences, in Sir G. C. Lewis's 'Treatise on the Methods of Observation and Reasoning in Politics.'

modes, actions, and affections,—say, as thinking, feeling, resolving.

I am convinced that from these two sources we obtain not all our knowledge, but all the knowledge we have of separately existing objects. We do not know, and we cannot, as will be shown forthwith, so much as conceive of a distinctly existing thing, excepting in so far as we have become acquainted with it by means of sensation and reflection, or of materials thus derived. Here Locke held by a great truth, though he did not see how to limit it on the one hand, nor what truths required to be added to it on the other. For man has other sources of knowledge.

THIRDLY, by a further Cognitive or Faith exercise we discover Qualities and Relations in objects which have become known by the senses external and internal. Of this description are the ideas which the mind forms of such objects as space, time, the infinite, the relation between cause and effect, and moral good. There is a wide difference between this Third Class and the Second, though the two have often been confounded. In self-consciousness we look simply at what is passing within, and as it passes within. But the mind has a capacity of discovering further qualities and relations among the objects which have been revealed to it by sensation and consciousness. This third kind of knowledge seems to be what is referred to by those who represent the mind or intellect itself as a source of ideas. But this account can be admitted only on its being understood that the mind notices these qualities and relations as in objects which have been made known by sensation and reflection.

FOURTHLY, the mind can reach truth necessary and universal, that is, universally true. This may be regarded as knowledge, and it is knowledge which goes far beyond that derived from the other sources. We are sure that these two straight lines which go parallel for the smallest possible space, may be extended infinitely, without being ever nearer each other. We are certain that gratitude and holy love, which are good here, must be good all through the wide universe. But this fourth kind of cognition is not independent of the other three kinds. All the necessary truth we can reach bears a reference to objects which have become known directly, or by a discursive process through perception and consciousness, either to these objects, as primarily known, or to the qualities and relations in them discovered by a further cognitive or faith process. The knowledge attained from the first three sources is, as I have repeatedly had occasion to remark, all concrete and individual. But we discern a necessity in certain portions of the individual knowledge or convictions, and we can proceed to generalize these; and so far as we abstract and generalize properly, we are sure that what is true of the singular is true also of the universal; that what is true of these two lines is true of every set of lines exactly like them which we could contemplate; that what is true of this effect, namely, that it must have a cause, is true of every other, that is, if we have accurately determined it to be an effect. By this process we reach universal truth, of which we know that it must hold good in all times and at all places.

Such seem to be the sources of human knowledge. We can add to the original stock got from all these quarters. Thus, we can add to what we have through the senses by observing other and new objects. We can know more of our minds by carefully noting their actions. The mind, too, can rise to clearer and nobler views of intellectual and moral qualities by meditating on the proper objects and themes. We can widen and consolidate our acquaintance with necessary and universal truth by a careful inspection and generalization of our individual convictions.

The question of the origin of our ideas is substantially the same with that of the sources of our knowledge; but in discussing this second question, it is of all things essential to have it fixed what is meant by 'idea.' Plato, with whom the term originated as a philosophic one, meant those eternal patterns which have been in or before the Divine mind from all eternity, which the works of nature participate in to some extent, and to the contemplation of which the mind of man can rise by abstraction and philosophic meditation. Descartes meant by it whatever is before the mind in every sort of mental apprehension. Locke tells us that he denotes by the phrase all that the schoolmen designated both by the phantasm and the universal notion. Kant applied the phrase to the ideas of substance, totality of phenomena, and God, reached by the reason as a regulative faculty going out beyond the province of experience and objective reality. Hegel is for ever dwelling on an absolute idea, which he identifies with God, and represents as ever unfolding itself out of nothing into being, subjective and objective. Using the phrase in the Platonic sense, it is scarcely relevant to inquire into the origin of our ideas; it is clear however that Plato represented our recognition of eternal ideas as a high intellectual exercise, originating in the inborn power of the mind, and awakened by inward cogitation and reminiscence. In the Kantian and Hegelian systems the idea is supposed to be discerned by reason; Kant giving it no existence except in the mind, and Hegel giving it an existence both objective and subjective, but identifying the reason with the idea, and the objective with the subjective. Using the phrase in the Cartesian and Lockian sense, we can inquire into the origin of our ideas.

In accordance with modern usage in the English tongue, it might be as well perhaps to employ the word 'idea' to denote the reproduced image or representation in the mind, and the abstract and general notion. Thus explained, it would exclude our original cognitions on the one hand, and also the regulative principles of the mind on the other. An idea, in this sense, would always be a reproduction in an old form, or more commonly in a new form, of what has first been known. We first know objects, external or internal; and then we may have them called up in whole or in part, magnified or diminished, or mixed and compounded in an infinite variety of ways; or, by an intellectual process, we may contemplate one of their attributes separately, or group them into classes. Our ideas, in this sense, are ever dependent on our cognitions; we cannot have an idea, either as an image or a notion, of which the materials have not been furnished by the various cognitive powers, primary and secondary. It is always to be remembered that by increase and decrease, by intellectual abstraction and generalization, our ideas may go far beyond our knowledge; still, as our ideas in the last resort depend on our knowledge, they must be drawn from the same quarters. When the question is put then as to the origin of our ideas, we are thrown back on the Four Sources from which all our knowledge is derived. So far as our ideas of distinctly existing objects are concerned, they are all got ultimately from the outward and inward senses: to this extent the doctrine of Locke is unassailable. We cannot imagine or think of any other kind of existence than matter and mind, with space and time, though, for aught we know, there may be other substances and beings in the universe with a far different nature. But then we are led by our cognitive and faith powers, intellectual and moral, to clothe the objects, thus known, with qualities and relations which cannot be perceived either by sensation or reflection. It is not by one or other of these, or by both combined, that I come to believe that space and time are infinite, that this effect must proceed from a cause, that this benevolent action is good, and that this falsehood is a sin; nor is it by either or by both that I can rise to the conviction that the effect is for ever tied to its cause, and that lying must be a sin in all time and in all eternity.

The principle "*Nihil est in intellectu quod non prius fuerit in sensu*" has been ascribed to Aristotle, but most certainly without foundation, as the great Peripatetic everywhere calls in intuition in the last resort, and is ever coming to truth which he represents as self-evident and necessary. The maxim has been fathered, I do not know on what authority, on the Stoics. It is assuredly not the principle adopted by Locke, who is so often represented as favouring it; for the great English philosopher ever traces our ideas, not to one, but to two sources, and delights to derive many of our ideas from reflection. It is however the fundamental principle of that school in France and in Britain which has been called Sensational. There are three very flagrant oversights in the theory of those who derive all our ideas from sensation. *First*, there is an omission of all such ideas as we have of spirit and of the qualities of spirit, such as rationality, free will, personality. *Secondly*, there is a neglect or a wrong account of all the further cognitive exercises of the mind by which it comes to apprehend such objects as infinite time, moral good, merit, and responsibility. *Thirdly*, there is a denial, or at least oversight, of the mind's deep convictions as to necessary and universal truth. Sensationalism, followed out logically to its consequences, would represent the mind as incapable of conceiving of a spiritual God, or of being convinced of the indelible distinction between good and evil; and make it illegitimate to argue from the effects in the world in favour of the existence of a First Cause.

Locke is ever to be distinguished from those who derive all our ideas from the senses. He takes great pains to show that a vast number of the most important ideas which the mind of man can form, are got from reflection on the operations of our own minds. His precise doctrine is that the materials of the ideas which man can entertain, come in by two inlets, sensation and reflection; that they are first perceived by the mind, and then retained; and that they are subsequently turned into a great variety of new shapes by the faculties of discernment, comparison, abstraction, composition, and the power of discovering moral relations. The ideas being thus obtained, he supposes that the mind can perceive agreements and disagreements among them. In particular, it is endowed with a power of intuition, by which it at once perceives the agreement and disagreement of certain ideas, discovers these to be in the very nature of ideas, and necessary. Such being the views of Locke, they are as different from those of the Sensationalists on the one hand, as they are from those of Descartes, Leibnitz, and Kant on the other. Indeed the most careless reader cannot go through the 'Essay on the Human Understanding' without discovering that, if Locke has a strong sensational, he has also a rational side. He will allow no ideas to be in the mind except those which can be shown to spring from one or other of the inlets, and yet he resolutely maintains that, with these ideas before it, the mind may perceive truth at once; he thinks that morality is capable of demonstration, and in religion he is decidedly rationalistic. So far, it appears to me, we can easily ascertain the views of Locke. It is more difficult to determine how far he supposed the mind to be capable of modifying or adding to the materials derived from the outward and inward senses. It is quite clear that he represents the mind as having the power to perceive and compound and divide these ideas, and discover resemblances and other relations; but there are passages in which, consistently or inconsistently, he speaks of the mind having something more suggested to it, or superinducing something higher.*

Confining our attention to the points which are clear, I think we may discover—not certainly such grave errors as in the doctrines of the sensationalists, but still—several oversights. *First,* he overlooks the cognitions and beliefs involved in the exercises with which the mind starts. This has arisen, to a great extent, from his attaching himself to the theory that the mind begins not with knowledge, but with ideas, which are first perceived by the mind, and then compared, upon which comparison it is that the mind reaches knowledge. He has never set himself to inquire what is involved in the sensation and reflection which give us our ideas. He takes no notice of intuition enabling us to look directly at the very thing, and of our intuition of extension, and of a cognitive self-consciousness, and of the beliefs gathering round space and time and the infinite. *Secondly,* he has not given a distinct place and a sufficient prominence to the ideas got from the mind observing certain qualities and relations in objects made known by sensation and reflection. The defects of his system, in not giving an adequate account of our idea of moral good, which he gets from our

* Locke speaks of certain ideas being 'suggested' to the mind by the senses (a phraseology adopted by Reid and Stewart), 'Essay,' ii. vii. 9; and of 'relation' as "not contained in the real existence of things, but extraneous and superinduced," ii. xxv. 8. (See Webb on 'Intellectualism of Locke,' v.) He maintains that morality is capable of demonstration, iii. ii. 16, etc. For other passages illustrative of Locke's precise views *supra,* pp. 18, 31, 104–106, 133, 154, 166, 172 (especially), 218, 239.

sensations of pleasure and pain, with a law of God superinduced, without so much as his trying to prove how we are bound, on his system, to obey that law, was perceived at an early date by British writers, who adhered to him as closely as possible; and Shaftesbury and Hutcheson called in a Moral *Sense* (as an addition to Locke's outward and inward sense); while Bishop Butler called in conscience, which he characterized as a "principle of reflection." *Thirdly*, he has not inquired what are the laws involved in the Intuition to which he appeals in the fourth book of his Essay as giving us the most certain of all our knowledge. Had he developed the nature of intuition, and the principles involved, with the same care as he has expounded the experiential element, his system would have been at once and effectually saved from the fearful results in which it issued in France, where his name was used to support doctrines which he would have repudiated with deep indignation. He is right in saying that the mind has not consciously before it in spontaneous action such speculative principles as that "Whatever is is," or moral maxims in a formalized shape; but he has failed to perceive that such principles as these are the rules of our intuitions, and that they can be discovered by a reflex process of generalization. It is but justice to Locke to say that he acknowledges necessary truth, but it does not form a part of his general theory: his professed followers have abandoned it; and sceptics have shown that he cannot reach it in consistency with his system.

Sect. III. Limits to our Knowledge, Ideas, and Beliefs.

It is instructive to find that not a few of the most profound philosophers with which our world has been honoured, have been prone to dwell on the limits to man's capacity. The truth is, it is always the smallest minds which are most apt to be swollen with the wind engendered by their own vanity. The intellects which have gone out with greatest power to the furthest limits, are those which feel most keenly the barriers by which human thought is bounded. The minds which have set out on the widest excursions, and which have taken the boldest flights, are those that know best that there is a wider region lying beyond, which is altogether inaccessible to man. It was the peculiarly wise man of the Hebrews who said, "No man can find out the work that God maketh from the beginning to the end." The Greek sage by emphasis declared that, if he excelled others, it was only in this, that he knew nothing. It was the avowed object of the sagacious Locke to teach man the length of his tether, which, we may remark, those feel most who attempt to get away from it. Reid laboured to restrain the pride of philosophy, and to bring men back to a common sense, in respect of which the peasant and philosopher are alike. It was the design of Kant's great work to show how little speculative reason can accomplish. In our own day we have had Sir W. Hamilton showing, with unsurpassed logical power, within what narrow bounds the thought of man is restrained.

We have already in our survey gathered the materials for enabling us to settle the general question, in which however are several special questions which should be carefully separated.

1. What are the limits to man's power of acquiring knowledge? The answer is, that he cannot know, at least in this world, any substance or separate existence other than those revealed by sense and consciousness. There may be, very probably there are, in the universe, other substances besides matter and spirit, other existences which are not substances, as well as space and time,

but these must ever remain unknown to us in this world. Again, he can never know any qualities or relations among the objects thus revealed to the outward and inward sense, except in so far as we have special faculties of knowledge; and the number and the nature of these are to be ascertained by a process of induction, and by no other process either easier or more difficult. This is what has been attempted in this treatise, it may be supposed with only partial success in the execution, but, it is confidently believed, in the right method. A more difficult process need not be resorted to, and would conduct us only into ever-thickening intricacies; and an easier method is not available in the investigation of the facts of nature, in this, nor, indeed, in any other department. After unfolding what seems to be in our primitive cognitions, I gave some account of the primitive faiths which gather round them, and classified the relations which the mind can discover, and unfolded the moral convictions which we are led to form. Such are the limits to man's original capacity, of which there are decisive tests in self-evidence, necessity, and catholicity.

Within these limits man has a wide field in which to expatiate; a field, indeed, which he can never thoroughly explore, but in which he may discover more and more. What he may discover, and what he may never be able to discover, are to be determined by the separate sciences, each in its own department. Thus, what he can find out of mind, of its various powers and original convictions, is to be determined by the various branches of mental science. What he can ascertain by the senses, aided by instruments, must be settled by the physical sciences.

2. The limits to man's capacity of knowledge being ascertained, it is easy to determine the limits to his power of forming ideas. The materials must all be got from the four sources of knowledge which have been pointed

out. There are two classes of powers employed in enlarging and modifying these. The one is the imagination, which can decrease, as when on seeing a man it can form the idea of a dwarf; and increase, as when it can form the idea of a giant; or divide, as when it sees a man it can form an image of his head; or compound, as when it puts a hundred hands on man, and forms the idea of a Briareus. The mind can further discover a number of relations among the objects primitively known. These I have endeavoured to classify. In particular, the mind can out of the concrete form innumerable abstracts, and from the singulars construct an indefinite number of universals. It should be observed that man's power of imagination and correlation extends over his moral convictions as well as his intellectual cognitions. Thus, he can clothe the hero of a romance in various kinds of moral excellence of which we have discovered the rudiments in ourselves or others, and perceive relations among the moral properties which have fallen under his notice. These are the limits to man's capacity of forming ideas, determined first by his powers of cognition and secondly by his powers of belief and correlation.

3. Our beliefs, it is evident, may go beyond our cognitions. Nay, there is a sense in which they go beyond our very phantasms or notions. Still there are stringent limits set to them in our very nature and constitution. Thus, we can never believe anything in opposition to self-evident and necessary truths. In regard to at least some of these truths, we cannot so much as imagine them to be false. Thus, we cannot conceive that we ourselves while we exist should at the same time not exist. There are beliefs which are in our very mental make and frame, and which are altogether beyond our voluntary power. If we except these, however, our power of possible belief is wide as our capacity of forming ideas. If it is asked

what we should believe within these limits? the answer is, only what has evidence to plead in its behalf, what has self-evidence or mediate evidence. Metaphysics, with its tests, can determine what truths are to be received on their own authority; as to the kind and amount of evidence required in derivative truth, this can be settled only by the canons of the special departments of investigation, historical or physical.

But do our beliefs ever go beyond our ideas? This is a very curious question, and different persons will be disposed to give different answers to it. It is quite clear that we can, and do, believe in much of which we can form no adequate conception in the sense of mental image; thus, we believe in the existence of an infinite God, who is not picturable in the imagination. But the more difficult question is, Can or should we believe in aught of which we have no apprehension of any kind? I am inclined to think that there is always a conception of some sort at the basis of every belief; and that when there is no positive conception, then faith ought to cease, and must cease. But this doctrine is liable to misapprehension unless certain very important modifications and explanations be conjoined.

It seems clear to me that every belief must be a belief in something of which we have some sort of conception. A belief in nothing would not deserve to be called a belief, and a belief in something of which we have no apprehension would be equivalent to a belief in nothing. But it will be urged that every man must believe in certain great truths regarding eternity, of which he has no conception, and that the Christian in particular has such a truth in which he firmly believes, in the doctrine of the Trinity. Still, I maintain that even in such a case there is an apprehension or conception. Thus, in regard to infinity, we apprehend space or time, or God, who inhabits all space and time, stretching away further and further; but far as we go, we apprehend and believe that there is and must be a space, a time, a living Being beyond. Or we apprehend a spiritual God, with attributes, say of power and love; and we strive to conceive of Him, and of these perfections; and we believe of Him and His power and goodness that they transcend all our feeble attempts at comprehension. In every supposable case of belief we have an apprehension of some kind. A traveller tells us that he saw in Africa some strange monster which he cannot describe so as to enable us to comprehend it; we understand this man's language, and if we have reason to look upon him as trustworthy, we believe his statement; but still our belief goes upon our apprehension. An inspired writer tells us something about there being three persons in one God; and, having evidence of his inspiration, we believe him: but even here there is an apprehension; there is a conception of the God of truth as revealing the truth. There is more: this revelation is contained in words of which we form some sort of apprehension. Thus, we are told that Jesus Christ is God; that he became man; and yet we discover that he is somehow or other different from God the Father. Thus in all our beliefs there seems to be a conception of something, and of something real and existing; but still it may be of something conceived by us as having qualities which pass beyond our comprehension, or qualities of which we have no comprehension.

Some of these conceptions, with their attached beliefs, are those which raise up within us the feeling of the sublime, and are, of all others, the most fitted to elevate the soul of man. Need I add that it is possible for us to believe in truths which we cannot reconcile with other truths of sense or understanding. It is wrong in us, indeed, to believe in a proposition unsupported by evidence; but when it is thus sustained, and when especially it is seen to have the sanction of God, then the mind asserts its prerogative of belief, even when the truth transcends all sense, all personal, all human experience, nay, even when it is encompassed with darkness and difficulties on every side. Faith feels that it is in its highest exercise, when founding on the authority of God, it believes not indeed in contradictions (which it can never do), but in truths which it cannot reconcile with the appearances of things, or with other truths which the reason sanctions.

Sect. IV. Relation of Intuition and Experience.

We must now dive into the subject whose depths the great Teutonic metaphysician sought to sound; not that Kant spoke much of it in the intercourse with his friends, but he was for ever pondering on it as he sat in his bachelor domicile, as he paced forward and backward in his favourite walk in the suburbs of Königsberg, as he lectured to his class, or elaborated his published writings. The general question embraces several special ones, which must be carefully distinguished. In seeking to settle these, we must always have it fixed in our minds in what sense we employ the word 'experience;' for the phrase may be understood in narrower or in wider significations. It may be confined to the outward fact known or apprehended, or it may also embrace the inward consciousness. It may mean mere personal experience, or it may contain the whole gathered experience of mankind. It has been employed to stand for the experience of sense, and it has been so enlarged as to comprise all that we can know or feel by any or all of our cognitive powers, such as consciousness and conscience. In this Section I use it to express all that comes into consciousness; for, properly speaking, there is no experience till the fact is apprehended within. Taken in this sense, it would be nearer the truth, that is, would embrace a larger portion of truth, were we to say that our knowledge and ideas are drawn from the experience of consciousness, rather than from the experience of sense. We cannot reproduce things in idea, we cannot generalize any conglomerate of facts till they have been in consciousness, into which however they must have come by a cognitive power, which is therefore the true source of knowledge. When I limit the phrase 'experience' to a particular class of apprehended facts, I will give notice by an epithet or explanatory clause. If it be needful to fix steadily in how wide a sense we use 'experience,' it is still more essential to determine under what particular aspect we view intuition, when we would consider its relations to experience. We have seen, in an earlier part of this Treatise (Part I. Bk. II. Ch. I. s. ii.), that Intuition may be contemplated under three general aspects,—as a body of regulative principles, as spontaneous convictions, and as generalized maxims. Under each of these, Experience stands in a different relation to Intuition.

I. Let us consider the relation of Experience to Intuition, considered as a body of Regulative Principles. In this sense intuition, being native and original, is prior to experience of every kind, personal or general. So far from depending on what we have passed through, our intuitions are a powerful means of prompting to the acquisition of experience; for, being in the mind as natural inclinations and aptitudes, they are ever instigating to action. All of them seek for objects, and are gratified when the proper objects are presented. Just as the eye was given us to see, and light is felt to be pleasant to the eyes, so the cognitive powers were given us in order to lead us to the acquisition of knowledge, and they are pleased when knowledge is furnished. Our belief as to the boundlessness of space is ever alluring us to explore it in earth and sea, and in the deep expanse of heaven; and our belief in time without beginning and without end, is ever tempting us to go back through all the years which human history opens to us, and, beyond these, through all the ages which geology discloses, and to look forward, as far as human foresight and Bible prophecy may enable us, into the dim events of the future. Thus too our minds delight to discover substances acting according to their properties, and plants and animals developing according to the life that is in them, to find species and genera in the whole organic kingdoms, to trace mathematical relations corresponding to our higher intellectual cravings among all the objects presenting themselves on the earth and in the starry heavens, and to rise from near effects to remote causes in space and time. Nor is it to be omitted that our moral convictions prompt us to look for, and when we have found him, to look up to a Moral Governor of the universe, and to anticipate of him that he will be ready to support the innocent sufferer, and to punish the wicked. It should be added, that in experience we are ever finding a gratifying exemplification of our native tendencies, and a satisfying corroboration of our intuitive expectations. We expect a cause to turn up for this mysterious occurrence; we are disappointed at first, but in due time it appears. We anticipate that this secret deed of villany will be detected and exposed; and so we are amazed for a season when we hear of the perpetrator flattered by the world, and seemingly favoured in the providence of God; but our moral convictions are vindicated when the wicked man is at last caught in the net which had all along been weaving for him, and all his ill-gotten spoils are made to add to the weight of his ignominy, and to embitter his disgrace.

II. Let us consider the relation of Experience to our

Intuitive Convictions as these are manifested in Consciousness. We have now a more complicated series of circumstances to look at and to weigh. Under this head we cannot speak of intuition and experience as being opposed; every conviction, be it of sense or consciousness, of the understanding or of conscience, is an experience. It is in itself an experience, and it is an experience which can be generalized.

So far, all is clear enough. The difficulty and the confusion arise when we contemplate the relation of experience to the forthcoming of the regulative principle into action, and into consciousness. There is a sense in which experience is required in order to such manifestation. Thus, in some cases the mental intuition is called forth by an external stimulus; it is thus that our knowledge of body is evoked by an action of the bodily senses. It is to be observed however, in regard to all such cases, that it is scarcely correct to represent the intuition as depending on experience; it depends, no doubt, on an outward stimulus as an essential part of the concause, but the action can scarcely be called experience, for there is nothing in consciousness till the intuition is in energy. The proper statement is that there must be the concurrence of an outward action, in order to the rise of the inward conviction. Again, it is a fact that all our intuitions relate, directly or indirectly, to objects which have become known by sensation and reflection, in the sense explained in the two preceding Sections. But in estimating this circumstance, it is to be remembered that sensation and reflection are themselves intuitions, and comprise very deep convictions. Once more, there are cases in which the intuition is called into exercise by the representations or apprehensions that have risen up in the mind. This is the case with all our primitive beliefs, judgments, and moral convictions: they all depend on previous cognitions, and our judgments may further depend on beliefs. Thus it is when we contemplate an object as extended, and an event as happening in time, that our intuitive convictions as to space and time spring up; it is when we consider two straight lines, that we proclaim that they cannot enclose a space. Thus it is when we look to objects grouped into classes, that we declare that whatever is predicated of the class may be predicated of all the members of the class. Thus it is when we look to certain voluntary acts of intelligent beings, that we regard them as good or evil, rewardable or punishable. In regard then to all intellectual beliefs and judgments, and to all moral cognitions, beliefs, and judgments, there must always be an experience on which they proceed. But, in making this statement, let it be observed first, that the experience may not be one of sense. Thus, our moral convictions proceed, not on an outward sensation, but on a voluntary action being presented to the moral power. It is to be further taken into account that the beliefs and judgments may often proceed on an experience which is itself intuitive. I proceed upon an intuitive conviction regarding time when I declare it to be infinite, and on an intuitive knowledge of extension, when I affirm that the shortest distance between two points is a straight line. It thus appears, in regard to our spontaneous convictions, that there is no proper opposition between experience and intuition; that we must beware of making sweeping declarations in the idea that they will apply to all instances; that in most cases there is a complex co-operation of the two; and that we must consider each class of cases separately, in order to determine what is the precise nature of the relation.

III. Let us consider the relation of Experience to our Generalized Intuitions. To reach these, experience is always necessary, is indeed an indispensable condition.

The maxim is just the generalization of the experiences. But let us keep a steady apprehension of the distinction between the generalizations fashioned from two different sorts of experience. One kind of general maxim is obtained from facts external and internal which may have fallen under our notice, no matter how, through our own experience or the experience or authority of others. Thus, we have discovered that the positive poles of magnets repel each other; that dicotyledonous plants are exogenous; and that ideas which have at any time co-existed tend to recall each other. But the mind can reach a higher order of maxims; I may give as examples, that two parallel lines cannot meet; that every quality implies a substance, and that sin is of evil desert. This second class of axioms implies a generalization equally with the other, but it is from a very different sort of singulars. Of the first class of maxims we may be able to say that they seem to be true within the cosmos open to our observation; but whether they hold good in all parts of the universe, we cannot dogmatically affirm. Thus, there may be metals in other worlds which follow very different magnetic laws, and there may be intelligent beings in them whose ideas follow a different order of association from those with which we are acquainted on earth; but it is as certain in those other worlds as in this, that the whole is equal to the sum of its parts, and that ungodliness is a sin.

SECT. V. ON THE NECESSITY ATTACHED TO OUR PRIMARY CONVICTIONS.

We have seen throughout the whole of this Treatise that a conviction of necessity attaches to all our original cognitions, beliefs, and judgments, both intellectual and moral. But we may find ourselves in hopeless perplexities, or even in a network of contradictions, unless we determine precisely to what it is that the necessity adheres. The proper account is, that the necessity covers the ground which the conviction occupies,—neither less nor more. We may err, either by contracting it within a narrower, or stretching it over a wider surface. It follows that if we would determine how far the necessity extends, we must carefully and exactly ascertain what is the nature of the native conviction, and what are the objects at which it looks.

Beginning with our Cognitions, the conviction is that the object exists at the time we perceive it, and has the qualities we discover in it. This implies, according to the law of identity (in the form of *non-contradiction*), that it is not possible that it should not be existing, and not in possession of these qualities at the time it falls under our notice. But it does not imply that the object has a necessary or an eternal existence. It does not imply that the object must have existed in all other, or in any other, circumstances. For aught our conviction says, the object in other positions, or with a different set of pre-existing causes, might not have existed at all, or might have had a different set of qualities. But while the necessity does not reach further, it always extends as far as the perception: thus it demands that body be regarded by us as extended and as resisting pressure, that self be looked on as capable of such qualities as thought and feeling, and that the properties of body and mind are not produced by our contemplation of them.

Coming now to our original Beliefs and Judgments, it has been shown, as to the Beliefs, that while they proceed on our Cognitions, they go beyond them, go beyond the *now* and the *present*,—declaring, for instance, of time and space, that they must transcend our widest phantasms or conceptions of them, and that they are such that no space or time could be added to them. And as far as the conviction goes, so far does the necessity extend.

The necessity attached to our Judgments is in like manner exactly coincident with them. These imply objects on which they are pronounced. At the same time the judgment, with its adhering necessity, has a regard not to the objects directly, but to the relation of the objects. These objects may be real or they may be imaginary. I may pronounce Chimborazo to be higher than Mont Blanc, but I may also affirm of a mountain 100,000 feet high that it is higher than one 50,000 feet high. As to whether the objects are or are not real, this is a question to be settled by our cognitions and beliefs, original and acquired, and by inferences from them. But it is to be carefully observed, that even when the object is imaginary, the judgment proceeds on a cognition of the elements of the objects. Thus, having known what is the size of a man, we affirm of a giant, who is greater than a common man, that he is greater than a dwarf, who is smaller than ordinary humanity. Still, the necessity in the judgment does not of itself imply the existence of the objects, still less any necessary existence; all that it proclaims is, that the objects might exist out of materials which have fallen under our notice, and that the objects, being so and so, must have such a relation. In a sense, then, our judgments are hypothetical; the objects being so, must have a particular connection. There may be, or there may never have been, two exactly parallel lines: what our intuitive judgment declares is, that if there be such, they can never meet. A similar remark may be made of every other class of primitive judgments. There may or there may not be a sea in the moon; but if there be, its waters must be extended, and can resist pressure. There may or there may not be inhabitants in the planet Jupiter; but if there be, they must have been created by a power competent to the operation. It is on this account, I suppose, that such truths have been called abstract or hypothetical, inasmuch as they deal with abstract relations, not implying the existence of the things. But it is to be borne in mind, that when the objects exist, the judgments, with their accompanying necessity, apply to them.

It holds good also of our Moral Perceptions, that the necessity is as wide as our conviction, but no wider. It implies that the good or evil is a real quality of certain voluntary acts of ours, and this whether we view it or not, and independent of the view we take of it. It involves that certain actions are good or evil, whenever or wherever they are performed, in this land or other lands, in this world or other worlds. Rising beyond cognitions and beliefs, the mind can pronounce moral judgments on certain acts apprehended by it. These judgments do not imply the existence of the objects; but the decision will apply to the realities, if there be such. Thus, there may or may not be ungodliness or ingratitude in the planet Saturn; but if there be such a thing, we declare that it must be evil and condemnable. It is to be noted that our moral convictions do not imply that we shall certainly practise the good, or that all must be morally good which men declare to be so.

As soon as our original cognition or belief assures us of the existence of an object with certain qualities, or as a judgment affirms a necessary relation, the law of identity comes into operation, and insists on our keeping truth consistent with itself; and in particular, the law of non-contradiction restricts us from thinking or believing the opposite of the truth apprehended. When we know that self exists, we cannot be made to think that self does not exist. Constrained to look on time as without limits, we at once deny that it can have limits. Deciding that every effect has a cause, we cannot be made to believe that it has not had a cause. We have a conviction that murder is a crime, and cannot be made to decide that it is not. We have this necessity in two forms as a test of fundamental truth; in its original or positive, and also in a negative form, founded on the law of non-contradiction. In no case can the conviction be wrought in us that what we intuitively know or believe to exist does not exist, or that the contradictory of a primitive judgment can possibly be true.

A different impression might be left by an account often given. A distinction has been drawn between self-evident truths which relate to matters of fact, such as that body exists and that self exists, and necessary truths, such as that a quality implies a substance, and that the whole is equal to the sum of its parts. Of the latter it is supposed that we cannot conceive or think the opposite, whereas it is supposed that we can of the former. But there is confusion in this representation. Thus, it is said that we can easily conceive that the self of which we are conscious might never have existed. The statement is correct, but it does not go to establish the general doctrine. For our intuition is not that self must have existed in all possible circumstances, but it is that it exists with certain qualities at the time we contemplate it. We may think a great many things about it, but the exact opposite we cannot be made to think or believe; in this respect our cognitions are on the same footing as our judgments, and all our intuitions are alike.

And this leads me to specify with precision what it is that we cannot do in regard to necessary truth. A common account is that we cannot *conceive* the contradictory of such a truth. But the word 'conceive' is ambiguous, and in itself means nothing more than 'apprehend,' or even than 'imagine;' and it is not mere apprehension or imagination that we use as a test. The exact account is that we cannot realize in consciousness the exact opposite of the intuitive conviction, whatever that be; that whatever we *know* intuitively as existing, we cannot be made not to know as existing; whatever we intuitively *believe*, we cannot be made not to believe; and when we discover an agreement, we cannot be made to *judge* that there is not an agreement.* The test of necessity thus employed admits of an application at once easy and certain.

It should be noticed that the conviction of necessity follows conviction wherever it is found. In what is technically called demonstrative or apodictic reasoning, all the new steps are seen to be true intuitively, and the necessity goes through the whole process step by step. Thus the necessity adheres not only to the axioms of Euclid, but goes on to the last proposition of the last book. It is the same in all other sciences which are demonstrative, as Ethics and Logic are to a limited extent; the necessity adheres to whatever is drawn from first truths by intuitive principles. It is needful to add, that in mixed processes, in which there is both intuition and experience in the results reached, the necessity sticks merely to the intuitive part, and does not guarantee the whole. I suppose there is no doubt of the accuracy of the mathematical demonstrations employed by Fourier in his disquisitions about heat, but there are disputes as to some of the assumptions on which his calculations proceed. We have here a source of errors. In processes into which intuition enters, but is only one of the elements, persons allot to the whole a certainty which can be claimed only in behalf of one of the parts.

* There are acute and profound remarks on the various kinds of necessity of thought in Mansel's Proleg. Log.

SECT. VI. (*Supplementary.*) ON THE DISTINCTIONS BETWEEN THE UNDERSTANDING AND THE REASON; BETWEEN *A PRIORI* AND *A POSTERIORI* PRINCIPLES; BETWEEN FORM AND MATTER; BETWEEN SUBJECTIVE AND OBJECTIVE; BETWEEN THE LOGICAL AND CHRONOLOGICAL ORDER OF IDEAS; BETWEEN THE CAUSE AND OCCASION OF INNATE IDEAS.

We are now in circumstances to examine certain distinctions which have been drawn by the supporters of innate ideas, or intuitive reason, mainly in order to reconcile their views with the claims of experience.

I. THERE IS THE DISTINCTION BETWEEN THE UNDERSTANDING AND THE REASON.—Milton draws the distinction between reason 'intuitive' and 'discursive.' Beattie and Reid represent Reason as having two degrees: in the former, reason sees the truth at once; in the other, it reaches it by a process. There is evidently ground for these distinctions. But the distinction I am now to examine was first drawn in a formal manner by Kant, and has since assumed divers shapes in Germany and in this country. According to Kant, the mind has three general intellectual powers, the Sense, the Understanding (*Verstand*), and the Reason (*Vernunft*); the Sense giving us presentations, or phenomena; the Understanding binding these by categories; and the Reason bringing the judgments of the Understanding to unity by three Ideas—of Substance, Totality of Phenomena, and Deity—which are especially the Ideas of Reason. The distinction was introduced among the English-speaking nations by Coleridge, who however modified it. "Reason," says he, "is the power of universal and necessary convictions, the source and substance of truths above sense, and having their evidence in themselves. Its presence is always marked by the necessity of the positions affirmed" (Aids to Reflection, i. 168). It has become an accepted distinction among a certain class of metaphysicians and divines all over Europe and the English-speaking people of the great American continent. These parties commonly illustrate their views in some such way as the following. The mind, they say, must have some power by which it gazes immediately on the true and the good. But sense, which looks only to the phenomenal and fluctuating, cannot enable us to do so. As little can the logical understanding, whose province it is to generalize the phenomena of sense, mount into so high a sphere. We must therefore bring in a transcendental power—call it Reason, or Intellectual Intuition, or Faith, or Feeling—to account for the mind's capacity of discovering the universal and the necessary, and of gazing at once on eternal Truth and Goodness, on the Infinite and the Absolute.

Now there is great and important truth aimed at and meant to be set forth in this language. The speculators of France, who derive all our notions from sense, and those of Britain, who draw all our maxims from experience, are overlooking the most wondrous properties of the soul, which has principles at once deeper and higher than sense, and the faculty which compounds and compares the material supplied by sense. And if by Reason is meant the aggregate of Regulative Principles, I have no objections to the phrase, and to certain important applications of it, but then we must keep carefully in view the mode in which these principles operate.

We may mark the following errors, or oversights, in the school referred to. (1.) Intuitive Reason is not, properly speaking, opposed to Sense, but is involved in certain exercises of sense. There is knowledge, and this intuitive, in all sense-perception. It may be proper indeed to draw the distinction between the two elements which are indissolubly wrapt up in the one concrete act. Kant endeavoured to do so, but gave a perversely erroneous account when he represented intuition as giving to objects the forms of space and time; whereas intuition simply enables us to discover that bodies are in space, and events in time. There is certainly a high intuitional capacity involved in every exercise of mind which takes in extension or regards objects as exercising property. And then it is altogether wrong to represent sense as the one original source of experiential knowledge, which is derived from consciousness as well as from perception through the senses. (2.) It is wrong to represent Intuitive Reason as opposed to the Understanding. There is intuitive reason involved in certain exercises of the understanding, as when we infer that what is true of a given class must be true of each of the members of the class. Nor is it to be forgotten that the understanding can abstract and generalize upon a great deal more than the objects of sense; it can do so upon the materials supplied by consciousness, and by all the further convictions of the mind, such as the conscience. (3.) It is wrong to represent the mind as gazing immediately and intuitively on the true or the good, upon the necessary or the universal. It can indeed rise to the conception of these, but, in order to its doing so, it has to engage in abstraction and generalization, which makes the truth gained no longer a truth of pure reason, but of reason and understanding combined. It is not consistent with the natural history of the mind to represent it as at once rising to the contemplation of some ideal of the fair and good, which it is able to look at when the spirit is not agitated by passion or bedimmed by earthliness. We are undoubtedly led by native taste to admire the beautiful, but it is when embodied in a lovely object. We are constrained, in spite of a rebellious will, to approve of the good, but it is when a good action, or rather, a good being performing a good action, is presented to the mind. The general ideas of the true, the fair, and the good, do not spring up intuitively in the mind, but are fashioned out of intuitive elements by those addicted to reflection. (4.) It is preposterously wrong to suppose that the mind can employ intuitive convictions in philosophic or religious speculations without any associated exercise of the logical understanding. Not being immediately conscious of the Regulative Principles of the mind, we cannot employ them in discussion till we have first inquired into their nature by induction, and embodied their rule in a clear definition or a precise axiom.

II. Distinction between '*a* Priori' and '*a* Posteriori' Principles.—Prior to the time of David Hume, the phrase *a priori* was applied to the procedure from principle to consequent, and from cause to effect, using the word cause in a wider and looser sense than in these times; while the word *a posteriori* was employed to characterize the procedure from consequent to antecedent, or from effect to cause.* Since the publication of Hume's philosophic works, and more especially since the 'Kritik of Pure Reason' came to have such extensive influence, *a priori* denotes whatever is supposed to be in the mind prior to experience; and *a posteriori* whatever has been acquired by experience. The distinction thus indicated and designated may be admitted without allowing that it probes the subject to its depths, and certainly without admitting all the views usually associated with it. Even in regard to knowledge acquired by experience, I maintain that, prior to its acquisition, the mind has the power of acquiring it. The bodily frame has certainly the organs of sense prior to seeing, hearing, tasting, touching, or smelling. The mind has certainly the capacity of perception before it actually observes any external object, and the power of comparison before it can notice relations. And, in acknowledging the distinction, we must ever protest against the idea that any universal or necessary truth can be discerned by the mind without a process of *a posteriori* in-

* Cudworth's language is, "The abstract universal rationes, 'reasons,' are that higher station of the mind, from whence, looking down upon individual things, it hath a commanding view of them, and, as it were, *a priori* comprehends or knows them" (Immut. Mor. i. iii. 2).

duction and arrangement. So far as the phrase is applied to general maxims, it should be on the understanding that they have been drawn by a logical process out of the individual *a priori* convictions.

Closely allied to the question of *a priori* truth is the question, Can there be an *a priori* science? This is a topic which will come more fully before us in certain of the Chapters of the next Book. There is a sense in which certain sciences are *a priori,* that is, the principles of them are in the constitution of the mind, and are ready to manifest themselves in individual acts. In another sense there can be no *a priori* science, for science employs general principles, and there are no such principles known *a priori.* But there are sciences, the ground-principles of which are not the generalizations of a gathered experience, but of the necessary decisions of the mind, and these sciences may be called *a priori* with perfect propriety, provided always that it be understood, that while the general law is in the mind prior to its manifestation, it is discovered by us only through the generalization of its individual exercises.

III. Distinction between Form and Matter.—This phraseology was introduced by Aristotle, who represented everything as having in itself both matter (ὕλη) and form (εἶδος). It had a new signification given to it by Kant, who supposes that the mind supplies from its own furniture a form to impose on the matter presented from without. The form thus corresponds to the *a priori* element, and the matter to the *a posteriori.* But the view thus given of the relation in which the knowing mind stands to the known object is altogether a mistaken one. It supposes that the mind in cognition adds an element from its own resources, whereas it is simply so constituted as to know what is in the object. This doctrine needs only to be carried out consequentially to sap the foundations of all knowledge,—for if the mind may contribute from its own stores one element, why not another? why not all the elements? In fact, Kant did, by this distinction, open the way to all those later speculations which represent the whole universe of being as an ideal construction. There can, I think, be no impropriety in speaking of the original principles of the mind as forms or rules, but they are forms merely as are the rules of grammar, which do not add anything to correct speaking and writing, but are merely the expression of the laws which they follow. As to the word 'matter,' it has either no meaning in such an application, or a meaning of a misleading character.

IV. Distinction between Subjective and Objective.—The word 'subject' has a diversity of meaning in the English language.

In logic it denotes the term of which predication is made; in common discourse, it means the topic about which affirmations are made; and in metaphysics, the mind contemplating an object. The term 'object' too is not without its ambiguity. Sometimes it stands for a thing contemplated by the mind, and sometimes for a thing considered in itself, and often it denotes the aim or end which the mind has in any of its pursuits. I am afraid it will be impossible, in common discourse, to deprive the phrases of any one of these various significations. The adjectives 'subjective' and 'objective' have not had such a variety of meaning, and the nouns 'subject' and 'object,' when used together, in philosophic discussion, should be limited so as to be exactly coincident with them. They should, in my opinion, never be used except as correlative phrases; the terms 'subject' and 'subjective' being employed to designate, not the mind in itself, but the mind as contemplating a thing; and the terms 'object' and 'objective' to denote, not a thing in itself, but a thing as contemplated by the mind. It is clear that if the phrases were employed in this sense when used at the same time, we should be saved an immense amount of word-warfare, in which subject and object, subjective and objective act so prominent a part. We should be prevented from speaking, as is so often done, of the mind as subject or subjective, except when it is looking at something, or of the thing as an object or objective, except when it is contemplated by a thinking mind. We would also know at once what is meant when it is said that the subject implies the object, and the object the subject. It does not mean that the existence of mind implies an external thing to contemplate it, or that a thing, as such, implies a mind to consider it; it signifies simply that the one implies the other, as the husband implies the wife and the wife a husband, from which we cannot argue that every man must have a wife and every woman a husband, but merely that when the man is a husband, he must have a wife, and when the woman is a wife, she must have a husband. The subjective implies the objective merely in the sense that when the mind is contemplating a thing, it must be contemplating it, and that when a thing is contemplated, it must be contemplated by a contemplative mind.

With a large school of metaphysicians and divines the words subjective and objective are used in a Kantian sense, and are made, without the persons employing them being aware of it, to bring in the whole peculiarities of the critical philosophy. In the philosophy which has germinated from Kant, the *subject mind* is supposed to have a formative power, and the *object thing* is supposed to be a thing, or phenomenon, *plus* a shape or a colour given it by the mind. Proceeding on this view, the phrase 'subjective' comes to express that which is contributed by the mind in cognition. Thus by a juggling use of these phrases, persons are being involved, without their having the least suspicion of it, in a philosophy which makes it impossible for us ever to know things except under aspects twisted and distorted no man can tell how far from the reality. We can be saved from this only by using them as correlatives, and insisting when we do so that the subjective mind is so constituted as to know the object as it is under the aspects presented.

V. Logical and Chronological Order of Ideas.—Sir W. Hamilton quotes a saying of Patricius, "Cognitio omnis a mente primam originem, a sensibus exordium habet primum." The distinction is deep in Kant, and has been fully and skilfully elaborated by M. Cousin. It is said that there are ever two factors in the formation of our *a priori* ideas, reason and experience; and that logically reason is first, whereas chronologically experience comes first. The distinction is not clearly nor happily drawn by such phraseology. For it is difficult to understand what is meant by 'origin' as distinguished from 'beginning;' and what is meant by 'logical' in such an application; it cannot mean, according to the rules of formal logic, it must mean, according to reason; and then comes in the important fact that reason and experience are not, properly speaking, opposed. The distinction, however, points to a truth, inasmuch as our intuitions, as mental faculties, laws, or tendencies, are in the mind prior to the exercise of them. There is a difficulty, however, in apprehending what is meant by the logical or reason element being first, but not chronologically. The intuition as a law is in the mind prior, chronologically, to the experience of it. The individual exhibition of the conviction and the experience of it come chronologically together. It is true, however, in the fullest sense, that an experience is necessary in order to our being able to present the necessary conviction in the form of an abstract definition or general maxim. This distinction connects itself with another, which I am now to examine.

VI. Distinction between Reason as the Cause, and Sense and Experience as the Occasion.*—It is allowed that, apart

* Cudworth refers to ideas of a high kind, which he admits are "most commonly excited and awakened occasionally from the appulse of outward objects knocking at the doors of the senses," and complains of men not distinguishing "betwixt the outward occasion, or invitation, of these cogitations, and the immediate active or productive cause of them" (Immut. Mor. iv. ii. 2).

from sense and experience, the mind cannot have any ideas; still, it is not experience which produces our necessary ideas, it is merely the occasion of them, the true cause being the reason. Thus, without an exercise of sense, there could be no idea of space in the mind; but then the operation is merely the occasion on which the idea of space is produced by an inherent mental energy. Aloof from a special event, there could be no idea of time; but then it is affirmed that upon an event becoming apprehended, the idea of time, already potentially in the mind, is ready to spring up. Without the observation of contiguous concurrences, there could be no idea of cause; but on such being presented, the mind is found to be already in possession of an idea of cause by which to bind them in a necessary connection. Till some human action is presented, there could be no idea of moral good; but on a benevolent action being apprehended, the idea of moral good is ready to spring up.

There is important truth which this account is intended to express, but it es no t bring it out accurately. It is not so easy to settle precisely the difference between cause and occasion: the occasion is, in fact, one of the elements of unconditional cause, or rather, concause, which produces the effect. In regard to the original faculty or law of the mind, it is undoubtedly the main element of the complex cause which issues in a spontaneous intuitive conviction. But there is need of a concurrence of circumstances in order to this faculty operating. But instead of confusedly binding all these up in the one expression 'occasion,' it is better to spread them out individually, when it will be found that each acts in its own way. Thus we should show that an action of the organism is needful to call our intuition of sense-perception into exercise. We should show, too, that an apprehension of an object or objects is needed, in order to call into action our intuitions as to the infinity of time, and eternal relations, and moral good; and then we may see that this apprehension may not have been got from sense, and that in our primary cognition of the object there may have been intuition,—thus, it is because we intuitively know every object as having being, that we declare its identity of being at different times. Again, in respect to the generalized maxim, or notion, the account is fitted to leave a very erroneous impression, for it makes it appear as if it were upon the occasion of the presentation of a material object, that there springs up the abstract idea of space, and of an event becoming known, that there arises the idea of time, or of a succession of events being apprehended, that the mind forms an idea of cause. It is all true that there must be experience in order to the construction of the abstract or general notion, but the notion is formed, after all, by the ordinary process of abstraction and generalization.

CHAPTER III.

ONTOLOGY.

Sect. I. On Knowing and Being.

These are topics which the subtle Greek mind delighted to discuss from the time that reflective thought was first awakened within it,—that is, from at least five hundred years before the Christian era. I confess I should like to have been present when they were handled on that morning when Socrates, as yet little more than a boy, met the aged Parmenides, so venerable with his noble aspect and hoary locks, and Zeno, tall and elegant, and in the vigour of his strength, in the house of Pythodorus, in the Cerameicus, beyond the walls at Athens.* At the same time I fear that, after all, I could have got little more than a glimpse of the meaning of the interlocutors. It is clear that even Socrates himself is not sure whether he is listening to solid argument, or losing himself among verbal disquisitions and dialectic sophistries. And who will venture to make intelligible to a modern mind—even to a Teutonic mind—the arguments by which Parmenides and Zeno prove that Being is One, and the impossibility of Non-Being; or translate with a meaning, into any other tongue, the subtleties of those Dialogues, such as Parmenides and the Sophist, in which Plato makes his speakers discourse of the One and of the Existing? The grand error of all these disputations arises from

* See the opening of the Parmenides of Plato.

those who conduct them imagining that truth lies at the bottom of the well, whereas it is at the surface; and in going past the pure waters at the top, they have only gone down into mud and mire. We are *knowing*, and knowing *being*, at every waking hour of our existence, and all that the philosopher can do is to observe them, to separate each from the other, and from all with which it is associated, and to give it a right expression. But the ancient Greeks, followed by modern metaphysicians, imagined that they could do more, and so have done infinitely less. They have tried to get a more solid foundation for what rests on itself, and so have made that insecure which is felt to be stable. They have laboured to make that clearer which is already clear, and have thus darkened the subject by assertions which have no meaning. They have explained what might be used to explain other truths, but which itself neither requires nor admits of explanation, and so have only landed and lost themselves in distinctions which proceed on no differences in the nature of things, and in mysteries of their own creation.

Knowing, in the concrete, is a perpetual mental exercise, ever under the eye of consciousness; and we can by an intellectual act separate it from its object, and contemplate it in the abstract. In all acts of knowledge we know Being in the concrete; that is, we know things as existing, and we can separate in thought the thing from our knowledge of it, and the thing as existing from all else which we may know about the thing. The science which treats of Being, or Existence, is Ontology. In a loose sense, every real science,—that is, every science which treats of existing objects,—might be called an ontological science. But every one sees that it would be preposterous to represent astronomy and geology and agriculture as departments of ontology, for these sciences treat not so much of the mere being of objects generally, as of certain qualities and laws of special classes of objects. We must therefore confine the science within more stringent limits. If we define Ontology as the science of what we know of things intuitively, we are giving it a precise field, which can be taken in from the waste, and cultivated. Gnosiology and Ontology may be treated to a great extent together in a Metaphysics which unfolds, as has been attempted in this treatise, the original convictions of the mind. Still they can be distinguished, and the distinction between them should be steadily kept in view. The one seeks to find what are our original powers, the other to determine what we know of things by these powers.

In order to reach this second end, we must go over, one by one, the various classes of objects known by our intuitive powers; but this not, as in Gnosiology, to determine what the power is, but what is the object which it looks at. I have been seeking to accomplish the one as well as the other of these all throughout this treatise. By simple cognitive, or presentative powers (as Hamilton calls them), we know objects in the singular and in the concrete: by consciousness we know self as having being, and capable of thought and feeling; by perception we know body as extended and resisting pressure; and by both we know self and not-self as having an existence independent of the contemplative mind. By the reproductive powers we are led to believe in the past event recalled by memory as real, that is, as having occurred in time past; and round space, known in the concrete in perception, and time, known with the event in reminiscence, there gather a number of beliefs which can be ascertained and expressed. Among the objects thus known or believed in,—and it should be added, imagined out of the materials supplied by the cognitive and reproductive powers,—the mind can discern necessary relations, that is, arising from the very nature of the objects. The mind, too, is led to know and believe in a moral excellence in the voluntary acts of intelligent beings, and to discover the bearings and relations of moral good and evil.

Such a survey as this enables us to determine what are the kinds of reality which the mind is able to discover. In sense-perception and consciousness it is a real thing, known as having certain qualities. In our beliefs, too, we look to a real thing having attributes. We believe, we must believe, space and time to have an existence, not as mere forms of thought, but altogether independent of the contemplative mind. Our judgments may or may not look to a reality, for we may discover relations among imaginary as well as among actual objects. But when the objects are real the relations discovered are also real, —not indeed independent realities, but real relations in the actual objects. The reality discovered by the moral power lies in a quality of certain voluntary acts performed by persons possessed of conscience and free will. We thus see how such an inspection settles for us not only that there is a reality, but what is the sort of reality; whether a present or an absent reality, whether an independent reality or a reality in objects. Thus we maintain that abstract and general notions have a reality when the objects from which they are drawn are real; but we are not to understand, as Plato's language would lead us to believe, that they have a reality independent in some intelligible world. The relations of quantity treated of in mathematics have a reality, but it is only in space and time, and in bodies as occupying space and existing in time. Cause and effect have a reality independent of the mind which observes them; but this is, after all, in the substances which act and are acted on. Moral good and sin are certainly both real, but their actuality is in the dispositions of responsible beings.

But it will be urged that all this proceeds on the idea that our original convictions can be trusted. I might maintain, in reply, that whether our convictions can be confided in or not, it is at least a matter of speculative interest to determine what our convictions say. But I do hold that our original convictions must be held as a sufficient guarantee of the truths for which they vouch. The objections which may be advanced against this view will be answered in the Sections that follow, on Idealism and Scepticism. It will be seen that, so far as they have any plausibility, they are all removed when we take along with us accurate conceptions of what it is that our original convictions depone to.

Sect. II. On Idealism.

Two questions here press themselves on us, and seem to raise up clouds in which dimly-seen objects look like spectres.

I. Does the subject never add to the object something not in the object? Does the eye, in looking at a scene, never impart a colour to it, a glow or a gloom? The mirth is not in the merry peal, nor the melancholy in the funereal toll of the bell, nor is the music in the flute or organ, but in the soul which rings and breathes and beats in harmony with the external movements. The view differs according to the point from which men take it, according to men's natural or acquired temperaments, tastes, and characters, and according to the circumstances in which they are placed. How different the estimate which is formed of a neighbour's character, according as he who judges is swayed by kindness or malignity, by charity or suspicion! The scene varies according to the humour in which we happen to be, quite as much as it changes according to the light or atmosphere in which we survey it. Hope gladdens everything as if it were seen under an Italian sky, whereas disappointment wraps it in mist and cloud. Joy steeps all the landscape in its own rich colours, whereas sorrow wraps it as in the sable dress of mourning. Do not such facts, known to all observers of human nature, and dwelt on by poets as being largely their stock-in-trade, prove that in all our ideas, views, notions, opinions, there is a subjective element no less potent than the objective? And if there be, what limits are we to set it? Is our metaphysical philosophy agreed with itself on this subject? Or, with all its refinements, can it draw a decided line which will for ever separate the one from the other?

1. All knowledge through the senses is accompanied with an organic feeling, that is, a sensation. Our immediate acquaintance with the external world is always through the organism, and is therefore associated and combined with organic affections pleasing or displeasing. Certain sounds are felt to be harsh or grating, others are relished as being sweet or melodious or harmonious. Some colours, in themselves or in their associations, are felt to be glaring or discordant, while others are enjoyed as being agreeable or exciting. In short, every sense-perception is accompanied with a sensation, the perception being the knowledge, and the sensation the organic affection felt by the conscious mind as present in the organism. He who is no philosopher, finds little difficulty in distinguishing the two in practice; and it ought not to be difficult for the man who is a philosopher to distinguish the two in theory. Every man can distinguish the sugar in itself from the sweet flavour which we have in our mouth when we taste it, or the tooth and gum from the toothache which is wrenching them; and the metaphysician is only giving a philosophic expression to a natural difference when he distinguishes between sensation and perception.

2. Certain mental representations are accompanied with emotion. Thus the apprehension of evil as about to come on us or those whom we love, raises up fear; the contemplation of good, on the other hand, as likely to accrue to us or those in whom we feel an interest, excites hope. This is only one example of the kind of emotions which attach themselves to all mental pictures of objects, as having brought, or as now bringing, or as likely to bring pleasure or pain, or any other sort of good or evil, and which steep the objects in their own waters, and impart to them their peculiar hue. Hence the gloom cast over scenes fair enough in themselves—as by a dark shadow the effect of the interposition of a gloomy self obstructing the light; hence the splendour poured over perhaps the very same scenes at other times—as by light streaming through our feelings, as through stained glass or irradiated clouds. Hence the pleasure we feel in certain contemplations, and the pain called forth by others. Hence the fear that depresses, that arrests all energy, and at last sinks its victim; hence the hope which buoys up, which cheers and leads to deeds of daring and of heroism. But while the two are blended in one mental affection in the mind, it is not difficult, after all, to distinguish between the object known, and the accompanying emotion; between the trumpet sounding, and the martial spirit excited by it; between the canvas and oil of Titian, and the feeling which his ascending Mary raises within us, glowing and attractive as the splendours of the dying day; between our friend as he is in himself, and the deep and tender regard which we must entertain towards him.

3. Certain ideas are associated with other ideas which raise emotions. It does not concern us at present to explain the nature of the laws which govern the succession of our ideas. It is certain that ideas which have at any time been together in our mind, either simultaneously

or successively, in a concrete or complex state, will tend to produce the one the other or the others; and an idea which has no emotion attached, may come notwithstanding to raise up feeling through the idea with which it is associated, and which never can come without sentiment. Thermopylæ, Bannockburn, and Waterloo, look uninteresting enough places to the eye, and to those who may be ignorant of the scenes transacted there, but the spots and the very names stir up feeling like a war-trumpet in the breasts of all who know that freedom was there delivered from menacing tyranny. Thus it is that the buds and blossoms of spring, and the prattle of boys and girls, call forth a hope as fresh and lively as they themselves are. Thus it is that the leaves of autumn—gorgeous though they be in colouring, and the graveyard where our forefathers sleep—clothed though it be all over with green grass, incline to musing and to sadness. But neither is it very difficult to distinguish between an apprehension or representation and its associated feeling, to separate between the primrose and the buoyant emotion which bursts forth on the contemplation of it, between the grave of a sister and the sorrowful tenderness which it evokes.

4. The mind of the mature man cannot look on any one object without viewing it in a number of relations. A house presented to an infant may be nothing but a coloured surface with a certain outline; to the mature man it is known as a house possibly, with a loved dweller within. An apple falling to the ground is known intuitively simply as an object in motion; but by the educated man it is known as a vegetable fruit falling to the ground in obedience to what seems a universal law of matter. Does not the mind, in such cases, add to the object relations imposed by itself? To this I answer, that all that the mind does, is to add to its original a further knowledge of relations discovered in the objects themselves. The

object before us is not merely a coloured shape, it is a house, and as a house we are entitled to regard it. The apple falling to the ground is in fact a fruit obeying a power of gravitation. The letters of a book are to the infant mere black strokes; to the child learning to read they are figures, signs of sound; to the grown man or woman they are signs of thoughts or feelings, addressed by a writer to a reader: but the truth is, the letters are real things under all these aspects, real strokes, real signs of sound and sense. So far as we proceed accurately, according to the laws of thought using experience, and are employed in discovering the actual relations of things, the conceptions reached imply a reality quite as much as the intuitions with which the mind starts.

I am not prepared to say that these are all, but they are the more important of the natural influences which operate to colour or enlarge our knowledge. The Author of our nature certainly means us to add to our knowledge by observation, and to graft the acquired on the original stock; and he has superinduced these attached sensations, and made the very laws of our nature to call in associated thoughts and feelings in order to intensify and elevate our enjoyment, and in some cases to be a prognostic of evil, which should ever be associated with offence and disgust. So far as music gives us more pleasure than wire vibrations;—so far as a Swiss valley, guarded by Mont Blanc, or Mont Cervin, or the Jungfrau, is finer than an accumulation of grass, trees, stones, and snow;—so far as the spot where a great and a good man was born, is more stimulating than would be the uninteresting hut, which is all the bodily sense perceives,—we owe it to the beneficence of God, who has made us sensitive as well as cognitive beings. So far as we are led to shrink from baser scenes, it is by a provision which is intended to keep us back from what might issue in pain or in sin. It should be added that while this is no doubt the original intent of these peculiarities of our constitution, they may, in the voluntary and sinful abuse of them, become a seduction to evil, and a scourge to inflict the keenest misery. They may lead man, through a misgoverned imagination, to paint in glowing colours a fictitious object, and then pursue it, when he

> "Sees full before him, gliding without tread,
> An image with a glory round its head;
> This shade he worships for its golden hues,
> And makes (not knowing) that which he pursues."

Thus it is that the mind irradiates with a romantic tinge objects unworthy in themselves, and then goes on to love them and delight in them. Man may thus come, too, to be haunted by spectres of his own creation, to be mocked by his own shadow seen across some of the deeper gorges of the earth, and striding opposite as he himself moves. Thus it is that there are to us, for our gratification, glowing colours, burnishing what are in themselves only mists and damps, and spanning the heavens above us with a bow of hope, assuring us that these waters which threaten will not overwhelm us; thus it is, too, that there are hideous mock suns personating the very brightest light which God has planted in these heavens. Still the man of good sense and of simple honesty will find no difficulty in distinguishing practically between things which I have been seeking to separate theoretically in this Section.

II. But is not an imperfect knowledge an erroneous, a delusive knowledge? A rock seen in outline between us and the sky, seems like a man's face; as we approach it, the features, chin, nose, and brow vanish, and we discover it to be an unshapely mass. To the common apprehension the sky looks concave, with a sprinkling of stars sparkling at night like diamonds on its surface, and it is only further consideration which brings us to regard it as a vast expanse, in which great luminaries are moving. The boy feels as if he might mount to the moon, and bring it down; and as if he could hold the sun in his hands like an orange, provided it did not burn him. In such instances our further experience on earth sets aside our first beliefs; and is it not possible that many of the favourite opinions entertained by all men on earth may be set aside by the wider and ever widening experience of heaven? Is it not conceivable that the very strongest and most universal convictions of humankind may seem altogether erroneous to beings in a different constitution of things, and with other principles of knowledge and belief?

1. I answer that many of the inferences we draw from our original and acquired knowledge, and the applications we make of it, are erroneous. It is ascertained, for instance, that absolute size, distance, and direction, are not original endowments of the sense of sight; all that we intuitively perceive by the eye is a coloured surface. It follows that when we are judging of the magnitude or locality of objects, we are drawing inferences from our original perceptions. We found these conclusions on rules which are correct enough for ordinary cases, or cases similar to those from which they were derived, but which may be altogether wrong or deceptive when applied to other or peculiar cases. We are not warranted to allege that our intuitive perceptions through the senses deceive us: we have been led astray by rules laid down by ourselves; and further knowledge enables us to correct them, or rather, to show under what restrictions they hold good. But the increase of knowledge does not set aside the primary knowledge; on the contrary, it might be shown that it proceeds on the original stock.

I am inclined to think that all the errors into which we fall are of a similar character. We draw rash inferences from our real knowledge, original or acquired, and then charge our errors on our constitutions. Still more frequently we illegitimately extend rules correct enough in themselves to cases to which they do not apply. In some of these instances the generalizations we form, or the conclusions we draw, may serve some good end, even though they cannot be regarded as positively true. Thus we suppose the sky to be a concave sphere; thus, too, scientific men of the most rigidly positive class are obliged, when referring to the last resources of decomposition, to call in indivisible particles, molecules, monads, or atoms. But these are mere suppositions to aid our conceptive power, and enable us to think or talk intelligibly of objects of which we have no intuitive, and, in the latter case, no certain knowledge whatsoever. These convictions cannot be described as primary or fundamental, and we can easily deliver ourselves from both the one and the other. In such cases, increase of knowledge constrains us to modify or correct some of the conclusions illegitimately drawn from data which are sound.

2. I answer, that further knowledge is ever adding to our original or acquired stock, but does not set it aside. Were we to look upon our knowledge as being absolute and perfect, we should, in the very act, be falling into error; we should be drawing a conclusion unwarranted by facts. I am convinced that much of the supposed illusion into which we fall arises from this cause. We suppose that we know all about an object, whereas we may know it, after all, only under one aspect, or in the exercise of but a very few of its many and varied properties; but, imagining we know its whole nature, we set about constructing theories regarding it, and pointing out its relation to all other objects. I acknowledge that such speculations may be set aside by further knowledge, even as they would be seen all along to be erroneous by

persons of higher intelligence. Those who imagine that they have cleared up all the mysteries of the Divine nature and decrees, of the soul of man and the nature of spirit or of body, may be astonished and humbled to find, when they reach the land of brighter light, how crude their theories have been. But their mistakes have arisen, not from their constitutions or their experience deceiving them, but from the unwarrantable additions made by their own ingenuity. But so far as our knowledge proceeds from intuition, and is guaranteed by our nature and constitution, it will be found that further knowledge, natural or supernatural, imparted in this life or the life to come, serves only to enlarge our original stock, and make it more solid and congruous. The new aspects now presented will not be inconsistent with the old, but will rather enable us to make a more extended use of them. Here we see as in a glass darkly ; still, what we see is a correct representation, so far as it goes; and what we are to discover in a clearer light, may often be the full lineaments and features of what we saw here so very obscurely. All existing objects may be represented as polygons,—some perhaps with a hundred sides, some with a thousand, and the Supreme Being with an infinite number; and of these man may see only a few, perhaps half-a-dozen or a dozen; still, what he sees is real. The knowledge may not be sufficient to enable him to construct the mathematics of the figure, or to discover all the relations of side to side and side to centre ; still, what he sees are real sides of the very thing; and if we could see other sides, or all the sides, it would not even modify this first knowledge, it would simply enlarge it.

Conceive a savage, just taught to read simple words of one or two syllables, poring over the pages of a full Bible, which a missionary has presented to him. A few chapters in Genesis or John is all he has read or can yet read.

What he has thus learned is truth, and if he keep to what he has read and understood, he has committed no error. But mingled with this there may be suppositions, guesses, conclusions, expectations, as to the general contents of the book, and associated with the whole, superinduced feelings of wonder or awe, and these, were he to open them up, would in all probability appear sufficiently ludicrous to one who has perused the whole volume. It appears to me that the wisest man in this world stands in relation to the whole body of truth in very much the same relation as the savage does to the truth in the Bible. Let this wise man, if he would deserve the name, keep to what he does know, and he is on safe ground; but if he begins to speculate beyond, his conjectures will in all probability appear most preposterous to higher intelligences, and his most confident assertions may turn out to be contradictions. Still, when he keeps within the precincts of knowledge given in intuition or acquired by experience, what is revealed to him is as certain as it is valuable, valuable in itself, and valuable as the foundation on which further acquisitions may be built, without limits and without end. I do believe that in the region, wherever it be, to which man is carried after death, new objects will be disclosed to him which he could not so much as conceive on earth; and the very objects which he knew before, divine or created, will be seen clothed with new qualities, as different from any which have come under his notice when on earth, as colours are to the man born blind but whose eyes are opened, or as musical sounds are to the man whose ears have been unstopped, and that these new kinds of knowledge will open new sources of enjoyment, ever-during and ever-increasing, but all this without any of our genuine earthly knowledge or experience being nullified or cancelled.

We are now in circumstances to judge of idealism. But let us first speak of the ideal spirit. It is truly an elevated and an elevating one, if at all restrained within proper limits. There are elements in human nature fitted and intended to produce and foster it. It is meant that sensations should warm our knowledge into a glow, that feelings should buoy up our intellectual notions into a higher region than they themselves can reach, and that our colder apprehensions should be linked to others which are more fervent. The glory thus cast around objects, commonplace enough it may be in themselves, renders them more lovable and beloved. The melody which the ear gives to the sound, increases our interest in the thought or sentiment uttered, and turns, if I may so speak, prose into poetry. The ideal spirit may be an incentive to glorious enterprise; it steeps the country before us—mountain, vale, sea, and island—in sunlight, and thus allures us to explore it. It is especially elevating when it takes a moral direction, when it places before us a high model to which we ever look, and to which we would become assimilated; and sets us forth amidst sacrifices made, to accomplish some high end reaching forth far in time or into eternity. Still, it is of the utmost moment that the person steadily draw the distinction between our knowledge of the object and the light in which we view it. Without this, the unrestrained spirit will be apt to break forth into extravagance, which will end in a collapse and a reaction; foolish hopes will be excited which can never be gratified, and when this comes to be realized, the issue is the blackest disappointment, not unfrequently *ennui*, apathy, and chagrin,—at times, sourness, bitterness, or despair.

While we can with truth say so much of the ideal spirit, I can bestow no such commendation on idealism as a philosophic system, that is, the system which would raise our associated sentiments to the rank of cognitions. I allow that it is vastly superior to sensationalism, which acknowledges only the visible and the tangible; but, in making this allowance, it is proper to add that, on the principle that extremes meet, it sometimes happens that there are persons atone and the same time sensationalists and idealists, believing only in the physical, and yet not believing the physical to be real.* But, speaking of idealism in itself, it is an unphilosophic system, and, in the end, has a dangerous tendency. Its radical vice lies in maintaining that certain things, which we intuitively know or believe to be real, are not real. I say, certain things; for were it to deny that all things are real, it would be scepticism. Idealism draws back from such an issue with shuddering. But, affirming the reality of certain objects, with palpable inconsistency it will not admit the existence of other objects equally guaranteed by our constitution. This inconsistency will pursue the system remorselessly as an avenger. Idealism commonly begins by declaring that external objects have no such reality as we suppose them to have, and then it is driven or led in the next age or in the pages of the next speculator to avow that they have no reality at all. At this stage it will still make lofty pretensions to a realism founded, not on the external phenomenon, but on the internal idea. But the logical necessity speedily chases the system from this refuge, and constrains the succeeding speculator to admit that self is not as it seems, or that it exists only as it is felt, or when it is felt; and the terrible consequence cannot be avoided, that we cannot know whether there be objects before us or no, or whether there be an eye or a mind to perceive them. There is no way of avoiding this black and blank scepticism but by standing up for the trustworthiness of all our original intuitions, and formally

* See a review of Mr. Mill, *infra*, Sect. VI.

maintaining that there is a reality wherever our intuitions declare that there is.

The idealist has indeed a truth, which he weaves into the body of his system, but that truth is misapprehended and perverted. There are impressions and inferences ever mingling, naturally or inadvertently, lawfully or unlawfully, with our knowledge; and he confounds these, when it is his business, as a professed philosopher, to distinguish them in theory, as men of common sense ever distinguish them in practice. His system is not clearness, but confusion. He has dived below the surface, but has not, after all, gone down to the bottom so as to see all, and his view of the deep is more obscure than if he had remained above. Amazed or enraptured with the discovery of certain facts immediately below that which is patent to the vulgar eye, he looks on them as the main or sole facts, and henceforth overlooks all the superficial ones, forgetting that it is true in philosophy, as in geology, that the rock strata which jut out into the most prominent peaks are those which, if we follow them, dive down the deepest. He has sought to attain a higher position, but has stopped halfway, and his views, after all, are not so clear as those obtained further down, and they are certainly much more confusing than those which he might have had, had he reached the clear height above all dimming influence; they are at best like those which the traveller gets on cloudy days when he has climbed a certain elevation up the Alps, and, in the midway mists, catches occasional glimpses of the green valleys below him, and of the imposing mountain-tops and sky yet far above him.

Sect. III. On Scepticism.

Scepticism may assume a variety of forms, which however differ only in some being more thorough-going than others, some denying the veracity of certain of our cognitions, others denying the trustworthiness of all. Like most kinds of folly, it commonly does not reach its last stage at once, but advances step by step. Some philosopher of eminence sets aside one of our intuitions, and then an advancing thinker, impelled by logical consistency, or by the sharpness of his mind, or by levity, or wantonness, or by the love of paradox or of notoriety, shows how on the same ground we may deny them all. It was thus that Berkeley, in denying the substantial existence of body, prepared the way for Hume, who denied the substantial existence of spirit; and thus that Kant, in affirming that space and time had no existence out of the mind, opened a path for Fichte when he declared that the external object in space might also be the creation of the mind; and for Schelling and Hegel when they made mind and matter, creator and creature, all and alike ideal.* I have already discussed scepticism disguised as idealism; I am now to offer a few remarks on an avowed scepticism.

Let us understand precisely how far a sceptic may go. In doing so it is essential to remember the distinction between the spontaneous and reflex use of our intuitions. Under the first of these aspects they not only claim authority, they secure concurrence and obedience. Every man knows that he has a bodily frame, and believes that it exists in space, and that if he would go in the nearest way to a given point, he must walk in a straight line. Doubt and denial are possible only in regard to the reflex statement of intuitive principles. Every man is in

* It is thus that the speculations of Professor Ferrier as to our cognition of the external world being the cognition of the object *plus* self, is holding out a great temptation to some vain and conceited youth to go a little further in the same direction, and maintain that all truth, all reasoning, that our very belief in God, are mixed up with some subjective element, are, in short, object or truth *mecum*.

fact convinced that he has a solid bodily frame, and that the nearest way to a particular place is a straight line; but it is possible for him, if he chooses, to deny the propositions in which these truths are conveyed; it is quite competent for him speculatively to assert that he has not a body, and that the shortest road to a given point is a crooked line.

And this leads me to point out in what respects scepticism may be allowable, and wherein it may even be beneficial. The dogmatist often lays down and employs for purposes lawful and unlawful, principles represented as indisputable, which have not the sanction of our constitution, or which may be expressed in a form only partially or approximately correct. Great interests may often be involved in having these principles doubted or disputed. Without this we may find, before we are aware of it, great moral or religious truths assaulted or undermined; or we may set up for defence of the citadel of truth a crazy and insecure turret, which is a positive weakness, and which, as it falls, may give an easier inlet to the enemy. This then is the special mission of the sceptic: it is to lay a restraint on the dogmatist; at times, if need be, to assail or to lash him. It would be wrong to affirm that the scepticism of Hume has not cleared the philosophic atmosphere of many weakening and deleterious influences which had been gathering for centuries. The great sin of scepticism lies in this, that it attacks indiscriminately the good and the evil, and would destroy both as by a consuming fire. But surely there may be a means of securing all the good ends which scepticism has produced, without the accompanying destruction of the good. Socrates seems to me to have succeeded in this, when he attacked the pretentious systems of his age, at the same time that he held resolutely by every great moral and spiritual truth. Let it be admitted that our spontaneous convictions guarantee a truth, but let it be avowed at the same time that any given philosophic expression of them is fallible, and may be doubted, disputed, and denied. Let it be understood, as to every philosophic principle proffered, that we are entitled, nay, in duty bound, to examine it before we assent to it, and that the burden of establishing that it is a thorough transcript of the law in the mind lies on him who employs it. By this simple rule, rigidly enforced and scrupulously followed, we might have all the benefits which have arisen from the siftings of scepticism, without its fearful throes, and its destructions—terrible as those of a battle-field—of noble credences and inspiring hopes.

But what are we to do with the sceptic, that is, with one who speculatively denies intuitive truth?

1. There are some things which we *ought not* to do with him. We should not waste our precious feeling in professing to sympathize with him, as if he were practically troubled with doubts as to the existence of himself, or his friends, or his enemies, or his food, or his money, or his earthly interests; for in respect of all these he is quite as firm a believer as the man who comes to convince him with an apparatus of argument. Nor need we be at the trouble of appointing a guard to watch him lest he run against a carriage, or step into a river, or fall over a precipice. For whatever he may profess to us or to himself, he believes in the existence of the carriage, the river, and the precipice, and has a salutary awe of their perilous power. Nor would there be any propriety in declaring him mad, and sending him to Bedlam, for he only pretends to have lost his senses, or rather, never to have had them, and in his simulation has over-acted his part, and gone beyond the madman, who never sets himself against intuitive truth.*

* M. Morel was asked to examine a prisoner who pretended to be

2. There are some things which we *cannot* do with the sceptic, and therefore should not attempt to do. We cannot answer him by argument, that is, mediate proof; for this, if followed sufficiently far back, will conduct us to a principle which cannot be proven, and which therefore the sceptic will deny. It can scarcely be regarded as a complete refutation to demonstrate that his sceptical denials are inconsistent with certain affirmations made by him; for he may admit the inconsistencies, and then found his argument against the possibility of discovering truth on the circumstance that he and every other must inevitably fall into contradictions. It is not even a confutation when it is shown that his scepticism is suicidal, or violates the law of contradiction, for he may find no position so suited to him as that which maintains that all knowledge is contradictory.

Still there are some things which we can do for or with the sceptic.

I. We may make use of any admissions avowed by him or incidentally made, in order to shut him up into truths which he denies. Sometimes we may be able to show that the truth which he allows implies the truth which he disallows. In other cases we can ask him on what principle or ground he assents to certain truths; and when we have his answer, we may be able to show how, on the same grounds, he must admit other propositions. Thus we ask the Berkeleian on what ground he admits the existence of the subject mind; and, whatever it be, we may show that the same ground supports the doctrine of the

deranged, and asked him how old he was; to which the prisoner replied, "245 francs, 35 centimes, 124 carriages," etc. To the same question, more distinctly asked, he replied, "5 mètres, 75 centimètres." When asked how long he had been deranged, he answered, "Cats, always cats." M. Morel at once proclaimed his madness to be simulated, and states,—"In their extreme aberrations, in their most furious delirium, madmen do not confound what it is impossible for the most extravagant logic to confound." (See 'Physiological Journal,' Oct. 1857.)

existence of the object matter. Thus too we may ask how it is that Kant admits the existence of a thing behind the phenomenon, and by help of this process prove that the phenomenon is the thing. If Fichte admit an ego, or a self, or a belief, it is competent to proceed thereon to show that we are thereby constrained to believe in the existence of objects out of self and independent of our belief.* This *argumentum ad hominem* is perfectly allowable. We can say to him, If you admit *this*, you must also admit *that*. If he is so guarded and stinted in his admissions as to say that he allows *this* merely practically and not theoretically or absolutely, we are entitled to demand of him that he believe *that* practically. Thus, if he admit practically that he has at any time had (what Hume allows at the outset) an impression, or idea, we may show him that he should also admit practically that he has an abiding and an identical self, and that he contemplates objects out of him, and independent of him, and, as more important, that he should admit practically that he is a responsible being, and must give account of himself. Should he try to save himself, by declaring that he believes the first, or second, or third of those truths, only because obliged to do so, we may show that there is a similar necessity requiring him to believe the rest. This is a telling argument, which has been used with great skill and power by many of the opponents of scepticism in all ages. It is emphatically an *argumentum ad hominem*, for it is one which may be used not merely against a particular individual, but with men as men, with every man. No man but admits something, and

* It is thus that when Professor Ferrier declares that we know the object *mecum*, we can show that on the same ground, whatever it be, he should admit an object independent of the *me*. He says (Scottish Philosophy, pp. 19, 20) that "no man in his senses could require a proof that it [that is, real existence] is." I am glad of this appeal. A man's senses tell us that the stone before us has an existence independent of the contemplative mind.

that something may be employed to make him admit something else. It can be shown that he who doubts believes, that he who denies affirms, and that he who doubts or denies that he doubts or denies, is in the very act making an affirmation. Such a process goes at least to shut the mouth of the sceptic, for if he open his mouth, it is to let out a weapon which you can turn against him. His only refuge is in a thorough-going scepticism, which affirms that man's supposed knowledge is contradictory, and that all argument is delusive. You can at least insist on this scepticism that it remain silent, and not advance arguments which are inconsistent with that judgment or belief to which it would appeal.

II. We can carefully explain the nature of a primitive conviction. The method referred to under last head is one which we may quite legitimately employ in dealing with the sophist or the caviller, we may always kill him with his own weapons. But we have a more satisfactory mode of dealing with the truth-seeking and the truth-loving. We can ask them to examine the nature of the convictions to which we invite them to yield.

1. It can be shown that the mind declares of itself that its primitive perceptions contain knowledge. I do not urge this as a mediate proof, or a new and independent proof, it is simply the statement of a fact, that the mind, in contemplating its original convictions, affirms that there is knowledge in them. As to some of its states, it finds that they contain sensations, sentiments, imaginations, but in every one of them, at the same time, a cognition of self, and in certain of them a cognition of an object or truth external to self and independent of it. It is to these that we ask consent without the aid of further evidence.

2. It may be shown that the intuitive principles of the mind are native, catholic, necessary. It is not truth merely

to the individual man, but to all men; not merely to all men, but to all intelligent beings. It is certain not only to me but to all beings throughout the universe who have capacity to understand it, that if two straight lines proceed an inch without coming nearer, they will proceed a million of miles without coming nearer, and not only is the wilful infliction of pain a sin on earth, it is a sin in every other part of the universe.

3. The mind declares of certain truths that they need no other truth to support them. There are cases in which it feels that it needs evidence in order to gain its assent. It does not allow that there was such a man as David, king of Israel, or Philip, king of Macedon, till proof is brought forward. It may remain in doubt as to what truth there is in the poetical accounts of the siege of Troy, because no valid evidence is produced. But it draws a distinction between these cases and others in which it needs no evidence. When it is asserted that the moon is inhabited, the mind asks proof, but it asks none when it is affirmed that I am the same person yesterday as I was to-day. It is conceivable that the first of these assertions might be substantiated by evidence which would command our assent, but it would not, after all, be a more rational assent than that which we give at once to the other.

4. The mind knows self-evident truth to be the most certain of all truths. What is it that the sceptic demands? It is all-important to put this question, and to fix him down to a specific answer. Does he demand proof or argument? Then it implies that he would be satisfied with argument. But it can be shown him that in argument there is a first principle involved, the dependence of conclusion on premisses, and in the last resort we come to a premiss not admitting of probation. But surely he who admits argument must admit all that is in

argument; but as to the premiss with which we set out, it is not less evident, it is more evident than the conclusion. It is so far a weakness in a proposition, or rather, of our mind in reference to it, that we do not see it to be true or false immediately. The mind declares that the most certain of all truths are those which are seen to be true at once and in themselves.

III. It can be shown that there is a congruity and consistency among the original and derivative convictions of the mind. This is not urged as if it were an independent and unassailable demonstration. It is conceivable that the power from which human power derives its power might have made all men liable to a deception, incapable of being ever detected, in consequence of its being carefully provided that no inconsistencies should creep in. This is certainly possible, though it is by no means probable, according at least to our laws of judgment. For, if this power be a Being possessed of goodness and truth, it is not conceivable that he should form any creature liable to be deceived: and, if it be a capricious or malignant power, it is by no means probable that all the deceptions would turn out to be congruous: here or there would come out an original conviction in manifest contradiction to another original conviction, or a derivative principle openly inconsistent with both. The consistency of the parts is thus a sort of corroboration of the truth of each part and of the whole. To give only two examples. It is by intuition I have endeavoured to show that the intellect, on discovering an effect, looks for cause, and it always finds, in fact, that for every effect there is a cause; and as it finds this again and again, in an extended and invariable experience, it has in this, not a primary proof, but a secondary confirmation of its intuition. Again, we expect that sin will not go unpunished; from time to time we find it punished in this life, and are thus strengthened in our convictions that it will all be punished at last. All the intuitions have such corroborations in the daily experience of every man, and these are felt to give a satisfaction to the mind.*

IV. When we reach the great truth, that there is a righteous God, we can plead the Divine veracity in favour of the trustworthiness of the intuitive convictions planted by Him in our constitution. Not that even this consideration can be adduced as a primary or an absolute proof; for it is only on the supposition that a God exists that it can be legitimately employed, and our conviction of the Divine existence presupposes a confidence in the veracity of our intuitions and arguments founded on them. But this truth, being once admitted, becomes henceforth the keystone which keeps all the separate and independent parts of our constitution in one compact and stable whole, which can never be broken down, but will be felt to be the stronger the greater the weight that is laid upon it.

V. No truths, recognized by the mind as such, can be shown to be contradictory. In this line of thought a sound metaphysics may accomplish some good ends. Scep-

* Speaking of primary convictions of the mind, Hamilton says: "They are many, they are in authority co-ordinate, and their testimony is clear and precise. It is therefore competent for us to view them in correlation; to compare their declarations; and to consider whether they contradict, and, by contradicting, invalidate each other. This mutual contradiction is possible in two ways. 1st, It may be that the *primary data themselves* are directly or immediately contradictory of each other. 2nd, It may be that they are mediately or indirectly contradictory, inasmuch as the *consequences* to which they *necessarily* lead, and for the truth and falsehood of which they are therefore responsible, are mutually repugnant. By evincing either of these, the veracity of consciousness will be disproved; for, in either case, consciousness is shown to be inconsistent with itself, and consequently inconsistent with the unity of truth. But by no other process of demonstration, is this possible." He adds, "No attempt to show that the data of consciousness are (either in themselves or in their necessary consequences) mutually contradictory has yet succeeded" (Reid's Works, pp. 745, 746).

tics have laboured—and others not sceptics have done their best to aid them—to prove that certain propositions approved of by the mind are contradictory. But in this attempt they have failed, as can be shown, I believe, of every case in which they have tried.* It can be proved, in regard to the opposed propositions, that, in some cases, they have no meaning; that, in other cases, the mind pronounces in favour of neither the one nor the other; that, in several cases, the propositions seem to be contradictory only because improperly stated, and when they are properly enunciated, the difficulty disappears; and that, in the remaining cases, there is merely a difficulty in proposing a positive reconciliation of the propositions, but no real inconsistency.

There is little risk of scepticism producing any injurious influence in the common business of life. The reason is, that circumstances ever pressing on the attention constrain men to proceed on their spontaneous principles, which are sound, even when the speculative principles are altogether infidel. He who is hungry will partake of food, he who sees an offensive weapon about to strike him will avoid it, even though he be not prepared to avow, as a philosopher, that there are any such gross things as bread or iron in the universe, or though he may doubt, as a metaphysician, whether food be fitted to nourish, or a sword to kill him. It is not in such urgent matters of animal comfort and temporal interest that scepticism is wont to manifest itself, but in far different subjects, and especially in leading persons to doubt of the great truths of morality and religion, the practical action in which is more under the control of the will. Even here there will be times when the spontaneous belief or impulse will overmaster the speculative unbelief, as when moral indignation, implying a belief in the reality of sin, is excited

* See an examination of Kant's attempt, *infra*, Sect. V.

by a mean or dishonest action, or when disease has seized us, and death seems in hard pursuit, and threatens to hurry us to the judgment-seat. Such circumstances as these will call forth the action of conscience, in spite of all efforts to repress it. But when there is nothing of this description to arouse the native feeling, unbelief may succeed in keeping us very much out of the way of all that would call the internal sentiment into activity, and for days, or weeks, or months together it may seldom arise to utter a protest or create a disturbance of any description; and, even when the deeper moral or religious powers come forth to assert their authority, there may be a vigorous, and, so far, a successful warfare waged with them; that is, they may be so far repressed as not to command the will, or lead to any practical operation. Hence the evil of scepticism, in chilling the ardour of youth, and confirming the hardness of age, in repressing every noble aspiration and every high effort, while it leaves the soul the servant or slave of the lower, the sensual, the ambitious, the proud, or the selfish impulses of the heart.

Sect. IV. On the Conditioned and the Unconditioned.

Leibnitz complained of the Electress of Brandenburg that she asked the *why* of the *why*. There are some truths in regard to which we are not warranted to ask the why. They shine in their own light; and we feel that we need no light, and we ask no light, wherewith to see them, and any light we might seek to aid us would be felt only as an encumbrance. In all such cases the mind asks no why, and is amazed when the why is asked; and feels that it can give no answer, and ought not to attempt an answer. Other truths can be known only mediately, or by means of some other truth coming between as evidence. I need no mediate proof to convince me that I exist, or that I hold an object in my hand which I call a pen; but I need evidence to convince me that there are inhabitants in India, or that there is a cycle of spots presented in the sun's rotation. In regard to this class of truths I am entitled—nay, required—to ask the *why*. Not only so; if the truth urged as evidence is not self-evident, I may ask the *why* of the *why*, and the *why* of that *why*, on and on, till we come to a self-evident truth, when the *why* becomes unintelligible. Now we may say of the one class of truths that they depend (to us) on no condition, and call them Unconditioned; whereas we must call the other Conditioned, for we require another truth as a condition of our assenting to them.

But this is not precisely what is meant, or all that is meant, by conditioned and unconditioned in philosophic nomenclature. We find that not only does one truth depend on another as evidence to our minds, but one thing as an existence depends on another. Everything falling under our notice on earth is dependent on some other thing as its cause. All physical events proceed from a concurrence of previous circumstances. All animated beings come from a parentage. But is everything that exists thus a dependent link in a chain which hangs on nothing? There are intellectual instincts which recoil from such a thought. There are intuitions which, proceeding on facts ever pressing themselves on the attention, lead to a very different result. By our intuitive conviction in regard to substance we are introduced to that which has power of itself. True, we discover that all mundane substances, spiritual and material, have in fact been originated, and have proceeded from something anterior to them. But then our intuition presses us on, and we seek for a cause of that cause which is farthest removed from our view. Pursuing various lines, external and internal, we arrive at a substance which has no mark of being an effect; to a substance who is the cause, and, as such, the intelligent cause, of all the order and adaptation of one thing to another in the universe; who is the founder of the moral power within us, and the sanctioner of the moral law to which it looks, and who seems to be that Infinite Existence to which our faith in infinity is ever pointing; and now the mind in all its intuitions is satisfied. The intuitive belief as to power in substance is satisfied; the intuitive belief in the adequacy of the cause to produce its effects is satisfied; the native moral conviction is satisfied; and the belief in infinity is satisfied. True, every step in this process is not intuitive or demonstrative; there may be more than one experiential link in the chain; but the intuitive convictions enter very largely, and when experience has furnished its quota, they are gratified, and feel as if they had nothing to demand beyond this One Substance possessed of all power and of all perfection.

If we would avoid the utmost possible confusion of thought, we must distinguish between these two kinds of conditioned and unconditioned; the one referring to human knowledge, and the discussion of it falling properly under Gnosiology; the other to existence, and so falling under Ontology. The conditional, in respect of knowledge, does, if we pursue the conditioned sufficiently far, conduct at last to primary truths, which are to us unconditioned. These are the first truths which we have been seeking to seize and express in this treatise. We cannot be made to think or believe that these primary truths should not be positive truths, and regarded as truths by all other beings capable of comprehending them as well as ourselves. But it is to be carefully remarked, and ever allowed, that some of those truths which are original and independent to us, may be seen by higher intelligences to be dependent on, or to be necessarily interlinked with, other truths. We may by patient induction ascertain what are to us unconditioned truths; but it would be presumptuous in us to pretend to determine what truths are so in themselves, and are seen to be such by the omniscient God. Again, as to conditioned and unconditioned existence, it is quite clear that nothing falls under our notice in this world which is absolutely unconditioned. But the intuitive convictions of the mind, proceeding on a few obvious facts, lead us by an easy process to an unconditioned Being,—that is, whose existence depends on no other.

But the question is started, Can we conceive of the Unconditioned? Of truth unconditioned to us we can conceive: it is the generalization of those truths on which we are ever falling back in the last resort. But can we conceive of unconditioned existence? I find no difficulty in doing so. My intellectual and moral convictions are not satisfied till I do so. But is not our conception, after all, merely negative? I admit that my conception of unconditioned is negative, is a conception merely of the removing of a restriction; and I am not aware that we have any intuitive conviction as to unconditioned such as we have in regard to infinite. But pursuing every one of our native convictions, cognitive, fiducial, moral, they conduct us to a positive conception of a Being from whom all conditions are removed, and whose existence and perfections are themselves underived, while they are the source of all power and excellence in the creature.

SECT. V. (*Supplementary.*) THE ANTINOMIES OF KANT.

Kant tries to show that the speculative reason conducts to propositions which are contradictory of each other (Kritik d. r. Vern. p. 338). It follows that it cannot be trusted in any of its enunciations. Kant extricates himself from the practical difficulties in which he was thereby involved by declaring that the speculative reason was not given to lead us to positive objective truth, and by appealing from it to the practical reason. It is however always competent to the sceptic to maintain that, if the speculative reason deceive us, so also may the practical reason. The doctrine which I hold is, that the reason does not lead directly nor consequentially to any such contradictions. In regard to some of the counter-propositions, Reason seems to me to say nothing on the one side or the other. In regard to others, there seem to be intuitive convictions but the contradiction arises from an erroneous exposition or expression of them. It is of course easy, on such abstruse subjects, to construct a series of propositions which may seem to be contradictory, or in reality be contradictory, if they have a meaning at all. But these propositions will be found not to be the expression of the actual decisions of the mind. Let us examine the contradictions which are supposed to be sanctioned by reason. I am to content myself with looking at the propositions themselves, without entering on the elaborate demonstrations of them by Kant. These demonstrations proceed on the peculiar Kantian principles in regard to phenomena, space, time, and the nature of the relations which the mind can discover, and these I have been seeking to undermine all throughout this treatise. It will be enough here to show that Reason sanctions no contradictions on the topics to which Kant refers.

FIRST ANTINOMY.

The world has a beginning in time, and is limited in regard to space.

The world has no beginning in time, and no limits in space, but is in regard to both infinite.

Now upon this I have to remark, first, that, as to the 'world,' we have, so far as I can discover, no intuition whatever. We have merely an intuition as to certain things in the world, or, it may be, out of the world. Our reason does declare that space and time are infinite, but it does not declare whether the world is or is not infinite in extent and duration. We shall find under another antinomy what is our conviction as to God. Reason does not declare that space or time, or the God who inhabits them, must be finite.

SECOND ANTINOMY.

Every composite substance consists of simple parts, and all that exists must either be simple or composed of simple parts.

No composite thing can consist of simple parts, and there cannot exist in the world any simple substance.

Our reason says nothing as to whether things are or are not made up of simple substances. Experience cannot settle the question started by Kant in one way or other. We find certain things composite: these we know are made up of parts; but we cannot say how far the decomposition may extend, or what is the nature of the furthest elements reached.

THIRD ANTINOMY.

Causality, according to the laws of nature, is not the only causality operating to originate the phenomena of the world; to account for the phenomena we must have a causality of freedom.

There is no such thing as freedom, but everything in the world happens according to the laws of nature.

Here I think reason does sanction two sets of facts. One is the existence of freedom; the other is the universal prevalence of some sort of causation, which may differ however in every different kind of object. These may be so stated as to be contradictory. But our convictions in themselves involve no contradiction: it is impossible to show that they do by the law of contradiction, which is that A is not Not-A. "There is some sort of causation even in voluntary acts;" and "the will is free:" no one can show that these two propositions are contradictory.

FOURTH ANTINOMY.

There exists in the world, or in connection with it, as a part or as the cause of it, an absolutely necessary being.

An absolutely necessary being does not exist, either in the world or out of it, as the cause of the world.

Our reason seems to say that time and space must have ever existed, and must exist. When a God is found, by an easy process the mind is led by intuition to trace up these effects in nature to Him as the underived substance. No contradictory proposition can be established either by reason or experience.

A little patient investigation of our actual intuitions will show that all these contradictions, of which the Kantians and Hegelians make so much, are not in our constitutions, but in the ingenious structures fashioned by metaphysicians to support their theories.

Sect. VI. (*Supplementary.*) Examination of Mr. J. S. Mill's Metaphysical System.

By far the ablest opponent of intuitive truth in this country in our day is Mr. John Stuart Mill. It will be necessary to examine his own metaphysical system. I speak thus because he has in fact a metaphysics underlying his whole logical disquisitions. He says, indeed, in the introduction to his Logic, that "with the original data or ultimate premisses of our knowledge, with their number or nature, the mode in which they are obtained, or the tests by which they may be distinguished, logic in a direct way has, in the sense in which I conceive the same, nothing to do." Yet Mr. Mill is ever and anon diving down into these very topics, and uttering very decided opinions as to our knowledge of mind and body, as to the foundation of reasoning and demonstrative evidence, and as to our belief in causation. This I exceedingly regret; the more so that his logic in topics remote from first principles is distinguished for masterly exposition, for great clearness, and practical utility.* If it be answered that a thorough logic cannot be constructed without building on the foundations which metaphysics supply, then I have to regret that Mr. Mill's metaphysics should be so defective. His philosophy might seem to be that of Locke, but in fact it omits many truths to which Locke gave prominence, as, for example, the high function of intuition. Mr. Mill's metaphysical system is that of the age and circle in which he was trained; it is derived in part from Dr. Brown, and his own father, Mr. James Mill, and to a greater extent from M. Comte.

The only satisfactory metaphysical admission of Mr. Mill is, "Whatever is known to us by consciousness is known beyond the possibility of question" (4th edit. Logic, Introd. p. 6). What does this admission amount to? First, as to self, or mind, he says, "But what this being is, although it is myself, I have no knowledge, other than the series of its states of consciousness." As to body, he says the reasonable opinion is that it is the "hidden external cause to which we refer our sensations" (Logic, i. iii. 8). Sensation is our only primary mental operation in regard to an external world, and perception is discarded "as an obscure word" (compare Dissertations, vol. i. p. 94). "There is not the slightest reason for believing that what we call the sensible qualities of the object are a type of anything inherent in itself, or bear any affinity to its own nature." "Why should matter resemble our sensations?" (Logic, i. iii. 7). Speaking of bodies, and our feelings or

* Mr. Kidd, in his very able work on the 'Primary Principles of Reasoning,' chap. iii., has examined Mr. Mill's Attributive theory of reasoning, and has shown that when he puts the major premiss in the form of "Attribute A is a mark of Attribute B," it means that "the class of things that possess A also possess B," and that we have thus the *Dictum* which he so much disparages brought in surreptitiously.

states of consciousness, he says, "The bodies, or external objects which excite certain of these feelings, together with the powers or properties whereby they excite them; these being included rather in compliance with common opinion, and because their existence is taken for granted in the common language, from which I cannot deviate, than because the recognition of such powers or properties as real existences appears to be warranted by a sound philosophy." It is curious to see how extremes meet. Mr. Mill seems in every way the opponent of the Kantian school. Yet he quotes with approbation and evident delight the words of Sir W. Hamilton, "All that we know is therefore phenomenal,—phenomenal of the unknown" (i. iii., 5).

I have to ask my readers to compare this philosophic system with the account I have submitted in this treatise, and judge for themselves in the light of consciousness. He admits that whatever is known by consciousness is beyond possibility of question; but I hold that by consciousness we know much more than he admits. He allows that we know Feelings—the favourite but most inadequate language of the French Sensationalists, and of Brown. I maintain that our consciousness is of Self as Feeling, and not of Feelings separate from Self. If he ask me to define Self, which I maintain that we thus know, I ask him to define Feeling, which he acknowledges that we thus know. It will then be seen that neither can be defined, because both are original perceptions of consciousness. He admits as indisputable only what we are conscious of. I maintain that we must admit all we intuitively know, and that we know body immediately. Mr. Mill, following Brown, maintains that we know body by inference, as the cause of what we feel. Brown can get the inference; for he holds resolutely by the doctrine that we intuitively believe that every effect has a cause; and discovering phenomena in us which have no cause in us, he seeks for a cause without us. This process would, I think, leave the external world an unknown thing, and could never give us a knowledge of extension (which not being in the effect we could not place in the cause;) still we might thus argue that an external world existed. But how can Mr. Mill, who denies intuitive causation, get the external world at all? Where, indeed, is he to get even his causation as an experiential law? For in a mind shut up darkly from all direct knowledge of anything beyond, the most common phenomena must be sensations and feelings of which we can never discover a cause, or know that they have a cause. I agree with an able critic ('National Review,' Oct. 1859), that the logical result of such a system is painfully blank. Kant saved himself from the consequences of his speculative system by calling in the Practical Reason, and Hamilton accomplished the same end by calling in Faith. I think that these great men were entitled to appeal to our moral convictions and to our necessary faiths. These I hold to be beyond dispute, no less than our consciousness or our feelings. But Mr. Mill makes no such appeal to save him from the void; and he avoids expressing any opinion as to the great fundamental religious truths which men have in all ages intertwined with their ethical principles, and from which they have derived their brightest hopes and deepest assurances. He is silent on these subjects, as if on the one hand unwilling to deny them, and as if he felt on the other hand that by his miserably defective philosophic principles he had left himself no ground on which to build them.

Mr. Mill's derivative logic is admirable; but it is difficult to find to what the final appeal is to be. "There is no appeal from the human faculties generally; but there is an appeal from one faculty to another, from the judging faculty to those which take cognizance of fact, the faculties of sense and consciousness" (iii. xxi. 1). This would seem to make sense and consciousness the final appeal. But all that sense gives, according to him, is an unknown cause of feelings, and all that consciousness gives is a series of feelings. He says, very properly, that we should make "the opinion agree with the fact;" but he seems to leave us no means of getting at any other facts than floating feelings.

I have already noticed his defective account of our moral perception (see *supra*, p. 304), and of our belief in causation (p. 276), and I may yet have occasion to refer to his theory of mathematical axioms. It now only remains at this place to show that he has given an utterly erroneous account of the tests or criteria of primitive or fundamental truth. He is obliged, as for himself, to admit some sort of test: we must admit, he says, "all that is known by consciousness;" and he says there is "no appeal from the human faculties generally." I do regret that he has never patiently set himself to inquire what is the knowledge given by "consciousness," and in the testimonies of the "faculties generally." This would have led him to truths which he ignores, or contemptuously sets aside. He examines the views of the defenders of necessary truth on the supposition that the test of such truth is that "the negation of it is not only false but inconceivable" (Logic, ii. v. 6). He then uses the word "inconceivable" in all its ambiguity of meaning. By "conceivable" he often means that which we can apprehend, or of which we may have an idea, in the sense of an image,

"When we have often seen or thought of two things together, and have never in any one instance either seen or thought of them separately, there is, by the primary law of association, an increasing difficulty, which may in the end become insuperable, of conceiving the two things apart." He then proceeds to show that what is inconceivable by one man is conceivable by another; that what is inconceivable in one age may become conceivable the next. "There was a time when men of the most cultivated intellects, and the most emancipated from the dominion of early prejudice, would not credit the existence of antipodes" (iii. v. 6). I acknowledge that the tests of intuition have often been loosely stated, and that they have also been illegitimately applied; just as the laws of derivative logic have been. But they have seldom or never been put in the ambiguous form in which Mr. Mill understands them, and it is only in such a form that they could ever be supposed to cover such beliefs as the rejection of the rotundity of the earth. The tests of intuition can be clearly enunciated, and can be so used as to settle for us what is intuitive truth. It is not the power of conception that should be used as a test, but it is self-evidence with necessity,—the necessity of cognition, if the intuition be a cognition; the necessity of belief, if it be a belief; the necessity of judgment, if it be a judgment. There was a time when even educated men felt a difficulty in *conceiving* the antipodes, because it seemed contrary, not to intuition, but to their limited experience; but surely no one knowing anything of philosophy, or of what he was speaking, would have maintained, at any time, that it was self-evident that the earth could not be round, and that it was impossible, in any circumstances, to believe the opposite. The tests of intuition, clearly announced and rigidly applied, give their sanction only to such truths as all men have spontaneously assented to in all ages.

BOOK II.

METAPHYSICAL PRINCIPLES INVOLVED IN THE VARIOUS SCIENCES.

CHAPTER I.

DISTINCTION BETWEEN THE DEMONSTRATIVE OR FORMAL AND THE MATERIAL OR INDUCTIVE SCIENCES.

The distinction between them is so obvious that it has been very generally acknowledged. Every one sees the difference between such sciences as mathematics and the Aristotelian logic on the one hand, and zoology and botany on the other. Different accounts however have been given of the grounds of the distinction. Here, as in so many of the other topics which have fallen under our notice, there has been much confusion, issuing in partial truth and positive error. Thus, it is often said that the one class has to do exclusively with abstract truth, and the other with facts which it seeks to classify and arrange. But there are generalizations, and therefore abstractions, in all science ; and if there be any truth in the account given in this treatise, even the sciences which proceed on intuition have to commence with facts which they generalize. Again, the one class is said to be concerned with *a priori* and the other with *a posteriori* truth. But then truth can be available in such sciences only in a general form, and in order to reach the general truth there must be a process of induction. Still there is truth in both these statements. All that is necessary is to explicate it clearly, and make it stand out separate from associated errors.

One class of sciences have evidently to do throughout with facts which they seek to correlate by observing the relations among them, say of form, of property, or of cause and effect. When these facts are external, the sciences are material, such as physiology and chemistry and geology. If the facts be internal, then we have the science of psychology, with its several subdivisions. In these sciences the inquirer always starts with individual facts, but he aims to discover resemblances or other relations, to abstract the points of correlation, and at last to arrive at general laws or causes ever rising in generality. The other class of sciences, if there be any accuracy in the fundamental principles of this work, must also, begin with facts, but they are facts of a different order. The investigator seizes on the original convictions of the mind on the given set of objects, discovers their rule, or the principle involved in them, by a process of abstraction and generalization, and then constructs his science by combining them, and carrying them out deductively. I am to show, in the Chapters which follow, that this is what is done in the science of mathematics, and to some extent also in logic and ethics.

The distinction between the two is thus sufficiently marked. Both must start with facts, but the one starts with the individual convictions, which are native, original, and necessary—or, to speak more accurately, with the facts and truths thus revealed,—and formalizing the principles involved in them, it adopts these as its fundamental maxims, and is now ready to begin its proper work of combining its truths and deducing consequences. The sciences which use only such principles are very properly called apodictic, or demonstrative. They may also be called, in an especial sense, abstract sciences, inasmuch as they deal with principles in an abstract form. Logic is frequently called formal, because it proceeds on such rules; and the appellation might be applied to other sciences, such as ethics, and even mathematics. But it is not to be forgotten, that, after all, these sciences do start from facts, though from facts of a particular kind, and if there be any dispute as to their fundamental principles, the appeal must be to these facts, that is, to the original convictions of the mind. These facts have all a conviction of necessity in them, and on the condition that they be properly generalized, the necessity goes up with each case into the general axiom, and all the truths may be represented as NECESSARY TRUTHS. The maxims with which these sciences start are all generalizations of our primitive cognitions, beliefs, or judgments, and these with the furthest deductions reached have all a reference to objects, and these are the particular kind of objects contemplated in the original conviction. The propositions of geometry have a reference to space. The maxims of ethics have a reference to voluntary actions. Logical formulæ have a reference to the notions of the mind and the objects apprehended in these notions. We may at any time apply the abstract deductions of any of these sciences to cases which fulfil the conditions. They are all true, necessarily true, of their corresponding objects. Thus all the conclusions of mathematics in regard to the ellipse must hold good of the planets, so far as they move in an elliptic orbit. The special rules of the syllogism must hold good of our reasoning about every sort of things. It is to be remembered, however, that most of the axioms of the sciences are generalizations, not so much of our primitive cognitions or beliefs, as of our primitive judgments, and these, while they have a reference to objects, may have a reference to such merely potentially. There may be no such thing as a perfectly elliptic curve in the planetary movements; still, even in such cases, the abstract truth has a respect to a possible ellipse mathematically correct.

And here the question is started, How can demonstration be carried so far in certain departments, while in others it can proceed only a very little way? To this it must be answered, first, in a general way, that demonstration, as proceeding on intuition, is possible only in those departments in which we have intuition, and in these only so far as the special intuition will carry us. In mathematics we have the necessary relations of space, time, number, and quantity to proceed on. The simplicity of the objects allows of great accuracy of expression, which again admits, and all but necessitates, great clearness of notion and comprehension, and thus error is rendered all but impossible, except from the grossest carelessness. An encouragement is given to the prosecution of mathematical deduction, by the circumstance that the truths reached admit of an application to so many departments of nature which in respect of form, time, and quantity are constructed on rigidly mathematical principles. In formal logic too, and in ethics, the laws of thought and of our moral convictions being detected and rigidly expressed, may be carried out to a considerable length by rigid deduction. In mechanics and dynamics the intuition of mind regarding force may admit of a very limited union of demonstration with experiment. But in cases in which the intuition is of a very bare character, the number of relations which can be discovered is necessarily very limited. Thus the relation of identity can afford little matter for demonstration. Again, when the intuition mixes itself closely with other mental acts, it is difficult to reach its precise rule, or get a rule sufficiently clear and definite for demonstration. Thus, our intuition as to cause, the causes being so often dual or plural, does not admit of so satisfactory deduction as our mathematical intuitions. Yet further, demonstration, however far it might be carried in an abstract form, admits of few applications to nature when the circumstances become very complicated. Mathematics can determine very definitely what will be the path of a body when it is attracted by only one other, but it can settle the problem of three bodies only approximately. Formal Logic is greatly hampered by the complexity of thought and the variety of the objects of thought, and a demonstrative ethics becomes valueless in the complicated affairs of human life. By far the greater number of the phenomena of nature within and without us, are so involved and intricate that the abstract truths of intuition and demonstration admit of no application to them.

In the other class of sciences the inquirer begins with facts, these not being the necessary convictions of the mind. He has first and mainly to observe them carefully, and, if need be, to work experiments so as to elicit them fully, and discover the special action of each agent working in the complex operation; and he aims by the "necessary exclusions," and by co-ordination, to reach a general law or a general cause. This law, however, has in it no necessity, and no absolute universality, or universality beyond the knowable cosmos. Having reached the law, the science is satisfied in regard to that department of facts. At the same time it may employ the law as a means to further ends; say, by deduction to ascertain unknown facts, or to reach some further law. These deduced particulars, or laws, can of course have only the certainty of the law from which they are drawn, and this only on the condition that the derivation is properly made. The truths in these departments of knowledge are all EXPERIENTIAL OR CONTINGENT.

It should be noticed that some sciences are of a mixed character, partaking of the nature of both classes. Of this description are mechanics, astronomy, and optics, in each of which there is a union of the generalization of outward facts with the generalization of the intuitive convictions of the mind regarding space, number, and force. In ethics too there is an observation of the characters and circumstances of men, combined with original moral principle. Logic, taken in a large sense, may be considered as not only the science of the generalized operations of thought, but of the laws of thought as applied, say, to necessary truth in demonstration, and to contingent truth in induction.

Nor should it be omitted that in most sciences there are metaphysical principles involved, though these are seldom noticed by physical inquirers. In the Chapters which immediately follow, I am to refer first to the sciences in which intuition and demonstration are the all-important instruments, and then to those departments of knowledge in which intuition enters, often tacit and unseen, as an element.

CHAPTER II.

THE MENTAL SCIENCES.

SECT. I. CLASSIFICATION OF THE MENTAL SCIENCES.

ALREADY five mental sciences have emerged, and these will come each to be subdivided into special departments as the study makes progress.

There is Psychology, which inquires into the operations

of the mind of man with the view of discovering its laws and its faculties. The founder of this science is undoubtedly Aristotle in ancient times. Locke may be described as its second founder in modern times. It is a science throughout of facts and the co-ordination of facts. As a whole, it has made a gradual progress since its origin in Greece, and its second rise in the seventeenth century.

There is Logic. There were helps and preparations towards its construction in the discussions of earlier speculators, but Aristotle may be regarded as the founder of this science also. In modern times it has had a special province allotted to it by Kant, who defined it as the science of the laws of the understanding and of the reason. Those who do not acknowledge the distinction, as drawn by Kant, between the understanding and the reason, but who adopt Kant's general view of Logic, describe it as the Science of the Laws of Thought. It should seek first to seize the laws of thought as in the mind of man, but its main office is to analyze and formalize and apply them.

There is the science of Ethics. The founder of it is undoubtedly Socrates. It is the science of the laws of the Morally Good. It should endeavour to seize the laws of man's moral nature, especially of the conscience, and thence proceed, as its more particular work, to analyze them into forms or rules, and apply them to the peculiarities of human character and the specialties of human life.

There should be a science whose object-matter is the laws of the feelings. Already have we a science for an important part of this general subject, the science of Æsthetics, which would determine the laws of the beautiful. But we should have a science seeking to discover the laws of the feelings generally, and to trace them in their influence, as directed to various classes of objects within and without us. Plato is entitled to be regarded as the founder of this science, from his frequent and often profound inquiries into the nature of the τὸ καλὸν, or 'the fair.' I am inclined to call this scarcely formed science Kalology, or Kallisophy.

There is the science of Metaphysics. In some of its inquiries it appeared earlier than any of the others, going back to the age of the Eleatics. Yet it will be one of the latest to come to any degree of perfection, owing to the subtle and deeply seated nature of the objects at which it looks. It has generally had far too wide and ambitious a province allotted to it. I have sought in this treatise to confine it to a special field, and defined it as the science of the intuitive convictions of the mind, and made the science of knowledge and the science of being as two compartments of it. Its office is by induction to determine what are the laws of the intuitions, and to reduce them to general expressions. It cannot attain anything like a scientific form, till psychology has made some progress, and taught us to distinguish between intuition and associated and allied states of mind.

Sect. II. Logic.

I am disposed to define Logic as the Science of the Laws of Discursive Thought. It presupposes that certain materials are supplied to the mind, say, by sense and self-consciousness, and by the reproductive powers bringing them before the mind even when the objects are not present. Thought works on these materials discursively, that is, from something given it draws or derives something else. In doing so it follows certain laws. It is the office of Logic to seize these laws, and to derive rules from them which may guide and guard thought in its various applications.

Logic is described by those who take much the same

view of it as I do, as an *a priori* science. But this account cannot be allowed to pass without an explanation. It may be called an *a priori* science, inasmuch as it deals with laws which are in the mental constitution prior to all experience. But in another sense it is not an *a priori* science, nor can there be an *a priori* science, for there is no department in which general laws can be discovered independent of experience. While the laws of thought are *a priori*, we cannot discover them *a priori*. It is quite conceivable, indeed, that man might have been so framed that he could discover the laws of thought by immediate consciousness or intuition. His mental constitution might have been such as to enable him at once to enunciate the laws of contradiction and excluded middle, and the *Dictum de omni et nullo*. But it is very evident that man has not been so constituted by his Maker. The only method available to us of discovering the laws of thought, is to observe their spontaneous operations, separate by analysis the invariable from the accidental, and by a process of induction collect the law from its individual acts.

Logic thus throws us back on Psychology, and on an inductive psychology, not indeed to justify the laws, but to discover them. Not that psychology and logic are identical, or that they should be mixed up with one another. Psychology, in treating of the operations of the mind generally, will fall in with thought, and will seek by classification to discover the faculties of thought, and these are specially the comparative or correlative powers. It will seek even to discover in a general way the laws involved in thought. But when it has gone so far in this direction, it will stop. It does not make a very minute analysis of these laws, it does not seek to present them in all possible forms, it does not make an application of them to discursive investigation. It leaves this to logic as its special province. Nor should logic enter generally into the nature of the human mind, its faculties and laws. It should confine itself to one single department. Nor does it in this department seek to investigate faculties and their mode of operation. It looks at the human mind merely with the view of discovering the laws involved in the discursive exercises, and when it has detected them, it puts them in convenient formulæ, and applies them to all various discursive investigations. If psychology were in a more perfect state, it would save logic from nearly all psychological inquiry by handing over to it certain truths which it might at once adopt, and use for its own special purposes.

Logic has points of relation to metaphysics. Certain of the fundamental principles of logic are intuitive. These must fall under the province of metaphysics, which should generalize them out of their individual operations and express them, and show what is their precise nature in the human constitution, and their objective validity, and the relation in which they stand to the other intuitive principles, and to the experiential exercises of the mind. But having finished this work, it hands over these principles to logic, to make a more specific use of them by presenting them in divers formulæ, and following them out in discursive investigation. On the other hand, logic does not consider these intuitive principles as intuitive. If they are admitted, it does not care whether they are intuitive or experiential; it does not trouble itself to inquire about their origin, foundation, or guarantee, or their relation to other exercises of the mind. But while logic is not to be confounded with psychology or with metaphysics, yet in all disputes as to its fundamental principles, it is necessarily thrown back on both. In particular the disputes as to the nature of the abstract and general notion, and all the discussions in the present day as to whether the predicate ought or ought not to be qualified, as to whether the dictum is or is not the ultimate expression of the universal law of reasoning, are to be settled by psychological and metaphysical investigation.

From a very old date, Logic is represented as having to do with the Notion, with Judgment, and Reasoning. Its special province is to discover the laws of thought involved in each of these, to formalize and apply them. The investigations pursued in this treatise have brought out a number of truths capable of furnishing principles in each of these departments. But it would carry us into another science altogether, were I to proceed in this treatise to specify the logical applications of metaphysical truth.

In addition to the Universal Logic discovering and applying the laws of thought, whatever be the objects, there may also be a Particular Logic unfolding the laws of discursive thought as addressed to particular classes of objects. Under this head such subjects as demonstrative and probable evidence, induction, and analogy would be discussed. In this eminently practical department, metaphysics should be able to show, in every branch of inquiry, what principles are intuitive,—by the tests which I have so often specified,—and, by consequence, what must be made to rest on experience.*

* I am aware that there are some who deny that there can be such a department of logic. Logic, they say, has to do with thought, and not with objects, and can take no cognizance of the difference of objects. I admit that logic has to do with the laws of thought, and not with the nature of objects. But then thought has always a reference, avowed or tacit, to objects. There is a subtle error lying here in the account given of universal logic by Kant, who says that it makes abstraction of all content of the cognition (Kritik, Trans. Logik). It is all true that logic looks to the thought, but it is also true that thought has a content. The difference between universal and particular logic lies in this, that the former looks to thought, whatever be the content,

Sect. III. Ethics.

Ethics is in every respect an analogous science to Logic. The difference lies in the difference of the matters with which they deal, the one aiming to find the laws of discursive truth, the other the nature of moral good; the one seeking to attain its end by generalizing the operations of thought, the other by generalizing the exercises of the motive and moral powers of man. Ethics, like Logics, is in a sense an *a priori* science; it finds and it employs principles which are valid independent of our experience. In another sense, it is *a posteriori*, inasmuch as these principles and their laws can be discovered by us only through observation of their individual manifestations; and thus far it is dependent on an inductive psychology. We must begin with inquiring, *Quid est?* and then we find that the thing reached relates to the *Quid oportet?* It is the special office of ethics to ascertain what is involved in the *oportet*, and apply its formulæ to the conduct of responsible beings.

It has to look to three special classes of objects, in order to discover the laws which it employs. It has to look to the motives addressed to the mind, with the view of gaining its consent, and, it may be, of inducing it to form a determination to act. It has to look to the will or the mind deciding upon the motives addressed to it. Further, and specially, it has to look to the conscience

and the latter to thought, directed to special classes of content. This leads me to point out another error which has crept into the Kantian Logic from the Kantian Metaphysics. It is that the laws of thought are mere forms in the mind. True, they are rules in the mind, but they are rules which refer to objects, and they do not give the objects anything that is not in them. True, all discursive thought implies materials supplied to it. If fable or error be given it, what it reaches may also be fabulous or erroneous. But on the other hand, if it start with fact or with truth, and proceed according to logical laws, all that it reaches will also be real and true.

intimating to the will when it should yield to motives addressed to it, and when it should resist. The mind discerns moral good as a quality of certain voluntary acts, and it pronounces a number of decisions in regard to moral good in itself, and these can be abstracted into definitions or generalized into laws which are the fundamental principles of the science. The mind too has a set of primitive judgments, which it forms in regard to the connection of moral good and happiness, and these can also be made to assume a general form. The general principles thus obtained can be put, by analysis, into an immense number of specific forms, to suit special purposes scientific or practical. They can be put in the form of ethical principles, to meet prevalent errors, such as those of the utilitarian or of the sensationalist. Or, again, they can take the form of general or specific precepts, such as, "Thou shalt love the Lord with all thy heart;" "Thou shalt not covet anything that is thy neighbour's." In regard to the will, our intuitive convictions declare that in all moral action the deed must be voluntary, and the will must be free.

But a science of ethics fitted to serve any useful purpose cannot be constructed from the mere native convictions of the mind. We do obtain a few most important general principles from this source exclusively, and these underlie the whole science, and bear up every part of it. But, in order to serve the ends intended by it, ethics must settle what are the duties of different classes of persons, according to the relation in which they stand to each other, such as rulers and subjects, parents and children, masters and servants; and what the path which individuals should follow in certain circumstances, it may be, very difficult and perplexing. In consequence of the affairs of human life being very complicated, demonstration can be carried but a very little way in ethics. In order to be able to enunciate general principles for our guidance, or to promulgate useful precepts, the ethical inquirer must condescend to come down from his *a priori* heights to the level in which mankind live and walk and work. Even in the most practical departments of ethical science, the grand fundamental laws of our moral constitution must ever be the guiding principles, but we have to consider their application to an almost infinite variety of earthly positions and human character.

In these investigations metaphysics, were it diligently to cultivate its own field, and confine itself to it, should be able greatly to serve the science of ethics. It should be in a position to show what is the nature of our intuitions, how these intuitions differ from one another, wherein our intellectual differ from our moral intuitions, and what sort of objective reality each class of our intuitions guarantees, and it should show how we may draw the general law out of the individual convictions. But metaphysics and ethics are not, after all, the same science, nor should ethics be regarded as a branch of metaphysics, nor should metaphysics profess to be able to construct an ethical science. Some of the fundamental principles of ethics are certainly metaphysical, but ethics consists mainly in the construction of a science on these principles as a basis.

Of all the sciences, ethics is that which comes into closest relationship with Christianity and the Word of God. The reason is obvious. It deals with the law and the very character of God; it deals with man as under law, and with man as having broken the law. It thus prepares us, if it faithfully fulfil its functions, to believe in a religion which shows us how the sinner can be reconciled to God. When the great doctrine of the Atonement is embraced, a new and most important element is introduced into ethics. It should no longer be a science constructed, on the one hand for pure beings, nor on the other for persons who must ever be kept at a distance from God. This new reconciling and gracious element turns a pagan into a Christian ethics; it turns a cold and legal, into a warm and evangelical obedience.

CHAPTER III.

MATHEMATICS.

It has been shown by Kant that the axioms of geometry are synthetic and not analytic judgments.* Thus, in the axiom, "Two straight lines cannot enclose a space," the predication that "they cannot enclose a space," is not contained in the bare notion of "two straight lines." Starting with axioms which involve more than analytic judgments, we are reaching throughout the demonstration more than identical truth. The propositions in the books of Euclid are all evolved out of the definitions and axioms, but are not identical with them, or with one another.

The question is keenly agitated as to axioms, whether they are or are not the result of the generalizations of experience. It will be found here, as in so many other questions which have passed under our notice, that there is truth on both sides, error on both sides, and confusion in the whole controversy, which is to be cleared up by an exact expression of the mental operation involved in passing the judgment. A mathematic axiom, being a general maxim, is the result of a process of generalization. If we look to what has passed within our minds, we shall

* Kritik d. r. Vern., p. 143. Mr. Mansel (Proleg. Log., p. 93) maintains that such axioms as that "Things which are equal to the same are equal to each other" are analytic. But does not this confound equality with identity?

find that it has been by the contemplation of individual instances that the mind has attained to the comprehension and the conviction of the general proposition, that "If equals be added, the sums are equal." The boy understands this best when he is in circumstances to use his marbles, or his apples. The youth who is finding his way through Euclid does not feel that the axiom adds in the least to the cogency of the reasoning; on the contrary, it is rather the case before him that enables him to comprehend the axiom and to acknowledge its truth.

But it does not follow that the axiom is a mere generalization of an ordinary or an outward experience. It is not by trying two straight rods ten, twenty, or a thousand times that we arrive at the general proposition that two straight lines cannot enclose a space, and thence conclude as to two given lines presented to us that it is impossible they should enclose a space. It is certainly not by placing two rods parallel to each other, and lengthening them more and more, and then measuring their distance to see if they are approaching that we reach the axiom that two parallel lines will never meet, and thence be convinced as to any given set of like lines that they will never come nearer each other. Place before us two new substances, and we cannot tell beforehand whether they will or will not chemically combine; but on the bare contemplation of two straight lines, we declare they cannot contain a space; and of two parallel lines, that they can never meet.*

* Mr. Mill maintains (Logic, ii. v. 4, 5) that the proposition, "Two straight lines cannot enclose a space," is a generalization from observation, "an induction from the evidence of the senses." That observation is needed I have shown in this treatise; but there is intuition in the observation. That there is generalization in the general maxim I have also shown; but it is not a generalization of outward instances. Observation can of itself tell us that these two lines before us do not enclose a space, and that any other couplets of lines examined by us

In mathematical truth the mind, upon the objects being presented to its contemplation, at once and intuitively pronounces the judgment. It conceives two straight lines, and decides that they cannot be made to enclose a space. What is true of this case is seen to be true of this other case, and of every other, and of all cases. There is thus generalization in the formation of the axiom, but it is a generalization of the individual intuitive judgements of the mind. Hence arises the distinction between the axioms of mathematics and the general laws reached by observation. If we have properly generalized the individual conviction, the necessity that is in the individual

twenty, or a hundred, or a thousand, do not enclose a space; but experience can say no more without passing beyond its province. An intellectual generalization of such experience might allow us to affirm that very probably no two lines enclose a space on the earth, but could never entitle us to maintain that two lines could not enclose a space in the constellation Orion. Mr. Mill, in order to account for the necessity which attaches to such convictions, refers to the circumstance that geometrical forms admit of being distinctly painted in the imagination, so that we have "mental pictures of all possible combinations of lines and angles." We might ask him what he makes of algebraic and analytic demonstrations of every kind, where there is no such power of imagination and yet the same necessity. But without dwelling on this, I would have it remarked that in the very theory which he devises to show that the whole is a process of experience, he is appealing to what no experience can ever compass, "to all *possible* combinations of lines and angles." Intuitive thought, proceeding on intuitive perceptions of space, may tell us the "*possible* combinations" of geometrical figures, but this cannot be done by observation, by sense, or imagination. Supposing, he says, that two straight lines after diverging could again converge, "we can transport ourselves thither in imagination, and can frame a mental image of the appearance which one or both of the lines must present at that point, which we may rely on as being precisely similar to the reality." Most freely do I admit all this. We may 'rely' on it, but surely it is not experience but thought which tells us what must be at that point, and that it is a 'reality.' The very line of remark which he is pursuing might have shown him that the discovery of necessary spatial and quantitative relations is a judgment in which the mind looks upon objects intuitively known, and now presented, or more frequently represented to the mind.

goes up into the general, which embraces all the individuals, and the axiom is necessarily true, and true to all beings. But we can never be sure that there may not somewhere be an exception to experiential laws. We are sure that two straight lines cannot enclose a space in any planet, or star, or world, that ever existed or shall exist. But it is quite possible that there may be horned animals which are not ruminant, or white crows in some of the planets; and that there may come a time when the law of gravitation shall no longer operate.

In the case of our intuitive convictions regarding space, number, and quantity, the simplicity of the objects makes it easy for us to seize the principle, and to put it in proper formulæ, which can scarcely fail to be accurately made, Hence these convictions came to be expressed in general forms, in what were then called Common Notions, at a very early age of the history of intellectual culture. The disputes among mathematicians in regard to axioms, relate not to their certainty and universality, but to the forms in which they ought to be put, and as to whether what some regard as first truths may not be demonstrated from prior truths. Such, for instance, is the dispute as to how the axioms and demonstrations as to parallel lines should be best constructed. But in regard to our convictions of extension, number, and quantity, it is not difficult to gather the regulating principle out of the individual judgment, and the expression is commonly accurate. It is different with other of our original convictions, such as those which relate to cause and effect; the greater complexity of the objects renders it more difficult to seize on the principle involved, and there is greater room for dispute as to any given formula whether it is an exact expression of the facts.

Another interesting and still disputed topic in the metaphysics of mathematics, relates to the nature and value of Definitions. Mathematical definitions seem to me to be formalized primitive cognitions or beliefs regarding space, number, and quantity. In their formation there is a process of abstraction involved. A point is defined "position, without magnitude;" there is no such point, there can be no such point. "A line is length without breadth;" there was never such a line drawn by pen or diamond point. But the mind in its analysis is sharper than steel or diamond. It can contemplate position without taking extension into view. It can reason about the length of a line without regarding the breadth. In all these definitions there is abstraction, but I must ever protest against the notion that an abstraction is necessarily something unreal. If the concrete be real, the part of it separated by abstraction must likewise be real. The position of the point is a reality, and so also is the length of a line; they are not independent realities, and capable of existing alone and apart, but still they are realities, and when the mind contemplates them separately, it contemplates realities. So far as it reasons about them accurately, according to the laws of thought, the conclusions arrived at will also relate to realities, not independent realities, but realities of the same nature as those with which we started in our original definitions. Thus whatever conclusions are arrived at in regard to lines, or circles, or ellipses, will apply to all objects, so far as we consider them as having length, or a circular or elliptic form. We find, in fact, that the conclusions reached in mathematics do hold true of all bodies in earth or sky, so far as we find them occupying space, or having numerical relations.

If this view be correct, we see how inadequate is the representation of those who, like D. Stewart and Mr. J. S. Mill, represent mathematical definitions as merely hypothetical, and represent the whole consistency and necessity as being between a supposition and the consequences drawn from it.* This is to overlook the concrete cognitions or beliefs from which the definition is derived. It is likewise to overlook the fact that these refer to objects, and the further fact that the abstractions from the concretes also imply a reality. This theory also fails to account for the circumstance that the conclusions reached in mathematics admit of an application to the settlement of so many questions in astronomy, and in other departments of natural philosophy. Thus, what is demonstrated of the conic sections by Apollonius, is found true in the orbits of the planets and comets, as revealed by modern discovery. All this can at once be explained if we suppose that the mind starts with cognitions and beliefs, that it abstracts from these, and discovers relations among the things thus abstracted: the reality that was in the original conviction, goes on to the furthest conclusion.

I am inclined to look on the primitive cognitions as constituting, properly speaking, the foundation of mathematics. The mind, looking at the things under the clear and distinct aspects in which they are set before it by abstraction, discovers relations between them, and can draw deductions from the combination. In this process the mind proceeds spontaneously, without thinking of the general principle involved in the reasoning. It finds that A is equal to B, and B to C, and it at once concludes that A is equal to C. It does not feel that in order to reach this conclusion it needs any generalized maxim, such as that "Things which are equal to the same things are equal to one another." The reasoning appears clear anterior to the general principle being announced; and when the principle is announced, it does not seem to add to the force of the ratiocination. It does not, in fact, add to the cogency of the argument; it is merely the

* Stewart's Elem. vol. ii. p. 53. Mill's Logic, ii. v. 1.

expression of the general principle on which it proceeds. Still, it serves many important scientific purposes, as Locke and Stewart admit, to have this general principle expressed in the form of an axiom.* It allows the reflective mind to dwell on the general principle underlying the spontaneous conviction; by its clearness it enables us to test the ratiocination; and it shows what those must be prepared to disprove who would dispute or deny the conclusion. If this view be correct, the abstracted cognitions or beliefs in the definitions constitute the proper foundation of mathematical demonstration, while the axioms being the generalizations of our primitive judgments pronounced on looking at the things defined, are the links which bind together the parts of the superstructure added.†

CHAPTER IV.

INTUITIVE PRINCIPLES INVOLVED IN THE PHYSICAL SCIENCES.

THESE sciences must ever be conducted in the method of induction, with sense and artificial instruments as the agents of observation. But almost all these sciences do at times go down to first principles, and the inquirer is obliged, in the last resort, to appeal to what the mind

* Locke's Essay, iv. vii. 11. Stewart's Elements, vol. ii. p. 25.

† There is truth, then, in a statement of D. Stewart: "The doctrine which I have been attempting to establish, so far from degrading axioms from that rank which Dr. Reid would assign them, tends to identify them still more than he has done, with the exercise of our reasoning powers; inasmuch as instead of comparing them with the *data*, on the accuracy of which that of our conclusion necessarily depends, it considers them as the *vincula* which give coherence to all the particular links of the chain; or (to vary the metaphor) as *component elements*, without which the faculty of reasoning is inconceivable and impossible" (Elements, vol. ii. p. 38).

sees to be true. At the same time, it is not the special business of these sciences to inquire into the nature or guarantee of ultimate truths ; this it leaves very properly to metaphysicians, who should be prepared to announce laws of intuition, which the physicist might profitably employ to suit his purposes. They might be more profitably employed in such a work, which lies exclusively within their own province, than in pursuing speculative ends which can never be attained by human reason.

In all the sciences which meet in their researches with regular forms, and correlated numbers, and constant or periodical motion,—such as mechanical science, statics and dynamics, and certain departments of astronomy, optics, and thermotics,—mathematics have an important part to act, and they come in with all their intuitive axioms and demonstrations. On these I need not dwell further. I leave them, to refer to those sciences in which intuition enters otherwise than in a mathematical form.

Most, if not all, of our intuitive convictions enter, in a tacit way, into physical investigation. Thus, the conviction as to the identity of being leads us to chase the substance through the various forms it may assume, and constrains even those who are most opposed to hypotheses, to speak of ultimate molecules or atoms, which change not with changing circumstances. The intuition of whole and parts prompts us to seek for the missing part after we have found certain parts which have been separated by analysis, and it constrains us to look on the abstract as implying the concrete. Our intuitions as to space make the physicist certain, when he sees body now in one place and again in another, that it must have passed through the whole intermediate space ; and it should prevent him from ever giving in to the theory which represents matter as consisting merely of points of force ; these points cannot, properly speaking, be unextended, and there must always be space between. Our conviction as to time assures us that there can be no break in it, and that when we fall in with the same object at two different times, it must have existed the whole intervening time. Our intuitions as to quantity, or to number and proportion, enter more or less formally into all natural investigation. Our intuition as to generalization insists that, in division, the subclasses should make up the class. Our conviction as to substance and property prompts us, when we discover a new object, to look out for the exercise of its properties; and leads the physicist, when he meets with such agencies as electricity and galvanism, to declare that they must either be separate substances (which is very improbable), or properties or states of substances. Finally, the fundamental law of causality directs us to seek for a cause to every effect. The physical investigator, engrossed with external facts, and seeking to clear them up, will seldom so much as observe these fundamental principles, which are unconsciously guiding him; and only on rare occasions will he find it necessary to make a formal appeal to them. Still, there will be times when those most prejudiced against metaphysics will be tempted or compelled to fall back on them, when going down to the depths of a deep subject, or when hard pressed by an opponent. It often happens that, when they do so, their expression of the principle is sufficiently awkward and blundering; and I think they have reason to complain of the metaphysician that he has been wasting his ingenuity in unprofitable and unattainable pursuits, and has done so little to aid physical investigation in a matter in which he might have lent it effectual aid.

It has been shown by Dr. Whewell, in his great work on the Philosophy of the Inductive Sciences, that each kind of science has its special fundamental idea at its basis, and he classifies the sciences according to the ideas which regulate them. The phrase "ideas" does not seem a good one to express the intuitive convictions of the mind, either in their spontaneous exercises or formal enunciation, and I think he is altogether wrong in supposing that these ideas "superinduce" on the facts something not in the facts. But he has in that work developed great truths, which physical investigators were almost universally overlooking. I do not mean to follow him in his elaborate exposition of the ideas and conceptions involved in the various sciences; I must content myself with showing how certain intuitive principles enter into special sciences.

There is a class of sciences which proceed on our intuition as to the resemblances among objects and classes. These have been called the classificatory sciences by Whewell; they embrace zoology and botany, and mineralogy so far as it is not a branch of chemistry, and geology so far as it deals with organisms. In all these the mind is guided and guarded by our convictions regarding individuals, classes, genera, and species. Another class of sciences have underlying them our conviction as to substance and property; of this description is chemistry, and the sciences which treat of electricity and magnetism and the cognate agencies. A number of sciences proceed on the conviction as to causation; such are all departments of natural philosophy, as it seeks to determine the laws which regulate force; and such too is geology, so far as it strives to find the circumstances and agencies which have brought the earth's surface to its present state. In physiology too there is an inquiry after the properties, be they mechanical or chemical or vital, which have brought the organism into the state in which we find it.

The metaphysician should in no case pretend to be

able to construct any department of natural science; but, keeping within his own province, it is competent for him to furnish an expression of the fundamental principles of cognition, belief, and thought, and the physicist might then be able to use them under the forms which are best suited to his special purposes.

CHAPTER V.

APPLICATION TO THEOLOGY.

SECT. I. FAITH AND REASON.

THE word Faith is used in various senses, some of them sufficiently wide and loose, and others extremely narrow and stringent. But there is a common mental property to which the phrase points in all its shades of meaning. This quality cannot be positively defined; but we may bring out in clear relief its peculiarity as known to consciousness, and show what it is not by distinguishing it from other exercises of mind. It is that operation of soul in which we are convinced of the existence of what is not before us, of what is not under sense or any other directly cognitive power. It is a native energy of the mind, quite as much as knowledge is, or conception is, or imagination is, or feeling is. Every human being entertains, and must entertain, faith of some kind. He who would insist on always having immediate knowledge, must needs go out of the world, for he is unfit for this world, and yet he believes in no other.

It is in consequence of possessing the general capacity that man is enabled to entertain specific forms of faith. By a native principle he is led to believe in that of which he can have no adequate conception,—in the infinity of space and time; and, on evidence of His existence being presented, in the infinity of God. This enables him to rise to a faith in all those great religious verities which God has been pleased to reveal.

There is faith, always along with other exercises, involved in nearly every act of human intelligence. There is faith, I acknowledge of a simple kind, even in the very acts of memory, for in every exercise of memory we believe in that which is not before us. In many, indeed in most of our judgments, there is faith implied, as when on seeing an effect we look for an unseen cause. There may be faith wrapped up even in the very operations of inference, as when from data before us we infer something not before us; as when we see the tide ebbing now, and argue that it will be flowing so many hours after; or, as when Columbus reasoned himself into the belief that there was a world lying far to the west of the lands known to civilized men.

Not in any way psychologically different from these exercises of faith is that which leads us to believe in the testimony of others, a kind of belief to which the word Faith has often been specially appropriated. I am not inclined, with some, to look on this faith in testimony as originating in any intuitive or necessary conviction. I think it indeed very likely that there is a native tendency in children to give credit to the narratives told them by those whom they love or esteem; but this is not of the nature of a fundamental or irresistible conviction. Our common and settled belief in testimony is the result of observation, induction, and reasoning. We have found by experience that we can trust our fellow-men, at least some of our fellow-men. In all this there is inference proceeding on an induction, the issue being not a faith in all men, or in all statements, but a belief in certain men and in certain narratives.

When we rise from faith in man to faith—I mean natural faith—in God, there are the same elements with certain new ones. The new ones arise from the convictions regarding morality and infinity which attach themselves to the good, the omnipresent, and eternal God. We believe that this omniscient God must know the truth; that this infinitely righteous God is incapable of falsehood. At the same time this faith is not without reason, for what are our intuitions about infinity and goodness but primary exercises of reason? This faith is not even without reasoning, for I am inclined to think that there is a single link of ratiocination in that mental exercise by which we rise from the works of God to God the worker, and there is certainly deduction implied in the process by which we reach the conclusion that the declaration of this God of truth must be true.

The word Reason has been employed in as great a diversity of significations as the term Faith. Sometimes it stands for the faculty which reasons or draws inferences. With other writers, reason, as distinguished from the understanding, denotes the power which sees necessary truth at once, without an intermediate process. With certain English writers it stands for that aggregate of qualities (unspecified) which distinguishes man from brutes. Very often it is a general name for intelligence, or for the cognitive powers of man. When persons compare or contrast the exercises of reason with those of faith, they should be careful to understand for themselves, and to signify to others, the senses in which they employ the phrase. In the remarks which I have to offer, I use it as embracing every form of human intelligence, and I attach particular epithets to it when I refer to certain more special exercises.

It is wrong to represent faith as in itself opposed to reason in any of its forms. Faith may go far beyond intelligence, but it is not in itself repugnant to it. There is belief involved in all kinds of intelligence except the primary ones, those in which we look on the object as now present; and in all the higher exercises of reason there is a large faith-element which could be taken out of reason only with the certain penalty that reason would be stripped of all its soaring capacities. What could cognition say of duration, expansion, substance, causation, beauty, moral good, infinity, God, if faith were denied its proper scope, and forbidden to take excursions in its native element?

But if reason is not independent of faith, so neither is faith to proceed without reason. In particular, it would be far wrong to insist on any one believing in the existence of any object, or in any truth, without a warrant. True, the mind is led to believe in much intuitively, but it is because the objects or verities are self-evident, and reflexly can stand the tests of intuition. And in all cases in which we have not this self-evidence, it is entitled to demand mediate evidence, and should not concede credence till this is furnished. It is not indeed justified in insisting that all darkness be dispelled, but it is abandoning its prerogative when it declines to demand that light be afforded; either direct light, which is the most satisfactory, or reflected light, where direct light is unavailable, as it is in by far the greater number of instances. An allowable faith has thus ever the sanction of reason, and in some cases it is the issue of a consequential reasoning. Faith is thus liable to be tested, even as reason is; nor are we at liberty to lay reason aside on the pretence of following a faith which will not allow itself to be examined. Where the truth is alleged to be intuitive, it must submit to be tried by the marks of original convictions. Where it professes to be the conclusion of reasoning, the process may be subjected to the crucible of the logic of inference. Where it claims to be the result of a gathered experience, it must be prepared to stand an examination by the canons of induction.

It is not good either for reason or faith that it should "be alone." The former is in itself hard, bony, angular; and, unmarried to the other, is apt to become opinionative, obstinate, and dogmatic; the latter, without her partner to lean on, would be facile, weak, and impulsive. The one is a help-meet provided for the other, and let there be no divorce of the firmer from the more flexible, or the more devout and affectionate from the more considerate and resolute.

When faith has evidence, intuitive or derivative, in its favour, by all means let us follow it, and this however far on it may lead us, however high it may lift us. As a general practical rule, we are to yield to what has fair *prima facie* evidence in its behalf, without waiting till every objection is removed. Those who act thus will find as they advance that difficulties are removed, and further light furnished. This is easily explained. It arises from the knowledge of the subject and of its relations which is being acquired, and from the suggestions flowing in upon a mind whose intellectual senses are open to receive knowledge. Thus children, confiding in the information conveyed by parents whose veracity they have reason to trust, and pupils believing, on the testimony of a judicious master, in the utility of branches of knowledge which are at present felt to be irksome, will find as they make progress that confirmations ever come in to strengthen their primary trust. In like manner those who follow such light as they have in religious matters, will find further light as they grow in an acquaintance, speculative and practical, with the truths to which they are thus brought into closer propinquity. Those who allow the star set up in the sky to guide them, will fall in with more formal testimonies to direct them as they go on, and will at last reach the very spot where truth —it may be in humble guise—is waiting to gratify their vision and to receive their homage. On the other hand, those who refuse or decline to act on the evidence supplied, may find themselves landed in hopeless darkness. The rationale of this can also be given. They have refused to follow light, and in the very act they have given offence to the conscience, which will fill the soul with reproaches whenever the attention is forced upon the object, from which, therefore, the mind will ever be tempted to turn away as from a personal enemy, whose presence reminds us of ill usage in the past, and possible mischief for the future. Hence, I suspect, the unwillingness of many to consider even the claims of religion, whose initiatory evidence they have refused to look at, and the further evidence of which is therefore denied them. They have turned away from the object, and to look upon it produces only irritation, and so they cannot see it, as they might have done, under its pleasant and its profitable aspects, and at length it is associated in their minds with humiliation and bitterness. There is but one way of delivering themselves from this unbelief and its ever widening shadows, and this too many of them are unwilling to submit to; they must come, like the Apostle Thomas, to the very place of intercourse which they originally avoided, and there a gracious invitation will be given them to search the object round and round, and in every part, till, as they find unmistakable marks, every doubt vanishes, and they exclaim, "My Lord and my God." We see the difference between the two classes. The one class, under the influence of pride, have turned their backs on the light, and they have the shadow caused by their obstruction of it before them, and they go out into the darkness and are lost. Whereas the other and wiser class keep the light before them, and they leave their shadow behind them, and they go on towards the light, and as they approach nearer, the shadow lessens, till as they stand immediately under it, and look up to it, all blackness and darkness are dispelled.

But on the other hand, we should not place ourselves for one hour under the guidance of a faith which has no evidence to furnish. There cannot be a more perilous advice than that which has been given by certain parties to the doubting and inquiring, when they exhort them to force themselves to believe, when as yet they feel that they have no convincing evidence, or to profess a creed in order to get one as they fall in with evidence in advancing. It will be seen at once wherein this case differs from the other previously put. In the one we walk with reason from the beginning, though we do not just know whither it may lead us; in the other we are without reason from the beginning, and cannot expect reason to aid us in our difficulties. In the one we set out with light, and wait for more; in the other we set out without light, and necessarily at random, and if we fall in with light, it must be by the purest accident. There cannot, as it appears to me, be a more likely means of leading faith into temptation, than by counselling her to yield to the first party who pays address to her; for speedily finding herself deceived, she may refuse to put confidence in any other; or, being seduced or debauched, she loses all purity of discernment, and runs from one lover to another, and the issue is commonly either a scoffing infidelity or a restless flitting from creed to creed, and from one observance to another, and not unfrequently a ridiculous combination of the two, and the soul is taking refuge in, and seeking repose under the nearest and most imposing superstition, in order to avoid a blank and horrid scepticism.

There is indeed a sense in which there may be said to be an opposition between faith and reason; but it is as there may be an inconsistency between one dictate of reason and another. There occur times and circumstances, in the life of every one, when reasons are addressed to the intelligence in favour of inconsistent courses, and when the reasonable man decides, it is in favour of the one for which the reasons are the strongest. So there may also be times when man is required to believe, in opposition to many appeals to the sense, and even to the understanding. But in all such cases reason in a higher sense comes to the aid of faith, and announces that we ought to believe in spite of the appearances of mere sense, and of a quibbling intellect.

It is further to be taken into account that there are truths to be believed which are not and cannot be reached by any native shrewdness of intelligence, or by the consecutive deductions of reasoning. Of this description are some of our convictions as to infinity. Of a similar character are many of the doctrines which God has revealed in His Word. In regard to some of these, not only is a deductive reasoning incapable of demonstrating them, reason in its highest degree is incapable of fully comprehending them. When it labours to do so, it is encompassed in darkness, and finds itself utterly at a loss as it would seek to reconcile them with other truths sanctioned by reason or experience. But still, even here, faith is not without reason; for in regard to certain of these truths, the intuitive reason which commands us to believe in them is above all derivative reason; and in regard to truths revealed to us supernaturally by God, reason calls on us implicitly to submit to them as to an intelligence which cannot err. Reason always demands that we should have evidence, immediate or mediate, in order to believe; but it does not insist that the truth be completely within the comprehension of the reason, or unclouded by mystery of any description. Faith has ever the support of reason; yet it goes far beyond reason, and embraces much which is far beyond the conceptions of the intellect in its widest grasp and excursions. It is because man has a natural capacity of faith in the unseen and unknown, that he is able to cherish a faith in the supernatural truths of God's Word. It is because he has the natural gift of faith, that he is capable of rising to the supernatural grace.

Sect. II. Natural Theology. The Theistic Argument.

The idea of God, the belief in God, may be justly represented as native to man. We are led to it by the circumstances in which we are placed calling into energy mental principles which are natural to all. Man does not require to go in search of it: it comes to him. He has only to be waiting for it and disposed to receive it, and it will be pressed on him from every quarter; it springs up spontaneously, as the plant or animal does from its germ; it will well up from the depths of his heart; or it will shine on him from the works of nature, as light does from the sun.

But, while the conviction is natural, this does not prove that it is simple, original, unresolvable, unaccountable. The knowledge of distance by the eye is undoubtedly natural to man; there is a provision made in the organism for its attainment, and all who have an eye acquire it; yet it is not original, but the result of a variety of processes, physiological and psychological, which can be pointed out. Our conviction as to God seems to me to be of a like nature; it is not a single instinct incapable of analysis, but is the proper issue of a number of simple principles, all tending to one point. Such being its nature, the process admits of explicit statement and satisfactory defence.

Among metaphysicians of the present day it is a very common opinion that our belief in God is intuitive. In particular this is the view set forth by a school in Germany and in this country, which allows to Kant that the speculative reason can find or devise no valid argument in favour of the Divine existence. Left without mediate proof, they have called in a special cognition, intuition, or feeling, under the name of 'God-consciousness' or 'Divine Faith.' If there be any validity in the conditions laid down in this treatise, as to the logic of intuition, those who advocate this view may be called on to show that such an intuition exists; that it is original—that is, incapable of being resolved into anything else; and fundamental—that is, leaning on nothing else. It may be further demanded that they explain the precise law, that is rule of the intuition's operation. Is it of the nature of an intellectual cognition, or is it a mere feeling, or is it a faith? What, in particular, is the precise object which it perceives and which it reveals, and how much is revealed regarding that object? Is God revealed as a being, or a person, or a substance? Is he revealed as a power or a cause? or is he revealed simply as a life? Is he revealed as a living God? or as an infinite God? or as a holy, that is, sin-hating God? It behoves those who invoke a separate intuition to reply to such questions as these, in a way that is at least approximately correct; and, in giving the answers, it will be needful to reconcile the replies with the known facts of history, and, in particular, with the degraded views which have been entertained, in most countries, of the Divine Being. If it be a partial or mutilated God that is revealed,—say, a bare abstraction without qualities, or a brute force, or a vague life or activity,—we are left, after all, to depend on other processes when we would clothe him with perfections. If, on the other hand, it be a full-orbed light, shining in all the glory of wisdom and excellence and infinity that is hung out in the firmament before the mental eye, the question will have to be answered, How have the great body of mankind come to see Him in such distorted shapes and in such dark or hideous colours?

I am not convinced that we are obliged to call in a separate intuition to discover and guarantee the Divine existence. I agree, with the majority of philosophers and divines in all ages, that the common intelligence, combined with our moral perceptions and an obvious experience, lead to a belief in God and his chief attributes. But in the process there may be, and there commonly is, a variety of elements conspiring.* In particular, there are both experiential and *a priori* elements.

I. There are facts involved. These become known to man in the ordinary exercise of his faculties of knowledge. In observing them, he discovers phenomena which bear all the marks of being effects. Everywhere are there traces of plan and purpose; heterogeneous elements and diverse agencies conspire to the accomplishment of one end. They are made, for example, in the organs of plants and of animals, to take typical forms, which it is interesting to the eye, or rather, the intellect, to contemplate, and which look as if they were built up by a skilful and tasteful architect. Then every member of the animal body has a purpose to serve, and is so constructed as to promote, not merely the being, but the well-being of the whole. Even in the soul itself there are traces of structure and design. Man's faculties are suited to one another, and to the state of things in which he is placed; the eye seems given him to see, and the memory to re-

* The whole theistic argument is expounded with admirable judgment in Buchanan's 'Faith in God, etc.' There is vigorous thinking in Dove's 'Logic of the Christian Faith.' It is not necessary to do more than refer to the Burnett Prize Essays, by Thompson, Tulloch, Orr, etc.

member, and the laws of the association of his ideas are suited to his position, and his disposition to generalize and his capacity of grouping enable him to arrange into classes, in due subordination, the infinite details of nature. If once it be admitted that these are effects, it will not be difficult to prove that they do not proceed from the ordinary powers working in the cosmos. No doubt there are natural agencies operating in the production of every natural phenomenon which may be pressed into the theistic argument; but the agencies are acting only as they operate in the works of human skill, which are most unequivocally evidential of design. In the construction and movements of a chronometer there is nothing, after all, but natural bodies, and the action of mechanical forces, but there is room for the discovery of high purpose in the collocation and concurrence of the various parts to serve an evident end. It is in the same way that we are led to see traces of design in the works of nature; we see physical agents made to combine and work to accomplish what is obviously an intended effect. Just as in the construction of a timepiece we discern traces of an effect not produced by the mere mechanical laws of the parts, so in the construction of the eye we find marks of plan and adaptation which do not proceed from the potency of the coats and humours and muscles and nerves, but which must come from a power above them, and using natural agencies merely as a means to accomplish its end.

Facts illustrative of order and adaptation furnish the stock of the common treatises of Natural Theology. Most important ends are served by having them advanced in great number and variety. For not only do they give a religious direction to physical science, not only do they help the devotion of those who are already believers, not only do they confirm the conviction already produced,—they tend to produce the conviction. I am aware that there are intuitions involved in the process, and in particular the intuition of causation. But the intuitions are called forth by facts. It is the trace of effects which evokes the intuition of causality. A son of the desert being asked how he came to believe that a God existed, replied, that he knew it as he knew from traces on the sand that a beast or a man had passed. By all means then let works unfolding marks of design in the universe be multiplied, and let each take up its own department and yield its peculiar contribution. Nor let it be urged that one case is as good as a thousand or a million. There are, I admit, single cases which are decisive,—such, for example, is the construction of the eye,—but in all these the adaptations are numerous, and they should be carefully unfolded. It is by the number and diversity of instances that the possibility of doubt is precluded. The single trace of a foot in the desert might scarcely have seemed conclusive to the savage; the presence of many would have settled the question beyond all dispute. It is the multiplicity and variety of traces that show so clearly and satisfactorily that nature is the effect of construction. It is a happily ordered circumstance that every man has evidence, and evidence in proportion to the extent of his knowledge. The common man, the peasant, the artisan, is furnished with abundance of traces in the portions of nature which fall under his immediate inspection,—in the revolving seasons, in the grass and grain, in the instincts and organs of animals, in his own bodily frame, in the provision made for his wants, and the events of an overruling Providence, now encouraging and now punishing him. The man of science, according as he widens his sphere, finds further evidences; and in proportion as he penetrates deeper, he falls in with more recondite proofs.

I cannot then agree with those metaphysicians who look on the presentation of instances, or at least the multiplication of them, as useless, and who would have writers on Natural Theology to be threading their way for ever among the intricacies of abstract discussion. The fact is, in order to a spontaneous conviction, we do not require to have the mental principle enunciated. The unsophisticated mind will have the belief produced more readily and effectually by reading such a work as that of Paley, than by the subtlest exposition of the metaphysics of the argument.

Still, there is a metaphysical principle involved, and this should be brought out in every professedly scientific statement of the complete argument. The belief will spring up of its own accord when the facts are presented, and this whether the mental law is or is not formalized and expressed; but those who would review the conviction must have the mental principle as well as the facts unfolded, and it is the office of metaphysics to furnish it to natural theology.

II. The principle of causation is involved. The object being offered, the intuition is ready to act. The object presented is an effect, and the intuition demands a cause. It may be admitted that there is a possibility of doubt as to whether the phenomenon is an effect. It is conceivable that the stones, lime, wood, and slates might, without any power beyond themselves, have met to form the house in which I dwell; and it is equally conceivable that the flesh, bones, skin, ligaments of the human frame, might also have congregated into my bodily frame without any higher power contriving their harmony. This link of the argument is not intuitive. The evidence is just so much short of demonstration as to allow the possibility of doubt. But it is a probability, a moral certainty of the highest order. It is quite as certain that the eye is a construction, as that a watch is so, or a house is so, or a steam-engine is so. This being admitted, the phenomenon comes under the mental law, and we are necessitated to believe, that this, being an effect, must have a cause.

It may be demanded of those who profess to expound the whole argument, and who appeal to the principle of causation, that they should specify the nature of the principle and show wherein lies its validity. If they derive it from an extended experience, it will always be competent for the sceptic to urge that the widest experience of human science and of history cannot justify the universality of the law. True, in this world every effect seems to have a cause, but our experience in the cosmos does not entitle us to go beyond it, as we must do, when we seek a cause of the cosmos. Hence the importance, if we would bind firmly the ligaments of the theistic argument together, of showing that the principle of causation is a primary one, prior to experience and above it. It may be further required of those who appeal to the principle, that they unfold its precise nature. In doing so they will find that every joint of the reasoning is firm, and capable of repelling all the weapons which have been directed against it.

It is an essential part of the internal law that it requires the cause to be adequate to produce the effect; it must be a power to produce the effect, the given effect.* Here again an experiential element must, I should suppose, enter. Experience must tell us what the precise effect is. Experience, too, must tell us that there is no power in the common agencies of nature, without an arrangement made for them, to run into these typical forms and beneficent collocations. The intuition, meanwhile,

* I have endeavoured to establish the positions here used, P. II. B. III. C. II. s. 8.

insists not only on a cause, but a competent cause for this effect, and for every separate effect, and for the whole effect in its beautiful co-ordination and harmonious adjustment. Our idea of the cause thus grows and accumulates with our idea of the extent of the effect, till at last it is felt to be far beyond human comprehension.

It is an essential element of the law of causation that if the effect be a real thing, the cause must also be real quite as much so as the effect. Hence the importance of adhering to the doctrine of natural realism as opposed to idealism. For when the effect is supposed to be in part or altogether a creation of the contemplative mind, the cause is apt to be regarded in the same ideal light.

It is of the nature of the law of causation that it looks for the cause in a substance, in an existing thing having power and capable of action. The intuition does not say what the nature of the substance must be: it says, however, that it must be a substance with a power commensurate with the effect. And what is the effect? It is an harmonious adjustment, a union of agency, a combination of effort far beyond our power of comprehension, and the cause, whatever it be, must reside in an existence competent for all this. So far the mental principle, proceeding on very obvious facts, can carry us. Perhaps it can conduct us no further without the aid of other intuitions employing other facts. But in guiding us so far it has fulfilled its function and discharged an important office in God's service.

It will be observed that the principle of causation, while it constrains us to seek for a power in a substance, does not, when properly interpreted, necessitate us to look for an infinite series of causes. The intuition is satisfied when it reaches a Being with power adequate to the whole effect; and if, on the contemplation of the nature of that Being, we find no marks of His being an effect, the intuition makes no call on us to go further. It feels restless indeed till it attains this point. As long as it is mounting the chain, it is compelled to go on; it feels that it cannot stop, and yet is confidently looking for a termination; but when it reaches the All-Powerful Being, it stays in comfort, as feeling that it has reached an unmovable resting-place.

III. Other intuitions take hold of other facts, and confirm the argument, and clothe the Divine Being with a variety of perfections. The argument is a cumulative one. It gets materials from a great number and diversity of quarters, indeed from every quarter. It is the business of natural theology as a science to spread out these, and of metaphysics to give an exact expression to the intuitive elements.

(1.) There is the conviction which we have of self as a being, intelligent, thinking, loving, willing. It is the knowledge which we have of ourselves as spiritual beings which suggests the idea of God who is a spirit. Those who, like Hobbes, or like the French Sensationalists, make sensation the only inlet of knowledge and ideas, can never consistently reach a spiritual God. The possession of a soul by us justifies us in regarding God as a being with intelligence and personality. We are constrained to look for an adequate cause of the marks of design in the universe, and we cannot rest till we call in a Designing Mind. Besides, this self is an important part of the effect, and we look for intelligence as alone capable of producing intelligence. Our idea of the Great Original Cause of all things is thus at one and the same time enlarged and rendered more definite.

(2.) I have shown that man has a very peculiar class of intuitive convictions bearing on the subject of moral good. In particular, every one has a conscience, which declares that there is an indelible distinction between good and evil. Surely the God who implanted that conscience must himself love the good which it would lead us to love, and hate the evil which it would impel us to hate. This moral power in man manifests itself in leading us to cherish a conviction of obligation to a law above itself, independent of itself and of the mind which looks to it, and having authority or right to enjoin and forbid. I shall not go the length of positively affirming that this binding law of itself implies a lawgiver, but I do maintain that the mind feels something wanting till it hears of a Moral Governor who is ever ruling, and is ready to reward and punish.

(3.) The mind has a strong conviction that there is an infinite existence. Space and time are conceived by themselves as unbounded, and wherever they are, there may be substance dwelling in them. But infinite extension and duration, and our belief regarding them, are felt to be void and empty till we are able to place in them infinite substance with infinite attributes ; but when it has done so, the mind feels that it has found the wanting truth, and is satisfied supremely and to the full.

Thus it is that I would build up the cumulative idea. But I would have it remarked that what I have sought to construct so systematically, is spontaneously reared in a much more irregular or piecemeal manner ; that which I have placed first coming last ; or, in too many cases, very important elements, such as the recognition of the high spirituality and holiness, or even the unity of the Divine plan and personality, being altogether omitted, so as to exhibit a partial, or broken, or distorted image ; or the whole may happily be reared at once by the strong intuitive energy, evoked and trained by a Christian education.

Several advantages arise from giving this account of the genesis of the conviction. The argument thus built postulates no new or peculiar intuitions other than those which guide us in all thought of a lofty or a profound character. Our appeal is to the universal principles of humanity, on which all men act in other matters, and which they are not at liberty summarily to discard when it would constrain them to believe in a Great and Good Being, the Author of their own being and of the universe. It embraces the same mixture of elements, experiential and intuitive, as is found in the arguments which carry conviction in the more important transactions of life. It carries with it the sanction of our constitution, and yet allows observation to contribute out of its ever-accumulating stores. When ingenious men make the inference demonstrative, it holds out incitements to other ingenious men to detect weaknesses and breaks in the links of the chain. When there is a loose appeal to consciousness or faith, there is always a possibility of persons urging in reply, 'You may have such a sentiment, and I allow you freely to indulge it, but do not impose it on me;' or more frequently this vague feeling may be satisfied with a God as vague and empty as itself. If the account given above be correct, then the grounds of our belief can be spread out, and the argument defended, the experiential elements by the logic of induction, and the mental elements by the logic of intuition; and the whole pressed home, in an appeal which no one is at liberty to decline to look at or to accept.

The account given shows how the argument may be resisted. The conviction springs up naturally, but not necessarily. Men may overcome it, being led into a labyrinth of sophistry from which they discover no outlet, or, more frequently, being hardened by an encouraged pride, or sensualized by a course of vice. An atheist is a phenomenon which rarely presents itself; and when it does, it is to be viewed with a feeling of humiliation and compassion. It may be allowed, I think, that there have been persons who have strived hard to persuade themselves that there is no God, and have so far succeeded that they are troubled with the conviction only at some of the more lucid or awful moments of their lives.

We see how man is responsible for his belief in God. Were the argument altogether apodictic, there would be no possibility of doubt, and therefore no room for the consent or dissent of the will. But the argument being moral, and not demonstrative, there is room for the exercise of an evil heart in rejecting it, and therefore of a candid spirit in falling in cheerfully with it.

The account given shows not only how we can build up on defensible grounds the argument for the Divine existence, but also how we can construct a defence of His more peculiar perfections, such as His goodness, justice, and infinity. Those who describe the whole process as one of feeling, are apt to take a very light and loose view of the Divine Being; they talk of Him as mere power, or mere activity, or mere life. But when we give a wiser and juster view of the conviction, we see that the same considerations which lead us to believe in his existence also constrain us to believe in his unbending righteousness and his spotless holiness.

Following out the theory, we can account for the low, the unworthy, the perverted representations taken and given of the Divine character. When the higher intuitions of the mind are not called into exercise by proper training and the appropriate objects, they lie, to a great extent, dormant, and so God, or the gods, come to be largely stripped of spiritual or moral qualities. As men's minds became barbarized and narrowed, their attention was confined to a very limited class of objects as being the proper effects of the Divine power. God came to be contemplated not as the author of creation, or as the actor in it throughout, but as an agent merely in certain portions of it, which were contemplated with peculiar wonder or fear; and as these portions were viewed as inconsistent with each other, there arose gods many and lords many. The doctrine of the unity of God, and of the spirituality of God, being lost sight of, the gods came to be multiplied indefinitely, according as it suited the impulses, the fears, the superstitions of the votaries, or the interests of the priests and their temple. The distinction between God and His works being lost sight of, distorted traditions, and baseless fables and myths, the natural expression of human wants and wishes, clustered in ever-increasing intensity round the gods, and their places of worship, and certain awful spots in nature, or mysterious agents operating in it; and these were handed down from mother to son, ever growing in waywardness and strength. In the history of religion we have two classes of phenomena to be accounted for by those who would give an explanation of the nature and genesis of the religious conviction. We have an all but universal belief in a God, or in gods, with nearly as universal a degradation of the character of Deity. The double phenomenon can be explained only by supposing that there are native religious tendencies in the mind, ever working but ever liable to be abused and perverted, and requiring to be called forth into healthy exercise by the presentation of suitable objects, and indeed to be guided and directed by a standard revelation.

We see how the conviction is to be called out, strengthened and refined. It is by the presentation of objects fitted to awaken the intuitions into energy and to keep them in proper exercise. The idea of a moral and spiritual God is to be aroused and kept alive by the attention being directed to moral and spiritual truths. This is what is done, in the best of all modes—in the concrete mode, in the Word of God—which ought therefore to be thrown open to children at an early age. This is what is done in a religious training, conducted according to the Word of God. A God who is at once Light and Love is set before us, and he is represented as revealed to fallen man in the face of his Son; holy precepts are enjoined by Him as the guardian of duty; and thus is generation after generation reared, the child being trained by the parent, and the child becoming the parent in order to train the child. Natural Theology is also fitted to confirm and widen this conception among the comparatively few who may be expected to study it. According as men are taught to look on their own nature as spiritual, so will they be disposed to look on God as a Spirit; and according as they are educated to look on the conscience as an undefeasible property of humanity, so will they be led to look on God as essentially holy. Still it is only, I believe, by an abiding written revelation that the truth can be made patent to the great mass of mankind, or saved from perversion by the fancies, the foolish speculations, and the infidelity of the educated. Only thus can we get light admitted into the dwelling of the poor man, and into the heart of the busy man of the world, and only thus get it handed down from age to age. I am aware that even though the Bible were withdrawn, the religious conceptions would go down, in lands which had once enjoyed its light, to the next age in comparative purity. But as generations succeeded which had not been trained in its lessons, I am convinced that the great mass of the people would speedily lapse into some degraded worship, probably of the Mormon type, and that the philosophers, pursuing their own favourite ideas, would exercise little influence, certainly little influence for good, and care little to put forth what little they have over an unthinking multitude, who would appreciate their distant and refined speculations only by evincing at times their shrewd sense of their practical absurdity. It is by a permanent Luminary being kept up in the sky that we expect light to be so diffused over our world that all men may behold it, and walk in it, and see objects in it.

Sect. III. On the Immortality of the Soul.

The doctrine of the soul's immortality cannot be established by rigid demonstration any more than that of the Divine existence. But in the one as in the other there are necessary principles involved, which look to obvious facts, and issue in a conviction which may be described as natural. The expounded argument is the expression of processes which are spontaneous. It draws materials from a variety of quarters and admits of accumulation. No one of the elements is in itself conclusive, but in the whole there is a high probability quite entitled to demand belief and practical action. There are three intuitive elements involved.

I. There is the intuition of self as a being, a substance, a spiritual substance. Every one is immediately conscious of a self different from the material objects which press themselves on his notice, and of the action of mental attributes in no way resembling the properties of matter, of lofty thoughts and far-ranging imaginations and high moral sentiments, of lively and fervent emotions and of a power of choice and fixed resolution. The circumstance that the bodily organism is dissolved at death is no proof that these qualities or the existence in which they inhere shall perish. We see the body die, but we never see the spirit die. We know that the soul has existed; we have no evidence that it ceases to exist. The burden of proof may legitimately be laid on those who maintain that it does. The soul exists as a substance, and will continue to exist unless destroyed by a power from without capable of producing this special effect. I doubt whether the argument can be stretched further. It is possible to conceive that the dissolution of the body may be an adequate cause of the destruction of the soul, and the idea could not be repelled by any positive demonstration. It could only be urged in reply that there is no necessary connection between the breaking-up of the bodily organism and the death of the soul, and that the soul is convinced that it may look on in the midst of the struggles of the material dissolution and survive when they are ended.

And here it is worthy of being noticed that we have no experience of any one thing being absolutely annihilated. Man knows no such thing even among material objects. He casts wood into the fire, and the existing combination of its elements is destroyed, but the elements themselves are not lost; one part has gone down into the ashes, another has gone up into the air, and not one particle has perished. What is true of material particles is no less true of physical forces. Man cannot create a physical force, and as little can he destroy it; if it be in a statical state, he may bring it forth into a dynamical one; if it be in activity, he may contrive to counteract it; but he cannot create it on the one hand, not put it out of existence on the other. The force which came from the sun to the plants in the form of heat in the geological age of the coal-formation is not lost; it was received by the vegetable organisms, it was laid up in the strata of the earth, and is ready to burst forth, on the needful conditions being supplied, in fire and flame, and be a source of mechanical force in steam. And if no material particle is ever lost, and no physical force lost, is it consistent with the analogy of nature to suppose that mental force is lost? If mind is extinguished on the dissolution of the body, it is the only force known to us as being absolutely annihilated, and yet it looks and feels as if it were the most imperishable of them all.

II. There is the conviction of moral obligation and responsibility pointing to a judgment day and a state of righteous retribution. The argument built on this ground is felt by many strong minds to be the strongest of all. Kant, so severe in his criticism of the psychological argument, yields to the moral one. Chalmers fondly dwells on it as the one which actually carries weight with mankind. It proceeds on the existence of a moral faculty; but its validity does not depend on any peculiar view which may be taken by us of the moral powers in man. It is enough that man be acknowledged to be under moral obligation—under moral law: that law is imperative—it commands and it forbids: it is a supreme law—claiming authority over all faculties and affections, over in particular all voluntary desires and acts. This law in the heart points to a lawgiver who hath planted it in our constitution, and who sanctions and upholds it. Upon our recognizing God as lawgiver, the conscience announces that we are accountable to him; "so then every one of us shall give account of himself to God." But if we are to give account to God, there must be a day of reckoning to arrive—in this life, or, if not in this life, in the life to come. He who hath appointed the law must needs be judge; He who has appointed it so authoritatively, and proclaimed it so publicly, must needs inquire whether it has or has not been obeyed. But this judicial work is not fully discharged in this present state of things, and therefore we look for another. There are times when God seems to set up a throne of judgment on the earth, and call men before it. There are ever and anon instructive examples of studiously concealed wickedness being brought to light and exposed; of the arm of violence being arrested, when the blow was about to descend; and of the deceitful man being caught in the net which he laid for others. These cases however are not uniform, or without palpable exceptions; they are corroborations of our moral decisions, but they do not come fully up to the demands of our constitution, which is thereby only strengthened in the conviction and expectation that what is only partial here will, at last, be universal.

Our moral nature, giving these general intimations as to the world at large, seems to carry a more special message to every man,—that he must submit to the judge. This is a feeling which may lie very much dormant in many states of the existence of man; as when he is engrossed with business, or absorbed in schemes of earthly ambition; but it seizes many a quiet moment to insinuate the truth committed to it; it awakes with terrible power in the state of relaxation which succeeds the fever heat of the evil propensities; it issues its lightning flashes in the dark hour of disappointment; it raises its sharp voice in the stillness of the sick chamber; and gives forth foreboding utterances, which few dare despise when they realize the thought that the time of their departure is at hand. I am not seeking to disturb men by dreams in the night, which have no corresponding realities in the day; I am not raising up ghosts in the darkness to frighten men, as if they were children, into a salutary fear; I am asking them to read what is graven, as by a chisel on a rock, on the constitution and heart of all men. The conscience in this life is the anticipation of the archangel's trumpet summoning all men to the judgment, and in the other world may become the worm that never dies, and the fire that is not quenched.

III. There is the intuition of personality guaranteeing that the self that lives and sins and the self to be judged is the same being. I am not advancing this as a primary proof that this self must abide after death; I urge it simply to prove that, if the soul outlives the body, it must carry with it its essential personality. The soul which lives after death is the same as lived before.

I have previously noticed the circumstance that there

is nothing lost in this world. In particular, the soul carries with it the conviction that it should abide. This feeling being perverted has led to a doctrine which has been widely entertained in various ages and nations, that the spirit passes from body to body. But in this doctrine of transmigration there is a serious mistake, arising from materialistic ideas, that is, from attaching to the soul ideas which have a meaning only when applied to bodily force. It is easy to conceive of physical force migrating from body to body, losing meanwhile none of its essential qualities. But in supposing that mind thus travels we are obliged to strip it of one of its essential attributes: we suppose that it has a different consciousness in its different habitations, and thus deprive it of an abiding personality. It is curious to notice that a similar error has made its appearance of late among a class of thinkers who profess to be looking into great depths, but in so doing have overlooked a truth near at hand. According to the pantheistic doctrine of these times, the soul at the separation from the body goes out as it were into a great ocean of spiritual existence. This doctrine is also materialistic. We can conceive of air thus rushing into air, and of a bucketful of water losing itself in a river; and why? because neither air nor water ever had a separate and conscious personality. The soul as long as it exists must retain its personality as an essential property, and must carry it along with it wherever it goes. The moral conviction clusters round this personal self. The being who is judged, and saved or condemned, is the same who sinned and continued in his sin, or who believed and was justified when on earth.

Upon these arguments others grow which have more or less of force. There is, for example, the shrinking from annihilation, the longing for immortality,—a feeling which seems to guarantee the veracity of the expectation cherished. Then there are affections, pure and holy, springing up on earth but not allowed to be gratified on earth, but we may hope to have satisfied to the full in heaven. There are attachments and profitable friendships firmly clenched only to be violently snapped asunder by the stroke of death, but which we expect to have renewed in a place where there are no breaches. Do not those swelling feelings which agitate the bosoms of friends when one of them is summoned away seem to show that these divided waters are yet to meet? Then we see from time to time intellectual powers cultivated to the utmost, but blasted in the flower when they seemed to promise a large fruit. May we not believe that in a universe in which nothing is made in vain, and nothing of God's workmanship lost, these powers have been nurtured to serve some great and good end in a future state of existence? These facts combined seem to show that there are means instituted in this world which have their full consummation in the world to come.

Sect. IV. Pantheism.

Pantheism has some qualities to recommend it to our favourable regard, especially when it is viewed at a distance. To be able to reduce the multiplicity in the universe to unity may seem to be about the highest achievement of human ingenuity, and the end to which every separate science points. To represent every existing thing as a modification of the one God seems to account on the one hand for the variety which we find in nature, and on the other hand for the wonderful mutual connection and dependence of all the parts. The system fosters the admiration which the enlightened mind feels in the contemplation of the beauties of nature and art, and thus falls in readily with those æsthetic feelings which become stronger in every nation as it advances in refinement and civilization. It allows too of the outpouring of some of the devout sentiments of our nature. It leads us to connect God with his works, and makes us feel as if our admiration of beauty were an act of devotion paid to God, of whom this beauty, whether it proceed from the forces of nature or the ingenuity of man, is an exhibition. If it does not compel us to fall on our knees in prayer, it at least encourages praise, for what is all this admiration, whether merely heaving in the breast or expressed in glowing language, of the loveliness and grace of the objects around and above us, and of the order and harmony of the powers in nature, but just a hymn of praise to Him who lives and acts in them and indeed constitutes them? Pantheism calls forth and fosters these feelings because of the truth which it has retained,—truth often left out or rejected in certain mechanical systems of nature, in which, to use the strong language of Thomas Carlyle, God is represented as "sitting as it were apart, and guiding it, and seeing it go." As embracing these truths it can use, though often in a hypocritical sense, the profoundest phraseology of the Bible, and speak of God as incarnate in his works and especially in man.

But it must be added, that there are other considerations which recommend pantheism to not a few. Under some of its forms it fosters the deepest pride; as, for instance, in the system of Spinoza, where man is represented as a mode of Deity, and in that of Hegel, where human intelligence is represented as identical with the Divine. Under every form it delivers mankind from a sense of personal responsibility to God, who may call his intelligent creatures to account; and from all sense of guilt and fear of punishment in a future life. Being a modification of Deity, we are not called to cherish any deep sense of dependence on Him, and we have no motive to pray to Him; more especially as His whole procedure is an eternal flow in a predetermined channel beyond the control of our prayers. No doubt we are liable, even according to this system, to be, not exactly punished, but exposed to suffering if we pursue certain courses; but all this does not imply that we have given offence to a living being, that we have raised up by our conduct a holy indignation in the breast of any one, or that we shall have to appear at last at a throne of judgment. What we have to bear (this is the sort of spirit which Carlyle has caught from feeding on the German pantheists), let us bear in a spirit of manly pride, as knowing that we cannot by any entreaties influence a power whose movements are fixed from eternity. And as to the world to come, doubtless there is such a world, but there God is as unpersonal as He is here, and we become like Him by casting off our supposed personality, and, like the burst bubble, become swallowed up and lost in the awful ocean of Being, out of which we were blown to float for one brief hour as a spectacle on the surface.

These are the considerations which have recommended it to some of the best and some of the worst principles of our nature. It is needful to examine it, and yet it is difficult to do so, for, Proteus-like, it takes a new shape as we seize it, cloud-like it eludes us as we would grasp it. Few of those attached to it have ever attempted to give it a defined shape, and most of those who have attacked it have had no fixed or conceded points from which to assail it, and the weapons that they shoot neither wound nor slay. "They fight in vain; the shadows which they destroy spring up again in a moment, like the heroes in Valhalla, again to be able to amuse themselves in bloodless conflicts."

There have been very exaggerated statements made as to the extent of the prevalence of pantheism, and this both by its foes and its friends. Some, in a sensitive apprehension of it, have discovered it in systems which have not avowed it, and in which there is an open acknowledgment of the existence of a personal God. The historians of philosophy of the school of Hegel discover pantheism, even in the Hegelian form, in almost every system of philosophy, Asiatic or Grecian. I grant that in the great majority of the popular superstitions and pagan philosophies there has been no sharp line of demarcation drawn between God and his works, and in most of them there is supposed to be some matter coeval with God, and independent of him. This arises certainly not from an elevating, but from a degrading tendency in the human mind, which has a difficulty in conceiving of a spiritual God, the creator of all things. Acknowledging that this confounding of God and his works is nearly universal in all systems of religion or philosophy not derived directly or indirectly from revelation, I am persuaded that comparatively few have allowed themselves to sink so far in the bogs of metaphysics as not to look on God as a person, or to believe that God is in no way distinct from his works. The number of avowed pantheists must ever be very few, fewer than belong to Buddhism, Brahminism, Mahometanism, or even Mormonism, and they are to be found exclusively in the narrow circle of the refined and the idle. The creed is of far too subtle and cobweb a texture to stand the rude jerks and the storms of common life.

It has assumed an immense number of shapes, if shape it can be said to have, whose very nature is to be shapeless. The following seem to be the more decided.

1. There is Material Pantheism. According to this, it is the mere matter of the universe, with its forces, its life, its thought, as the result of organism, which constitutes the One All, that may be called God. This is the lowest sort of pantheism, indeed it scarcely deserves the name, for it has no proper unity amidst the diversity. Yet

I suspect it is, after all, the most prevalent among those who are inclined to pantheism in this country or in France, and in the extreme left of the school of Hegel,—and this has as many supporters in Germany as the higher forms have. It has something to recommend it to vulgar minds, which dislike a living God, and yet are not prepared to give up all belief in Deity. It admits nothing but what can be made patent to sense, and yet it has a way of deceiving itself, by speaking of the aggregate of material existences as if they were one existence, capable of something like order and intelligence.

2. There is Organic or Vital Pantheism. The difficulty which we have in defining life, or in apprehending it, holds out a temptation to many to explain all things by it, which, in fact, is to explain the *ignotum per ignotius*. All nature, they say, is full of life; and this statement is doubtless true, if by life is meant simply activity. The old Cartesian doctrine, according to which matter is mere extension, and is in itself utterly sluggish and inert, cannot stand in the midst of the discoveries of modern science, which show us the chemical, electric, and calorific forces all characterized by incessant activity. But while matter is active in a sense, this does not show that any one particle of it, or that the material world as a whole, has life, meaning organic life. The mystical view that nature is a plant, an animal, or an organism, appeared in various forms of Platonism; the equally unintelligible idea that all nature has life, comes out in the writings of certain physical speculators of the school of Schelling, and has passed over into the poetry and the poetical prose of this country, and in all cases tends to substitute some sort of impersonal power for a personal God.

3. There is the One Substance Pantheism. Persons begin first by declaring that the material universe is the body, and God the soul. This is an error, for God acts

independent of the universe, which is his creation. It is not, however, pantheism; for persons may hold this view, and yet maintain that the two are distinct. It however prepares the way for pantheism, which maintains that there is a spiritual power acting in the material form, the two being all the while one substance. We owe the introduction of this system, as a system, to Spinoza, who tried to found on certain views of Descartes as to the nature of substance. According to this shy, thought-bewildered man, there is but one substance, which substance has attributes which the mind can conceive as its essence and modes, being the affections of the substance. This substance is infinite, a part of it is substance finite, and man is such a part of the Divine Substance. This system has been set forth in his Ethics in a terrible array of confused and confusing definitions, axioms, and demonstrations, in which things that should be distinguished are confounded, and propositions that should be proven are unconsciously assumed. Perhaps no one, except Spinoza, ever held his precise doctrine; but it was eagerly grasped at by those who, towards the end of last century, were seeking to introduce pantheism in a more shadowy form. It might be shown, in opposition to it, that whatever considerations are urged to prove that there is one substance, may be employed to prove that there must be two.

4. There is Ideal Pantheism. It is the issue reached in the course of ages by a process of philosophical speculation, starting with improper assumptions, and conducted in a wrong method by persons of consecutive and systematic minds, who will follow out their favourite notions, however preposterous the conclusions to which they lead. Kant began with making time and space subjective forms, and Fichte went on to make matter and God himself a subjective creation of the mind. Schelling

sought to enlarge the system by making mind and matter, God and the universe, at one and the same time ideal and real,—ideal on the one side, and real on the other; and Hegel came forward with an artificial dialectic, to show how nothing could become something, and how God becomes conscious in humanity. These systems differ widely; indeed some of them are absolutely inconsistent with the others. In particular, an ideal pantheism is incompatible with a materialistic, organic, or substantial pantheism. Yet among those who are inclined to these views there is a constant propensity, when attacked, to flee from the one to the other. When we prove that there is a material world, they assert that this external world intellectualized is God; and again, when we prove that there are laws, typical forms, ideas, above the mechanism of nature, they solemnly announce that these objectified constitute the universe. But we cannot allow the system thus to transmigrate from body to body; I insist on its abiding in some one of its shapes while we subject it to examination. In the course of our extensive survey we have attained principles quite sufficient to exorcize it, whatever be the form which it assumes. It will be instructive to find that the intuitions of the mind, while they conduct, with the aid of obvious facts, to a belief in the Divine existence, are utterly inconsistent with pantheism.

1. Pantheism is inconsistent with the intuitive knowledge which we have both of mind and matter. The universe cannot all be matter, for we are conscious of ourselves possessing thought and intelligence, and of planning, designing, and executing in the exercise of free will. It cannot be a mere organism, for we see material objects which are beneath the organic state, and we are conscious of souls which are above it. It cannot be one substance, for we are as sure that there are two substances as that there is one. It cannot be all idea, or

mere idea, for we are cognizant of the object as well as of the thought; and ordinary experience, with the laws of thought building on it, carries us from object to object, from quality to substance, and from effect to cause, the one being real as much as the other.

2. Pantheism is inconsistent with the consciousness of self, with the belief in our personality. It may seem a doctrine at once simple and sublime to represent the universe as *Ἓν καὶ πᾶν*, but it is inconsistent with one of the earliest and most irradicable of our primary convictions. If it can be shown that there are two or more persons, it follows that all is not one, that all is not God. According to every scheme of pantheism, I, as a part of the universe, am part of God, part of the whole which constitutes God. In all consciousness of self we know ourselves as persons; in all knowledge of other objects we know them as different from ourselves, and ourselves as different from them. Every man is convinced of this; no man can be made to think otherwise. If there be a God, then, as all His works proclaim, He must be different from at least one part of His works, He must be different from me. In the construction of his artificial system of *a priori* forms, Kant most unfortunately omitted the knowledge of a personal self, and thus speculation, in the hands of his successors, was allowed to flow out into a dreary waste of pantheism. When we restore the conviction of the separate existence of self, and the belief in our continued personality to its proper place, we are rearing an effective barrier in the way of the possible introduction of any system in which man can be identified with God or with anything else.

3. Pantheism is inconsistent with man's possession of a will, and a free will. It is the circumstance that man is possessed of a distinct will which suggests the idea that God is not a mere law or principle, but a person

with a power of voluntary determination. It is in consequence of his possessing an inherent and positive freedom that man is led to look upon God as also free, and this in a higher and more absolute sense, inasmuch as there can be nothing to lay restraint upon His liberty. May we not go a step further, and maintain that the possession of voluntary power and freedom on the part of man, is not only fitted to suggest, but is a proof, that the God from whom they proceeded has a will, and that this will is free? It is not easy to determine, as to certain forms of pantheism, whether they attribute free will to God, or in what sense they affirm or deny it. The doctrine of Hegel, that God awoke to consciousness, and acquired a will in the consciousness and will of man, seems to me to be utterly inconsistent with the essential principles of reason, which requires that the cause be adequate to produce the effect. But what adequacy can there be in a power without will to produce will? All forms of pantheism which do not ascribe a separate will to God are liable to the objection that they suppose God to produce in man a free will not possessed by Himself from eternity. If the other alternative be taken, and will be ascribed to Deity, then have we two wills in the universe, the will of God and the will of man, and it follows that all is not one in any intelligible sense, for we have now two distinct wills, which may run counter to each other. Whatever be the philosophic system adopted, we have, as matter of fact, the hundred of millions of distinct wills possessed by human beings. These separate wills show by one process that God must have a distinct will, and by another process that there must be more than one will in the universe, and both conclusions are inconsistent with a system which says all is one.

4. Our sense of accountability to God as Judge is inconsistent with pantheism. There is in man, we have

seen, a native principle, which leads him to distinguish between good and evil, which indicates not unobscurely that the evil will be punished, and points to One ready to inflict the penalty. Natural religion, it is true, can say little as to the time and manner of the judgment, but it does announce that the sustainer of the moral law must, among other offices, exercise that of Judge. But the feeling with which we look at the judgment plainly intimates that we must submit to the trial in our individual capacity. It is utterly inconsistent with the sentiment to suppose that, prior to the final judgment, man is to be absorbed into Deity. God, as Judge, must be distinct from the persons judged, and we who are judged must be the same as those who committed the deeds. In particular, they who sinned, and they only, are liable to punishment. We have only to follow out the doctrine of personal responsibility to find it setting aside every form of pantheism.

Having thus inquired into the truth of pantheism, we are now at liberty to look at its consequences.* And this, it may be remarked, seems to me to be the proper order in which to proceed in all investigation. The argument from consequences may very properly make us suspicious of a doctrine, but cannot absolutely disprove it. It may be one of the very objects of those who propound an erroneous dogma, to deliver us from the fear of God and the obligations of morality, and they are to be met by proving, not that their opinions are injurious, but that they are unsound. But when we have first shown that a doctrine is untrue, we may then point out the evil consequences which flow from it. It will be found, in fact, that the true always leads to beneficent, and the false to pernicious results. This does not seem

* There are fine remarks on the Pantheistic spirit in the First Essay of Bayne's 'Christian Life.'

to arise, as some have supposed, from the true and the good, from the false and the wicked, being identical, but rather from the pre-ordained connection instituted between them by Him who hath marked His approbation of the true and the good by making them yield happy fruits, and hath branded the false with His disapprobation by causing it to be followed by a train of disastrous consequences.

In weighing the results to which the system leads, I would not wish to be indiscriminate in the censure bestowed; I by no means charge it with leading to every sort of evil. As containing some important elements of truth, it may, under some aspects, have rather an elevating tendency, more especially when compared with those systems in which God is separated altogether from the universe, and made an idle spectator of its mechanism, or those other and superstitious systems in which he is pictured as guilty of favouritism and caprice. But in comparing it with an enlightened theism, in comparing it with revelation, which it would set aside, it is chargeable with certain very grave consequences.

It is supposed to be one of the special advantages of the system that, teaching us to discover God in all his works, it leads us to cherish a perpetual affection towards Him. But in this representation there is as grievous a misunderstanding of the character of man as there is of the character of God. It proceeds on a mistaken view of emotion, and of the objects which call it forth. The sentiment raised by inanimate beauty is a mere æsthetic feeling, and has nothing in it of love, in the adequate sense of the term. The feeling with which we contemplate a lovely natural scene, such as Loch Lomond or the Trossachs, or a great monument, such as that of Rauch at Berlin, or that of Canova at Vienna, or of Thorwaldsen at Lucerne, is not that required of us when we contemplate the Divine Being. Then it may be doubted whether any abstract truth or general principle is fitted to kindle emotion. Analysis and classification are intended to deepen and amplify our intellectual conceptions, but are by no means fitted to rouse feeling. It is not by dwelling on the grand ideas of the lovely and the good that sentiment is evoked, but by the contemplation of a lovely object or a good individual. These ideas may serve to widen our views and raise our minds above a weak superstition, but they are not fitted nor intended, by Him who hath given us the capacity to form them, to create and cherish affection in our bosoms. It is when a lovely object, a fine statue or painting, is presented, that feelings of admiration are called forth; and in like manner, it is when a person supposed to be possessed of good or amiable qualities is brought under our notice that we are led to love him. It follows that in very proportion as we take away the individuality of God, we make it more and more difficult for man to love him; and if we strip Him of personality altogether, we make it impossible for the human heart to cherish any affection towards Him. Hence we find that the pantheist, when he would create a passing feeling of gratitude or affection towards the God of his system, is obliged to personify him. Were he to look upon God as a mere principle of law or order, as a procession of processes, he would find his heart continuing cold and blank as he contemplated Him, and so he uses a species of deception, or yields to a delusion, and represents Him as having consciousness and life, nay, as the only consciousness and the absolute life. In this way he may succeed in exciting a sort of mystic feeling, radiant as the evening sky; but as the body of the luminary, which alone can keep up the glow, is gone, it soon sinks into darkness. Even when the feeling is warmest, there is an idea ever pressing itself on the mind, that the whole representation is fictitious, and hence the glow produced has as little of permanence, and exercises as little control over the practice, as that called forth by a theatrical show or the scenes of a novel.

Failing as it does in this its supposed advantage, the system is chargeable with stripping religion of all those severe truths and elevating sentiments which practically influence the minds of men for good. The feeling of personality having been destroyed so far as it is possible for an artificial system to destroy it, he who has imbibed the spirit of pantheism will not be distinguished by much determination, activity, or practical philanthropy. The energetic and devoted character of Fichte may seem to be an example to the contrary; but, as Archdeacon Hare remarks, "To form a correct judgment concerning the tendency of any doctrine, we should rather look at the fruit it bears in the disciples than in the teacher. For he only made it, they are made by it." We see the true influence of pantheism in the indolent and dreamy character of the Brahmins and Buddhists of the East. It is scarcely conceivable that there should arise among pantheists a great reformer, an energetic philanthropist, a self-devoted martyr. Along with personality there must depart all feelings of responsibility, all sense of obligation, all consciousness of guilt, all apprehension of a judgment-day; and when these are gone, there can remain no very acute perception of the distinction between right and wrong, between good and evil. This feeling is promoted by the representations given of the eternal ideas, processes, and laws, which are supposed to move on in one everlasting stream, raising up, bearing along with them, and turning to their own use, every event, the important and the unimportant, the evil and the good. Viewed in this light, evil comes to be esteemed the lesser good, or rather, as merely the lesser good for the present; for in the end it may come to be the greater, or the very greatest good. It is a necessary tenet of this system that the evil equally with the good is a part of God,—some one speaks of the "good as God's right hand, and the evil as the left." It is vain to suppose that under such a system God can seriously purpose to punish the sin, or that he can so much as condemn it. Those who are thoroughly imbued with the spirit of the system, will be led first of all to excuse evil in themselves, and then they will be led to palliate it in others. One of the issues will be very perverted views of contemporaneous society and of past history. The responsibility of the individual will be lost sight of in the contemplation of the vast processes and sweeping cycles which move like gigantic wheels, apparently as well without as with individual effort; and crime, especially brilliant and successful crime, will be spoken of with little or no condemnation, because regarded as a step necessary to great and good results. Nor is it to be forgotten that pantheism, in nearly all its forms (if not in all), rejects the doctrine of the immortality of the soul, at least of a personal immortality. Our personality in this life is an illusion, or rather, a delusion, and at death the deception ceases, and the reality commences in the soul being swallowed up in the all-absorbing One, and lost in its individuality, as the river is when it flows into the ocean. It should be the grand aim and the holy office of religion to raise the downward tendencies and to lay a restraint on the evil propensities of humanity; and this it can do only by the holy truths which it proclaims, and the self-sacrificing sentiments which it calls forth. But so far from providing or fostering these, pantheism seems rather to remove them out of the way, or destroy their force; and instead of stemming the stream of evil, it rather sails along with it, and helps to swell its waters.

Such, if I do not mistake, is the influence of pantheism on the individuals who are under its sway. Equally pernicious would be its influence upon any country in which it might prevail to any great extent. It is foolish indeed to expect or to fear that the majority of any people will ever attach themselves to so mystical, and yet, withal, so artificial a system. The great body of mankind must—happily or unhappily—be far too much engrossed with realities, will be far too eagerly bent on seeking calculable gains, and exposed to far too many real sorrows, to allow of their wandering into this land of dreams and shadows. But if ever pantheism should come to be favourably received or extensively adopted among those addicted to reflection, or possessed of abundant leisure, in any modern nation, the effect on the character of the people would be most pernicious. It would necessitate an immediate revival of the old distinction, done away with by Christianity, of an esoteric doctrine for the thinking few, and an exoteric doctrine for the unthinking many. The inner doctrine of the select class would be an airy pantheism scarcely differing from a blank atheism, and the outer doctrine of the multitude would be a hero-worship, a nature-worship, or an idol-worship; in short, some description of creature-worship, with all its degrading tendencies. All this would take place without any attempt on the part of the learned to restrain the evil; nay, the learned would join in the evil and encourage it; and this worship would be defended by them as a homage paid to the part of the One All as representative of the whole. They would acknowledge that the mass of the people are incapable of seeing any such meaning; but then, it is by this very circumstance that they themselves are separated from the vulgar, who must necessarily be doomed to act without knowing the significance of their acts. "Posterity," says Jacobi, "will not wonder, if in the desert of unbelief, men raise serpents and pray to golden calves once more, and if in this serpent and calf service philosophers tend the altars." In such a state of things it is evident we should have the idle and the educated classes proud, haughty, self-righteous, mostly pleasure-loving and dissolute, and the great body of the people abandoned—without any serious attempt being made to elevate them—to the grossest darkness and the most grovelling superstition, relieved only by a love of imposing spectacles which impress the senses or excite the imagination; while now and then, and here and there, we should have some earnest or malicious sceptic attacking the hypocrisy of the one class and the ignorance of the other, and troubling both, without being able to improve either by supplying anything more solid or satisfying. So far as I can see, the more advanced nations of modern Europe are to be saved from such an issue only by the active and earnest propagation of Scriptural light.

Sect. V. Christian Divinity.

It has been found in all ages, that there are intimate points of affinity between Metaphysics, that is, our generalized intuitions, and Theology, that is, the systematized expression of the concrete and scattered truths of revelation. In the first speculations of mankind theology and philosophy are indissolubly intertwined in what has been called Theosophy. At a very early age of the Church of Christ, the Eastern theosophies and certain forms of Platonism became associated with Bible doctrine. This arose partly from the circumstance that a number of eminent Christian Fathers had, prior to their conversion to Christianity, been attached to philosophy, Asiatic or Grecian; and partly, I am convinced, by the fact that there had been wrought, even into the pagan philosophic systems, a large body of truth, either springing from the native convictions systematized by the inherent sagacity of the mind, or derived from a tradition which had kept afloat a remnant of primitive truth. Platonism, in particular, had many interesting points of correspondence with Christianity. The lofty genius of Plato, nurtured in Eastern as well as Western learning, and drinking deeply of the moral spirit of Socrates, had succeeded in seizing on some of those great natural truths which come closest to Inspired Revelation. In the scholastic ages the logical forms of Aristotle were employed to mould into a certain shape every known truth of religion (as well as of secular knowledge), and may be traced at this day in not a few distinctions and technical phrases of theology. In modern times famous divines and schools of divinity have delighted to couch their expositions of doctrine, and their defences of Christianity, in accordance with the favourite principles and often in the very nomenclature of particular philosophers of eminence. The influence of Descartes is visible in the rigid, dogmatic, and deductive method of not a few theological treatises of the second half of the seventeenth century. Even the philosophy of Locke, though possessing little affinity to the profounder truths of Christianity or sympathy with them, may be detected as regulating the defences of religion, and the manner in which it was recommended during last century,—as when it is shown us that experience, external or internal, is in favour of Christianity, and that piety promotes the happiness of the possessor. The speech of those who talk much of a moral sense "bewrayeth" them, and shows that they have taken their views directly or indirectly from Shaftesbury or Hutcheson. In the United States of America the metaphysics of Jonathan Edwards were incorporated for two or three ages with New England theology. The formidable nomenclature and the bristling distinctions of Kant, as also the subtle and glowing intuitionalism of Schleiermacher (the two being often mixed incongruously together) may be traced in almost every theological work published in Germany for the last half-century, and come out in the writings of not a few British and American divines who have felt the impulse of the great Teutonic invasion of thought. The airy spirit of Coleridge has been caught by a considerable body of English divines of high literary reputation.

It may be doubted whether religion has not, on the whole, been injured to a greater extent than it has been benefited by its close association with philosophy. The gnosticism of the East introduced the earliest formidable heresies into the Christian Church, and drew many away from the simplicity of the truth into mystic speculations. In the writings of Origen, and others of a kindred spirit, the statements of the Word were thought to be of little value in their literal interpretation, and are sublimated into gorgeous theories, constructed in a region of gilded clouds. No doubt many of those who thus introduced the gentile philosophy into the religion of Jesus, imagined that they might thereby benefit Christianity, but in fact they corrupted it,—quite as much as those who with like intentions introduced pagan rites into Christian worship, and pagan statues into Christian temples. In the medieval ages the scholastic bandages, when they did not positively strangle the vital truths, did yet set them in so rigid a shape as to injure the life, and made them repulsive to many souls which might have been attracted by the same truths presented in a so much more rounded and flexible and altogether natural form in the pages of the living Word. The professed demonstrations and deductions, conducted in the mathematical mode of Descartes and Samuel Clarke, were guilty of many a paralogism, and this often tempted shrewd men to doubt of the whole system which had been supported by such brittle buttresses. The philosophies of Locke and of Hutcheson could not appreciate one-half of the great soul of Christianity; the sanctifying truths of revelation assumed a clipped, a bare, and a dry appearance in the pages of those whose appeal was to sense, and in whose view happiness is the greatest good. Edwards had undoubtedly a spirit of angelic brightness and depth of penetration, yet it may be doubted whether certain profound and mysterious doctrines of Christianity are most expediently defended by being identified with his speculations as to necessity and original sin. The theologies which have ramified from the trunk of Kant, or sprouted from the germ of Schleiermacher have laboured to move Christianity from the old foundation of faith in the testimony of God, on to a new ground in the Practical Reason, or a God-consciousness; and the issue is that those who have felt their influence have been seeking to construct each one a religion for himself, retaining only so much of revealed truth as may please his heart and fancy or suit his purpose. The school of Coleridge has experienced how difficult it is to serve two such masters as religion and literature, and in its airy excursions has had a tendency to fly off from some of those truths—such as the Inspiration of Scripture and the Atonement of Christ—to which unsophisticated minds have ever clung most resolutely as feeling that their soul's peace is involved in them.

Can no method be devised of making philosophy and theology co-operate without their being confounded? In particular, is there no way by which religion may call in philosophy to her aid in fighting her battles against error, and yet prevent the powerful and ambitious ally from settling in her country and lording it over it? The following rules might at once guide and guard religio-philosophic speculation.

I. Metaphysics have important negative purposes to serve in theology.

1. Sound metaphysics may be employed to meet unsound metaphysics. When Scriptural truths are assailed on professedly philosophic grounds, by philosophy may these foundations be examined. Thus some object to the Scriptures that they represent God as cherishing moral indignation against sin; their views may be counteracted by showing that, if we are entitled to argue from our mental nature that God is a good God, we are authorized on the same ground to look upon him as hating iniquity. If it be maintained that the Scripture doctrines are not to be believed because they land us in speculative difficulties, and cannot be fully comprehended, philosophy is at hand to show that the truths which are most fully believed by us, such as those relating to being, cause, infinity, to the growth of the plant and of the animal, and even to such agents as heat, light, and electricity, all go out into mystery.*

But in performing this office of expulsion, philosophy should not be allowed to take the place which had been usurped by the power which it has driven out. What I mean may be illustrated thus. Certain doctrines regarding necessity and free will have found their way into theology, and wrought not a little mischief. Some have given such an account of man's freedom as to make him independent of God, and to set aside the Scripture doctrine of his being enslaved by the influence of sin. At the opposite extreme some have gone so far as to deny to man all proper freedom of will, and some have identified their doctrine of an iron necessity with the Bible doctrine of the Divine Sovereignty. Both of these extreme errors may

* See 'Glauben und Wissen,' von Dr. H. Ulrici.

be removed, as I think, by a judicious exposition of the true facts of human nature, by proving on the one hand that there is a causation *sui generis* in the human will, and by showing on the other hand that consciousness testifies to an essential freedom in every genuine exercise of the voluntary power in man. But when this end has been accomplished, let metaphysics henceforth retire into its own territory, and let not the peculiar views which we may entertain in regard to the will, or the precise psychological nature of freedom, be allowed to rule in Divinity proper, and to overawe the honest interpretation of Scripture, according to exegetical principles.

2. Metaphysics may be pre-eminently useful in keeping metaphysics in their own place. For it is the tendency of metaphysics to be ever pressing beyond their own domain, and encroaching on their neighbour's territory,—sometimes avowedly and as claiming a right, more frequently in a covert manner, denying that they are metaphysics, to which they may even profess an antipathy;—but under whatever pretext they come, if they propose to settle in theology, they must be driven out as intruders. Metaphysics have a very important province—not all truths, but first truths—and to that province they must be confined. No one will now tolerate for a moment any claims which they may put forth to construct a natural philosophy, a botany, or a chemistry. A primary philosophy may do some little in the way of setting fast the foundations of these sciences, but they must be built up by materials got from other quarters. And just as little is it capable of rearing a theology, and determining every question which may be started as to God and man and nature, and their reticulated mutual relations. History, the history of all ages and countries, gives a testimony as decided as it is uniform, that human reason is incapable of forming a religion which can stand the tests of reason

and meet the felt wants of man. He who would construct a physical science must go to the volume of nature; he who would construct a theology must go to the volume of revelation. It is no disparagement to metaphysical science that it cannot do what it is the province of other sciences to accomplish. It is no disparagement to geometry that it cannot draw out a system of anatomy, nor in any way to the discredit of chemistry that it cannot build up a science of geology. Nor is it any degradation to speculative philosophy that it cannot rear a science of Divinity. Each science, like a planet, has its own orbit, and when it keeps to this it has good purposes to serve; but if it passes beyond, it will fail to accomplish its proper ends, and may come into destructive collision with other powers. "We do not enlarge the sciences," says Kant, "but disfigure them, when we suffer their boundaries to run into one another." He who would seek for a quickening religion among the maxims of philosophy, is, as Bacon says, seeking the living among the dead, and must ever come back with an aching heart and a feeling of disappointment. A wise metaphysics, which knows its own place, which is the place of principles, will find it to be for its interest—indeed absolutely essential to the preservation of its influence, and the protection of its own territory, in the present day, when it has so many enemies—to rebuke every attempt which may be made by its less prudent but more ardent supporters to make it intrude into the province of other sciences.

II. Metaphysics, without entering Theology, may lend it some aid.

1. It may show that the difficulties and mysteries which meet us in theology are the same as those which come up in metaphysics, being those which arise from the limitation of our faculties, and the imperfection of our knowledge. "No difficulty," says Sir W. Hamilton,

"emerges in theology, which has not previously emerged in philosophy." The difficulties of Revealed Religion chiefly congregate round the doctrines of the Trinity, of the Decrees of God, and Original Sin. The difficulties of the first arise simply from the mystery which attaches to this, but also to every other doctrine regarding the Divine Nature; we can understand so much, but learn of vastly more, beyond our comprehension. Those who would doubt of the triune nature of God because they cannot fully compass it, will find themselves landed in precisely the same difficulties when they would fathom the infinity, or indeed any of the perfections of God. The difficulties which may spring from the doctrine of the Divine Sovereignty are no other than the old ones which philosophers have met with from the beginning, as they sought to reconcile freedom with causation. The doctrine of Original Sin does raise up difficulties, and may seem to bear hard against the character of the Creator; but an analogous insoluble problem presents itself in Natural Religion. How has sin been permitted under the government of a God at once Omnipotent and Good? Nay, it is the very same difficulty which presses on us when we ask the question, How does it happen that all human beings, left though they be to the freedom of their own will, do in fact begin to sin as they begin to act for themselves? He who would answer this question and not avoid it, must come to an original sin, encompassed with all the difficulties of the Bible doctrine; but if he discard Christianity, he has no relief from the evil, he has no light to set over against the darkness. Metaphysics are competent to demonstrate that no man can deliver himself from these difficulties by fleeing from Christianity to what may be represented as a Rational Theism.

2. Metaphysics may furnish not a few evidences in favour of Christianity. Thus it supplies the main ele-

ments in the proof of those great doctrines which the Word of God presupposes, such as the existence of the infinity and unity of God, and the immortality of the soul, and a judgment-day,—truths very much lost sight of in heathenism, and the prominence given to which in the Jewish Scriptures is a proof of their being divinely inspired. All works of Natural Theology properly constructed have a tendency to strengthen the foundations of Christianity. In particular, the inductive investigation of the moral faculty in man may yield a number of evidences in favour of the Divine origin of our religion. The conscience declares that there is an indelible distinction between good and evil, and conducts by an easy process to the conviction, that God approves the good and hates the evil. The moral power points to a law, holy, just, and good, a law which all men have broken, and which no nation shut out from supernatural light, and no pagan philosophy, has ever exhibited in its purity. When that law shines forth in the Word, and when, in particular, it is manifested in the character of the God-Man, the conclusion is forced on us that those who make it thus shine upon us in its brightness, must have had an express vision from heaven. The conscience, rightly interpreted, declares that all men have sinned, and so given offence to God. The same moral power indicates, not obscurely, that sin deserves to be punished, and points to God as ready to inflict the penalty. Great service, as it appears to me, is rendered to Christianity, when it is shown, by means of an inquiry into the nature of conscience, that these are truths of natural religion. For being once established on an independent basis, they prepare us to welcome the grand doctrine of Revealed Religion, that the Word has become flesh, and tabernacled on the earth, suffering in the sinner's room and stead, and thus opening a way by which sinful man may be restored to the favour and image of a sin-hating God. Verily those rationalists or intuitionalists who would set aside or explain away the doctrine of the sinner being reconciled by the blood of Jesus, are overlooking what is about the deepest and strongest conviction of moral reason or intuition in the breast of man. In these, and in a variety of other ways, illustrated by such writers as Pascal, Butler, and Chalmers,* a sound philosophy may show us light shining through chinks upon us in the darkness, to allure us to look out for the great luminary which God has made to shine upon our world.

3. Metaphysics can give a philosophic method and manner to the treatment of theological topics. It may do so without intruding beyond its province, or introducing any of its peculiarities. It may appear in its mode and in the results, without troubling us with all the processes. How often does it happen, in theological discussions, that there are laboured attempts to prove what need not and cannot be proven, while other propositions, which ought to be demonstrated, are left unsupported! How often are derivative propositions left without a support, while primary principles are made to lean on secondary ones! A mind trained to philosophy will avoid these errors; as knowing what propositions require not probation, and how to make such shine in their own light, and generally, how to build up an argument of original and derived truth consecutively from the foundation.

But are metaphysics to be absolutely precluded from entering the domain of divinity proper? If a philoso-

* The intimations of conscience were long neglected in the philosophies and speculative theologies of Germany, which in this respect were behind those of Britain. A better tone was commenced by Julius Müller, in his great work on 'Sin;' and of late we have, in 'Die Christliche Dogmatik vom Standpunkte des Gewissens, von Dr. Schenkel,' an admirable account of the relation of the conscience to God.

phic thought occur to a youth in the freshness of his observation, or to an old man in the ripeness of his wisdom, is he not to be allowed to bring it into the temple, and lay it on the altar, because these are too sacred? In reply, I observe that,

III. Metaphysics are to be allowed to enter theology only under certain conditions.

1. The metaphysical principle advanced must be shown to be sanctioned by the very constitution of the mind, and by Him who has granted it to us. It is thus only that we can lay an arrest on fancy, conceit, and prejudice, and prevent persons, when pushed hard for a defence, from taking refuge in a principle which they declare to be above argument. There are truths above probation, but there are no truths above examination, and the truths above proof are those which bear inspection the best. If persons appeal to first principles, avowedly or unavowedly, the burden lies on them of showing that the principles they employ are first truths. Those who adopt this rule for themselves are entitled to insist that those who oppose them, or oppose religion, should submit to the same restrictions. It may certainly be demanded of those who set themselves against Christianity, or any of its peculiar doctrines, on professedly philosophic grounds, that they show that their objections are founded on principles which are fundamental, and not drawn from the prejudices of the heart or the pet opinions of some small knot of thinkers.

2. The precise nature of the fundamental principle employed must be specified, so far at least as it is brought to bear on the topic discussed. For it is quite possible that the principle, though in itself a legitimate one, may be illegitimately employed, and how can this be ascertained except by a precise enunciation of its rule? Thus, I believe that there is a principle of causation ope-

rating in all creature-action, even, I believe, in acts of the will; but then it would be wrong to infer from this that the mode of causal action is the same in our voluntary as in physical, or even as in our intellectual nature. Yet, again and again have writers maintained that man must be a machine, because the principle of causation is universally operative, even in the will, as is shown by predictions founded on statistics which can be given forth as to crimes and other voluntary acts. The fallacy at once appears when we properly interpret the principle of causation, which announces indeed that every event has a cause, but leaves the nature of that cause to be determined by experience, which shows that causation in the will is entirely different from causation in other action. Some go to the other extreme, and insist that the possession of freedom by man is inconsistent with the universal reign of causation. This misapprehension may be removed by a correct exposition of the intuitive principle of freedom, which affirms indeed of every action of the will that it is free, but says nothing, and can say nothing, as to whether it is or is not caused. These are illustrations of the way in which a philosophic principle, sound in itself, may issue in illegitimate consequences because its rule has not been ascertained.

I have so far limited the rule as to say that the intuitive principle employed must be precisely enunciated, so far at least as it is brought to bear on the topic we are discussing. This is all that can be legitimately insisted on. Every time that we argue that an effect has a cause, or that a quality implies a substance, we may not be bound rigidly to announce the formula. But in all perplexing questions and doubtful references, the law must be given in express terms, for it is quite possible that it may not admit of a legitimate application to the case before us. Fortunately the questions in which such rigid accuracy requires to be insisted on are comparatively few. Unfortunately for the theologian it so happens that among these are the very questions which fall to be discussed in deeper divinity. The rule is that the principle must be correctly expressed so far as it relates to the topic to which it is applied, and if it is possible that an expression in part may be an inaccurate one, there is no help for it, the law must be fully and rigidly unfolded.

But it will be urged that such a caution must often necessitate the inappropriate discussion of a metaphysical question in the midst of a theological exposition. I admit that this shows that the introduction of metaphysics into theology has its difficulties and inconveniences. Nothing can be more unsatisfactory than the practice by many theologians of laying hold, without examination, of a supposed philosophic principle which serves their end, using it to help their immediate purpose, and then passing on to another topic, which is treated in the same manner. All ingenuous minds feel this method to be most confusing and uncomfortable; even the professed metaphysician will often be stirred up to oppose it, as the metaphysics may not be his own. If metaphysics are to venture into the theological field, let them come in openly and not furtively, and let them conform to the rules of the logic of intuition. And if the investigations thus necessitated cannot come in gracefully in the heart of a Scriptural exposition, let them be handed over to an appendix, or appear in a separate treatise, the merits of which will be more readily ascertained from the circumstance that the philosophical stands out separate from the religious element. This leads to another rule.

3. There must be a careful separation of the Scriptural truth from the supposed metaphysical principle employed to illustrate or defend it. The great body of practical

thinkers, especially in England, have ever entertained, and this not without grounds to go on, a suspicion of metaphysical theology. In the exposition of the doctrines of the Bible, not only in sermons, but in practical divinity, the introduction of metaphysical discussions may be declined with great wisdom, except when the metaphysical objections of opponents necessitate it. The great body, even of thinking men, will be vastly more pleased, and in a still higher degree more profited, by clear statement and spontaneous reasoning, than by abstruse discussions. A calm reverence for Scripture, a careful collation of passages, an enlarged acquaintance with the whole volume, sound sense, clear statement, direct argument, in which there is but a link or two between the first premiss and the final conclusion, a knowledge of human character in its practical operations, and, above all, genuine faith, an attachment to the truth, and a love to God and man, will do vastly more than metaphysical subtlety or lengthened deduction, in explaining, enforcing, and defending Divine truth.

But are metaphysics therefore to be absolutely banished from theology? I lay down no such stringent rule; the very objections of the heretic and the rationalist, and the cavils of the infidel and the scoffer, compel divines, whether they will or no, to enter the regions of metaphysics. The God who gives to all men their gifts, is to be praised because he has raised up from time to time persons of great intellectual stature, who have defended the grand essential doctrines of Christianity in learned and elaborate philosophical treatises. Philosophy should acknowledge that some of the works of which she has most cause to be proud were constructed with the avowed design of defending the foundations or strengthening the fortresses of religion.

But in professedly theological works there should be a studious distinction drawn between the philosophy and the religion. This is needful, in order that we may satisfactorily examine both, and be able on the one hand to determine whether the author has laid hold of a correct metaphysical principle, and been legitimately applying it; and, on the other hand, to view the religious doctrine apart from the philosophic speculation. The caution now enforced will not forbid philosophy from attempting to aid religion, to furnish to it evidences, to confirm its doctrines, and systematize its scattered truths; but it will secure that the two be not confounded; in particular, that philosophy do not represent itself as religion but as metaphysics; that it do not claim for its speculations the authority of the Bible or of God, or advance them as an essential part of religion, or place them on the same level as the truths of the Divine Word; and, above all, that it do not make religion lean upon them, so that if they should break down religion would be supposed to have suffered a defeat.

The rule laid down demands that the two be seen to be different. Not that it should insist that they be discussed in separate treatises, or each in separate chapters of one treatise; this might look too like that formal accuracy of demeanour and character which often conceals the worst inaccuracies. But it rigidly exacts that the two be distinguished in the mind of the writer, and that the discussion be conducted so that the difference cannot be lost sight of by the most careless reader; so that the philosophy may be recognized simply as philosophy, and the religion be seen to be independent of the philosophy; and so that, should the philosophy be set aside by new systems, the religion may remain entire and uninjured. Bishop Butler, I may remark, has set a noble example in this respect both in his 'Analogy' and in his 'Sermons:' his philosophy, whether employed in illustration or defence, is always so brought forward that it can never be confounded with the religious truth, which it is meant to aid, and never to injure. As neighbours, the two may have much pleasant and profitable communion, and many interchanges of good offices; but still, they should keep their separate domiciles; without this there will sooner or later be misunderstandings, jarring, and disputes, and in the end suspicions and cruel separations.

These restrictions, I am aware, lay the axe to the root of many a tree which those who planted it will be unwilling to see cut down; but they are necessary to the clearing of a dreadfully intertangled forest, and to allow the trees which are entitled to remain to have free breathing-space, and thus attain their full growth, and stand out in their proper form.

Sect. VI. Man as a Religious Being.

There is a sense in which man is certainly not a religious being. He is inclined to avoid God, and to live unmindful of Him; and when constrained to look at His purity, his eyes are so dazzled that he pays Him a blinded and superstitious prostration. When left to himself, he has ever been degrading the Divine nature and character, and whether blessed or not with a supernatural revelation, he has ever been breaking the commandments of God. But there is a sense in which man is a religious being. All nations have had a religion of some kind, and the number of professed atheists is so small that some have doubted whether there has ever been such a monster as a sincere atheist. The Psalmist seems to give the true account when he describes the fool as saying in his heart there is no God. There are intuitions, processes of thought, natural observations, and deep feelings, which all tend, even when restrained and degraded, towards a conviction of the existence of a Supernatural Being, to a faith in Him or a fear of Him, to adoration, and a sense of responsibility. Every deeper intuition of the soul goes out towards God. Created being, as we follow it down, is felt to be fixed and permanent only in uncreated being. The objects around us are felt to be so fleeting that our conviction of reality is satisfied only when we reach self-existent substance. Our conviction of substance is not content till it comes to One who has all power in himself. Infinite time and space are felt, after all, to be only infinite emptiness till we fill them up with a living and loving Being. All the beautiful relationships in nature, all the order in respect of form, time, and quantity, all the adaptations of means to end, seem but the scattered rays from an original and central wisdom. The impulse which prompts us to search after causes will not cease its cravings till it carries us up to a first cause in a self-acting substance. Earthly beauty is so evanescent that we rejoice to learn that there is a Divine beauty of which the other is but a flickering reflection. Our moral convictions especially mount towards God as their proper sphere, their source, and their home. Our sense of obligation connects us by stronger than physical bonds with Him who is the author of our moral nature, the sanctioner of the moral law, and who is at last to be our judge. I do not go so far as to say that any one of these does of itself prove the Divine existence. I do not even affirm that all of them together would enable us to construct a logical argument in behalf of the being of God. These intuitions are expected to look to certain very obvious facts pressing themselves on the attention of all; but I maintain that, being thus stimulated and supported, they do lead to certain deep feelings and impressions in the minds of all, and to a most reasonable belief in God. Every one of them, like the plant, is sending down roots towards this ground, is shooting out points towards this light. We feel that this world has no stability till we make it rest on God. In particular, we feel as to ourselves that we are in a state of dependence; as having derived our being from another; as needing a supply for our ever-craving wants; as having our destiny swayed by events arranged without consulting us; as being ever under an eye that inspects us; and as having at last to appear at a judgment-seat; and we cannot be satisfied till we learn that we hang on a Great Central Power and Light, round which we should revolve, as the earth does round the sun.

These convictions, and the feelings growing on them, are deep down in the bosoms of all; and like waters which have descended from the heavens and penetrated into the hills, they will ever tend to burst out, and if restrained in their legitimate channels, they will find vent in others. Ever craving for something, they will be in pain and uneasiness till the appropriate object is presented. Their cry indeed will often be like the infant's cry in the night, a cry in the darkness for something unknown. And as the appetite of hunger in its eagerness may lead us to grasp at a sad mixture of food and earth, nay, of food and poison when it is presented, so our natural religious faith may often be taken in with a sad medley of truth and error, of earnest godliness, and debasing superstition. Still, while they eagerly devour such, they will not be satisfied therewith, but, feeling restless and troubled, they will still crave for something, they know not what, and look for a remedy to their experienced ills.

It follows from this account that these instincts and feelings may be perverted and abused. Man is allured, not compelled, to be religious. True piety is always a holy act, to which there is the consent of the will. Man, if he is bent upon it, may become unbelieving or superstitious. As having committed sin, he will ever be prompted, like Cain, to go out from the presence of the

Lord, and to strain after a forgetfulness of Him. Or, as oppressed with a secret consciousness of sin, and as unable to look on the holiness of God, he will ever be tempted to form a god to his own taste, and who may not dazzle and blind him by the brightness of his purity. The majority of mankind flit between these two states; between a stubborn forgetfulness of God and desire to be independent of Him, and a superstitious prostration before a god, or more frequently gods, fashioned by them according to the crude cravings and cherished wishes of their hearts.

But in this state of half-conscious sin there is a powerful intuition awakened, and though to a large extent blind, and to some extent incapable of hearing, it will at times cry terribly for its object. There will rise up a conscience of guilt and an apprehension of an unknown danger, like the sullen roar of ocean waves evidently at hand, but not seen in a murky and stormy night; and this will be followed by an anxious though possibly very ignorant and perplexed looking round for a way of escape. While men are engrossed with the cares and climbings and fears and gratifications of this world, these apprehensions may to a large extent be suppressed; still they are there deep down in the heart, and at times they will breathe out in yearnings after some help, to come we know not whence, or burst forth in dreadful cries and alarms; or if these natural outlets be closed by a cherished unbelief, it will only be to make the restrained feelings spread like a disease and burn like an internal fire. It is this sentiment which keeps alive a sense of sin and a fear of God and of a judgment-day among all nations, and which so far prepares the heathen to listen to the tidings of a provided Saviour. But this instinct may likewise be misled, because of its blindness, and may be directed to objects which seem fitted to gratify it, but which in the end disappoint it. It may tempt the man who is moved by it to picture God as a vindictive being, or it may prompt to acts of laceration, supposed to be fitted to appease the anger of God. Still, the anxious spirit, even after the most horrid and excruciating acts have been performed, will not be satisfied, for it will still be in doubt whether, after all, that terrible God be pacified. These sentiments and cravings will always feel that there is nothing to meet them in a deistic or rationalistic creed, and that there is nothing to give them peace in pagan ritual and sacrifices. I believe they can be met, and gratified, and brought to composure only by the view, presented in the Word, of God reconciling man to Himself by the blood of His Son.

SECT. VII. RATIONAL THEOLOGY.

Attempts have often been made, by persons professing a great respect for Christianity, to construct a religious creed by human reason; sometimes using 'reason' in the larger and looser sense, to stand for all the intellectual powers, together with the moral faculty, and sometimes confining it to the mere logical understanding. It is not proposed to discard the Bible, but to found the doctrines believed in on a rational basis; and most commonly all tenets are rejected, or at least omitted, which cannot be thus supported. In this country this theology usually borrowed largely from Locke, and appealed much to experience and man's desire to secure happiness. In Germany it proceeded on the fundamental principles of the critical philosophy of Kant, and especially on certain *a priori* notions of the sufficiency of virtue. Its oversights are many and glaring.

1. While professing to appeal to human nature, it has commonly overlooked some of the very deepest intuitions and the most characteristic feelings of the soul, such as

the sense of sin and the terror of a sin-hating and sin-punishing God. These have been studiously omitted, because they are palpably and uncompromisingly opposed to the self-righteous, self-sufficient spirit which the builders of the system wish to be allowed to cherish.

2. There have been not a few gaps and flaws in the structures reared. These have proceeded from the determined purpose of the builders to erect a system of theology without accepting aid from Divine authority. They have been triumphantly pointed out with a sneer by the sceptic, who shows that objections can be taken to many of the pretended demonstrations of religious truths, as, for example, to the doctrine of the resurrection of the body, and all that depends on that doctrine in regard to the world to come. By all means let the analogies and illustrations which may be drawn from nature in favour of such doctrines be urged, but the truths rest, after all, most securely on the authority of God. The rational theology, which would move them from this foundation, is in every respect most irrational.

3. It errs most egregiously in casting aside the truths of the Word, which are most suited to the deeper wants of man, such as those which tell us of reconciliation through the Son of God, of the work of converting grace, and of restoration to communion with God. These doctrines cannot be discovered by human reason in its highest or deepest researches, yet they are the truths which when revealed commend themselves most forcibly to the heart of man.

4. It has been powerless in calling forth deep feeling, in rousing the soul to enthusiasm and devotedness, or in urging it on to deeds of heroism and self-sacrifice. The heart of man, especially at those times when it is awed by a sense of the Divine majesty and purity, or struck with a sense of its own sinfulness, or elevated by aspira-

tions after a holier state, has ever turned away from it with abhorrence and scorn.

SECT. VIII. INTUITIONAL THEOLOGY.

The icy and rigid rationalism of last age has dissolved in the heat of a warmer season, and of late we have had a time of wading deep in melted matter; and now we are in an atmosphere of sultriness and dimness, of haziness and dreaminess. It is universally acknowledged that the logical processes of definition and reasoning can do little in religion; and those who, in days bygone, would have appealed to such forms, are in these times betaking themselves to something livelier,—to Feeling, Belief, Inspiration,—or, in one word, to Intuition, which looks at the truth or object at once, and through no interfering process or dimming medium. In last age, certain of our "excelsior" youths were like to be starved in cold; in this age, they are in greater danger of having the seeds of a wasting disease fostered by lukewarm damps and gilded vapours.

The clearest views they show are those which we obtain by gazing immediately on the object. Have not, they ask, the seers and sages of our world, poetic and philosophic, seen further than other men by direct, and not by reflected or introspective vision? Does not our own consciousness witness that we get the furthest-reaching glimpses when we are wholly engrossed in looking out at things, without being at the trouble to analyze our thoughts? There are moments when all thinkers, or certain thinkers, have seen further than in their usual moods; and this by overlooking all interposing objects, and gazing full on the truth. Some seem to have experienced ecstatic states, in which, being lifted above themselves and the earth, and carried—whether in the body or out of the body they know not—into the third heavens, they behold things which it is not possible for man to utter. An entranced minute of such bursting revelation is worth, they say, hours or years of your logically concatenated thought. The soul is then carried as to a great height, above the clouds that rise from the damps of earth, like unto Mount Teneriffe, from which ardent gazers thought they saw land lying to the far west ages before the practical Columbus actually set foot on America. As there are sounds, such as the sighings of the stream, heard in the stillness of evening, which are not audible in the bustle of the day, so there are voices heard in certain quieter moods of the mind which cannot be discerned when the soul is being agitated by discussion and ratiocination. As there are states of our atmosphere in which remote objects seem near, as there are days in which we can look far down into the ocean and behold its treasures, as the night shows us heavenly lights which are invisible in the glare of common day, so there are day moods and night moods in which we look into great depths, and see the dim as distinct, and behold truths glittering like gems, and brilliant as constellations. At these times it looks as if a veil or cloud were removed, and we see, as it were by polarized light, the inward constitution of things which usually expose but their tame outside; and we gaze on naked truth without the robe which it commonly wears, but which conceals what is infinitely more lovely than itself. Our eye can then look on pure light without being blinded by it; and we stand face to face with truth and beauty and goodness, and, in a sense, with God Himself.

This is a view very often presented in the present day; and it should be admitted at once that it is by spontaneous, and not by reflective thought, that the mind attains its clearest and most penetrating visions of things. Our mental powers operate spontaneously, and act most faithfully when we are taking no notice of them, but are influenced by a simple desire to discover the truth; when the mind is in its best exercises, the interposition of metaphysical introspection and syllogistic formulæ would tend only to dim the clearness of the view. It may be allowed farther, that there are times in every man's thinking when great truths come suddenly upon him; times when he feels as if he were emerging at once from a tunnel into the light of day. These are states to be cherished, and not curbed. But it is of vast moment that we understand their precise nature, and the value to be attached to them, and the restrictions to be laid upon the confidence we put in them.

I. In these visions, clear or profound, there are commonly other processes besides simple intuition. Almost always there is involved in them the gathered wisdom of long and varied and ripened experience; very often there are analyses more or less refined, generalizations of a narrower or wider scope; and not unfrequently ratiocinations, passing so rapidly, that the processes are not only not analyzed, they are not even observed. When Archimedes broke out into such ecstasy on discovering a law of hydrostatics; when the thought flashed on the mind of Newton that the power which draws an apple to the ground is that which holds the moon in her sphere; when Franklin identified the sparks produced by rubbing certain substances on the earth with the lightning of heaven; when it occurred to Watt that the steam which moved the lid of a kettle might be turned to a great mechanical purpose; when the Abbé Haüy, in gathering up the fragments of a crystal which had accidentally fallen from his hands, surmised that all crystals were derived from a few primitive forms; when Oken, on looking at the bleached skull of a deer in the Hartz Forest, exclaimed, "This is a vertebrate column!" every one acknowledges that there was vastly more than intuitional power involved: there were presupposed large original talents of a peculiar kind in each case, habits of scientific research, and long courses of systematic training and observation; while at the instant there were the highest powers of comparison and computation in exercise. It will be readily allowed that there was a similar combination of native gift, of accumulated experience, and connected ratiocination, implied in the discoveries made by Adam Smith and others in political and social science. But I go a step further, and maintain that the grand views of moral and religious truth which burst on the vision of our greatest philosophers were the result of rays coming from a thousand scattered points. When Socrates unfolded to an age and nation deprived of the light of revelation such elevated doctrines regarding a superintending Providence, and the intimate relation between virtue and happiness; when Plato showed that man participated in the Divine intelligence, and that the forms of nature partook of the ideas or patterns which had been in or before the Divine Mind from all eternity; when Leibnitz developed his grand theory of a pre-established harmony running through the mental and material universe,—there were in active exercise profound reflection, long observation of human nature and of the ways of God, searching analyses, and a cultivated moral vision. I am sure that there is a similar union involved in those far-reaching glimpses which more obscure men have had, at their better moments, of great moral or spiritual verities regarding the nature of man, and the character and dealings of God.

The leap of waters at the cataract of Niagara is on the instant, yet it is not, after all, a simple process: antecedent to it there have been rains falling from heaven, and these gathered into a river, and acquiring momentum as they move on, and a precipitous cliff formed for their descent; and in the fall, water, rock, and atmosphere mingle their separate influences. The flash of lightning across the sky is instantaneous, yet it is the produce of long meteorological operations, in which probably air, moisture, sunlight, electricity, and an attracting object, have each had its part; and it is only on the whole gathering to an overflow that the convulsive effect is produced. There must have been a similar collection of strength, and combination of scattered influences, in those sudden leaps which certain minds have taken; as when Augustine abandoned paganism, and Luther left ritualism; and there are the same in those movements of the spirit of man in which it penetrates to immense distances without our being able to follow it through all the intermediate space, and illumines as it passes the densest masses of darkness. It is the business of physical science to explain the one set of processes, and it shows that they are the result of a conspiracy of agencies. It is the office of psychological science to explain the other set of operations, and it can show that there is involved in them a variety of original and acquired endowments. A number of different rays have met in the production of this pure white light. The views are so wide-ranging, because all the inlets of the mind are open to receive impressions.

II. In all these higher visions there is apt to be a mixture of error. The glittering lustre in which the objects are seen is apt to dazzle the eye, and prevent it from taking too narrow an inspection. The rapidity of the mental process is favourable to the concealment of hastiness of inference, to which we are led by the influence of inferior motives, acting like concealed iron upon the ship's compass. With the desire to discover the truth there may be united the personal vanity or the idiosyncrasies of the individual, or the prejudices of the pledged partisan, or the proud and self-righteous temper, or a spirit of contradiction. How often does it happen, in such cases, that the conceits of the fancy or the wishes of the heart are attributed to the reason, that high feeling is mistaken for high wisdom, that what is dark is supposed to be deep, that what is lovely is supposed to be holy! In the region to which they have betaken themselves, objects seem gigantic because perceived in the mist, as they look through the openings in which persons mistake gilded clouds for sunlit islands, or for mountains based on the earth and piercing the sky.

Besides the error which may be in the original vision, there are apt to be additional mistakes when the individual would unfold it and put it into language. As Aurora Leigh says:—

> "It may be, perhaps,
> Such have not settled long and deep enough
> In trance, to attain to clairvoyance; and still
> The memory mixes with the vision, spoils
> And works it turbid."

The intuitionalist often has a genuine feeling; and when he confines himself to a simple description, his statement, if not altogether free from error, may be a correct transcript of what has passed in his own mind, and may have as vivifying an influence upon others as it has had upon himself. The glow which radiates from such men as Coleridge, when tracing the correspondences between subject and object, or Wordsworth, as he sketches the feelings awakened by the forms and aspects of nature, or Ruskin, as we gaze with him on the higher works of art, steeps all attendant minds in its own splendours,—as the gorgeous evening sun burnishes all objects, clouds as well as landscapes, in its own rich hues. The intuitionalist ever succeeds best in poetry, or in prose which is of the character of poetry, and might, if the father of it chose, be wedded to immortal verse. But when he attempts, as he often does, a systematic exposition, scientific, or logical, or philosophical, or theological, of his sentiments, there may now, with the errors of the original writing, be mingled the mistakes that arise from an unfaithful transcription. Every one knows that to feel and to analyze the feeling are two very different exercises; and it often happens that those who feel the most intensely, and even those who think the most profoundly, are the least capacitated for unfolding the process to others. In attempting to do so, they often mix it up with other elements, and the product is a conglomerate, in which truth and error are banded together without the possibility of separating them. In unwinding the threads, they have tangled them; and they become the more hopelessly entangled the greater the strength which they exert in unravelling them. The pool may, or quite as possibly may not, have been originally pure; it has certainly been rendered altogether turbid by the mud stirred up in the attempt to explore it. As the author of 'Hours with the Mystics' says, "This intuitional metal, in its native state, is mere fluent, formless quicksilver; to make it definite and serviceable, you must fix it by an alloy: but then, alas! it is *pure* Reason no longer; and, so far from being universal truth, receives a countless variety of shapes, according to the temperament, culture, or philosophic party of the individual thinker."

These visions, raptures, and ecstasies are most apt to appear in philosophy and theology; and it is there they work most mischief. The intuitionalist is ever placing things in their wrong category, dividing the things which should be joined, or mixing the things which should be separated. His analogies overlook differences; his distinctions set aside resemblances. His limitations are like the mad attempts of Xerxes to chain the ocean. His definitions are like the boundings of a cloud—while he is pointing to them they are changed; indeed his whole method is like a project to make roads and run fences in cloudland. In metaphysics, he represents as essences what are in fact nothing but attenuated ghosts, created by his own oppressed vision as it looks into darkness. The Neo-Platonists pretended to see the One and the Good by ecstasy; what they saw was merely an abstract quality separated from the concrete object. They tried to raise up emotion by the contemplation of the skeleton attribute, but in this they did and could not succeed; for it is not by abstraction that feeling is excited, but by the presentation of an individual and living reality. The attempt in the present age, by certain metaphysical speculators, to call forth feeling by the presentation of the True, the Beautiful, the Good, must terminate in a similar failure. It is not by the contemplation of truth, but of the God of truth; not by the contemplation of loveliness, but of the God of loveliness; not by the contemplation of the good, but of the good God, that feelings of adoration and love are called forth and gratified.

There are still greater perils attending the indulgence of these inspirations in matters of religion. The intuitionalist is tempted to ascribe to some higher influence the idea which arises simply from the law of association or organic impulse; to attribute to intuition what is mere floating sentiment; to pure reason what is the product of habit or of passion; nay, to God Himself what springs from the fallible human heart. The height to which the soul is carried in these elevations is apt to have a dizzying influence; and not a few have fallen when they seemed to themselves to be standing most secure. Some, pretending to a heavenly mission, have yielded at once to the temptation which the true Messenger withstood; and, without a promise of one to bear them up in their presumption, have cast themselves down from the pinnacle to which they were elevated, and been lost amidst the laughter of men. Some have claimed for their own conceits the inspiration of Heaven ; and have come to deify their own imaginations, and to sanctify their schemes of ambition, by representing them as formed under the sanction of God.

III. The error is to be detected by a careful reflex examination of the spontaneous process of intuition, or, what is more frequent, of the intuition with certain conjoined elements. That error may creep into these visions and raptures, is evident from the circumstance, that scarcely any two inspirationalists agree even when pretending to have revelations on the same point ; and when they do concur, it is evidently because of the dominant authority of some great master. How, then, are we to decide among the claims of the rival sages, or seers, or doctors, or schools ? Plainly by inquiring which of them, if any, are in fact under the influence of a native intuition ; and this is to be done by an inductive inquiry into the nature of our intuitions, and by trying the proposed dogma or feeling by the tests, thus discovered, of intuition.

In no other department of human investigation, except speculative philosophy and theology, will an indiscriminate appeal to intuition or feeling be allowed in the present day. Mathematics admit of no such loose methods of procedure. The fundamental principles of that science are, no doubt, founded on intuition ; but then it is on intuitions carefully enunciated and formalized, and the whole superstructure is banded by rigid logical deduction. Physical science will not tolerate any such anticipations, except at times in the way of suggesting hypotheses, to be immediately tried by a rigid induction of facts, and accepted or rejected only as they can stand the test. In political science there is a necessity for the weighing of conflicting principles, and room for clearness of head and far-seeing sagacity; but in these operations mere intuition has a small share, and is not allowed to pass till it is carefully sifted. It is surely high time that intuition were prevented from careering without restraint in the fields of philosophy and theology, and that rules were laid down, not for absolutely restraining it, but for confining it within its legitimate province.

The sole corrective of the evil, the only means of separating the error from the truth, is to be found in a cool reflex examination of the spontaneous process. This is needed, even when the idea is one which has occurred to our own minds; to protect them from the self-deception to which all are liable, to provide them with a safety-lamp when they would enter dark subterranean passages; or with a chart when they would venture on a sea of speculation; or with a compass to tell the direction when they would go out beyond the measured and fenced ground of thought into a waste, above which clouds for ever hover, and where are precipices over which multitudes are for ever falling. Needed to guard us even in our personal musings, it will surely be acknowledged that it is still more necessary when others demand our assent to their proffered vision, lest what we pick up be

> "Like cast-off nosegays picked up on the road,
> The worse for being warm."

Not that this review of the spontaneous thought should set out with the fixed purpose of rejecting all that has been suggested; on the contrary, it should retain and carefully cherish all that may be good, and cast away only what cannot stand a sifting inspection. But the testing, in order to accomplish these ends, must proceed on certain principles. So far as the spontaneous exercise professes to be guided by an induction of facts, it must be tried by the canons of the logic of induction. So far as it involves ratiocination, the approved rules of reasoning must determine its validity. So far as it claims to be intuitional, metaphysical science is entitled to demand that the principle involved be shown to be in the very constitution of the mind, self-evident, necessary, universal; and further, that its determinate rule be specified and formalized, so that we may see whether it covers the case in hand.

In moral subjects, *first thoughts* are often the best, because formed prior to the calculations of selfishness. They may not, however, always be the best; for they may proceed from passion, which in fallen man is as spontaneous and quite as quick as any moral impulse. As a general rule, neither the *first* nor the *second* thoughts are the best; but the *last* thoughts of a studious course of reflection, in which both first and second thoughts are reviewed, that which is good in each being preserved, and that which is evil rejected. The same remark holds good of the exercises of the intellect. The first views of the truth are frequently the freshest and the justest. It has been remarked, that the first view of the new-born infant discloses a resemblance to father or mother which the subsequent growth of the child effaces; and there is often a similar power of penetration in the first glance of the intellectual eye, directed towards a truth presented for the first time: the prominent features are then caught on the instant, and correspondences are detected which disappear on a more familiar acquaintance, being lost sight of among other qualities. But while these original glimpses are often very precious, and are to be carefully noted and registered, it is equally true that first impressions often contain large mixture of error. At these times of intense rapture and ardent longing, the mind seizes eagerly on what presents itself, and is incapable of drawing distinctions, and may utterly neglect other aspects, which are only to be detected by longer and more familiar acquaintance. Hence the need of cool reflection to come after, and retain only what can be justified by the rules of logic. As the first looks of the infant reveal features which are subsequently lost sight of, so the last look of the dying will call up once more likenesses which had escaped our notice in the interval. Let there be a similar holding of all the true analogies—caught in the first look—in those last looks, which, after many a survey, we cherish and retain for ever of the objects which excite our interests and claim our regards.

IV. In order to give the intuitions in the disordered soul of man a religious direction, there is need of a very special OBJECT to evoke, to harmonize, and centre them. Had man's nature been limpidly pure, I suppose he would have risen at once and spontaneously to the contemplation of God, and that his soul would have reposed with satisfaction on Him. But man ever feels, when he would thus mount, that there is a downward drag, when he would draw nigh to God that there is a repulsion, and he knows not what to do in order to reconciliation, and he either betakes himself to various sorts of supposed pacifications, but is left in painful uncertainty as to whether they can accomplish his ends, or he allows himself to sink into a godless indifference. In order to the restoration of peace, and to his heart being drawn forth towards God, there is need of some Reconciler being disclosed to the view; and this is what is so aptly provided in the Eternal Logos becoming flesh and working out a salvation. But in order that this Object be recognized, he must come before us with the authority of God; and in order to our being able to look to him, he must be set before us in such a way that we can readily and clearly see Him. It is thus that Jesus Christ comes before us, attested by prophecy and by miracle, thus that he is presented to us in the Word as in a glass. We have now the Object fitted to call forth the deeper moral intuitions into play, and to gratify them each and all to the full. We can now look to God, revealed in the face of his Son, without being scared or prostrated; and as we gaze, the pent-up and imprisoned religious affections are set free. The sense of sin, which before so bound the heart in icy hardness, is melted as by genial heat, and repentance bursts forth in copious streams to relieve the soul. Faith feels that it can repose on a pacified God, and love clasps and embraces Him who is now seen to be chiefest among ten thousand, and altogether lovely.

Need I add, that in order that the Object presented accomplish those ends he must be a real object. Were he a mere picture, or a fable, or a myth, the soul would be driven back by the idea ever pressed on it, that this is, after all, an illusion. The understanding would rebel against the imposture which had been tried upon it; and the faith would veer round by a polar reaction to a hardened scepticism; and the intuitions would refuse to appear on the idle summons given them; and the soul would in sulkiness, as it were, retreat into a dim cavern where it has only a flickering light, but from which it is morbidly indisposed to pass into the sunshine without.

It is, as I reckon it, a happy result of the development of principles in this treatise, that it shows how we must still go to the Word of God for our religion. All attempts hitherto made to construct a religion independent of Scripture have turned out acknowledged failures: the systems reared cannot stand a sifting examination by reason, and have been utterly powerless on human character. There was an expectation, long cherished by many, that something better than the old Christianity of the Bible, literally interpreted, might come out of the great German philosophic systems of Kant and Fichte,

Schelling, Hegel, and Schleiermacher; but these hopes have been doomed to acknowledged disappointment. The idea was fondly cherished by some that certain men of literary genius, who had caught more or less of the spirit of the German Metaphysics, such as Coleridge, and Goethe, and Carlyle, must have something new and profound to satisfy the soul in its deeper cravings, could they only be induced to utter it. Coleridge has played out his tune, sweet and irregular as the harp of Æolus, and all men perceive that he never had anything to meet the deeper wants of humanity, except what he got from the songs of Zion. It has long been clear, in regard to Goethe, and is now being seen in regard to Carlyle, that neither of them ever had anything positive to furnish in religion, and that all they had to utter was blankly negative, and I rather think that the last hope of drawing anything soul-satisfying from these quarters has vanished from the minds of those who have been most impressed by their genius. I freely acknowledge, as to some of the eminent men I have referred to, that they have given profound expositions of some of the deeper principles and feelings of the soul, and have thus furnished a contribution to philosophy and incidentally benefited theology. In particular, it may be admitted of a school of intuitionalist divines who have felt the influence of the Teutonic speculations, that they have called attention to foundations and impulses in our nature, which a narrow artificial theology—made up of coagulated abstracts of the supposed Christian system—had overlooked; but which, as these men have shown, had not been lost sight of in actual and living Christianity. The school has erred not in the positive views which the members of it have unfolded, but in what they have omitted and scornfully denied. In particular, they have lost sight of one of the deepest and most ineradicable of all our intuitions; they have taken no notice of that sense of sin and apprehension of God and of a judgment-day which make men feel dissatisfied with every form of natural religion, and bring them in helplessness to the Crucified Saviour and the written Word.* Intuitionalism has had its trial in the age now passing away as rationalism had in the previous one, and both have been found utterly insufficient. Rationalism reared a structure with regular walls and well-fitted gates, but the soul has ever felt it to be desolate as a prison. Intuitionalism has raised up a showy summer palace, but it is utterly and manifestly unfitted to withstand the winds and colds of winter.

There are some who imagine that we may now discard the Bible, and yet retain all the light and assurance and comfort which it has diffused. There were persons in the last century who thought they could dispense with the Scriptures, and yet retain among the people their high morality. The generation which had been piously educated did in many cases keep up to the high standard of morality; but the generation which succeeded, educated in mere morality, thought they had outgrown the rigid morality of their fathers, as these fathers had outlived the rigid orthodoxy of *their* fathers; and the race which was reared to be moral, turned out fearfully immoral. Men had cut down the tree on which the flowers grew, expecting they would still flourish, and were astonished when they faded. In the day which has now reached its noon, the corresponding class of thinkers are under a deep impression that there is need of feeling in order to incite to a living morality, and so must have

* In particular, Mr. Maurice, drawing from the schools in Germany which flourished prior to the later inquiries into Sin and Conscience, has, while developing some of the airier of our mental aspirations, overlooked the deeper convictions of the moral power, and thus been led to discard the Scripture doctrine of Atonement. There are important remarks in Rigg's 'Anglican Theology.'

sentiment, by all means and above all things a warm and glowing sentiment. But still they would rise above the inspired Word, and leave it behind, foolishly imagining that they may have a continuance of the diffused fervour, without the body from which the heat radiates. The issue of such an experiment is certain, and is already beginning to show itself. The race reared under such influences will go a step further in the direction in which they have been led, and will have no difficulty in discarding the feelings which are left without a basis, till we have a generation without creed, and without any semblance of piety, real or pretended. The evening sky, immediately after the sun has sunk, may be as lovely and gorgeous as when he was above the horizon; but it is only the child who will cherish the imagination, that after the illuminating body has gone the glow will not soon fade into gloom.

V. A theology which looks merely to that portion of Divine truth which is addressed to our intuitions must be very vague, loose, and unsatisfactory. If compelled to decide between a rationalistic and intuitional religion, I would infinitely prefer the latter, just as I would choose an idealistic view of nature rather than a materialistic or sensational or mechanical. But I am not bound to make a selection. It is all true that a logical divinity has ever been felt to be harsh and crabbed, and that there has been nothing in it to gain our deeper convictions or win our regards. But it is as true that intuitional theology gives mere cloudland, in which all is vapoury and hazy at the best, and in which we are at last apt to be drenched in rain and tempest. If the one looks so unattractive, as dyked so rigidly into rectilinear and rectangular figures, disregardful of all natural height and hollow, the other is a territory in an unmeasured and unenclosed waste.

In religion, in all its beneficent forms, especially in religion as set forth in the Bible, all the deeper principles and higher faculties of the soul are addressed, and, being combined, they keep each other in their proper position, while each fulfils its function the better by having the co-operation of the others. True religion certainly calls forth the intuitional power in its highest intensity, but it gives exercise to other powers of the soul. If there be need of an immediate reason to gaze on higher truth, and appreciate it, there is also a use for the logical understanding in examining and weighing the evidence, in distinguishing one truth from another, and in keeping truth consistent with itself; and there is a place for the affections as they collect an interest around it. Nor is it to be forgotten that the will, or the choosing and resolving faculty, has a very special work to do in following out the obligations lying on us in the discharge of duties, which are an essential part of religion, and react upon our whole intellectual and moral nature; "by works faith is made perfect." It is all true that a performance of duty without respect to God and godliness, will become empty formalism or self-righteous phariseeism, but it is just as certain that a mere gazing intuitionalism will end in idle musing, wasting itself and so dying out.

It was never meant that any one of the members of our psychical frame should act apart from the others in religious exercises, just as it is not intended that one limb of the body should act without the others, or that the eye should act without the ear, or the taste without the touch. In a sound piety the various powers act in combination, like the various elements—heat, colour, and chemical—of the sunbeam, and they are to be separated only for scientific ends by a scientific process. True, there may, even in natural operations, be a preponderance of one of the elements above the others, for the accomplishment of special ends; still, they are never altogether separated; and if studiously kept apart, or if certain of them be allowed to gather to excess, their action may become deleterious, or they may burst out in a destructive discharge. In particular, the contemplative element, if unduly fostered (like a plant in a stove), and dissevered from rigid thought and a resolute will, must issue in a mystic creed and a life of day-dreams. Revelation calls forth all the powers of the soul. The light of the Word, like the light of the sun, is one, but it has, after all, a number of elements, such as narrative, example, description, type, argument, appeal, exhortation, warning, precept, promise, presentations, and representations, in prose and poetry, each fitted to evoke a corresponding power in our souls, and to draw it forth in a proper direction, and give it the proper hue; and piety is in the healthiest and loveliest state when every essential principle of our constitution is exercised in due measure and proper proportion.

VI. In a living piety the intuitions have a very important place, being always associated with other mental exercises. All the deeper convictions of our nature rest on the objects which are presented in a living religion; indeed they can be satisfied with nothing else. The self-existent being, the self-subsistent substance, the inherent power, the loveliness, the love, the righteousness, the truthfulness of God, these, not in their abstract forms (which are far too like skeletons to delight the eye), but as embodied in full form in a Living Being, are objects on which the soul would gaze with rapture in its pure and unclouded moments; it would turn towards them as towards an attractive light; it reposes upon them as upon a mountain whose foundations can never be moved; and it expands towards them as towards the expanse of heaven, with its still stars away in the depths. We have never reached the proper objects of religion, nor even the region in which they dwell, if intuition has not been bearing up the soul. In our highest exercises of rapt devotion, other operations, though still present in their results, may disappear in their processes, to allow the soul to gaze without distraction, immediately, and, as it were, face to face, on God who is a Spirit, on God who is Light, on God who is Love.

INDEX.

Abelard, 199.
Abstraction and Abstract Notion, 16–19, 50–55, 68, 96, 103, 114, 157–161, 247–250, 413.
Æsthetics, 401, 446.
Analysis, 248.
Analytic Judgments, 245–247, 325, 409.
Anselm, 199, 221.
Antinomies of Kant, 388–390.
Appetencies, 279–284, 287, 406.
A priori, 19–21, 34–35, 111, 115, 317, 353–354, 395, 403, 406, 428–429, 453.
Aristotle, 13, 57, 66, 100–102, 137, 184, 186, 316–317, 331, 354, 401, 462.
Atonement, 307, 408, 464, 466, 480, 481, 493, 496.
Axioms, Mathematical, 50, 64, 68, 247, 249, 250–251, 255, 409–415.

Bacon, 1, 75, 317, 467.
Beattie, 110, 351.
Beauty, 288–290, 456, 477.
Being, 121, 149, 161–164, 165, 477.
Berkeley, 81, 129, 167, 375.
Body, 126–133, 170, 441–442, 452.
Brown, Thomas, 112–113, 204, 242, 252, 278, 292.
Buffier, 107–108, 153, 184.
Butler, 285, 293, 470, 475.

Calderwood, 215.
Campbell, 149.
Carlyle, 447, 448, 495.
Categories of Kant, 20, 110–112, 242.
Catholicity as a Test of Truth, 40, 41, 43, 49, 52–53, 107, 109, 220, 380.
Cause and Causation, 20, 23, 73, 79, 89–90, 109, 112, 113, 187–195, 258–278, 310–311, 316–317, 342, 353, 356–357, 390, 392, 417–418, 433–435, 471–472, 477.
Chalmers, 443, 470.
Classification, 418 (see *Generalization*).
Clarke, Samuel, 67, 211, 225, 464.
Coleridge, 351–353, 463–464, 487, 495.
Colour, 124, 140, 143, 144.
Common Sense, 55, 109–110, 112, 114.
Conscience, 285–288, 301–302, 385, 406–407, 435, 436, 443–444, 470, 496.
Consciousness, 21–23, 42, 44–50, 85–86, 88, 114, 121, 148–157, 340–341, 360, 392–393, 452–453.
Contradiction, Principle of, 66, 246, 325, 346, 348–350.
Contradictions, supposed, in Human Reason, 60–61, 200, 212–213, 218–219, 222–223, 227, 271–273, 382–384, 388–390.
Cousin, 62–63, 89–90, 113–114, 132–133, 164, 221, 268, 310–311.
Criterion of Truth, 325–326.
Cudworth, 57, 353, 356.

Definitions, 50, 66, 93–97, 412–415.
Demonstration, 350, 395–400, 438.

Descartes, 7, 79, 99, 102–104, 115, 119, 146, 152, 166, 168, 174, 184, 186, 209, 221, 317, 329, 450, 451, 462.
Design in Nature, 429–432, 435, 477.

Edwards, Jonathan, 462–463, 464.
Eleatic School, 98, 163, 174, 315–316, 358, 402.
Emotions, 283–284, 364–365, 456–457, 498.
Essence, 178–180.
Ethics, 64, 66–67, 70, 74, 279–307, 350, 400, 406–409.
Excluded Middle, Law of, 246, 325.
Experience, 4, 27–28, 104, 232, 258–262, 274, 305–306, 325–326, 340–345, 353–354, 356–358, 396–400, 410–412, 429–433, 437, 477.
Externality, 128.

Faculties of the Mind, 21–23, 72–73, 236, 279–288, 351, 360.
Faith, 196–202, 286–287, 327, 337–340, 341–342, 346, 348–350, 361–362, 393, 419–427, 428.
Ferrier, Professor, 129, 375, 379.
Fichte, 21, 75, 81, 112, 129, 181, 201, 278, 375, 379, 451, 458, 494.
Forms given by the Mind, 19–21, 110–112, 354, 453.
Fundamental Principles, 38, 53, 112, 115.

Generalization and General Notion, 16–19, 32–36, 50–55, 62–71, 97, 103, 114, 157–161, 255–257, 258–259, 409–412.
Gillespie, 207.
Gnosticism, 463.
Gnosiology, 320–362, 387 (see *Knowledge*).
Goethe, 495.
Hamilton, Sir William, 10, 13, 43, 52–53, 55, 106–107, 109, 114–115, 125, 127–128, 129–130, 138, 145–146, 153, 171–173, 197, 201, 205, 214, 217–219, 227–229, 238–240, 245–247, 312, 320–321, 356, 360, 383, 467.
Hegel, 75, 81, 115, 181, 227, 329, 375, 447, 449, 450, 452, 495.
Heraclitus, 57, 98, 173.
Herschel, Sir J., 206.
Hobbes, 435.
Hume, 81, 108–110, 119, 149, 166, 242, 272, 278, 353, 375, 376.

Idea, 1, 13, 15, 99, 115, 119, 329–340, 418.
Idealism, 5, 9, 129, 135, 363–375, 451–452.
Identity, 242–247, 325, 416.
Immortality of the Soul, 441–446.
Individuals, 29–36, 45–46, 68, 105, 110, 113, 114, 240–241, 244, 248.
Induction, 3–4, 101–102, 112, 114, 322–324, 423, 491.
Infinite, 32, 59, 113, 114, 208–210, 214–231, 436, 477.
Innate Ideas, 1, 15, 23–29, 42, 54, 103, 329–337.
Intuition, 29–36, 42, 44–50, 85–87, 104, 340–345, 351–353, 437, 439, 482–500.
Intuitional Theology, 470, 482–500.
Ionian School, 98.

Jacobi, 84, 200–201, 461.
Judgments, Primitive, 236–242, 287, 346–350.

Kalology, 401–402.
Kant, 19–21, 22, 43, 52–53, 65, 88–90, 105, 106–107, 108, 110–112, 115, 127, 128, 149, 152, 164, 166, 181, 204–205, 212, 242, 244, 245, 271–273, 309–310, 317, 329, 351, 353,

354–356, 375, 379, 388–390, 401, 405–406, 409, 443, 451, 453, 463, 464, 467, 480, 494.
Kidd, Mr., 391.
Knowledge, 38, 106, 119–122, 126–133, 148–157, 196–200, 322–336, 346, 358–362, 362–374, 387.

Leibnitz, 52, 106, 107, 147, 159, 166, 211, 221, 244, 385, 485.
Locke, 7, 9, 14, 15, 17, 18, 22, 23, 31, 97, 99, 107, 115, 120–121, 131, 132–133, 154, 167, 172–173, 179, 184, 186, 214, 217–218, 238–240, 241, 252, 329–335, 401, 415, 462, 464, 480.
Logic, 64, 66, 82, 250, 257, 351, 390–393, 400, 401, 402–405, 422–423, 437, 497–498.

Mackintosh, Sir James, 292.
Mathematics, 64, 68, 74, 255, 396–398, 409–415.
Mansel, Mr., 149–150, 181, 227–229, 238–240, 286, 409.
Maurice, Mr., 496.
Maxims, 18, 32–36, 50–55, 64–66, 106, 114, 344–345, 409-415.
Metaphysics, 6–7, 64–97, 315–394, 402, 404, 408, 416, 461–476.
Mill, Mr. J. S., 158, 236–237, 268, 276–277, 304–305, 326, 373, 390–394, 410–411, 413.
Miracles, 276–278, 493.
Mode, 173–175.
Moral Good, 23, 32, 58, 59, 66–67, 88, 290–297, 302–307, 342, 348, 357, 361, 393, 407, 435–438, 439, 443–444, 458–459, 477.
Motion, 185–186, 251.

Necessary Truth, 4, 26, 39–40, 47, 50–53, 56, 59, 100, 105, 107, 109, 111, 112, 113, 219–220, 260–262, 267–268, 298–299, 327–328, 345–350, 353, 380, 390, 394, 397.
Neo-Platonists, 100, 163, 489.
Newton, Sir Isaac, 67, 212, 213, 225.
Notion (see *Abstraction* and *Generalization*).
Number, 115, 184–185, 253–254.

Obligation, Moral, 292–295, 404–305, 443–444, 454–455, 459, 476–480.
Ontology, 315–316, 321, 358–388.
Original Principles, 48, 58, 63.
Original Sense-perceptions, 122–126, 134–138.

Pantheism, 166–169, 275, 446–461.
Pain, 306–307.
Perfect, 220–221.
Permanence of Substance, 128, 151, 166–169, 442-445.
Personality and Personal Identity, 112, 113, 180–182, 444–445, 448, 453, 457.
Phantasm and Phantasy, 13, 105, 115, 215.
Phenomenal Theory of Knowledge, 19–20, 127–128, 163, 204, 270.
Philosophy, 6-7, 33–36, 82, 316–319, 464–476.
Plato, 7, 16, 57, 66, 99–100, 115, 174, 289, 310, 324–325, 329, 358, 361, 450, 460–461, 485.
Physical Sciences, 250, 415–419.
Power, 130–133, 146–148, 153–155, 165–166, 178, 187–195, 257–258, 263–265 (see *Cause*).
Properties, 178, 257–258, 417–418.
Psychology, 400-404.

Quality, 20, 23, 113, 145–148, 176–178.
Quantity, 20, 66, 252–255, 417.

Rationalism, 468, 470, 480–482.

Reason, 20, 56, 72, 73, 104, 108, 110–112, 113, 199, 351, 353, 419–427, 498.
Reasoning, 28–29, 66, 405, 492.
Reflex use of Intuition, 62–69, 109, 113, 490–492.
Regulative Principles, 25, 33, 34, 42–43, 54, 59, 341–342.
Reid, 22, 108–110, 138, 149, 166, 167, 275, 322, 351.
Relations, 250–278, 365–366.
Resemblance, 255–257 (see *Generalization*).
Responsibility (see *Obligation*).
Revelation, 439, 440, 461–476, 482–498.

Scepticism, 135–137, 374–385.
Schelling, 75, 181, 375, 451–452, 495.
Schenkel, 470.
Schleiermacher, 201, 227, 463, 464, 495.
Schoolmen, 7, 462–463.
Self, Knowledge of, 58, 148–157, 243, 435, 441–442, 452–453.
Self-Evidence, 38, 56, 59–60, 100, 102, 103, 104, 108, 219, 381.
Sensation, 138–141, 324–325, 363.
Sensationalism, 5, 9, 57, 120, 331–332, 435.
Senses, 86–87, 122–144, 353, 357.
Sense-Perception, 86–87, 121, 134–145, 324, 325, 326, 353, 363.
Shaftesbury, 286, 462.
Sin, 297–302, 360–361, 470, 478–482, 496.
Singulars (see *Individuals*).
Socrates, 57, 66, 324–325, 358, 401, 462, 485.
Sophists, 57, 66.
Space, 20, 23, 32, 67, 88–89, 114, 115, 202–214, 215–223, 250–252, 262, 357, 360–361, 389, 416.
Spinoza, 74, 79, 81, 168–169, 174, 447, 451.
Spirit, 148–157, 170–171, 251–252, 435, 441–446, 452–453.
Spontaneous Convictions, 44–50, 54, 56, 59, 62–69, 82, 109, 113, 114, 342–344, 357, 490.
Stewart, D., 112, 128, 149, 205–211, 275, 320, 413, 415.
Subjective and Objective, 354–356.
Substance, 20, 23, 66–67, 89–90, 110, 113, 164–180, 263, 268, 416–418, 450–451, 477.
Synthesis, 248.
Synthetic Judgments, 245–247, 325, 409.
Superstition, 438, 457, 461, 478–480.

Testimony, 420.
Tests of Intuition, 37–41, 68, 109, 113, 231–233, 325, 326, 393, 394, 422, 492.
Theistic Argument, 271–273, 388, 427–441.
Theology, 70, 74, 383, 461–476, 482–498.
Time, 20, 23, 32, 67, 88, 89, 114, 115, 200–214, 222–225, 252, 263, 357, 360, 361, 389, 417.
Trendelenburg, 186, 205.

Ulrici, 166, 465.
Unconditioned, 272, 385–388.
Understanding, 72–73, 351–353.
Uniformity of Nature, 259, 275–278.
Unity, 113.
Universal Truth, 26–27, 52-53, 50–55, 57, 111, 113, 291, 321–328, 353, 380–381.
Utilitarianism, 303–305.

Whately, 158.
Whewell, Dr., 115, 253–254, 417–418.
Whole and Parts, 247, 416.
Will, 284–285, 295–296, 308–312, 390, 406, 453–454, 465, 471–472.

www.ingramcontent.com/pod-product-compliance
Lightning Source LLC
LaVergne TN
LVHW021317110826
845150LV00003B/603

* 9 7 8 1 4 2 5 5 5 7 1 3 3 *